The Church

Johann Auer
Joseph Ratzinger

Dogmatic Theology

Johann Auer

The Church

The Universal Sacrament of Salvation

Translated by Michael Waldstein
Translation edited by Hugh M. Riley

The Catholic University of America Press
Washington, D.C.

Originally published in German under the title *Die Kirche: Das allgemeine Heilssakrament*. Copyright © 1983 Friedrich Pustet Verlag, Regensburg

Copyright © 1993
The Catholic University of America Press
All rights reserved
Printed in the United States of America

The paper used in this publication meets the minimum requirements of American National Standards for Information Science—Permanence of Paper for Printed Library Materials, ANSI Z39.48–1984.
∞

LIBRARY OF CONGRESS CATALOGING-IN-PUBLICATION DATA

Auer, Johann, 1910–1989
    [Kirche. English]
    The Church : the universal sacrament of salvation / Johann Auer;
translated by Michael Waldstein ; translation
edited by Hugh M. Riley.
        p. cm. — (Dogmatic theology ; 8)
    Translation of: Die Kirche.
    Includes bibliographical references and index.
        1. Church. 1. Ratzinger, Joseph. 11. Riley, Hugh M.
III. Title. IV. Series: Auer, Johann, 1910–   Kleine katholische
Dogmatik. English ; v8.
BX1746.A9213 1993
262—dc20
91–44734
ISBN 0-8132-0684-7 (hard). — ISBN 0-8132-0685-5 (pbk.)

Dedicated to Joseph Cardinal Ratzinger
Prefect of the Congregation for the Doctrine of the Faith
on the occasion of his departure from Munich on
February 28, 1982

Contents

Part Three. Manifestations of the
Church's Being, Life, and Activity in the
Light of Its Sacramental Structure

Preface to the Original German Series

Dogmatic Theology is intended to be a series of textbooks for theology students—in brief compass. It has come out in a pocket book format because it is meant to accompany the student, not just in the classroom but on his or her meditative walks as well. Anyone who has had the task of preparing a three-year dogmatics course will know how impossible it is to achieve for each and every area of dogma that scientific presentation which can be expected from a multi-authored, collaborative work such as *Mysterium Salutis*. By way of compensation, textbooks which are concise, through their selectivity and inner coherence, may illustrate certain points more clearly than is the case in such team products.

We have decided to publish this series of concise textbooks because we believe they fill a gap. They are intended to provide a foundation which appropriate lectures can extend and build upon. In this way they will offer a basis for theological discussion, something which is meaningful in dogmatics only if it can presuppose a certain knowledge of the subject matter.

We have tried to pay special attention to three dimensions which are important for dogmatics today:

1. The biblical foundation of doctrine. This is why we cite biblical texts so frequently. The quotations are there in order to communicate not simply the doctrinal truths themselves but also their spirit.

2. The history of individual doctrines. The historian of

doctrine is well placed to show the many facets of the underlying problem as well as the multiplicity of human answers.

3. The systematic inner coherence of doctrine. Doctrinal formulations always tell us about some part of the whole, but the whole is more than the sum of its parts. In the exposition of the individual parts, it is vital to preserve the whole and keep it in view at all times. The main problem in teaching dogmatics is really this: by means of a large number of statements scattered through three or more years of the student's academic life, dogmatics must unfold before the learner's eyes a single reality and a single truth. This fundamentally single whole can stand before the student in its greatness and profundity only to the extent that he or she is able to absorb it in its unity at a single glance.

It is our hope that this series will be used not just as a series of textbooks but also as a collection of materials capable of enriching theological thinking, reflection and meditation. We hope, moreover, that the series may thus stimulate that attitude which all true theologizing requires. That attitude may be summed up under five heads: respect for the uniqueness of the object of theology; sensitivity to the various methods that object demands, and a readiness to employ them; the realization that faith must accompany knowledge, and that both life and action flow from this knowledge of faith; awareness that an individual's theological endeavor needs for its completion the achievement of others both past and present and will thus take its place in the noble history of theology in our Church and find its orientation there—and finally, the awareness that all theology, as reflection on the Church's teaching, shares in the "historicity" both of the Church itself and of the individual theologian within it.

It is our wish that this series, which in the spirit of the

Gospels attempts to present "old and new" (Matt 13,52), may be of service to theology and theologians in a time of widespread and rapid change.

JOHANN AUER
JOSEPH RATZINGER

Preface to the English Edition
of the Series

Dogmatic Theology of Johann Auer and Joseph Ratzinger is now being offered to an English-speaking public in the belief that the three characteristic emphases of the series mentioned in the German preface—informedness by Scripture, attention to the history of doctrine, concern with the systematic coherence of theological teaching—are as desirable in the Anglophone world, far-flung and diverse as that now is, as in the Bavaria which is the authors' home. Both men belong to the milieu of South German Catholic theology which has produced, over the last hundred and fifty years, several great schools or centers. In each of these, a rigorously academic theology, concerned to rise to the challenges of documentary accuracy and conceptual orderliness set by universities, was placed at the service of the Church—bishops, clergy and people—and hence obliged to meet the differing but no less exigent requirements of doctrinal orthodoxy and pastoral good sense. It is typical of German Catholic theological work in this inheritance that it is simultaneously open to biblical scholarship, to Church tradition in all its phases and monuments, and to the philosophical culture of its day which, however, it sifts critically, bearing in mind the Johannine dictum, "Test the spirits, to see if they come from God" (I John 4,1).

Students of dogmatic theology are frequently to be heard making three complaints about the state of the subject. First, they find it difficult to employ contemporary biblical criticism in a constructive fashion in the sphere of doctrine. This Dogmatic Theology, while showing no hostility to historical-critical tools as such, which occupy a limited but legitimate place in its enquiry, seeks to penetrate beyond the historical-critical problems to the revelatory witness that shines forth from the Scriptures. Secondly, students lament the sheer quantity of detailed monographs now available on the history of doctrine. Sinking as one may well do beneath this weight of erudition, the main contours of doctrinal development are easily lost to view. In the Dogmatic Theology, by a judicious selection of *topoi*, an attempt is made to point out the lie of the land to those who cannot see the wood for the trees. Or, to change the metaphor once again, theologically acute historical highlighting illuminates what is of lasting significance for the Church's sensibility, teaching and practice. Thirdly, students do not always find it easy to see how the different facets of doctrinal believing belong together as a unitary whole. Dogmatic Theology addresses itself to this problem in a conscious effort to lead back all the ways of doctrinal reflection to their living center, the Gospel of grace.

Although the series is aimed in the first place at the theological student, whether in university or seminary, the needs it tries to meet are felt much more widely by clergy and laity alike. May that "quest for understanding," to which all Christians are summoned by the gift of faith itself, be stimulated, assisted and brought closer to its goal in the vision of God by the contemplative study of these pages.

AIDAN NICHOLS, O.P.
Blackfriars, Cambridge
Memorial day of St. Isidore,
bishop and doctor of the Church,
1987

Preface to This Volume

The Gospel of Grace (volume 5) unfolded the basic message of Christian faith. *The Sacraments of the Church* (volume 7) and especially *The Mystery of the Eucharist* (volume 6) spoke of those events in Christian life wherein the believer receives and lives his or her Christian existence ever anew from the community and for the community—together with all those "human beings whom God loves" (Luke 2,14). The present volume (volume 8) treats of the Church as the "universal sacrament of salvation," a reality always present and involved in our earlier discussion.

One might ask why we are only now dealing with the Church in this particular place and somewhat tardily even though during the forty years that ecclesiology has formed part of dogmatic theology and not just part of fundamental theology it has been customary to offer one's portrayal of the Church immediately after a treatment of the central mystery of Christ himself. (One might compare in this connection the textbook series written by Michael Schmaus.) We must confess that one reason for the delay lies in the difficulties that the treatise on the Church currently entails. But in addition, right from the planning stage of this *Kleine Katholische Dogmatik*, we have had the idea that it is from this penultimate place in the dogmatic system that the special character of the Church may perhaps become more easily intelligible in our time. The mystery of Christ, out of which the Church lives, should first unfold itself before our spiritual eye in the concrete form it takes in human life as that form is displayed in the doctrine of the sacraments and the doctrine of grace, so as to clarify the goal of the divine *ensarkōsis*, the incarnation and the redemptive activity of God in Christ, the crucified and risen Lord, as well as of the Spirit's mission and indwelling. That goal is: the human person, in his or her immortality and ordination to everlasting glory with God. It is at this point, therefore, that we wish to speak of the community of such persons in the Church of Christ, and of the Church as the universal sacrament of salvation.

This reason for choosing the present sequence already betrays some of the considerable problems bound up with the dogmatic treatment of the doctrine of the Church today. Nowhere indeed does the Christian faith reach so deeply into the reality of the world as it does in this faith-reality of the "Church," which speaks of the Christian person in his or her common life in the midst of the world. This renders intelligible the tensions that arise not only within the biblical idea of creation, but also, and even more so, in the historical mystery of sin and redemption, and, finally, in the promised judgment and glorification of the entire world: tensions that convey the foundational theme of the divine history of salvation in this world. Because of the inner, human decision between faith and knowledge these tensions have always—but especially so in our own day—led to cleavages in basic outlook and the formation of parties, not only between believers and unbelievers but between Christians themselves. These divisions make it very difficult to sustain discourse about the faith-reality of the Church. One group judges that what has been said about the Church in the past is the static ideal image of a non-ideal worldly reality. Their opponents allege that new attempts at understanding the Church are based upon a world-view so thoroughly secularized and so strictly determined by an inner-worldly anthropocentrism that it is no longer capable of expressing adequately the salvation-historical arrival of the divine in this world, precisely in the realm of the Church.

We contemporaries experience the radical change of our times more as revolution than as evolution. For the world in which we and our Church live, a new, technological epoch has opened up, transforming the human world in a way that not only changes at a deep level the life and image of human beings but also begins to call into question our very existence in the world at all. Parallel to this event, there has been a profound shift in the understanding of society on the part of the people of our day. This shift is colored not only by novel, technologically determined features of science but also, and even more, by a Marxism that has affected the metaphysical depths of the understanding of the human being, and by the atheistic Communism that has built on that foundation. Technical, economic, and social changes originating in and guided by scientific progress and effective, above all, since the Second World War, call into question the bases of our Christian faith, not just by way of their elaboration in a metaphysical system of thought, but also in their objective and historical actuality. The contemporary world-picture has not found a metaphysics that could give appropriate expression to the fact that human beings are "persons" with a meaning inherent in themselves and that they are not obliged to receive that meaning first and foremost from the world. Only the happenstance that human life has a "double track," only the "contemporary character of what is not contemporary,"[1] keeps open the possibility of the Church's continued existence and of discourse about it in a world split into two parts, one nominally Christian, the other professedly opposed to Christianity.

This division and these tensions are rendered deeper still, in a decisive way, by the historical self-understanding of our time. Great discoveries and inventions, especially in the area of natural science and of technology, have led to a general belief in progress, which devalues and despises everything permanent, everything that understands itself more in terms of the greatness of a historical tradition than in terms of planning for a still undetermined future.[2] What the Church in its almost two millenia of history has been and achieved is regarded as a succession of failures. People say that the Church has not changed the world; that modern progress has had to make its way against the Church's judgment, and in the face of its anathemas; that the alienation of the present world from the Church, from its teachings and values, is the natural response to this inefficacy of churchly activity in this world.

This reproach will not convince those who are acquainted with the history of the West and its high culture and who live open-eyed in the present. But what do the values of intellectual culture mean for us today in comparison with the material and immediately, universally perceptible success of modern civilization? Moreover, the values of human culture, with which the Church is concerned in consequence of its Christian image of humanity, cannot be planned as can the objects of material, technical civilization. They are not performance or industry, but fruit and gift—they are something that is received by those human beings who, thanks to ever-new initiatives at their own conversion, seek to reach that deeper selfhood which alone can generate and give birth to human culture.

Admittedly there is one area where this modern reproach appears justified—and that is where the Church in the economic and social sphere of human life has not been sufficiently able, right up to our own day, to renew the social thinking and action of individual persons (though indeed such action has never been lacking in the Church's charitable outreach), especially in such great Christian countries as Italy and Spain and in South America. This inability is the result of a holding fast to the feudal system that originated in the Middle Ages and was at that period something significant for the Church regarded as a factor in the organization of secular power. To someone who lives in the shadow of these economic and social realities the theological image of the Church, viewed against the backdrop of the new picture of the social economy, can easily appear as an ideological quantity. Failure here cannot be excused by drawing attention to the lack of efficacy of the Church's teaching and planning, or to human lethargy and infirmity, or by pointing to the outside interference of secular powers which, as history often shows, can place major obstacles in the Church's way.

Against the background of this new non-metaphysical understanding of society and of the world numerous problems about the structure of our Church today are thrown into relief: the question of its constitution (hierarchical, conciliar, or democratic); of its dialectical structures of order (a Church authoritative and obedient; proclaiming and listening, and containing a necessary distinction of persons between the minister of a sacrament and its recipient); the question of the offices which pertain to its structure (the relationship of pope and bishops, of hierarchy and laity, of institution and charisms), and of the fundamental makeup of its unity (the ecumenical question, and the Church's relationship to the great non-Christian religions of the world).

In light of all these questions, the task of developing an understanding of the Church appropriate to our time seems to touch the foundations of our Christian faith at large, with the knowledge it brings of an inner identity to the picture of God as revealed to us and of the saving history he undertakes with humankind, as well as the inner identity of the human being as creature and image of God. Moreover, the Christian picture of God, of the world, and of the human being must be delineated against the background of a human understanding of the world, and the human being's place in it, which does not inquire about the true image of the human being, but rather about human freedom in the sense of the experience of freedom and human happiness in the sense that modern consumer society attaches to those words. For this kind of understanding God has largely ceased to be a question and actually appears to some extent (in, for example, the Marxist critique of religion) as the idol of an unjust economic and social order. As far as possible we must keep all this in mind as we unfold in theological terms the image of this Church of ours as a living and concrete image which, nevertheless, can only be conceived in faith.[3] In this connection allow me to refer to the latest proposals for a doctrine of the Church made by Hans Küng[4] and Michael Schmaus[5] as well as a volume of *Mysterium Salutis.*[6] The sketch offered in these pages has been influenced by these works; it was also challenged by them to say something both complementary and novel. While the text in accordance with the plan of the *Kleine Katholische Dogmatik* has had to be kept brief, the extensive bibliographies may help the reader to pursue the issues further.

I dedicate this volume to Joseph Ratzinger, the co-editor of the series ever since the appearance of its first volume (*The Gospel of Grace,* volume 5), and author of its final volume (*Eschatology. Death and Eternal Life,* volume 9).

JOHANN AUER
Regensburg
Feast of St. Joseph,
Guardian of the Holy Church,
1982

Editor's Note on This Volume

The present volume is the English translation of volume 8 of the Dogmatic Theology of Johann Auer and Joseph Ratzinger. Almost a decade has passed since the German original was published in Regensburg by Johann Auer. Given the nature of the work and the intention of the author, however, this translation will provide welcome assistance to those in the English-speaking world whose view of the Church has become increasingly fragmented, often by acrimonious debates on how the Church is to be perceived as it confronts a plethora of contemporary problems.

The violence done to a proper understanding of the Church when it is viewed merely as a phenomenon of secular society can be counteracted only by a contemplative view of it, which takes into account the fullness of its nature. Only in a full historical perspective, presenting biblical and theological material as an original whole and demonstrating in widest possible scope the many angles of vision in which human reason and imagination attempt to grasp in an ever-imperfect way what is ultimately a divine mystery, can a dessicated image of the Church engendered by all-too-subjective polemics and all-too-imperfect ministers be overcome. Such a work can help provide access to what the Church's Founder wanted it to do—to give us bread and not stones, to be for us the channel of that peace which surpasses all understanding.

Users of this English translation, especially teachers and students of theology, will be indebted to my friend and colleague Rev. Michael A. Fahey, S. J., Professor and Dean of Theology at the University of St. Michael's College, Toronto, for adding references to current English translations of works cited in the original German footnotes. Of even greater importance for the usefulness of this volume to the English-speaking reader is Father Fahey's thoroughly up-to-date Select Bibliography, which takes into account the development undergone in recent years in all the topics of Johann Auer's German original.

HUGH M. RILEY, EDITOR
Munich
Epiphany, 1992

An Introduction to the Work of Johann Auer

Johann Auer was a Bavarian theologian who, throughout a long life of literary production dating back to before World War II, took as his chief interest the theology of grace, placed now at the service of an entire dogmatics which moves from the triune God, through creation, to the person and work of Jesus Christ and the sacramental life of the Church. On his sixty-fifth birthday the editors of a volume of essays in his honor described his work as a celebration of theology as *Heilswissenschaft*, the knowledge and study of salvation.[1] For grace, as Heribert Rossmann and Joseph Ratzinger pointed out, does not merely bring human beings to a knowledge of their true selves, but, as understood by Auer, grants them a share in God's own divine life. If the Catholic Church, at the Second Vatican Council, understood itself as empowered to create unity and peace in the world, this can only be because it is, in Christ, a sign and instrument of the most inward community with God, which Jesus Christ brings us through his life and teaching, death and resurrection. God's gracious action for our re-formation serves to lead human beings, through the Church's community of salvation, to the Uncreated Grace which is the triune God himself.

Who, then, was the theologian of whose ideas this is the leit-motif? Johann Auer was born on May 15, 1910, near Regensburg.[2] He completed his secondary education at the *Humanistisches Gymnasium* in Straubing and went on to study theology at the University of Munich. Ordained a priest at Regensburg (whose cathedral city was one of the

cultural centers of southern Germany in the Middle Ages),
Auer continued his studies after ordination by specializing
in medieval philosophy and theology. His philosophical
dissertation on the freedom of the human will in Thomas
Aquinas and Duns Scotus was published at Munich in
1938.[3] Auer's study of human freedom, in the company of
these two masters, centers on two questions. First, what
must the freedom of the will be like if it is truly human
freedom and not a meaningless, blind arbitrariness unworthy of us? Second, how can the will so be determined as to
constitute meaningful striving, without doing damage to
its freedom? With a care to allow each author his particular approach within the ample space of Catholic thought,
Auer's study highlights the significant differences between Thomas and Scotus on these issues. Thus, for
Thomas the will is free insofar as it is *rational* appetite,
simply; Thomas is interested, above all, in the meaningfulness of human striving. For Scotus, on the other
hand, the will is, first and foremost, free with the primordial freedom of its own nature, from the superabundance
of its power; his interest lies in the experienceable *freedom* of a will that is, to his mind, identical with the soul
itself. Thomas' will is moved by something actual beyond
itself, Scotus' by its own inner force. To Thomas, the object of the will is the good in general, the ground of value—
and ultimately beatitude, which in the last analysis is an
act of the speculative intellect, the vision of God. To
Scotus, the will's object is, rather, being in general, its last
goal felicity, attained by love, necessitated by no object but
finding in God an object with a due proportion to its own
infinite striving. Auer concludes his comparison of the
two medieval thinkers by throwing light on the grounds of
their difference. Thomas' approach is by way of creation as
nature, an analogical family of realities of different kinds,
and he sets out to present experienced totalities in terms of
thinkable relationships and laws; Scotus, by contrast, approaches creation as existence—seeking what is particu-

lar, singular, concentrating on the phenomenon in its independence and individual wholeness. The entire human being philosophizes and, in the contrast between Thomism and Scotism, two types of scholar-saint are in play. Thus the mystery of the will's freedom (the subject of Auer's book) takes us back to the mystery of human personality itself.[4]

From this largely philosophical study, Auer then turned to theology proper, under the guidance of the great religious historian of the Middle Ages, Martin Grabmann, and of the dogmatician Michael Schmaus. A certain preference for the Franciscan school issued in his next book, a study of the development of the doctrine of grace in high medieval Scholasticism, with special reference to the teaching of the Franciscan cardinal Matthew of Acquasparta.[5] Here a philosophy of the human will drawn from Augustinian and Franciscan sources, and a theology of grace as supernatural love, are joined together. Matthew of Acquasparta, an Umbrian who lived from 1240 to 1302, had been almost forgotten until the late nineteenth century, but as teacher, minister-general of the Friars Minor, cardinal, and reformer he turned out to have been a major figure, outstanding among the young Bonaventurians of his generation. His interest for Auer lies in his combining a fundamental allegiance to the Franciscan tradition, largely Augustinian as this was, with an openness to Thomism. Like all the Franciscans from Alexander of Hales to Bonaventure, he asserted the primacy of will (love) over intellect (understanding), of experience over thought, of the person over the *res:* yet he accepted more of Thomas' theory of knowledge, and metaphysics, than had his predecessors.[6]

In Matthew we see an attempt to appropriate Aristotelian thought in a Franciscan spirit. The starting point was the teaching of the Master of the Sentences, Peter Lombard, that charity is the direct action of the Holy Spirit. Owing to the distinction between Creator and creature, however, such uncreated Charity must be received

by a human being. Some kind of accidental form is needful
if it is to belong to the created realm, however directly it
may be ordered to the divine. Earlier Franciscans had tried
to speak of this, in the imagistic language inherited from
Augustine, by a metaphysics of light. Matthew, however,
saw the importance of the new Aristotelian conceptual
language of form. Though Matthew was not a particularly
original thinker, Auer evidently admires him for holding
together the Bonaventurian stress on the role of grace in
our moral and religious existence, with the developing
Thomist inquiry into the metaphysical ground of the supernatural order. Now less optimistic about the benefits of
Scotist thought, Auer saw the strains in such Aristote-
lianizing Franciscanism as leading, however, to a tearing
apart of Creator and creature, a separation of faith and
knowledge, and, finally, a devaluation of the idea of the
supernatural in post-Scotist nominalism, since the basis
for a human understanding of the supernatural order is
lost. Auer drew two lessons from this research.[7] First,
though theological pluralism within the Church's communion may well help to preserve a desirable multiplicity
of illuminating perspectives, not all the aspects of each
and every theology can be underwritten without further
ado. Second, he saw the possibility of a dogmatics that
would take grace as its center, since from grace one may
move, as the history of theology could show, through the
doctrine of justification to an account of Christology and
the sacraments (and so the Church), while at the same
time, by way of the doctrine of election (and its shadow,
reprobation), one can move to an account of *theo*-logy
proper, the doctrine of God.[8]

After the years of wartime military service, which the
editors of Auer's *Festschrift* describe as "bitter" for him
and filled with extraordinary experience, he was enabled,
by the publication of his *Habilitationsschrift*, to become a
university professor at Munich in 1947, lecturing also
from 1947 to 1950 at the *Philosophische-Theologische*

Hochschule at Freising, the former primatial see of Bavaria whose name is still incorporated in the title of the arch-diocese of Munich and Freising. From 1950 until 1968 Auer was professor of dogmatics and the history of dogma at the University of Bonn, where his pastoral activities and contribution to the formation of the clergy were notable. In 1968, however, with the creation of the University of Regensburg, he was able to return to Bavaria and to his native city. After that his name would be linked with the series *Kleine Katholische Dogmatik*, although the many-sidedness of his interests in the history of doctrine and in contemporary theology was also manifested in a constant flow of articles on particular themes.[9] Johann Auer died in Regensburg on March 17, 1989.

What are the principal features of Auer's mature theo-logical work? They are, in the first place, the holding to-gether of the contributions of Scripture, the history of tra-dition, and systematic theology, a capacity for synthesis to which this *Dogmatics* amply testifies. And, in the second place, in the centrality of the topic of grace to which his earlier studies had directed him, whereby the Holy Spirit draws us to himself through faith, hope and charity, in contemplation and *askēsis*.

AIDAN NICHOLS, O.P

Abbreviations

AAS	*Acta Apostolicae Sedis* (Vatican City, 1900ff.)
Baraúna, Eccl.	G. Baraúna, *De Ecclesia: Beiträge zur Konstitution "Über die Kirche" des II. Vat. Konzils*, 2 vols. (Freiburg im Breisgau, 1966)
CSEL	*Corpus Scriptorum Ecclesiasticorum Latinorum* (Vienna, 1886ff.)
D	H. Denzinger, *Enchiridion Symbolorum, Definitionum et Declarationum de rebus fidei et morum*, 31st ed. (Freiburg im Breisgau, 1957)
DS	H. Denzinger and A. Schönmetzer, *Enchiridion Symbolorum, Definitionum et Declarationum de rebus fidei et morum*, 34th ed. (Freiburg im Breisgau, 1967)
DSAM	Dictionnaire de la Spiritualité Ascétique et Mystique (Paris, 1932ff.)
DThC	*Dictionnaire de Théologie Catholique*, 15 vols., 2 suppl. (Paris, 1903–1950)
EC	*Enciclopedia Cattolica*, 12 vols. (Vatican City, 1949–1961)
GNKR	*Grundriss des nachkonziliaren Kirchenrechts*, ed. J. Listl et al. (Regensburg, 1979)
HWPh	*Historisches Wörterbuch der Philosophie*, ed. J. Ritter (Darmstadt, 1971ff.)
KKD	J. Auer and J. Ratzinger, *Kleine Katholische Dogmatik*, 9 vols. (Regensburg, 1970ff.)
KlP	*Der Kleine Pauly, Lexikon der Antike* (Stuttgart, 1964ff.)
LThK	*Lexikon für Theologie und Kirche*, 2d ed., ed. J. Höfer and K. Rahner (Freiburg im Breisgau, 1957–1967)

LThK *Lexikon für Theologie und Kirche*, 2d ed., ed.
Concil. J. Höfer and K. Rahner, supplementary vols.
I–III (Freiburg im Breisgau, 1966–1967)

Mansi *Sacrorum conciliorum nova et amplissima collectio*, ed. J. D. Mansi, rev. ed., 60 vols. (Paris, 1899–1927)

MS *Mysterium Salutis, Grundriss Heilsgeschichtlicher Dogmatik*, 5 vols. (Einsiedeln and Cologne, 1965–1976)

NCE *New Catholic Encyclopedia* (New York, 1967)

PG *Patrologia Graeca*, ed. J. P. Migne (Paris, 1857–1866)

PL *Patrologia Latina*, ed. J. P. Migne (Paris, 1844–1855)

RAC *Reallexikon für Antike und Christentum*, ed. Th. Klausen (Stuttgart, 1950ff.)

RGG *Die Religion in Geschichte und Gegenwart*, 3d ed., 7 vols. (Tübingen, 1957–1965)

RNT *Regensburger Neues Testament*, ed. J. Eckert and O. Knoch (Regensburg, 1938ff.)

TDNT *Theological Dictionary of the New Testament* [ET of TWNT], trans. and ed. G. W. Bromily (Grand Rapids, 1964–1974)

TU *Texte und Untersuchungen zur Geschichte der altchristlichen Schriftsteller der ersten drei Jahrhunderte* (Leipzig and Berlin, 1882ff.)

TWNT *Theologisches Wörterbuch zum Neuen Testament*, ed. G. Kittel and G. Friedrich (Stuttgart, 1933–1974)

WA Martin Luther, *Werke. Kritische Gesamtausgabe* [=Weimarer Ausgabe] (Weimar, 1883ff.)

ABBREVIATIONS OF THE TEXTS OF VATICAN II

AA	*Apostolicam Actuositatem*	Decree on the Apostolate of the Laity
AG	*Ad Gentes*	Decree on the Church's Missionary Activity
CD	*Christus Dominus*	Decree on the Bishops' Pastoral Office
DH	*Dignitatis Humanae*	Declaration on Religious Freedom
DV	*Dei Verbum*	Dogmatic Constitution on Divine Revelation
GE	*Gravissimum Educationis*	Decree on Christian Education
GS	*Gaudium et Spes*	Pastoral Constitution on the Church in the Modern World
IM	*Inter Mirifica*	Decree on the Instruments of Social Communication
LG	*Lumen Gentium*	Dogmatic Constitution on the Church
NA	*Nostra Aetate*	Declaration on the Relationship of the Church to Non-Christian Religions
OE	*Orientalium Ecclesiarum*	Decree on the Eastern Catholic Churches
OT	*Optatam Totius*	Decree on Priestly Formation
PC	*Perfectae Caritatis*	Decree on the Appropriate Renewal of the Religious Life
PO	*Presbyterorum Ordinis*	Decree on the Ministry and Life of Priests
SC	*Sacrosanctum Concilium*	Constitution on the Sacred Liturgy
UR	*Unitatis Redintegratio*	Decree on Ecumenism

Introduction

Wherever genuine faith in a divinity is present, believers will form a living community which—so they are convinced—is neither a community determined by certain interests or purposes of a free, natural kind (a mere society or association), nor a purely natural community based on what is given in existence (for instance, a clan which exists in virtue of ancestry and history). On the contrary, believers know themselves to be united by the living divinity itself, the deity creating, determining and sustaining this community in a higher (supernatural) fashion. The way believers conceive this community will depend on the grandeur of their idea of God. That is why the idea of God has achieved its fullest development through divine revelation. The major tensions interwoven in all authentic religion have found here their strongest dynamism in their highest unity: the tension between individual and community, between the spiritual and the earthly political dimension, between what is one's own and what is Wholly Other, and between the human person and the divinity.

In such a way the revealed image of God in the Old Testament (Exod 3,2–6; 19,18; 20,1–7) has its counterpart in the covenant God made with his people (Gen 15,18; 17,2–14; Exod 19,4–6; 24,8). This covenant was inaugurated so that through this people all the nations might one day be blessed by God (Gen 22,18; Jer 31,31–34), the God who would become all humanity's king (Isa 11,1–6; cf. Luke 1,32) and establish his divine kingdom (Mark 1,15) through the instrumentality of the Son of Man (Dan 7,13ff.; cf. Mark 14,62).

The New Testament revelation of God, which in the

same way has given us the "depth of the riches and wisdom and knowledge of God" (Rom 11,33), as well as the mystery which is "Christ" (Eph 1,3–3,21) and the "Spirit of truth" (John 16,7–15), who proceeds from the Father and the Son, has also given us fresh knowledge of the nature of the community of believers, the Church. The supernatural character and the divine proportions of this community were disclosed to us, and the concept of the Church as an authentic mystery of faith and one of the most difficult of theological ideas gained clear contours. For this reason the Church from the beginning has been an object of the confession of faith in the Apostles' Creed.

This fact, as well as an analogy to the growth of a human being (coming to an appreciation and grasp of sociological realities not in early youth but only with the onset of maturer years), enables us to understand how the doctrine of the Church was explicitly unfolded by theologians only gradually, especially in the fifteenth century (around the time of the Council of Basel) as well as in the course of the last hundred and fifty years (since the Romantic revival). And yet the doctrine of the Church turns out to be one of the most important doctrines in the entire proclamation of faith. In fundamental theology this doctrine is the most important of all since the Church is the bearer and guarantor of revelation, and so too of the doctrine of the triune God and of Christ the Redeemer. The Church is also the universal mediator of salvation, the space in which Christ's saving action in word and sacrament has its effective subsistence and imperishable vitality.

A theological account of Christian doctrine (dogmatics) can best expound its doctrine of the Church if in its first part it clears pathways for the right understanding of the Church in our own time. This it will do by bringing to light the natural presuppositions and history of the image of the Church, as well as the foundation of that image in revelation. Part Two will then deal with the model of the Church to be proposed theologically, with the structures of the Church and its inner sacramental nature. Part Three will try to make intelligible the manifestations of its being, life and activity in the light of this essential image or structure of the Church. Finally, Part Four will explain the tasks of the Church in the world in the perspective of this same basic understanding.

At the end it will be clear that the living reality of this two-thousand-year-old Church can still be grasped in the early Christian statements of its apostolicity, unity, catholicity and holiness.

Part One

Pathways towards the Proper Understanding of the Church

In order to grasp the image of the Church or its theological concept in all its breadth and depth, we must first open up, and shed some light upon, three major approaches towards understanding the Church. The first of these proceeds from individuals and their natural relationship to communities in general and to the Church in particular. In other words, it consists of a basic sociological reflection (I). The second approach is found in the subject matter of our enquiry itself, in the image of the Church as has been revealed and continues to be revealed in its history (II). The third and most important approach can be found in the statements of revelation because the Church is a supernatural reality disclosed and bestowed by God (III).

Individual Approaches towards Understanding the Church

Here we shall ask the following four questions: First, why today, in the age of sociology, is human society endangered? Second, what, in fact, constitutes human communities? Third, by what routes do the various theological disciplines seek out their image of the Church? Fourth, what form of faith in the Church does the Apostles' Creed require?

I. THE SPIRITUAL SITUATION OF OUR AGE AND THE CATHOLIC IMAGE OF THE CHURCH

Everything that is Christian, and so too the Church, is, like the mystery of the cross, a scandal and folly for many believers and even more for unbelievers. The Church is a scandal for the "pious," whose self-knowledge is quite limited and who cannot reconcile the human frailty and weakness of the Church in the world with their spiritualistic and idealistic image of the Church. It is folly to the "learned," caught as they are in an individualistic moralism of the kind exemplified by Kant in his *Religion within the Limits of Reason Alone,* unable to fathom the depths of human community. Only those who live for community can understand it; only those who spend energy on community, sacrificing themselves for it, can draw personal riches from it. Paul's saying about the Cross of Christ has an application to the Church as well: "But to those who are called [it is] the power of God and the wisdom of God. For the foolishness of God is wiser than men, and the weakness of God is stronger than men" (1 Cor 1,24–25). What aspects of our age seem most significant if we seek to understand the Church today?

a) Sociology investigates why today such basic natural communities as marriage, the family, people, nation are no longer understood correctly. These communities seem questionable or lacking in credibility. The main reason may be that the typical person in the age of technology no longer understands with sufficient clarity that some values can be gained only through personal commitment. Community values, like moral values, are of this kind, and individualistic egotism cuts off access to them. At the depths of a person, where all genuine community has its origin and foundation, the capacity for, and inclination towards, joyful giving and grateful receiving must be alive if the life of the so-called natural communities is to be lived out.

b) In the most general sense, human community, or society, is a union of human beings (themselves embodied spiritual persons) for the realization of authentic values in human history. Materialism in all its forms (the individualist-capitalist, as well as the Marxist-socialist and historical-dialectical) so chains human beings to material goods that the freedom of the spiritual person, which alone can grasp and realize spiritual values and ideals, is paralyzed and blotted out.[1] Understanding of and sensitivity to genuine spiritual values, as correlatives to the free spiritual person, constitute the natural foundation for understanding and realizing in the world true religious values— and above all for grasping the holy.[2] The value of the holy, together with the inner freedom of the spiritual person for responding to this highest value in adoration and self-abandonment, is what makes possible the community we call Church. The continuing existence of natural communities, as well as the Church, in spite of the materialism of our age—in other words, the fact that marriage, the family and the Church have not been destroyed despite the grave errors of our time—is due only to the mystery of nature which was, in its totality, created by God and whose validity is ultimately indestructible. Horace's words have meaning here: *Naturam expellas furca, tamen usque recurret.*[3] Before nature can be completely corrupted, the individual will perish.

c) The Church in the Catholic sense, however, is not only a religious community concerned with the holy. It is an absolutely unique community. It is grounded in the mystery of the Creator, Lord and Father of all human beings, who determines the world and its history; in the Son, who has become both man and Head of the Church in Jesus of Nazareth, Messiah of the Old Covenant and founder of the New Covenant with God; and in the Holy Spirit of Jesus, Mediator between all beings and the living God and Father. The Church is a community in this world, yet at the same time it remains in its innermost essence an absolute mystery of faith, because the origin and foundation of this community lies in the triune God; it lies in God's historical action and being in this world, through Christ and his Spirit. Only where faith acknowledges and accepts the Wholly Other (absolutely transcendent) God in the world which is his creation; only where it acknowledges and accepts the absolutely supra-temporal (eternal) God as Lord, Governor and Judge in our human history; only where it acknowledges and accepts the mystery of Christ as the incarnate Son of God, as the historical God with us (Emmanuel: Isa 7,14); only where it acknowledges and accepts God as the final, and only, goal of humanity and of the whole world (cf. 1 Cor 15,25)—only there can the Church of Christ be fully lived and understood in this world.

d) At the root of all these present-day difficulties in understanding the Church lies the crisis of that fundamental human perspective known as "meta-physics." It was a perspective which tried to gain a unified, over-arching vision of thinking, willing, acting, of the human understanding of the world, and of man himself, of the human person, of being, and of the Absolute. Metaphysics formulated its questions in existential as well as object-oriented ways, and sought to give its answers in a fashion suited to such a vision of the whole. The loss of the "center" from which the "coincidence of opposites" (Nicholas of Cusa) might be seen; the loss of the "spirit of the whole" (Julius Langbehn, the "Rembrandt German") in which the basic tensions of personal existence could be endured, and notably that between knowledge and faith, between self-preservation and self-abandonment, has deprived a sound metaphysics of the ground on which to stand. It must, however, be admitted that some of the supporting structures of the old metaphysics have been destroyed by correct and important features of the modern age, together with progress in understanding the world and technological control over it built upon those features. A new metaphysics, taking into account the new picture of the world, has not yet been developed, and this is one of the main reasons for the general crisis of faith and theology today, as well as for the erroneous conceptions attached to current "secularism" and "anthropocentrism." All this has a decisive impact on the question of how, theologically, to understand the Church.[4]

2. THE FOUNDATION OF COMMUNITY STRUCTURE

As already indicated more than once, a natural philosophical understanding of community is a highest necessity if the Church as a unique form of community is to be properly understood. In an ontological understanding of all social formations, it is imperative to possess at least three vantage points which, together, offer an overview of this reality. These are: first, the foundation of community; second, the enactment of community by its members; third, the community structure which develops from these.[5]

a) In accordance with the essential structure of the human persons who make up communities, the foundation of human communities has many levels. An authentic "phenomenology of the community," based upon observation and experience, must mention several factors relevant to their rise. There are natural factors active in man, without their activity coming to his notice (factors, for example, stemming from biology, psychology and the history of culture, such as the founding of the family, the mother-child relationship, and family traditions).[6] One must also mention a host of values which become effective by way of conscious human experience (the experience, precisely, of value), even though they are not conscious in a reflective fashion. Here belong the values lived out and given shape in human society and human history, and which are thus determined by an overarching destiny. In German, *Gesellschaft*, "society," means literally a community of human beings who live together in a large common room where they grow up together sharing both joy and sorrow. Suffering, struggles, feasts and joys all shared in common have the effect of binding people together. Of course, factors grounded in value which form communities and societies can change very much, just as natural factors do. In particular, the generation gap contributes decisively to this change. Youth must detach itself from old communities in order to found its own new ones, under the conditioning pressure of nature and history. Over against the older generation, and before understanding the old communities and their foundation, youth sets up new ideas and ideals in which and through which it asserts itself and gains independence. Hence, in addition to these natural factors and factors grounded in value in the founding of communities, one must always recognize and acknowledge the personal foundations operative in human communities through human striving, interest, enthusiasm, creative action and personal gift of self.[7] In light of these basic elements we can understand especially family, clan, people and nation.

b) The personal foundation of which we have just spoken becomes manifest and effective only in a second element that is essential to a community's being: the free human enactment of community relationships on the part of individuals. Life in community as an enactment of human existence is not only the result of the factors which gave rise to community in the first place. Human beings are not just products of society or culture. Rather they must personally actualize those decisive factors which give birth to community. Forms of community such as acquaintanceship, comradeship, friendship, and especially courtship and marriage, should be mentioned here. For these communitarian forms to be vital, the realities and values which are their foundation must be grasped ever more consciously; they must be lovingly affirmed and brought about through action in the community setting. For this reason, only those who live for these communities can understand them; and only those who are ready to exert themselves and sacrifice themselves can draw on the personal wealth of the community. Freedom of the spirit is more determinative than natural disposition. Blood kinship is weaker by far than community of ideas and communion of love.

c) Social structures that possess real validity going above and beyond individual persons, making claims and demands on them, even while carrying them and forming them, are once again many sided. What they have in common is that relationships among the members of these communities are governed by institutionalized rules (rules of the game), determined apparently not only by the members themselves but even more by the reason and purpose of the community. In the first instance, the number of participating persons provides a criterion for distinquishing various types of such communities. There are communities which are basically two person communities, and in a special way marriage. But most human communities involve several other persons because they are grounded in economic, social, cultural and political values (as in the case of associations, leagues, political parties and all other special purpose communities). The only omni-personal community, the only community which embraces all human beings, is authentic humanism defined as the knowledge that all humanity is one—to the degree that such humanism produces community (for instance, by establishing human rights) rather than remaining simply at the conceptual or ideal level. In this sense, the Church must be included insofar as it is not only an institutional community defined by law, but a missionary community of love defined by a specific purpose. We will return to this point later.

Another way of distinguishing different types of communities is based on the fact that all human communities have not only rules of conduct (community rules) but also an established order and authority (institutions). For example, the authority-bearing *caste* society, as it existed in antiquity and still exists in India; the society composed of *estates*, existing in developed form in the guilds and estates of the Middle Ages and still of importance today; and, finally, today's society where position is determined by merit, with its trade unions.

Human community without authority is an impossibility. Even what is known as "democracy" must furnish itself with authorities, though it establishes authorities also with the help of its own social rules. The "classless" society sought by Marxism has not yet become reality anywhere. Indeed, it generally appears as the "absolutism of a single party." In our day, this range of problems is, in many ways, made manifest through the opposition of "state" and "society." "State" refers to a stable structure formed through power and legal order in the course of history, whereas "society" denotes the different groups engaged in living a communal life in which the various values of human society are cultivated and realized in history. For the most part, the personal element becomes effective vis-à-vis these two realities only by way of the formation of elites.[8] In our attempt to understand the Church as a society it will be of great importance to grasp correctly the natural as well as supernatural foundations, the necessary activities that flow from those foundations, and the values and realities which have their ground therein, and also to bring out the specific social form of the Church, so far as possible, in the natural sphere as well as in its being as an object of faith.

3. CONCRETE ATTEMPTS TO DEFINE "CHURCH"

Before unfolding the dogmatic vision of the Church, it may be helpful to point to the attempts of other theological disciplines to explain what "church" is. It should be stated from the outset that in "theology," as the science of faith, Church must be seen both in the light of faith in revelation, as well as from the standpoint of human experience. It must be regarded as a reality both supernatural and natural, a work of God entrusted to human hands. This is not possible for a purely immanent, empirical science such as sociology, in which Church is seen only as an immanent social formation, concerned with communication and action; it is understood in terms of its efficacy in today's organized human world. For this reason it has so far proved impossible to find a unified common denominator between the theological and the sociological understandings of Church. Sociology may point out defective attitudes within the Church, but it cannot form a valid concept of Church.[9]

a) Let us mention first of all research in religious studies. Its methodology leads to important insights (even though it does not arrive at an ontological determination of the Church), provided that its research does not rule out, as happens in "liberal" religious studies, supernatural realities that are accessible only to faith, including even God's self-revelation and the Incarnation in Christ. In this connection it is significant that the term "Church" is used only in the different expressions of the "Christian religion."[10]

b) The viewpoint of the Church historians takes us considerably further, inasmuch as Church history is concerned not merely to narrate the secular, sociological manifestation of the Church but also to attempt to portray its origin and activity based on its mystery and its understanding of the world.[11]

c) The traditional apologetic method, found in fundamental theology, made some further progress. In order to remove false objections, fundamental theology tried to understand the Church's manifestation from within (analytical method), and then it tried to support this deeper understanding by means of an interpretation of the nature of the Church in the world which comes close to that of dogmatic theology, especially in regard to the Church's four notes: one, holy, catholic and apostolic (synthetic method).[12]

d) Canon law, which in its self-understanding has been strongly influenced by the reception of Roman law into the Church's legal practice, has seen the Church rather as an organized, authority-bearing institution on the model of the State. In the new code of canon law, the Church's proper social basic structure should have been given better expression by accommodating canon law to the new formulations of the Second Vatican Council.[13] Nevertheless, it must be said that canon law in a special way has always had the totality of the Church in view. In its statements about persons and things it took account of the Church's inner, salvific structure, as well as its real external structure and, through legal norms, clarified and made tolerable the tensions between the divine and secular orders in its life.

e) Dogmatic theology's task is that of grasping the

Church's nature ever more profoundly on the basis of revelation, the self-definitions of the Church in the course of its history, and the living faith of the ecclesial present, which, during the Council, led to a new representation of the Church's self-understanding. Dogmatic theology must determine more exactly the Church's supernatural character which made its concrete appearance as early as the Old Testament revelation in the People of God, called and guided by God, and would, in the New Testament, find itself described as the body of Christ and the temple of the Holy Spirit. In pursuit of this goal, we cannot and should not overlook the fact that every supernatural reality in this world must be grasped in living union with the corresponding natural reality. Otherwise an image of historical reality will arise that is both ideological and unreal. This demand carries with it great difficulties, especially in the case of understanding the Church. In the Church, God entrusts himself and his work to sinful human beings, who not only commit their own mistakes and crimes but in their foolishness and wickedness even attempt to legitimize them with God's Word and God's authorization. And thus, in addition to the scandal of the Cross, there is the scandal of human weakness and wickedness as an obstacle to the credibility of the Church in this world.

4. THE CHURCH AS A MYSTERY OF FAITH

True access to the Catholic understanding of the Church is opened up only by faith, insofar as the Church, though it lives in this world and according to the manner of this world and is an object of human experience and of the historical and social sciences, is a supernatural reality bestowed and preserved by God himself, but not in the same way in which Christ is the head of the Church. Although Christ lived as a man of this world and as a part of this world, he was the Son of God, not only after his baptism and visibly so, through the exaltation which happened to him after death, but, much more, in his very essence as the pre-existent Logos who became man in him, the personally united God-man. The Church too is more than what is visible of it in this world. The risen Lord and his Holy Spirit are present and active in it, even if hidden from natural sight. The Church is not Christ; yet Christ is present in it, and without him it is not the Church in the fullest sense (Col 1,18; Eph 1,22ff.). And for this reason, since the time of Justin and Tertullian, the Church has been mentioned in the Apostles' Creed as an object of faith: "I believe (in) the holy Church." But what does this affirmation of the Creed mean?

a) According to the interpretation largely current today it means that the Church is an object of faith, not of natural experience and understanding only. This corresponds in some degree to the phrasing introduced around A.D 390 by Theodore of Mopsuestia, whose creed no longer uses the form "we believe in" (*pisteuomen*) but rather "we confess" (*homologoumen*): "We confess one baptism, one, holy, catholic and apostolic Church," etc.[14] A clear distinction is hereby drawn between "religious faith" in God the Father, Son, and Holy Spirit, and "confessing faith" in the gifts of salvation granted by God: the Church, baptism for the forgiveness of sins, and eternal life.[15]

b) To reach a judgment concerning the form of this "faith" we must look briefly at the history of this section of the Creed.[16] By the beginning of the second century, in all probability, the trinitarian baptismal formula was expanded by a statement about the "forgiveness of sins through baptism in the Church for life everlasting." Here the Church appears as the location and space in which we encounter the triune God and his salvation. Tertullian still calls the Church the "body" of the triune God.[17] Depending on the emphasis, the Church appears either as the *space* "in which" we believe in baptism, forgiveness of sins, and life everlasting,[18] or as the *location* "in which" the triune God acts through his Spirit,[19] or again, in the Roman version, as the *means* "through which" he acts.[20]

The occasion for this expansion of the baptismal formula in the baptismal creed may have been the struggle against the Gnostics in the second century.[21] Cyril of Jerusalem (d. 386) explains in one of his baptismal sermons[22] (even that late) that in the phrase "I believe in the holy Church" the candidate is admonished not to cling to heretical sects but to "adhere forever faithfully" to the one holy Catholic Church "in which you have been born again." And he calls it "the Mother of us all, just as she is also the bride of our Lord Jesus Christ, the only-begotten Son of God." In the Church all gifts and virtues are at home, "for God has made peace her borders."[23] Augustine says much the same.[24]

The formulation of this statement in the baptismal Creed was: "We believe in the Church," *eis tēn ekklēsian.* This was especially common in the East,[25] where the Church and the Kingdom of God were subsequently more and more identified. Ambrose, Priscillian, and Augustine, however, are still saying *Credo in Ecclesiam.* Finally, Rufinus omits the preposition *in.*[26] The Creed of the Council of Constantinople (A.D. 381) draws attention to the different forms of faith.[27] It subsumes faith in the three divine persons, and in the Church, under the phrase "we believe in" (*pisteuomen*) (religious faith), while baptism for the forgiveness of sins appears as an object of confessing faith (*homologoumen*) and the resurrection and life everlasting as the goal of our believing expectation (*prosdokōmen*).

c) How we are to regard the specific form of faith in the Church depends on how the Church itself is understood. As the special space of the divine saving action in this world, and the final eschatological hope for Christians— the New Jerusalem (Rev 21), as the column and foundation of the truth (1 Tim 3,15) and our mother (Gal 4,26), the Church is the *universale salutis sacramentum*, "the universal sacrament of salvation,"[28] which, to be sure, calls for a different, more personal faith than the objective sacrament of baptism and the promise of eternal life call for. One might ask, however, whether the term *sacramentum* refers more to the visible sign in this world or, rather, to the invisible reality of salvation made present through that sign. One might also ask whether the Church's sacramentality should be understood more in the sense of a sacrament which consists, simply, in our enactment thereof (our "practice"), for example, in confession, or, rather, in the sense of the Eucharistic sacrament, a reality itself "worthy of adoration," or, again, in the sense of marriage as a sacramental state ("practical theory"). For is this not true also of the Church as the "body of Christ," whose head is Christ (Col 1,18; Eph 1,22)? At any rate, faith in the Church must be understood in the specifically Christian sense as "saving faith," a faith which "acknowledges and grasps God's work of salvation in Christ."[29] One cannot rightly understand the Church on earth unless one also sees in it the Lord present in word, sacrament and office. For this reason, the Council of Toledo, meeting in A.D. 693, includes in its creed[30] a point later formulated in a still more exclusive way in the *Decretum pro Jacobitis*,[31] that there is "outside the Church no salvation." The Second Vatican Council, as well as Pope Paul VI in his personal *credo*, expressed this truth in an "inclusive" rather than "exclusive" sense. All salvation comes through the Church of Christ, a Church which must, therefore, be embraced in personal faith and affirmed in love.

d) Before addressing the question of faith in the Church, one must reflect on the problem raised today by criticism of the Church. Hans Küng expresses the viewpoint of many young people, called by Schelsky the "skeptical generation," when he writes: "Just as the Church can be an object of admiration to one, so it can be an object of scandal or at least of disappointed, irritated, sad or bitter criticism to another. . . . Just as one can admire the Church and still not belong to it, so one can criticize it and still belong to it.[32] Such an attitude has been termed, correctly enough, "a psycho-sociological phenomenon." And yet one cannot regard it as a matter of indifference vis-à-vis the Christian reality, for faith in the Church must also be called "religious faith." Psycho-sociological attitudes have to be themselves called into question and clarified by the realities which faith knows and embraces, on pain of the reduction of those realities to the mere play of illusion. Psychological processes must be subordinated to personal insights and decisions. The way towards the building of a community in which and from which we gain our essential life cannot be found in a criticism that is dominated by disappointment and irritation. Besides positive work for the Church, only personal suffering from the deficiencies of this community can be constructive here. Perhaps this too must be found in the Cross of Christ. Let us call to mind the *Rules for Thinking with the Church* in the *Spiritual Exercises* of St. Ignatius of Loyola.[33] Though their formulations are historically conditioned, they can still provide valid direction. Still, rules 1–13 must be read in the same critical spirit needed to read rules 14–17, which confront St. Thomas's teaching on grace.[34]

II

Foundations for Understanding the Church in the Revelation of the Old and New Testaments

INTRODUCTORY REMARKS

Our first task must be to discern the nature of the Church as found in the Scriptures of the Old and New Testaments. In those writings the self-understanding in faith of that reality which we call "Church" is presented in its historical genesis. At the same time, it will be shown how the Church which understood itself in this way, became historical reality in light of its own understanding. The image of the Church found in Scripture must serve as an orientation for the historical image of the Church at any time, especially our own. In this search for the biblical imagery of the Church three considerations must be borne in mind.

I

Holy Scripture is a collection of individual writings from different periods. In their historical, prophetic and paraenetic subdivisions these writings reflect the faith-grounded world-view and self-understanding of their authors as well as of their times. As we know, the writings of the Old Testament were first of all the national literature of ancient Israel, while the writings of the New Testament

were from the outset texts belonging to a supranational
Church. Yet, for Christians, all these writings, Old and
New, form a single whole which, in its variegated history,
is nevertheless unified through its orientation to God, the
one Creator and Lord of history, and his Son, our Redeemer
Jesus Christ, as well as through the teaching office of the
Church. Only a unified, salvation-historical overview of
these time-conditioned affirmations about the people of
God of the Old and New Testaments in its situation and
organization, as found in those times and places, can reveal to us the reality we call "Church" (Eph 1,3–14).

2

The word used for Church in Scripture (*ekklēsia*) appears frequently in the New Testament. In order to grasp
the reality to which the word refers, we should not start
from its conceptual content but from the various real historical images used in the different texts. Images are formally less precise than concepts but richer and fuller in
content. They express a living reality in the course of historical appearances, and they allow one to find formulations for this reality.

3

In accordance with the Eastern use of images, some may
be understood in a more objective relationship to reality.
They can be taken as models, or as structural elements for
a suitable model. An important task of scriptural ecclesiology today is the search for, and furthur development of,
such theological models used for the Church in the Old
and New Testaments.

Before we look at the various terms, concepts, and models (especially the term "Church"), let us briefly sketch
how the way was prepared for this reality "Church" during
the earthly life of Jesus. According to Acts 2, the Church

appeared in its earthly distinctiveness and divine power only at Pentecost, fifty days after Jesus' redemptive death and ten days after his ascension.

a) The Foundation of the Church in the Jesus Event

(1) From the beginning of his public ministry Jesus stands in the midst of the great messianic movement of his people. He accepts the baptism of repentance in the Jordan at the hands of the desert preacher John, his cousin, as a sign of his entry into the dawning "reign of God." After John's beheading, Jesus leaves Judea and goes to Galilee (Capernaum) in order to preach there, just as John before him had preached at the Jordan: "Repent, for the reign of the heavens (= the reign of God) is at hand!" (Mark 1,15; Matt 3,2; 4,17). The messianic eschatological rule of God (basileia tou theou), which Israel expected in this time of political oppression under Roman rule as a political libera-tion, became also the basic theme of Jesus' proclamation. But the human contrast between the ascetical John the Baptist and the ordinary man Jesus (cf. Luke 7,33f.; 7,28) is clear also in the understanding of the new "reign of God." The decisive point is that Jesus proclaims the eschatologi-cal reign of God as something which has arrived in his own person (Luke 11,20). His works are intended to show him to be the Messiah, a point stressed again and again in the discourses in John's Gospel (John 10,22–30,38; 14,1). He calls Yahweh his "Father" and he is one with his Father. For this reason it is in his own person that the reign of God has arrived in this world. Thus he is the new Moses (cf. Matt 5,21f.) and more than the promised Son of David (cf. Mark 12,35ff.). In this way Jesus relates the messianic ex-pectation of the reign of God to his own person.

(2) Like the prophets of the Old Covenant and the rabbis of his time he gathers pupils and disciples around himself. Luke tells of seventy-two disciples (Luke 10,1), just as

Moses had been supported by seventy elders. They followed Jesus, at least until the multiplication of loaves (John 6,66). From among them he selects the Twelve (Mark 3,13–19 par.), whom he calls apostles (Luke 6,13), and whom sends out to preach (Luke 9,1–6). After the Galilean turning point in which many of his followers, even the disciples, abandoned him after the multiplication of loaves (John 6), he begins to instruct these Twelve in a special way, foretelling his suffering and resurrection three times (Mark 8,31; 9,30ff.; 10,32ff., par.). They stay with him until they abandon him at the time of his arrest. In symbol and reality, the Twelve represent the new people of twelve tribes, the Church as the "new Israel" (Gal 6,15f.). Peter is given the promise that he will be the foundation, the steward of the new temple of God, the Church (Matt 16,18f.), and the risen Lord entrusts the whole flock into his charge (John 21,15ff.). All these images reflect promises of the Old Testament and bring them to fulfillment, as we will see below.

(3) The culmination of his life's work and thus the fulfillment of the entire Old Testament salvation-history becomes clear at the Last Supper that Jesus celebrates with the Twelve (Mark 14,12–26, par.). In one single cultic act, this Supper fulfills the Passover and thus the new exodus (Exod 12), the establishment of the covenant (Exod 24) and its fulfillment in the new covenant, and the mystery of the Servant of God in Deutero-Isaiah (cf. the Suffering Servant songs, Isa 42, 49, 50, and 52f.), who takes upon himself suffering and death for the people and who for this is exalted by God.

Now this Christ event is the content of the apostolic preaching as well as the content of the sacramental signs of baptism and the Eucharist. As the origin and ground of the Church, the Christ event constitutes the saving event of the new covenant, the spiritual space of the new people of God. The reality founded and given for all ages in Jesus' earthly life was revealed to the world on the day of Pentecost, when three thousand people accepted baptism after Peter's preaching, and when the mystery of the new salvific community, now known as "Church," came into existence (Acts 2,1,41–46).

We want to approach the mystery of this Church by reflecting on the names, the images, and the models that Scripture uses for it.

b) The term "ecclesia"

The first point of departure for grasping the biblical understanding of the Church must be the New Testament term *ecclesia* (*ekklēsia*). We can then proceed to investigate the images and models which correspond to it in Scripture. The term *ecclesia*[35] appears 114 times in the New Testament: 65 times in Paul, 23 times in Acts, 20 times in Revelation, and 2 times in Matthew (it is not used in Mark, Luke, and John). It can signify the whole Church (cf. Eph 1,22f.; Col 1,18; Gal 1,13; 1 Cor 15,9), as well as local churches (cf. the beginnings of epistles, 1 Cor 1,2; Rev 2,1.8.12, etc.) and particular house-churches (Phlm 1,2). The word did not have this meaning in its original Greek, where it simply means "public gathering." It was borrowed from the Septuagint, where it is used about a hundred times and most often signifies the cultic community or the whole community of God in the cult, the *qahal Jahweh* (this is also the meaning of *synagōgē*). The etymological derivation of *ek-klēsia* from "calling out" (out of the world) cannot be demonstrated.[36]

It is significant that in second-century Rome the original Greek word *ekklesia* was not replaced with a corresponding Latin term (such as *contio* or *commitia*), but was taken over as a fixed borrowed term, because the community of religion or faith had to be distinguished from the political community (which is what *contio* would have meant). The term *"Kirche,"* ("Church") which is used in the Slavic and Germanic languages (introduced into the

German-speaking regions at the time of the Merovingian kings) is also a borrowed term which derives from the Byzantine expression *oikia kyriake,* house (temple) of the Lord (cf. 1 Kings 8,10–53; 1 Cor 3,16f.).[37] It was from Byzantium in the sixth century A.D. that the Germanic peoples coming from Asia adopted this name, which expresses God's glory as well as his grace.

c) *The Church in the Old Testament*

Although the Church, as a community founded by Jesus Christ, appears only in the New Testament, it can be understood only in connection with the history of the people of God in the Old Testament. As believers, the Christians are "children of Abraham" (Gal 3,7).[38] Israel is the "noble olive tree" onto which the Gentiles, as wild shoots, were grafted (cf. Rom 11,17–24; 1 Kgs 8,41–43). Christ wanted to "create in himself one new man in place of the two (Jews and Gentiles), so making peace, and to reconcile both in one body through the cross," so that now "both have access in one Spirit to the Father" (Eph 2,16–18; quoted in the Vatican II "Declaration on the Relationship of the Church to Non-Christian Religions," 4). There are at least two basic notions of the cultic community of the Old Testament which have become important for the Church: the idea of the covenant with God, and the idea of the people of God.

These two ideas are inwardly united, even though the covenant comes first. For it is through the covenant that the community of twelve tribes becomes a people, the people of God. The covenant which the Lord made with Israel contains an element of mutuality like every human covenant (cf. the analogy with the covenant of marriage, Hos 1–3). Still, the covenant does not arise from a bilateral declaration. It is established exclusively as a gift of God's grace. God wants to be the Lord of this people, i.e., not only lawgiver and judge, but also warlord, protector, helper; and the people is to be his people, Yahweh's people, so that all laws and promises, all rewards and punishments, come from Yahweh. "The self-awareness of this people is a reflection of its faith in Yahweh."[39]

In the history of Israel and in its divine revelation, this covenant appears in at least four forms. In the oldest sources there are already two covenants: the covenant with Abraham (Gen 15; J) and the Moses covenant (Exod 24; E). The first is primarily the bearer of personal piety (faith and circumcision), while the second is more the foundation of the moral and religious order, and also the social, economic, and political order of the whole people. According to the various cultural situations, the different literary strata (Yahwist: Exod 24; 32; Deuteronomist: Deut 9,7–10,11; Priestly: Lev) portray the "covenant" differently. Only on the basis of the covenant do twelve tribes of the Hebrew people (cf. Acts 26,6f., *dōdekaphylon*) understand themselves as one people.

The Priestly Writing adds the covenant with Noah (Gen 9,1–17) which is understood as a covenant between God and humanity, as a covenant of peace in which the bow and arrow of war is replaced by the rainbow as a sign of peace and covenant.

Perhaps already in the period of the monarchy there appears the notion of the Lord's covenant with David and his house (cf. 2 Sam 7,12–16; 23,5) which is the basis, at least in the Hellenistic period, of the idea of the Messiah.

In the catastrophes of the Babylonian exile, faith in the covenant with Abraham and Moses had become so problematic to the prophets that they announced a New Covenant (cf. Jer 31,31; 32,37–41; Ezek 34,25–31; 37,23–28; Heb 8,6–13). According to Paul's account of the Last Supper (cf. Luke 22,20; 1 Cor 11,25; cf. Isa 52,13–53,12), Christ himself invoked this prophecy when he instituted the sacrificial meal of the Eucharist as the central cultic action of his Church. The apostles understand themselves as "ministers of the New Covenant" (2 Cor 3,6) just as they understand Christ as the "mediator of the New Covenant" (Heb 9,15; 12,24).

One partner in the covenant is God; the other is the people of God. Looking back to its nomadic origins, Israel understood itself as the fulfillment of a promise which had been given to Abraham, the forefather of the people: "I will make of you a great people. . . . In you all generations of the earth will be blessed" (Gen 12,1–4; cf. 17,1–8). Through his grandson Jacob = Israel (Gen 32,29) this promise was fulfilled when, according to the narrative of the hagiographers (perhaps from the period of the monarchy), Jacob's twelve sons (six from his wife Leah, and two from her servant Zilpah, two from his wife Rachel, and two from her servant Bilhah, Gen 29–35) became the forefathers of the twelve tribes of Israel. In its historical time, the people of the "Hebrews" (*Ibrim* = sons of Eber, Gen 10,21), as Israel originally called itself (Gen 40,15), and as it was called for the most part during the capivity or by its enemies, always referred to itself as "Israel" after its father Jacob, who had received the name Israel (the one who fights with God) from the Lord himself after wrestling with him by the river Jabbok (Gen 32,29; 35,10). According to the conception of the ancient Near East, Jacob continues to live in the people, just as the descendants live in their forefather (cf. Gen 25,23; 48,16; Rom 4,18f.; corporative personality: J. de Fraine). Israel is "the Lord's people," a point made especially clear by Deuteronomy (Deut 7,6; 14,21; 26,18; etc.). Yahweh is "Israel's God" (Deut 4,7; 32,43). The people's cult is directed towards him, and the *qahal,* the gathering of the tribes, is directed towards the cult, or towards judgment or war in the Lord's name (cf. Deut 23). Israel's war is therefore the Lord's war (cf. Exod 17,15f.). Especially after settling in Canaan, Israel understands law and custom as the Lord's decrees (cf. Gen 35; Exod 24, the Covenant Law; Lev 17, the Law of Holiness).

The primordial history of Israel's election by the Lord is and remains the foundation of Israel's national history. In

Deuteronomy, Moses summarizes this self-understanding in the words,

You shall love the Lord, your God, with all your heart, with all your soul, and with all your strength. . . . For you are a people consecrated to the Lord, your God. The Lord, your God, chose you so that from all the peoples on the earth you would become his own possession. It was not because you were greater than the other peoples that the Lord set his love on you and chose you. You are the smallest of all peoples. No, it is because he loves you and keeps the oath he swore to your fathers that the Lord has brought you away with a mighty hand and redeemed you from the house of slavery, from the power of Pharaoh, the King of Egypt. Know therefore that the Lord, your God, is God indeed, the faithful God who keeps his covenant and steadfast love for a thousand generations with those who love him and keep his commandments, but who immediately requites his enemy and destroys him. (Deut 6,5; 7,6–10).

This is also the foundation of Israel's "creed" (Deut 26,5–10), which was recited by the leader during the sacred meals after the first-fruit offering and the yearly Passover sacrifice (in this way it became the exemplar for the *anamnesis*, the Last Supper account, at the New Testament sacrifice in the Mass).

When Israel had forgotten its Lord in Canaan and had turned to the Baals, the prophets again preached faith in Yahweh, Israel's God of old, with threats and promises. Israel's history appears at this point no longer primarily as a "tribal history" or "national history," but as "Israel's history of sin" and as the history of punishment and forgiveness by the Lord ("the Lord's history of salvation"). From the very beginning, despite the idea that Israel alone had been chosen among the Gentile nations, God's salvation was intended through Israel for all peoples (cf. Gen 12,3: "All generations of the earth shall be blessed through you" and John 4,22: "Salvation comes from the Jews"). Christ insists on the universality of salvation through Israel against all limitations in the Judaism of his time (cf. Luke). After the Exile, the idea of the "remnant" (Isa: *shear;* Jer and Ezek: *sheerit*) gained increasing importance until apocalypticism turned the "remnant" into "the little flock" (cf. Luke 12,32) which believed that it alone would be saved (the eschatological history of Israel). The Pharisees as well as the Essenes and the members of the Qumran sect thought that they were this remnant. Fundamental for this concept of the "remnant" (Isaiah, Amos) was the teaching that "the many have to be saved through the few elect" (cf. Matt 20,16). In the Old Testament, the many were always led by God through elect individuals (kings, judges, prophets).[40] In this way, Israel's tribal and national history, with its history of salvation and its eschatological self-understanding, offers the preliminary sketch of the reality which we encounter, *mutatis mutandis,* in the Church of the New Testament.

d) The Church in the New Testament

We can trace these Old Testament antecedents right into the underpinnings of the New Testament Church. They were mediated by the communities of early Judaism and by various strands of Hellenistic influence in local New Testament communities. Of course, everything is transposed and raised to a new level through the mystery of the "Incarnation of God" in Christ. The Incarnation implies that things which were, in the Old Testament, moral tasks for human beings (although God's grace was a present aid and the community of the people supported the individual) became, in the New Testament, supernatural realities in this world if not of this world (cf. John 1,10f.; 8,23).[41] The "New Covenant" is no longer built upon "law and circumcision"; it has become real "in Christ," the Son of God made man, who calls himself the vine and Christians his branches (John 15,1–8). Paul says the same thing in the image of the Church as the "body of Christ" and of

Christians as "members" (Col 1,18; 1 Cor 12,1–12f.). In the New Testament covenant relation, the Old Testament relation between forefather and descendants has been raised to a new, supernatural level through personal Christ-mysticism and the real mystery of Christ as it is expressed, above all, in Pauline christology (Col 1,13–20). For this reason, the "new people of God" formed by Christians (cf. Rom 4,17; Gal 4,26–28) is the community of the true "descendants of Abraham," built upon the new twelve forefathers, the twelve apostles (cf. Luke 6,12–16; Eph 2,19f.), who have become forefathers of the new people of God in the Holy Spirit (cf. Acts 2,1–14). The new primogenitor of this new people of God is Christ. He remains the head of this people, his body. And he is present in this world and time until the end of the world as the "exalted Lord," source of the life of each and every Christian (cf. Matt 28,20). For this reason he is the ever living "mediator of the New Covenant" (Heb 9,15), and in him everything which belongs to him has become "a new creation" (Gal 6,15; 2 Cor 5,17). The decisive point is this: The Old Testament law is replaced in the New Testament by the perfect law of freedom (Jas 1,25) and the Gospel of love (1 John 4,7–16; Isa 61).

For this reason the notion "people of God" is replaced in Paul by the more important term "Church of God" (*ekklēsia tou theou,* cf. Acts 20,28; 1 Thess 2,14; 2 Thess 1,4; 1 Cor 1,2; 10,32; 11,16; 15,9; Gal 1,13—the last text applies above all to the community in Jerusalem). As we said above, this term refers to the cultic community which has its center "in Christ," the Son of Man (cf. Luke 12,8f.; Deut 7,13f.) and which is, therefore, the final, eschatological people of God. This conviction is clearly expressed in the institution of the "paschal sacrifice," the foundation of the New Covenant (cf. 1 Cor 11,25f.: "This cup is the New Covenant in my blood . . . as often as you drink it you proclaim the Lord's death until he comes"). The eschatological character of Christian existence and especially of the Church is expressed even more succinctly when Paul addresses the Christians in the various cities to which he sends his letters as "those who are called as saints," i.e., as the community of those who have become members of this Church by a special call in Christ. Thus he writes in 1 Cor 1,2: "To the church of God which is at Corinth, to those sanctified in Christ Jesus, called as saints, together with all those who in every place call on the name of our Lord Jesus Christ." Similarly, in Rom 1,7 he says: "To all who are in Rome as saints, beloved and called by God." The eschatological character of the Christian community had been expressed even more clearly in the letters to the Thessalonians (partly because of the theme of those letters; cf. 1 Thess 1,9f.; 2 Thess 1,3–12). In the synoptics, this eschatological election is expressed more in the call and mission of the disciples (Luke 10,1–24) in which the Church is prefigured and in which the "brotherhood of Christ" (cf. Matt 23,8; Heb 2,11 and 17) is presented as the fundamental characteristic of the first community.

The same eschatological character had become visible in Jesus' famous parables of the reign of God. This reign can be understood primarily in terms of the mystery of the Incarnation; and so we could express it in the following statements:

(1) The Church as the eschatological reign of God, i.e., as the space in which God comes to reign in this world, is introduced in the three parables of growth: the "seed which grows by itself" (Mark 4,26–29); the leaven (Matt 13,33); and the sower (Mark 4,1–9). The word of God and everything which God gives is represented as something supernatural, something which has its own inner life in human hearts and is effective through itself if no obstacle hinders it. Paul later expresses the same idea as follows: "Only God gives growth" (1 Cor 3,6f.). What is alive in the Church is a gift of God: it is the life of the exalted Lord and the Spirit. Every human work can be only a condition per-

mitted by God, not a cause of the new life. The divine Word and the Spirit of God want to transform the whole world, as a leaven transforms bread dough (Luke 13,20f.). They want to give life anew. And, small as the beginning may seem, its goal encompasses the whole world (cf. the parable of the mustard seed, Mark 4, 30–32).

(2) Jesus expresses the unique inner value of this gift of God, which bears the reign of God on earth, in the parable of the treasure in the field, and that of the pearl found by a merchant (Matt 13,44–46). One gives everything to gain this treasure, once one has realized what it is. For it is a treasure which means everything. It means authentic life.

(3) In addition, the synoptics report parables of Jesus which shed light on the earthly mystery of God's reign in a way which is binding for all times for understanding the Church, even if it is precisely these truths that are most often forgotten. The parable of the weeds in the field (Matt 13,24–30 and 36–43) and the parable of the net with good and bad fish (Matt 13,47–50) clarify what is meant by the "eschatological" element in the reign of God in this eon. The reign of God does not reach its goal in this world; it is always on the way. In this intermediate position it has an "enemy" who sows weeds among the wheat. Christ explicitly says, "Let both grow until the time of the harvest." And in the parable of the fishing net he says that the good will be separated from the wicked only at the end of the world; only then will they receive their reward and punishment, in the judgment which God will carry out through his angels.

(4) The eschatological character of the reign of God on earth, the Church, is not only affected by its intermediate state, but also by the fact that both, the good as well as the wicked, are still on the way. For the wicked, the path of conversion, of turning to God, is still possible; and the good must know, "He who thinks he stands, let him watch lest he fall" (1 Cor 10,12). What Jesus expressed in the parables of the lost drachma, the lost sheep, and the prodi-

gal son (Luke 15,1–32) applies not only to the historical
Jesus but also to the Savior above all time: he is and remains the good shepherd who brings home the lost sheep
(Matt 18,12–14). He gives his life for his own (John 10,11–
18).[42]

In addition to these parables there are many images,
models, and metaphors. Let us briefly reflect on five of
these.

e) Images

Besides "covenant" and "people of God" the New Testament uses many other images for the Church that have the
same salvation-history characteristics. The most important are the images "drawn from pastoral life, agriculture,
building construction, and even from family and married
life" (cf. LG 6).

(1) A first image for the Church born from the thinking
of the ancient near east and particularly suited to the economic and social conditions of Israel, is the image of
"shepherd and flock." The sheep was the most important
domestic animal; its importance goes back to the ancient
nomadic times of the patriarchs. Already in the Old Testament God proclaimed himself through his prophets as the
future "shepherd of his people Israel" (cf. Isa 40,11; Ezek
34,11ff.). And Peter says to his Christians, "You were
straying like sheep, but now you have come home to the
shepherd and guardian of your souls" (1 Pet 2,25). He is
referring to Christ, who called himself the "good shepherd," who knows his own and is recognized by his own,
who gives his life for his sheep (cf. John 10,1–18), and who
follows the lost sheep to carry it home on his shoulders,
full of joy (cf. Luke 15,4–7).

The basic elements of this image are the following: It
is to the shepherd that the sheep belong; he is their lord.
At the same time he cares for them with love and eager-
ness, because they are his wealth and his joy. Authority

and power (Homer: the kings are the "shepherds of the peoples") as well as loving care are expressed in this image (cf. Psalm 23). The flock needs its shepherd, lest it perish from its enemies (wolves) and from hunger. This is the reason for the frequent lament about "the sheep without shepherd" (Num 27,17; Ezek 34,5; Matt 9,36). It also explains God's threat to Israel, "I will strike the shepherd and the sheep will scatter" (Zech 13,7ff.; Matt 26,31) and God's mourning about the "wicked shepherds who pasture themselves" (cf. Ezek 34; John 10,12f.).

(2) A second group of images is taken from agriculture. Especially Jesus' parables about the "reign of God" frequently speak of the "field into which the sower sows his seed" (cf. Matt 13,1–23). The seed grows by itself (cf. Mark 4,26ff.), but many enemies endanger it (cf. Matt 13,24–30). The smallest mustard seed turns into a great bush (cf. Matt 13,31f.). Paul says to his Christians: You are God's field. Paul has planted; Apollos has watered. But the one who gives growth is the Lord (cf. 1 Cor 3,6–9). The human realm of the field and the divine gift of seed, God's action and the cooperation of those who are called by God (cf. Matt 9,38) are clearly expressed here.

Corresponding to the agricultural conditions of Palestine and the whole Mediterranean, and Mesopotamia as well, two plants are frequently mentioned in addition to wheat. They serve not only to maintain human life but to enhance the culture of the land and the vitality and joy of its inhabitants: the olive tree and the vine. The olive tree is in many ways important because of the oil which is pressed from its fruits. Oil was not only the most important fat for food; it was also the fuel for lamps, a cosmetic, a medicine, and a means for sacred anointing, as in the case of kings and priests. For this reason Heb 1,9 applies the word of "the king's anointing for his wedding" (Psalm 45,7) to Christ, the "anointed," the royal son of David. In Zech 4,11–14, the governor and the high-priest Joshua appear as "sons of oil" (cf. Rev 11,3–13). In Rom 11,17ff.,

Paul applies the image of the olive tree to the people of God, from which the Jews are broken off at the time of Christ and replaced by wild heathen grafts, in order that these wild shoots would be ennobled through the good olive tree (an inversion of the natural image). The most important element in this image is "joy and salvation" ("the oil of joy," Psalm 45,8).

More important still are the images of the vine and the vineyard which are metaphorical images for Israel (cf. Psalm 80,9–12; Isa 5,1–4;32,12; Jer 2,21; Hos 10,1; Ezek 15,2; 19,10). And thus the workers in the vineyard become an image of those who are called to work for the reign of God on earth according to their call and the commandment of God (cf. Isa 3,14; 5,1–7). Christ uses this image very often (cf. Matt 20,1–16; 21,28–32.33–41). In a unique application, Christ calls himself "the vine" and his father "the vinedresser" and the disciples "the branches" (cf. John 15,1–8). They must live from Christ who is the "tree of life." They are dead and sterile without him. To serve Christ's reign is possible only in Christ and through Christ.

All images from agricultural life are concerned essentially with this "service for the reign of God" in the community of Jesus, the Church on earth.

(3) A completely new group of images is connected with the construction of buildings and the most important buildings in Israel, the temple and the city Jerusalem. Paul, above all, uses these images very frequently. He expressly calls the Church a "building of God" (1 Cor 3,9). The true foundation (*themelios*) is Christ, the cornerstone (*kephalēgōnias*) which determines the floor plan of the construction (cf. Matt 21,42; 1 Peter 2,7; Psalm 118,22). The apostles and prophets are foundations (Eph 2,19–22; Rev 21,14). And Paul says of himself that he constructed the Church upon Christ (cf. 1 Cor 3,10ff.). This Church, which is built with human beings, is called "house of God" or "temple of God" (cf. 1 Tim 3,15) in which the "family of

God" lives, the family which is itself the dwelling place of God and his Spirit (cf. 1 Cor 3,16f.; Eph 2,19–22). When this earth perishes at the end of time, the same Church will descend as "the tent of God among us" like a bride who is adorned for her husband (Rev 21,2). It will be the "new Jerusalem," the "new holy city of God," in which God himself will be "light and temple."

Two terms which are especially important for understanding the Church are connected with this architectural allegory and reveal its deeper meaning. One of them is the word "build up, edify" (epoikodomeō: 1 Thess 5,11; 1 Cor 3,10.12; Eph 2,20; Col 2,7; 1 Pet 2,5) which signifies the outward growth of the Church through the addition of new members, as well as the inner renewal, vitalizing, and deepening of Christian life. Paul summarizes the dimensions of theological meaning contained in this image when he writes about his activity in the Church as an apostle:

We are God's fellow workers . . . you are God's building. According to the grace of God given to me, like a careful master builder I laid a foundation, and another man is building upon it. Let each one take care how he builds upon it. For nobody can lay any other foundation than that which is laid, which is Jesus Christ. Now if any one builds on the foundation with gold, silver, precious stones, wood, hay, straw—each person's work will become manifest. For the day (of the Lord) will disclose it, because it will be revealed with fire, and the fire will test what sort of work each one has done. If the work which anyone has built on the foundation survives, he will receive a reward. If anyone's work is burned up, he will suffer loss. Though he himself will be saved, it will only be as through fire. (1 Cor 3,9–15)

The second term is oikonomia (cf. 1 Cor 9,17; Eph 1,10; 3,29; 1 Tim 1,4), which refers to the "economy of salvation" according to the divine plan that determines and supports this community of God's household.

The decisive point in the whole architectural allegory is that what is meant is not an edifice built from stones but always a building composed of human beings, so that Peter can write: "Set yourselves upon the living stone [Christ] . . . and like living stones let yourselves be built up into a spiritual temple, into a holy priesthood, to offer spiritual sacrifices pleasing to God through Jesus Christ" (cf. 1 Pet 2,4–8). God is the master builder; he is always active and the building belongs to him. There are those who are especially commissioned to build up the Church, namely, the apostles (cf. 1 Cor 4,1f.: steward, *oikonomos*, of the mysteries of God). But every member of the Church must help in the construction, because this Church must always be built further and anew. Ignatius, martyr and bishop of Antioch (d. 116), says to the Ephesians that they are "stones for the temple of the Father, prepared for the building of God the Father, lifted up by the lever of Jesus Christ, which is the cross, while the Holy Spirit is the rope. Your faith is your guide to the heights, and love is the way" (cf. *Ad Eph.* 9). The *Shepherd of Hermas* (ca. 150) further elaborates these ideas of the building and of the Christians as living stones (cf. *Herm. Vis.* III 2,4–7,6): construction of a tower above the water (baptism) with stones from the water (the baptized), which always fit, and stones from the land (the unbaptized), of whom only a small number fit.

The image of the building shows that the Church is at the same time a fixed "institution" and again and again a living, new "event" for the individual. God dwells in this building and all of its stones belong to him; they are God's stones, just as Christ is the foundation and the cornerstone. These New Testament images are prepared in the Old Testament.

(4) A further group of images "personifies" the Church according to Near Eastern custom and speaks of "mother Church" or of the "Church as bride." Paul first calls the Church "our mother" when he compares the Old Covenant to Hagar, the servant of Abraham, who was dismissed with her son Ishmael, and the New Covenant with Sarah,

the rightful wife of Abraham, whose son Isaac became the forefather of Israel (cf. Gal 4,21–31). Here he calls the Church "the Jerusalem above, our mother, the free one." The author of the Apocalypse sees the old and the new Jerusalem in their unity when he speaks of the woman who gives birth to a son and who appears upon the heavens, surrounded by the sun, the moon, and the stars, pursued by the dragon.

The image of the Church as mother takes on special importance in the parallel between "Eve and Mary," which was introduced by Justin Martyr and fully unfolded and applied to the Church by Ambrose. Like Eve, the Church is the "mother of all the living," and, like Mary, she is the mother of all those who have the new life of Christ, a life received from the Church in the bath of baptism. The Church is "virgin and mother" like Mary, and the spiritual mother of those who are born again in redemption from Christ, her son (cf. *Comm. on Luke* II 7; *De Virg.* I 5,22; likewise Augustine *De l. origin.* I 2). Similarly, Ephrem the Syrian applies Isa 7,14 ("the virgin will conceive . . .") to the virginal motherhood of the Church. In his commentary on Revelation, Gennadius (d. ca. 500) says: "Continuously the Church gives birth in pain to the one Christ in his members" (PL 35,24–34). Ambrose does not tire of speaking about the "virginal mother Church" (*De virg.* I 6,31). In its Constitution on the Church, Vatican II unites the mystery of the motherhood of Mary and the motherhood of the Church by saying about the Church, "Through preaching and baptism she brings forth to a new and immortal life children who are conceived of the Holy Spirit and born of God" (LG 64). Of course, one must point out the fundamental difference between this Christian doctrine of "Mary and the Church" and the verbally similar doctrine of the founder of the Nazarean sect, Johann Jacob Wirz (1778–1858). His doctrine is essentially dualistic, built upon the Platonic-Kabbalistic myth of the androgynous man; it must be understood in metaphysical terms, not in terms of the history of salvation. This remark is important, because this androgynous idea becomes important again for the "concept of the Church" in Hegel's philosophy of religion (*Vorlesungen über die Philosophie der Religion*, Part 3, III), and because Hegel plays an important role in contemporary theology.[43]

Two further texts became important for the doctrine of the Church as bride of Christ or bride of God. The first is the Song of Songs, which describes the relation between Israel and the Lord as a dialogue between bride and bridegroom in the form of a collection of Near Eastern love songs. In the Christian period it was applied to the relation between the Church and Jesus, between the human soul and God. Origen was the one, above all, who introduced this interpretation of the Song of Songs into the Christian proclamation. And the later commentaries on the Canticle developed a special "Church-mysticism."

The second text is Rev 19,7f. (cf. 21,2 and 9), which describes how at the end of time the Church descends from heaven as the "bride (and wife) of the lamb, adorned for her husband." This image expresses the eschatological character of the Church as well as the unity between the triumphant Church in heaven and the earthly Church. At the same time it expresses the supernatural beauty and joy of the Church which she does not possess out of herself, but which is completely and in every respect a gift of God: love and belonging to Christ, her husband, and to God, her Lord. Paul applied the mystery of the union of love between Christ and his Church to the mystery of the sacramental union between husband and wife in the sacrament of matrimony (cf. Eph. 5,21–32). The medieval commentaries on Revelation unfold these ideas in detail. Jesus' great parables in which he depicts himself as the bridegroom for whom the Father has prepared a wedding feast point to the Church as bride (Matt 22,1–14; Luke 14,16–24; Matt 25,1–13).

Of course, the fact that this glorious bride of Christ presents a miserable distortion of herself in her earthly appearance and action, in the sinfulness of her members, and that she still remains the Church of Christ, because Christ loves her and accepts her by calling her to conversion,— this fact is expressed in another image, that of the "holy whore." The Fathers used this image, and it finds its biblical application to the history of salvation in the medieval controversies concerning the Church.[44]

(5) The most important New Testament image for the Church is Paul's image of the "body of Christ." Let us present it in its basic outline. The image appears in two forms which are fundamental for understanding the Church. It is not taken from everyday life, as Jesus' parables are, but from grand cosmic conceptions. The first form, which Paul uses above all in his major letters, comes from contemporary Stoic philosophy, which illustrates and understands community, especially the state, through the image of an organically structured body. Plato uses this image: *Laws* 829a; Aristotle does as well, *Politics*, 1253a; likewise Poseidonius of Apamea (d. 50 B.C.), and in dependence on him, Cicero, *De off.* III 19; Seneca, *De ira* II 31,7; Ep. 92,30; 95,51f.: *membra unius corporis magni*, the members of one great body; Epictetus, *Diatribai* II 5,24. In 1 Cor 12,12–26 (cf. 12,1–31) and Rom 12,4–8, Paul shows by means of this image that Christians, in their totality as Church, form one body of Christ, or one body in Christ (cf. Rom 12,5), whose Spirit they possess, and that, as individuals, they are "members of this body." The members of the body have different functions with different degrees of dignity; and yet they are equally necessary for the body. The same is true of Christians. The service of all members is a service for the one body, from which they all derive their life and without which they could not live (cf. 2 Cor 5,14–21; 8,9; 13,3–5; Gal 3,28; 6,2; cf. John 15,1–8). Paul excludes the pantheistic and naturalistic background of the Stoic doctrine by teaching that God (not nature) freely (not by necessity) gives the particular gifts and that a

person becomes a member of this body through his or her free personal relationship to Christ in faith and love and through baptism (cf. Rom 6,2–12; 13,14a; Gal 3,27).

In Paul's letters from captivity, the image of the "body of Christ" appears in a new form and with implications which suggest an understanding of this image in terms of a completely different background, namely, the gnostic image of the "primordial man" in whom all individual human beings find their salvation. Four times in the captivity letters, the Church is called "body of Christ" (Col 1,24; Eph 1,23; 4,12; 5,29); five times Christ is called "the head of the Church" (Col 1,18; 2,18f.; Eph 1,22; 4,15; 5,23). As head, Christ is the creator (Eph 2,15) and redeemer (Eph 5,23) of his body, the Church. In Christ dwells the fullness (*plērōma*) of divinity, and in Christ Christians are filled with this fullness (cf. Col 2,9f.; Eph 3,19; sacramental understanding). The parallel between Christ and Adam (Rom 5,15–19; 1 Cor 15,45–50: the idea of the primogenitor) as well as Paul's understanding of marriage (cf. 5,21–33; the motif of the "bride"), of the mystery of baptism (Rom 6,1–11; 1 Cor 12,13), and of the Eucharist (1 Cor 12,17; cf. the importance of baptism and meals in the Mithras cult) may have been a factor in Paul's adoption of the gnostic image. Paul overcomes the dualistic and pantheistic tendency of the gnostic image by insisting on the history of salvation in which every event is God's free deed and free human acceptance.

Vatican II summarized the wealth of the body allegory in *Lumen Gentium* 7. Because of its importance, let us look at this text as a whole.

In the human nature which he united to himself, the Son of God redeemed man and transformed him into a new creation (cf. Gal 6,15; 2 Cor 5,17) by overcoming death through his own death and resurrection. By communicating his Spirit to his brothers, called together from all peoples, Christ made them mystically into his own body.

In that body, the life of Christ is poured into the believers, who through the sacraments, are united in a hidden and real way to Christ who suffered and was glorified.[45] Through baptism we are formed in the likeness of Christ: "For in one Spirit we are all baptized into one body" (1 Cor 12,13). In this sacred rite, a union with Christ's death and resurrection is both symbolized and brought about: "For we were buried with him by means of baptism into death." And if "we have been united with him in the likeness of his death, we shall be so in the likeness of his resurrection also" (Rom 6,4–5).

Truly partaking of the body of the Lord in the breaking of the Eucharistic bread, we are taken up into communion with Him and with one another. "Because the bread is one, we, though many, are one body, all of us who partake of the one bread" (1 Cor 10,17). In this way all of us are made members of his body (cf. 1 Cor 12,27), "but severally members of one another" (Rom 12,5).

As all the members of the human body, though they are many, form one body, so also are the faithful in Christ (cf. 1 Cor 12,12). Also, in the building up of Christ's body there is a flourishing variety of members and functions. There is only one Spirit who, according to his own richness and the needs of the ministries, distributes his different gifts for the welfare of the Church (cf. 1 Cor 12,1–11). Among these gifts stands out the grace given to the apostles. To their authority, the Spirit himself subjected even those who were endowed with charisms (cf. 1 Cor 14). Giving the body unity through himself and through his power and through the internal cohesion of its members, this same Spirit produces and urges love among the believers. Consequently, if one member suffers anything, all the members suffer it too, and if one member is honored, all the members rejoice together (cf. 1 Cor 12,26).

The head of this body is Christ. He is the image of the invisible God and in him all things came into being. He has priority over everyone and in him all things hold together. He is the head of that body which is the Church. He is the beginning, the firstborn from the dead, so that in all things he might have the first place (cf. Col 1,15–18). By the greatness of his power he rules the things of heaven and the things of the earth, and with his all-surpassing perfection and activity he fills the whole body with the riches of his glory (cf. Eph 1,18–23).[46]

All the members ought to be molded into Christ's image until he is formed in them (cf. Gal 4,19). For this reason we who have been made like unto him, who have died with him and been raised up with him, are taken up into the mysteries of his life, until we reign together with him (cf. Phil 3,21; 2 Tim 2,11; Eph 2,6; Col 2,12; etc.). Still in pilgrimage upon the earth, we trace in trial and under oppression the paths he trod. Made one with his sufferings as the body is one with the head, we endure with him, that with him we may be glorified (cf. Rom 8,17).

From him, "the whole body, supplied and built up by joints and ligaments, attains a growth that is of God" (Col 2,19). He continually distributes in his body, that is, in the Church, gifts of ministries through which, by his own power, we serve each other unto salvation so that, carrying out the truth in love, we may through all things grow up into him who is our head (cf. Eph 4,11–16).

In order that we may be unceasingly renewed in him (cf. Eph 4,23), he has shared with us his Spirit who, existing as one and the same being in the head and in the members, vivifies, unifies, and moves the whole body. This he does in such a way that his work could be compared by the holy Fathers with the function which the soul fulfills in the human body, whose principle of life the soul is.[47]

Having become the model of a man loving his wife as his own body, Christ loves the Church as his bride (cf. Eph 5,25–28). For her part, the Church is subject to its head (cf. Eph 5,22–23). "For in him dwells all the fullness of the Godhead bodily" (Col 2,9). He fills the Church, which is his body and his fullness, with his divine gifts (cf. Eph 1,22–23) so that it may grow and reach all the fullness of God (cf. Eph 3,19). (LG 7)

What Vatican II says in this text is developed from rich scriptural images. It is quite understandable that the model of the Church expressed in these images underwent many shifts of emphasis in the course of history. For example, Augustine integrated his Roman idea of *civitas* into the doctrine of the Church; the Germanic Middle Ages introduced their sociological concept of the people into the idea of the body of Christ. Making use of the Stoic ideas in 1 Cor 12, they spoke of a *"corpus ecclesiae"* rather than of a *"corpus Christi."* One saw in this body the community of the faithful organized on earth, which struggles on earth for God's cause and for the salvation of its members. The Platonic-Augustinian doctrine that the *"civitas terrena"* is only a part of the *"civitas celestis"* still on pilgrimage was replaced by the Aristotelian-Thomistic conception of the *"praesens ecclesia,"*[48] and (since John of Salisbury, around 1160) by that of the *"ecclesia militans,"* which was seen as a community of faith and love, to which sinful members belong "in body, not in mind, in number, not in merit."[49] The Church as mystical body was thus itself seen as *sacramentum,* in the sense in which this term had been understood since the eleventh century. Its external legal constitution became more and more distinct as an outward sign of the sacramental reality. The view of the High Middle Ages arose in part against evangelism and the view of a pure Spirit-Church of the twelfth century (cf. Peter of Bruys, d. 1126; Arnold of Brescia, d. 1155; Waldes, after 1173). In a similar contrast, nineteenth-century Romanticism (C. Passaglia, 1853; Cl. Schrader, J. Franzelin, 1879) developed a more organic conception of the mystical body of Christ against the Enlightenment understanding of the Church as a human pedagogical institution and against the ecclesiology of idealism (cf. J. A. Möhler). It thereby wanted to stress once again the sacramental character of the Church. After the encyclical *Mystici Corporis* of 1943 (which was drafted by S. Tromp) there was a reaction against these "romantic elements" in the idea of the body of Christ, a reaction in the name of a new "theology of the Cross" versus the old "theology of glory."[50] The idea of the "people of God" was intended to be a cure for the excessive elements of Romanticism.[51]

One cause of this controversy was the modern objective-scientific mode of thinking, which misunderstood the symbolic thought of Romanticism. Many events in the Church of the last ten years may challenge us to see and acknowledge more clearly the supernatural reality of the Church, which can only be grasped in faith, as opposed to its external reality which is accessible to experience. The biblical idea of the body of Christ, which must always be a corrective for any subsequent development, cannot be made fruitful for today without the acknowledgment and integration of the development that has occurred in the two thousand years of history since then.

What has been said in Part One about the Church on the basis of natural sociology or Church history (I), and about its foundation in the biblical images of the history of salvation (II), is intended as a help for developing a "theological model" or "theological concept" of the Church in Part Two. But before we turn to that let us first give a brief overview of the development of ideas on the Church in its two thousand years of history (III).

III

A Brief History of the Development in the Catholic Understanding of the Church

I. FROM PENTECOST TO CONSTANTINE

The Church grew from the preaching and baptizing of the small group of Christ's twelve apostles on the feast of Pentecost (cf. Acts 2). Its members did not understand it as an "association," which is determined by a certain purpose and by certain conditions of membership. From the very beginning (cf. Ignatius of Antioch, *Smyrn.* 8,2), the individual communities understood themselves as "communities of the one Catholic Church." Each Christian saw his true center, the source of his life, in the "living Lord Jesus," who was present in the eucharistic celebration of the community: as a teacher in its liturgy of the word, and as sacrifice and priest in its paschal liturgy. The heads of the communities, the bishops, were understood as successors of the apostles and thus as bearers of the "divine mission" which Jesus had received and which he had passed on to his apostles (cf. John 20,21; Ignatius of Antioch in his letters; 1 *Clem* 42). The persecutions of the Christians by the synagogue (Saul) as well as by the Roman state (after Nero) helped the communities and the Church to unfold their religious depth as well as their outward organization.

Important in the Church's growth were the mentalities of the various peoples who were its mainstay. The first people to be mentioned in this context is Israel, the people which understood itself in its origin as "the people of God." According to Israel's faith, God himself let this people spring from the stem of Abraham and from the twelve sons of his grandson Jacob. God himself revealed his name "Yahweh" to this people through Moses. In a first exodus Moses liberated the descendants of Israel who had been oppressed in Egyptian slavery; at the will of God he transformed them on Mount Sinai into a people, through the "law of God" which governed the private and public, the cultural, economic and political dimensions of the people. God himself made his "covenant" with his people and transformed Israel into "his people." Israel, its history and its institutions, its cult and its religious convictions, in fact many elements of the mentality of this people which found living expression in its language, became the basis of the new "Church." Jesus of Nazareth, the founder of this Church, as well as his twelve apostles and his disciples are without exception children of this people. Nevertheless, Israel as a people and a state rejected Jesus of Nazareth as the Messiah. In addition, the Jewish element did not remain the only important foundation of the Church. Many other peoples, their spirit and their history, have further developed, actualized, and marked the Church.

Next to Israel one must mention the Semitic Syrian people. A center for Gentile mission under Paul and Barnabas grew up in Antioch, the capital of Syria. It was here that the members of the Church were first called Christians (Acts 11,19ff.). Because of their spiritual kinship with the Jewish people, the Syrians clearly understood and faithfully preserved the primordial elements of the Christian message. The Syrian Church played an important role also in later times: in the second century, the "catechetical school of Antioch" was founded. With the help of Aristotelian philosophy, it developed a very sober interpretation of the scriptural message of faith. From this people there came the great Fathers: Ephrem the Syrian (d. 373), whose mysticism continued to be influential for a long time, and John of Damascus (d. around 750, perhaps an Arab?), whose *De fide orthodoxa* remains to this day the theological textbook of the Greek churches. In the fifth and sixth centuries, Syria became for the most part Nestorian.

Because of their greatness as a people and their advanced culture, the Greeks were even more important as interpreters of the Christian message. It is in the Greek language, the international language of that time, that the New Testament has come down to us. Since the third century B.C., Jews had read and quoted the Old Testament in Greek (the Septaugint). Under the influence of Platonic philosophy, especially in the catechetical school of Alexandria (Clement and Origen), faith and knowledge became a fundamental question in Christianity, not only in theology, but in the Church's communities as well. The development of the Church in the fourth and fifth centuries was decisively shaped by the "excommunication of heretics," i.e., of those who did not agree with the interpretation of the faith given by the legitimate bishops and councils. The mystery cults of antiquity, which were used since Paul for understanding the Church (body of Christ: Eph 2; Col 1) and its cult (sacraments: Rom 6,2–12), have their roots in Hellenistic thought. It was in the world of Greek culture that the Church resolved its first great doctrinal controversies (the controversy with Gnosticism) and clarified its understanding of Christ (in Nicaea, 325; Ephesus, 431; Chalcedon, 451), its understanding of God (Constantinople, 381), and its self-understanding (in the canons of the first four councils). Besides the bearers of the office (the bishops as successors of the apostles), charismatics played a great role in this cultural setting. The mystery of the Church as the bride of Christ, the mother of Christians, and the queen of the world was expressed in the symbolic language of Alexandrian theology through the image of the moon (as opposed to the sun, Christ).[52] From John 19,33 (blood and water from the side of Christ), John Chrysostom (d. 407) developed his symbolic theology of the Church: the Church came to be from the side of Christ as Eve did from the side of Adam, and in particular, it came to be from "baptism and mystery" (the Eucharist), which are symbolically indicated in "water and blood" (*Cat.* 3,13–19; SC 53,174–77).

The world power of Rome introduced a new element into the understanding of the Church, not only by its encouragement of Christian persecution, but even more by the Roman idea of "law and order" (*ordo et lex*) and its consciousness of the state (*civitas*). This form of thought raised and sustained questions of power, rank and organization in the Church. Although the Roman province of Africa inclined more towards territorial independence (cf. Cyprian's view of the bishop's role), the centralist idea remained normative in Roman thinking. This was especially clear after Innocent I and Leo I. The Greeks considered this centralistic thought of the Romans a danger to their own independence (cf. Chalcedon, canon 28).

2. FROM CONSTANTINE TO THE EARLY MIDDLE AGES

The Emperor Constantine (312–37) effected a decisive shift in the understanding of the Church. Until his reign the Church had been persecuted by the Roman state. Now it was taken into its service. Poor missionary bishops and pastors were turned into high officials of the state. At this time the Church found its hierarchical order, and Byzantine ceremonial forms were introduced into the public life of the Church as well as into its worship. From the third century on, the "patriarchal sees" of Alexandria, Antioch, and Constantinople developed along with the See of Rome. In Constantinople the Roman emperor remained a political force in the Church until the fall of the Byzantine Empire in 1453. These factors still determine the relation between Church and state as well as that between priests and laity in the Eastern Church.

After Theodosius' division of the Roman Empire into East and West (395), and aided by the fall of the Western empire (476), a distinct Western Church developed in Rome. The end of the Roman emperors during the barbarian invasions led the bishops of Rome, the popes, to assume political power (beginning in the fifth century). The idea of "eternal Rome" and of "Rome, the world power" was linked to the idea of the Church. This gave rise to the new understanding of the "eternal Rome" as the "capital of the Church," although this conception had been introduced at least since the second century by the fact that Peter and Paul were buried there (cf. 1 Clem.), and by the universal recognition of Rome as a world power. In this way, beginning in the fifth century, the pre-eminence of Rome in the Church was also politically buttressed. The increase of power is especially clear in the pontificate of Pope Leo I (d. 461), and in the great missionary activity and organizational reform under Pope Gregory I (d. 604). This development of the Western Church must have seemed dangerous to the Eastern Church, especially when Leo III anointed the Frankish Charlemagne as emperor of the "Holy Roman Empire of the German Nation" and placed the territory of the popes, who had up to this point been subject to the Eastern emperors, under the protection of the Frankish emperors.

Under Photius (865) these changes prepared the separation of the churches of the West and the East, which became a political reality in 1054. In this way the one Church of Christ was for the first time divided. The political schism, sealed through the fatal calamity of the Fourth Crusade in 1204, was also rooted from the outset in the difference of the theological development of creedal affirmations in East and West. The legend of the "Donation of Constantine" and the "Pseudo-Isidoran Decretals" increased and fortified the power and the possessions of the bishops of Rome. The religious idea of the "city of God," which Augustine had added to the biblical images of the people of God, the body of Christ, mother Church, and the bride of Christ, became in a more secularized form (after Nicholas I, 858–867) the model of the Church of Rome.

Among the Germanic peoples, the fifth group that formed the Church, the inner structure of the Western Church received a new form through medieval "clericalism." Literary education as well as greater possessions and higher power became the prerogative of the clergy and a few noble families. In this way the Germanic feudal structure was supported and deepened through Christian ideas. The world Church seemed to identify itself more and more with the "Holy Roman Empire of the German Nation."

3. THE WESTERN CHURCH FROM THE EARLY MIDDLE AGES TO THE REFORMATION

Around the turn of the millennium, the Eastern Church came into contact with the slavic peoples, the sixth family of peoples that shaped the Church. It developed a spiritually new variant of its own nature in the Russian Church. After the fall of Byzantium, the "second Rome," Moscow, the city in which the tsars retained power until 1917, attempted to assume a leadership role in the Church as the "third Rome."

While the Eastern Churches remained in essential respects the same in their theological self-understanding after their independence through the schism of 1054, the Western Church continued to develop in important respects, especially in the time we call the Middle Ages. The Eastern Church did not experience Middle Ages of its own.

The special development of the Western Church has its root in the great internal reform movement of Cluny, which attempted to bring out the interior, supernaturally unique reality of the Church, and to free it from the strong influence of, and dependence on, powerful worldly princes. The reform, which the monks began and pursued as an internal reform, was given political secular contour through the external activity of the great reformers Popes Leo IX (1049–1054), Nicholas II (1054–1061), and Gregory VII (1073–1085). Beginning in the eleventh century, the Western Church supported this reform through a special "Church law" or "Canon Law," which was rooted not in the liturgy of the Church, as were the canons of the Eastern Church, but rather in the legal norms of the Roman state (*Corpus Juris Civilis Justiniani*, 533).

The extended controversies between the pope and the emperor about *sacerdotium* and *imperium* (the investiture controversy settled by the concordat of Worms in 1122) resulted by the end of the thirteenth century in a strengthening of the papacy. The title *vicarius Christi*, which from the time of Gregory VII had been applied to every bishop, was now reserved for the bishop of Rome, the pope. By the time of High Scholasticism, the Church had become not only the center of learning, but also the greatest economic and political power in the West. The power of the popes, which had been based since Leo I on the scriptural doctrine of primacy (Matt 16,18), was considerably strengthened and extended through the work of the reformer popes, through canon law, and through the new mendicant orders (Franciscans, Dominicans, Augustinians, and Carmelites) who placed themselves with their possessions and their obedience entirely under the papacy which resulted in a significant papal strengthening and expansion. This becomes very clear in writings about papal power between about 1300 and 1340.[53] The profound mystery of the Church was portrayed in dependence on the theology of the Fathers through the images of the "bride" of the Canticle, of the "whore" of the Old Testament, and the contrast between Church and Synagogue.[54] In scholastic theology (Thomas Aquinas and Bonaventure), the basic outline of the doctrine of the Church was developed on the basis of the image of the Church as the "body of Christ" and the *"gratia capitis."*[55] An additional factor of the ascendancy of the Church to world power was the adoption of the philosophy of Aristotle (Albert the Great) through which theology, and all of Western thought, was given a new relation to the non-human world, to critical thinking, and to science.

All of these factors tended toward a worldliness of the Church which produced great pressure for a radical turnabout. In the year 1302 (the year of the bull *Unam Sanctam* of Boniface VIII, which attempted to subject all secular power to the power of the Church) there began the great catastrophes of the Church in this time. Through them the people of the Church were given a new image and experience of the Church: the papal captivity in Avignon (1309–1377) and the Great Western Schism of 1378–1417. The impact of these catastrophes was strengthened through the nominalism of theologians of that period and the struggle of urban culture against aristocratic rule.

Against the Waldensians and other laicistic movements of the thirteenth century the image of the Church in the High Middle Ages was for the first time theologically articulated, for example, by Moneta of Cremona (1241) and even more so in the reign of Boniface VIII by the Augustinian Jacobus Capocci of Viterbo (d. 1308; in 1302 he wrote *De regimine christiano*). In contrast, the nominalism of the fourteenth century made the distinction between a visible democratic Church on earth and an invisible unified Church of the predestined or the saints. The new ideas were unfolded especially by John Wycliffe (d. 1384 in Oxford) and John Huss (d. 1417 in Constance, active in Prague). Beginning in 1377 they had been expressed by Wycliffe in his works *De ecclesia* and *De potestatae Papae.* The Lollards, Wycliffe's lay apostles, spread these ideas and imposed them with violence. The Roman Augustinian monk Augustinus and the bishop Dietrich of Nieheim (d. 1418; main work: *De modis uniendi ac reformandi*) further developed these ideas. They had already appeared in the spiritualistic ideas of Joachim of Fiore (d. 1202) and the *spirituales* of the Franciscans (John of Parma, d. 1289; Peter John Olivi, d. 1298).

The fifteenth century produced the most important works of conservative theology about the Church, written in connection with the councils of Constance (1414–1418) and Basel (1438–1443). The Carthusian Stephen of Dole wrote his famous apologetic dialogue *De ecclesia*[56] against Wycliffe and Huss, and Thomas Netter, called Waldensis (d. 1431), wrote his three books of *Doctrinale antiquitatum fidei ecclesiae catholicae*. The Dominican Heinrich Kalteisen (d. 1465) from Cologne and the Dominican John Stoicovic of Ragusa (d. 1443) worked and wrote for the Council of Basel. It was for the same Council that Cardinal Juan de Torquemada (d. 1468) summarized the doctrine of the Church in a strictly papalist tractate called *Summa de ecclesia*.

The characteristic mark of the doctrine of the Church in this time is the increasing separation between the political-legal foundation for understanding the Church and the question of justification. This situation was favorable to the idea of conciliarism (which originated in the erroneous *Defensor pacis* of Marsilius of Padua, completed in 1324). It was for practical reasons that the conciliarist tendency introduced by the first Roman canon lawyers (e.g., Huguccio, d. 1210) achieved absolute validity, especially at the Council of Constance.[57] Although secular conciliarism, which is foreign to the Church, was now overcome, the question of "executive power in the Church" in questions of faith and Church order (whether belonging to the pope, or to an ecumenical Council, or to the people of the Church) had not yet been completely answered, as the controversies and questions at Vatican II show).[58] The reason is that questions of power and majority overburdened this question, while it should be decided by the true understanding of the Church and of theological principles.

4. FROM THE REFORMATION TO VATICAN I

The Reformation attempted to realize the "reform" that had been again and again postponed by the Church, although there had been private efforts in all centuries since the eleventh. It led to a schism which separated a third of the Western Church from Rome. Further schisms in the Churches of the Reformation led to a multitude of churches, and in modern times to a multitude of sects. However, the decisive achievement of the churches of the Reformation at this time was that they retrieved the question of "justification" as the central question in the quest for a true understanding of the Church. Of course, the Reformation treated this question very one-sidedly. Luther expected and taught justification as coming only from the word of God: *Ecclesia est creatura verbi*, "The Church is the creation of the word" (WA 6,56of.). Calvin saw the guarantee of justification only in predestination. But the decisive point is that the focus of the question was no longer the supernatural nature of the Church but its outward structure and conditions: Church is where the Gospel is preached and where the sacraments, of which only two are left, are correctly administered. Ecclesiastical office as something stemming from the mission of Jesus, and the sacraments as the true gifts of salvation, were no longer sufficiently seen next to the word of God, which retained its importance only as the word of Scripture.

How much the self-understanding of the Roman Church had itself become externalized in this development is shown by the definition given by the Jesuit Robert Bellarmine (d. 1641): "The Church is the society of human beings which is linked by the profession of the same Christian faith under the rule of the legitimate pastors, above all the one vicar of Christ on earth, the Roman pontiff. These things are required as the minimum for someone to be of the Church."[59] The catechism commissioned by the Council of Trent (and written by Peter Canisius) defines

the Church in a similar way by expressing its nature
through the condition of belonging to the teaching,
priestly, and pastoral office (*Pars* I, *Cap.* 10). The attempt
of expressing what Church is was reduced to speaking of
the conditions required for belonging to it, instead of discussing the nature of the Church. With different interpretations on both sides, these three conditions of belonging to the Church were still used in the seventeenth and
eighteenth centuries against the Enlightenment systems
of Gallicanism, Febronianism, and Josephinism. The Enlightenment understood the Church as an "educational
institution or teacher of the peoples," a definition that can
still be observed in the nineteenth century (cf. Bishop Ket-
teler of Mainz.)

The image of the Church, which had been introduced in
the great Christian art of the fifth and sixth centuries as
"mother Church," was seen (after 1150) as *ecclesia imper-
atrix* (cf. the painting in the monastery Prüfening near Regensburg and the illustrations in the *Hortus deliciarum* of
Herrad of Landsberg, twelfth century) and, after the fifteenth century, as the crowned woman and mediatrix of
salvation, who receives the saving blood from the wound
of the crucified Jesus in the chalice of the Mass, in order to
mediate the redemption of Christ to all humanity in this
sacrifice. The period of the Counter-Reformation developed the image of the "triumphant Church" (on the triumphal chariot, victorious over its enemies) which remained
normative until the twentieth century. The image of the
Church's chariot in Dante had been quite different.[60]

The nineteenth century only deepened the doctrine of
the Church through Romantic reflection on High Scholasticism and its great theology, influenced by Hegel's idealistic philosophy of being and the state. The question
of salvation became again the basic question in the understanding of the Church. J. A. Möhler understood the
Church as "the realized reconciliation of human beings
with Christ, and through him with God and among them-

selves."[61] For this reason, beginning in 1848 public controversies between Protestants and Catholics were conducted
in a more objective and understanding manner, e.g., H. W.
Thiersch, 1845 (Protestant), and H. Denzinger, 1847 (Catholic). After 1848, and through Vatican I, this ecumenical
springtime was again lost to some extent. In 1859, in the
first "fundamental theology," Johann M. Ehrlich wrote
about the Church, "The Church is the supernatural communion of life between human beings and God, a communion which was newly instituted by the God-man . . . it
is the one and true supernatural communion between human beings and God and between human beings themselves, a communion which was originally willed and instituted by God, which has been re-established by the God-
man, and which can no longer be destroyed" (II,338). The
convert Friedrich Pilgram gave a similar definition in his
famous work *Physiologie der Kirche* (1860). Johannes
Hirscher (d. 1865) sought the fundamental idea for his image of the Church in the idea of the reign of God in the
Gospel of John. The proposed text for the Vatican I document on the Church (written by the Jesuits J. Franzelin and
C. Schrader) presented a definition of the Church's nature
through scriptural images. The idea that became dominant
was the Pauline idea of the "body of Christ." Because of
the interruption of Vatican I, the proposal could not take
effect in its entirety. Only chapter twelve, about the pope's
primacy of jurisdiction, and his infallibility were defined
in a revised and enlarged form. This incompleteness led to
a one-sided image of the Church, an image that had to be
rejected by the liberal world as a preservation of medieval
ideas of authority. An additional reason for this reaction
was that Vatican I had been preceded by the Syllabus of
Pius IX (1864) and the condemnation of thinkers like
Lamennais who wanted to lead the Church into the modern age, even if not always with appropriate means. The
first chapters of Schrader's proposal shaped the encyclical
Mystici Corporis by Pius XII (June 29, 1943). The spirit of

Pius IX and Vatican I remained alive also in the anti-Modernist struggles from 1900 to 1910.

5. FROM VATICAN I TO VATICAN II

Around the turn of the century important German theologians had attempted to reconcile the Catholic understanding of the Church and of the faith with the spirit of the times. H. Schell (Würzburg) wrote *Der Katholizismus als Prinzip des Fortschritts* (Catholicism as the Principle of Progress, 1897) and *Die neue Zeit und der alte Glaube* (The New Times and the Old Faith, 1898). In 1900 A. Erhart (Vienna) wrote *Der Katholizismus und das 20. Jahrhundert* (Catholicism and the Twentieth Century). Schell's Dogmatics was put on the Index and his works were prohibited, and Albert Erhart lost his title of Prelate.

It was only after World War I that there arose important intellectual movements which created a new climate for a new image of the Church. In 1922 the Protestant theologian and bishop Otto Dibelius could speak of a "century of the Church," and in 1924 Romano Guardini could say, "The Church is awakening in souls." Abbot Prosper of Solesmes (after 1870) initiated a liturgical movement. It was supported by Pius X and further developed in the Benedictine monasteries Maria Laach (Odo Casel) and Beuron (Abbot Ildefons Herwegen) and in the Augustinian monastery Neuburg near Vienna (Pius Parsch) as well as in the work of Romano Guardini (Burg Rothenfels). In the First World War the youth movement (Wandervögel, etc.) was born. It produced a new climate of the freedom of spirit, of affirmation of the world, and a new sense of community. Both of these movements shaped the biblical movement, which was especially furthered by Pius XII and the encyclical *Divino Afflante Spiritu* (1943). The biblical movement also has roots in the ecumenical movement which had been cultivated among Protestants since 1923 (cf. the works of the Protestant bishop Nathan Söderblom,

1866–1931). In the struggles of World War II, ecumenism became a general Christian concern, also among Catholics. During World War II, certain Jesuits in Lyons (e.g., Henri de Lubac) developed a new movement in theology which was condemned in 1948 under the title *la nouvelle théologie.* Although it often made use of inappropriate modern approaches, the aim of this new theology was to detach theology somewhat from the bonds of Greek philosophy into which it had been drawn more and more since the fifth century and even more so since the twelfth century, and to bring it back to a more scriptural mode of thinking and speaking. The thought of theologians before 350, which focused on the history of salvation, became normative again in contrast to the more philosophical thinking of later times. The spirit of these five movements was decisive for preparing the new image of the Church at Vatican II. During the Council an additional movement was born, namely, "The Church of the Poor," which was led by Cardinal Lercaro (Bologna) and supported especially by bishops from Communist countries. There was also the movement of the Jesuit P. Lombardi "For a Better World" (inaugurated by Pope Pius XII).

The new image of the Church in Vatican II in contrast to Vatican I can be characterized as follows: The classical image of the Church, which had been developed especially after the Reform movement of the eleventh century (its highest expression is in canon law and it focuses on issues of power and authority, was uniquely able to bring to light the Church's autonomy and independence vis-à-vis various secular powers. It also stressed the Church's worldwide task and its supernatural character. However, it tended to identify the transcendent nature of the Church with the political and social order of this world. Thus it no longer sufficiently showed the true inner tensions in the understanding of the Church: the tensions between natural appearance and supernatural nature, between inner doctrine and outward order, between universal and local

Church, between pope and bishops, between institution and spiritual essence, between office and charism. One reason for this defect lies in the character of the metaphysics of the High Middle Ages which had been maintained against all criticisms since the High Middle Ages without much change from the time of Ockham to the present. Its problems have become clear only today. The following particular differences must be pointed out:

a) In Vatican II the Church appears less as an institution than as an event in the history of salvation, as an action of the triune God with and through and for humanity in this world. The Church as a whole is now experienced as a missionary Church: mission is not a task, but a structural element of the Church.

b) In contrast to the involvement, particularly of the hierarchy, in worldly power since Constantine, Charlemagne, and Otto the Great, the pilgrim Church now appears more in focus as the eschatological community of Christ, without forgetting its role in the world.

c) The Church of power and glory is contrasted with the Church of the poor. While Vatican I used the titles *potestas* and *officium* for office, Vatican II uses as a matter of principle the term *ministerium* (service).

d) In contrast to the centralism which appeared in Vatican I, a new openness and diversity becomes visible and possible in the Church through the new view of the episcopal office, through the collegiality of the bishops, with the Pope as head, through the new view of the laity and its tasks in the Church, and through the introduction of the vernacular into the liturgy.

e) The period up to Vatican I laid special stress on the defense of the supernatural through dogma and canon law. Vatican II, on the other hand, declared no dogma, made no condemnation, and instead published a "Decree on Ecumenism" and a "Declaration on Religious Freedom." This shows that the Church wants to set out in a new way to gain the world, to open new regions (China, Africa) for

Christ which had not been included in its still medieval system. Of course, in doing so, the Church must not lose its continuity with the past, a continuity which belongs to any healthy living being.

f) Especially the "Dogmatic Constitution on Divine Revelation" shows that the ultimate reality is not the multiplicity of factors seen within the world, namely, Scripture and historical tradition, but rather the "living God" who reveals himself in Scripture and in the living Church with its worldwide mission. It also shows that charism, even of the laity, should gain importance besides ecclesiastical office. This is why Vatican II in a new way stresses the importance of the Holy Spirit for the growth and action of the Church and for the understanding of the Church.

g) Finally, one sees an ultimate openness of the Church for its missionary task. In a completely new way the Church expresses its position in relation to the world: in relation to secular science as well as the phenomenon of atheism and the non-Christian religions. The Church wants to begin a dialogue with these historical realities in order to become everything for everyone and to gain everyone and everything for Christ (cf. 1 Cor 9,19–22) who alone is Lord and Savior for everyone and everything. The new image of the Church in Vatican II, which does not repudiate anything contained in the old image, remains a great task for everybody who wants to serve the Church with his or her whole life and being.[62]

Part Two

Pathways towards a Theological Concept of the Church

Vatican II raised the question about the structures of the Church.[1] Subsequent to Vatican II and without the support and unifying power of the college of bishops at the Council, this question often led to interminable discussions among theologians and the faithful.

The first thing to notice in this new way of formulating the question is the use of "structures" (in the plural). This plural expresses the conviction that the Church exists at many levels and that it cannot be defined using the model of a single, natural social body. Part One prepared us for this insight. The Church is a community which has been founded by God for all human beings "from all tribes and languages, peoples and nations" (cf. Rev 5,9; 7,9; 13,7; 14,6). So as to see the order in the fullness of this Church, which is intended for all of humanity, one must see and acknowledge the manifoldness of human communities and social structures.

This implies that the various images we encountered in Scripture and in the history of the Church's self-understanding represent and express only single structural elements of this Church. These images cannot provide a comprehensive concept, although some affirmations, especially scriptural ones, can serve as models and are thus of greater importance than mere images.

What we said above (including the terminology of

"structures") shows that we must gather affirmations about the Church which express, as far as possible, the manifoldness of its structural elements. Still, our goal must be to grasp theologically the Church's being so as to allow us to understand its life and activity as the function of its being. This attempt is all the more important because the Church, in theological understanding, includes a supernatural element without which its appearance in the world and in history cannot be understood but will even be misunderstood.

Finally, the purpose of this attempt is to reach a genuine account of the Church's being which cannot be dissolved into a mere collection of statements about its functions. Some contemporary thinkers speak of the "primacy of praxis" without, of course, wanting to replace orthodoxy by orthopraxis. They express the primacy of love over theory and thereby address the role of the missionary Church in this world and the task of the individual in it. However, they fail to address the Church's very being. Church as a social entity is of its nature more than the sum of the activities of all its members. In fact, the activities of its members can be understood only in terms of the Church itself, its being and its powers.[2]

In order to achieve this grasp of the Church's being, or, in scientific language, a "theological concept of the Church," we will briefly reflect about the structural elements contained in the biblical images of the Church, especially the images of the people of God, the body of Christ, God's building, and the Kingdom of God (IV). Building on this foundation, we will then investigate the theological concept of the Church as the "universal sacrament of salvation," which has recently been presented in the Constitution on the Church of Vatican II (V). The meaning of the theological term "universal sacrament of salvation" is difficult to grasp, so we will clarify and concretize it by reflecting about its spatial and temporal dimension. First, we will investigate the relationship be-

tween congregation, particular churches, and universal Church in order to clarify the specific form of the Church's visibility (VI). Then we will deal with some questions about the timeframe of the Church and about the concept of the Church's temporality and historicity in general (VII).

Structural Elements for a Theological Concept of the Church, Taken from the Biblical Images of the People of God, the Body of Christ, God's Building, and the Kingdom of God

In order to reach an appropriate theological concept of the Church we must identify its most important elements. In the course of our discussion it will become clear that these elements usually appear in polarities or as dialectical elements of a unified historical whole.

a) Let us first take up the idea of the "people of God," which gained new importance through Vatican II. In early Christianity, at least until 70 A.D., the Church understood itself as the "people of God of the new Covenant." The Apostolic Fathers overlooked the link between the people of God in the New Testament and in the Old Testament. For them, the Jewish people were the type of apostasy: like Easu, they lost the primogeniture.[3] According to 2 Clem. 28, the true people of God remained hidden until Christ. Ignatius does not use the term "people of God" at all and speaks instead of the "catholic Church" (Ign. Smyrn. 8,2), which is for him "Christianity" (christianismos, i.e., communion with the glorified Lord). Marcion fails to understand even the continuity between the God of the Old Testament and the God of the New Testament. The development of a theology parallel to the word of revelation leads to a shift from a historical understanding to an understanding in terms of a theology of salvation. Despite Rom 9–11, Israel appears no longer as the chosen people, but as the rejected people.[4] The just men and women of the Old Testament were seen as pre-Christian members of the Church saved through their faith, not through Israel.[5] Especially in Augustine, the concept of the Church is lifted from the historical to the spiritual plane. This is the level on which he locates the *Civitas Dei*, as opposed to the *Civitas terrena*. Before his struggle against the Donatists, Augustine's underlying Neoplatonism made intellectual faith the decisive criterion for belonging to the Church (salvation is turning away from the visible world). Later he held that the one who possesses charity belongs to the Church. Cain and Abel are types of Judaism and Christianity, the Synagogue and the Church. At the same time, beginning with Augustine, the concept of the people of God, a concept rooted in the history of salvation, was replaced by the Roman juridical concept of *populus:* the Church is the Church of all peoples contained in the *Imperium Romanum.*[6] In the fourth century, due to the development of ecclesiastical hierarchy after Ignatius and Cyprian and especially in the work of Optatus of Mileve (d. 365), the concept of people of God was transformed more and more into a term for the laity as distinct from the bishops. From the fifth century on the true concept of the people of God, as rooted in the history of salvation thus disappeared almost completely. In its place the Augustinian concept of the *congregatio fidelium* asserted itself more and more.[7] In the Middle Ages, this concept was furthermore understood primarily in terms of the concept of the family and the political concept of the nation.[8] Especially the Crusades (beginning in 1096) and the negative judgment about the Jews, which the Crusades fostered, prevented an approach in terms of the history of salvation, which sees the unity of the people of God in the Old and New Testament in the biblical sense.[9] Although the Reformers used the terms "Christian-holy people" (Luther,

WA 50, 624) and "believing people,"[10] the scriptural sense of this concept does not come into play, neither at the Council of Trent nor in the *Catechismus Romanus*. Central to the Reformation churches is the idea of particular community and then the confession.

Only in the nineteenth century did the Romantic idea of the spirit of a people and the Enlightenment idea of the *societas humana* in the sense of an educational community come to the fore. However, it did not arrive at the historical concept of the people found in the Old Testament. The Tübingen school, especially in J. A. Möhler, understood the idea of the spirit of a people in part pneumatologically and in part christologically, and in this way so applied it to the Church. The secularization of Germany in 1803 and the end of the monarchy in France supported the concerns of Ultramontane circles: the Church was understood primarily as a *societas perfecta*. This way of thinking remained normative for the Roman school (Perrone, Franzelin, Schrader) and for the drafts and definitions of Vatican I. It was improved by the patristic concept of the mystical body of Christ, but this image did not receive sufficient emphasis. A new approach was opened up only after World War I. In the general collapse many looked upon the Church as a saving rock amid the turbulence of the times. The Romantic idea of seeing the inner human community behind external society gained increased importance in the Youth Movement. The idea of the universal priesthood of the baptized contributed to the overcoming of the idea of the clerical Church. The rediscovery of John Henry Newman brought the patristic idea of the people of God which preserves the true doctrine against the errors of the time (the struggle against the Arianism of the educated world of the fourth century) through its *sensus fidelium*. The reason for this stabilizing power is above all the connection of each individual Christian with Christ (personalism). Among Catholics the historical link between the people of God in the Old and the New Testament is increasingly stressed. The critique of the image of the body of Christ led to an image of the people of God which still lacked the dimension of the history of salvation. Protestant theology meanwhile developed the doctrine of a visible historical Church in which the invisible Church is present as the reign of God in the reign of Christ. Especially since the 40s, exegetical research has led to a new understanding of this historical people of God. Through a clearer grasp of the term "eschatological," among Catholics as well, the bases were created for a concept of the people of God based upon the history of salvation. It was this concept which became the basis of Vatican II's Constitution on the Church. M. Keller develops the basic structure of this people of God as a salvation-history concept of the Church when he notes that the Church is the chosen people of God. This definition stresses the gratuitous election and mission which is already present in the Old Testament people of God. "The New Testament Church is the people of God constituted through the revelation of God in Christ" (267). This definition clarifies the historicity of the Church and its place in the realm of earthly history. Of course, this insight does not imply that Paul's image of the body of Christ, when used as a model, is a monolithic block, as Keller supposes. The New Testament Church is the wandering people of God of the end times. This statement expresses the sinfulness of the individual and the Church, its future in the history of salvation together with Israel (cf. Rom 11), and the saving function of the people of God for the whole of humanity. The most important element in this model of the Church is historicity in the variety of its relations: back to the past of the Old Testament people of God with which the New Testament people of God will be judged and fulfilled in the coming end times; as a transformation in the present, in the conversion of the individual and the Church in the spirit of the call, through immersion in historical revelation and sanctification by the ever-active Spirit of God in the Church. The invisible in the visible, the past and future in the present, salvation in sinfulness, eternal election in the course of history, the individual and the community, all of these polarities in their dialogical unity in earthly history are expressed in the image of the people of God.

b) The biblical image of the "building," like that of the "people of God," is rich. However, even more so than the image of the people of God, this image lost its fullness of meaning and its application to the Church in the course of history. Only two marginal meanings were left: the term "building" for the cultic building which was constructed from wood or stone, and the term "edifying" used in the language of piety. The great importance of the "building" image will become clear only if we see the biblical term and attempt to summarize the elements which are most important for the theological understanding of the Church.

To begin with, the image of the building and that of the field are often seen together (1 Cor 3,9). This shows that they express the most basic conditions of human life, nourishment and shelter. Just as human life comes from God, so do nourishment and shelter. Both images therefore must not be seen in a modern sense as differentiated and externalized (cf. Jer 1,10: "See, I have appointed you this day to pluck up and to break down, to build and to plant." cf. Jer 24,6; Sir 49,7; 1 Cor 3,9).[11] The Old Testament develops most of the images for this building allegory. Yahweh is the founder and builder of the universe (Psalm 102,26; Amos 9,6), of Zion and of the people Israel (Isa 62 and 64; Ezek 40–48). God has co-workers in the world for this activity, especially the prophets, who are called "to build up the old ruins and rebuild the cities" (cf. Isa 54,13; 61,4). For Israel, God's people, Jerusalem, its capital, and its Temple are "God's city, God's house," and the inhabitants of this city are "God's community" (cf. Num 12,7; Amos 9,11). Especially after the Babylonian exile, the Temple and Jerusalem were seen as "messianic-apocalyptic" statements. The promise given already during the Exodus from Egypt, namely that God would dwell among his people, among the children of Israel (cf. Num 35,34), that he would walk among them (cf. Lev 26,11ff.), takes on an eschatological character (cf. Ezek 34–38, esp. 37,27). Particular elements of the building are described in more detail. God's building is a solid building which has been planned from the very beginning. The cornerstone, which determines the layout of the foundation and thus the whole building, is the stone rejected by the builders (Psalm 118,12f; Isa 28,16: "See, I am laying on Zion a stone, choice, precious, firmly founded. The one who trusts in it will not falter"). Yet, in God's hands, it has become the cornerstone of the whole building.

In the New Testament, the image finds a rich fulfillment. God himself is the unshakeable foundation of the Church as the house (temple) of God (cf. 1 Cor 3,9–13; 2 Tim 2,19–21). He founded it and he made Christ its foundation and cornerstone. For this reason, solidity and unshakeable strength, holiness and truth are anchored in this Church (cf. Heb 11,10). Thus Paul writes to the Corinthians, "For we are God's fellow workers; you are God's field, God's building. According to the grace of God given to me, like a skilled master workman I have laid the foundation, and another man is building upon it. Let each take care how he builds on it. For no one can lay any other foundation than that which is laid, which is Jesus Christ. . . . Do you not know that you are God's temple and that God's spirit dwells in you? If any one destroys God's temple, God will destroy him. For God's temple is holy, and you are that temple" (1 Cor 2,9–11 and 16–17). In this temple there are more precious and less precious vessels (2 Tim 2,20f.). Only if this view of the divine foundation is rightly seen can one correctly understand the second order of foundation, the foundation through God's coworkers (cf. 1 Cor 3,9).

In the earthly realm, in virtue of being sent by Christ, Peter becomes the rock (petra) upon which Christ builds his Church (cf. Matt 16,18) and Peter's fellow apostles become a foundation (themelion). But even in this founda-

tion, Christ remains the only foundation and cornerstone
(*akrogōaion*) "in which the whole building is joined together and grows into a holy temple in the Lord" (Eph
2,20–21; cf. Heb 3,6: "We are Christ's house") and in
which the former Gentiles are also built up to be a "dwelling of God in the Spirit" (Eph 2,22). In virtue of their mission, the apostles are "co-workers of God" in this construction of the Church (cf. 1 Cor 3,9; Col 4,11). They
contribute by preaching and by administering the sacraments in which Christ becomes over and over again the
living foundation of the community (cf. Heb 6,1f.). The
apostolic workers can build wrongly on the foundation
Christ, which has been laid once and for all. Then their
part of the building will be destroyed "as through fire" (1
Cor 3,11–17) in the judgment which is pronounced over
and over in history.

Especially 1 Peter uses this building allegory for the
community and its members when he writes to the communities in Asia Minor, "When you come to him, the
living stone, which has been rejected by men, but is chosen and precious in God's eyes, then, like living stones, let
yourselves be built into a spiritual house, into a holy
priesthood, in order to offer spiritual sacrifices acceptable
before God through Jesus Christ" (1 Pet 2,4–5). For unbelievers, Christ is the "stone of offense and the rock of
stumbling" (Isa 8,14). But Christians who believe in him
become "a chosen race" (Isa 43,20), "a royal priesthood, a
holy nation" (Exod 19,6), "a people chosen to proclaim the
glorious deeds of him" (Isa 43,21) who has "called you
from darkness into his marvellous light" (1 Pet 2,9).
Through their daily lives, Christians must silence the
wicked and the foolish who deny or despise God, and convince them of the truth of God (cf. John 17,20f.; 1 Pet
2,11–17). The believers must "build each other up" as
Paul says in his first letter: "Encourage–admonish–con-
sole [*parakeleite*] one another, and build each other up
[*oikodomeite*]." Immediately after this text, however, the
apostle says, "We beg you, brothers, respect those who

work among you who are over you in the Lord [*pro-istamenous en kyriō*]." All further admonitions addressed to the community are carried by this idea of the building (cf. 1 Thess 5,11–21). Everything is permitted to Christians in the freedom of their faith, but not everything builds up (1 Cor 10,23). "Let us pursue what makes for peace and for mutual upbuilding" (Rom 14,9; cf. 1 Cor 14,4.12.26: Let everything in the community be done by the individual for the building of all).

The building allegory is a rich contribution to the aspects of Church expressed in the following dialectical tensions: The Church is God's building as a fixed institution and as a living event for every individual; it has been founded from eternity and was instituted in the time of Christ, built upon the rock of Peter and the foundation of the apostles and prophets: yet God remains its living foundation, and Christ is the cornerstone, the permanent norm of the whole. It is towards him that the Church is continually built up by the work of God's co-workers, first by the apostles, who participate in Christ's special mission, then by all who are bound to Christ by baptism. The basic character of this building of God is eschatological, it is always a reality *in the process of coming to be*. Human contributions can be good or bad. Judgment will preserve what is good and consume what is bad in the fire of God. The Church stands in God's eternal grace. It continues to grow on earth, and God's judgment will separate the wheat from the chaff.

The *Shepherd of Hermas* elaborates the external building allegory, the construction of the tower, the fortress of God from the stones of the baptized Jews and Gentiles (cf. *Herm. Sim.* 9,3,1f.; 9,9,7; *Herm. Vis.* 3,2,4; 3,3,3). In the Letter of Barnabas we encounter the pneumatic-inward eschatological understanding of the allegory (cf. *Barn.* 16,1–8) and Clement of Alexandria writes that not only God, but also the building constructed in his honor, namely, the Church, is holy: "What I call Church now is not the room, but the community of the elect." Especially the "gnostics" are a dwelling of God, not only those "who are already gnostics," but also those who "are capable of becoming gnostics" (*Strom.* 7,5; 29,3–7).

Augustine does not tire of presenting the Christian community as the *domus Dei: Domus Dei nos ipsi* [*Sermo* 336, 337,338 (three sermons for the consecration of a Church); PL 38,1471: Faith hews wood and breaks stones in the mountains; the catechumenate with its instruction and baptism prepare this material; it becomes a house of God when all of this is firmly linked in love; cf. also *Sermo* 336, PL 38,1479]. Bernard of Clairvaux later applies the five rites of the consecration of a Church (*aspersio, inscriptio, inunctio, illuminatio, benedictio*) to the human beings who are received into the Church and thus form the Church (*Sermo de dedic. eccl.*, PL 183,520A). He calls the Church "temple of God through sanctification, city of the highest king through the communion of common life, bride of the immortal bridegroom through love" (*Sermo* 6, PL 183,535A). In John of Damascus, on the other hand, *ekklēsia* appears only as the church building (temple of God) in which the community gathers (*De fide orth.* I,13; ed. Kotter 13,22–24). The inner Church is described only by the image of the body of Christ.

After the Counter-Reformation, this image became very important through the application of Matt 16,18 to the papacy (cf. Vatican I).

c) New aspects for a theological understanding of the Church are contained in the Pauline image of the "body of Christ," which we discussed above when we quoted Vatican II's Constitution on the Church. Let us characterize the basic outlines of this image more closely.

First, it expresses the unique relationship between Church and Christ, while the images of the people and the building of God portray more the relationship of human beings to God as such. This relationship is viewed so profoundly that we must say already at this point: we encounter the great theological problems of Christology also in the doctrine of the Church. It is wrong to deny the true humanity of Jesus, as did the Docetists, Apollinarians, and Monothelites; it is also wrong to deny his true divinity, as did the Ebionites, Cerinthians, Paul of Samosata, and the Arians; the historical Jesus is misunderstood if one asserts, like Nestorius, that the two natures in him form only a moral unity, not a physical-personal unity, or if one asserts, like the Monophysites, that the human nature has been absorbed in the divine nature of Christ like a drop of water in the ocean. What remains is the paradoxical formula of Chalcedon which attempts to express the mystery as follows: "We confess one and the same Christ, the Son, the Lord, the Only-Begotten, as existing in two natures, without confusion or change, without division or separation" (*inconfuse, immutabiliter, indivise, inseparabiliter*; DS 302).

At the same time the following truth must be preserved: The dynamic unity in the Church between Christ and the Christians, their being towards each other, with each other, and for each other, is not an essential hypostatic unity, like the unity of the two natures in the historical person of Jesus, nor is it a merely moral unity of grace, like the unity visible in the cooperation between grace and freedom in each individual human being. Rather it is a unity determined through the mystery of Christ. This mystery unfolds its presence in the history of salvation in three events which are one in their effect: (1) in the incarnation (cf. John 1,14: ". . . and the Word became flesh;" Phil 2,5–11; Heb 2,11–13.14ff.), in which the Second Adam (cf. Rom 5,12.15) laid the "physical-supernatural foundation" for the Church; (2) in redemption [cf. Col 1,21–22: ". . . you who once were alienated and hostile in mind (against God) in your evil works he has now reconciled through the death in the body of his flesh, in order to present you holy and spotless and blameless before his (God's) face"; cf. Col 2,14f.; 2 Cor 5,21] in which he laid the "moral foundation of grace" (cf. Rom 5,18) for his Church; (3) finally, in the mission of the Holy Spirit (cf.

Acts 1,5: ". . . you shall be baptized with the Holy Spirit;" cf. Acts 2,1–4; John 14,26; 15,26f.; 16,13–15) in which he baptized the apostles as the foundation of the Church (cf. Eph 2,19f.) and prepared the "efficient foundation" for the biblical word of God and the sacraments of the Church and thus the "mystical-personal foundation" of the Church.

Through these events in the history of salvation the one Church was founded. Like Christ, it is a completely human reality in this world, and yet not of this world. The exalted Lord, his Spirit, and his Father belong to it so essentially that the failure of recognizing this unity necessarily leads to ecclesiological heresies one could call ecclesiological Arianism (which does not take the divine foundation seriously) or Docetism (which ignores the community of human beings as the body of Christ) or Nestorianism (which wants to separate the head from the body, Christ and the Christians) or Monophysitism (which looks for the glorified exalted Lord in the Church instead of looking for the body of Christ in this world). The Constitution on the Church (LG 8) expresses this truth in the following words:

The society furnished with hierarchical organs and the Mystical Body of Christ are not to be considered as two realities, nor are the visible assembly and the spiritual community, nor the earthly Church and the Church enriched with heavenly things. Rather they form one complex reality which grows together from a divine and a human element. For this reason, by an important analogy, this reality is compared to the mystery of the incarnate word. Just as the assumed nature inseparably united to the divine Word serves him as a living organ of salvation, so, in a similar way, does the communal structure of the Church serve Christ's Spirit, who vivifies it, for the growth of the body (cf. Eph 4,16).

In this way, in the order of the history of salvation, Christ has become the head of his Church. The Church is his body (cf. Eph 1,22f.: ". . . and he has given him as a head above everything to his Church, which is his body, the fullness of him who fills all in all," he "in whom dwells the fullness of the Godhead" (Col 1,19). The exalted Lord, of whom Paul once says that he is the *pneuma* (2 Cor 3,17) is here called the head of the Church. Through all centuries, especially since Peter Lombard (Sent III, d. 13), the dynamism of this assertion has given a special note to the doctrine of the Church as the body of Christ.

It is characteristic that High Scholasticism interpreted this doctrine in two ways. The Franciscan theologian Bonaventure is interested, above all, in the human being in whom the divine action is manifested. For this reason he explains: Christ is the head of the Church in virtue of being similar in essence to human beings (*conformitas:* John 15,1–8). Although he was equal to God, he took this nature upon himself and thereby became the principle of life for his members (*principium membrorum:* Col 2,18). Through his deed of redemption he has become the basic principle of all Christian activity (*influxivum principium sensus et motus*). He acts causally through his divine nature (*impartiens, conferens, efficiens ad remissionem culpae*), and he disposes us through his human nature (*praeparans, merens ad remissionem poenae*). The unity of believers with him is brought about through faith and love, not by nature (*caput spirituale non opportet uniri materialiter et naturaliter, sed spiritualiter per cognitionem et amorem; Sent. Com.* III, d. 13, a. 2, q. 1 and ad 4).

Thomas Aquinas, on the other hand, constructs his theology in terms of the creator God and develops it with the help of Aristotelian philosophy. For this reason he explains the doctrine of Christ as head in a way contrary to Bonaventure. The head excels the body through its superiority in value (*ordo:* cf. Rom 8,29; Col 1,18), through the fullness of its being (*perfectio:* all five senses are united in the head) and through its effective power (*virtus, motus, gubernatio* of members: cf. John 1,16; *Summa Theol.* III, q. 8, a. 1–6; *De Ver.* q. 29, a. 4–5). Later Thomism throws into relief the dependence of members of the body upon the head by pointing to the independence of the head from the body (cf. Cajetan: "Christ receives nothing from the members"). By doing so it probably goes beyond Thomas, although it follows his approach. To counteract this tendency, the encyclical on the Mystical Body of Christ, basing itself on Col 1,24 ("I want to complete in my flesh for his body, the Church, what is lacking in the suffering of Christ") and on 1 Cor 12,21 ("The head cannot say to the feet, I do not need you"), explicitly teaches that Christ desires the cooperation of the mystical body, the cooperation of its members in carrying out the work of redemption: "It is truly an awesome mystery, never sufficiently meditated, that the salvation of many depends upon the prayers and voluntary penances of the members of the mysterious body of Jesus Christ which they take upon themselves for that purpose, and upon the co-operation of pastors and believers, especially upon that which fathers and mothers must give to our divine redeemer" [AAS 35 (1943) 213].

In terms of his role as head one can understand Christ's role as mediator in the Church.[12] Mediator does not mean a static intermediate position between God and human beings (in the sense of the cosmic-soteriological intermediate powers of Gnosticism) but rather the activity of the God-man, especially his activity through his human nature. In the Old Testament, mediators are human beings sent by God (kings, prophets, priests).[13] Similarly, 1 Tim 2,5 says, "One is mediator between God and men, the man Christ Jesus" (cf. Heb 8,6; 9,15; 12,24). Also the New Testament uses the title "Son of Man" for Jesus (cf. Dan 7,13f.) and the Christ hymn of Philippians says that through his exaltation he has become the mediator. Even if the gnostic image of the "primal man" stood at the origin of this assertion, the meaning of the title is clearly non-cosmic. Christ's role as mediator is contained in his offices as teacher, priest, and pastor (cf. John 14,6: "I am the way, the truth, and the life"). They are offices rooted in his being the God-man, and yet they show their effect only in his activity as the Redeemer. The doctrine of Christ's offices will show this point in more detail.

In the communication of the "mission," which Christ received from the Father and gave to his apostles, his role as mediator becomes a foundation of the Church as the "body of Christ." This passing on of Jesus' mission is the reason why the body can appear as an "organ" of the head. Like "building," the body of Christ is not to be understood as a mere thing. The decisive point in the image of the body is the idea of "instrumentality." Everything in the body, all members, must and can serve the whole body. The point is thus not the organization of the body alone, but "the manifold service of the various members for the whole of the body," for the meaning of the body which is in turn fulfilled through the "service for each individual as a member of the body." The task of the members is to care in unity of heart for each other and thus for the body of the Lord; they exist for each other, for others, not for themselves (cf. 1 Cor 12,12–31). What Paul expresses in the model of the body does not happen by the mere fact that there are members; its condition is that each carries out the service appropriate to a member. In this action of the members for each other, Christ is active, the head, who was the first to see and to live the task and meaning of his life in this "for others." "The love of Christ urges us on when we reflect: One has died for all and so all are dead. But he died for all so that those who live live no longer for themselves, but for him who died and was raised to life for them" (2 Cor 5,14f.). Here too, the Apostle continues his teaching by pointing out that Christ has transferred this office of reconciliation to the apostles in particular: "Everything is from God who has reconciled us with himself through Christ and gave us the ministry of reconciliation. . . . We are ambassadors in Christ's stead, so that God makes his appeal through us. In Christ's stead we beg you, let yourselves be reconciled with God. . . . Him who knew of no sin he made to be sin, so that we might become justice of God in him" (2 Cor 5,18–21). For this reason Paul's great prayer at the end of all his letters is that God would fill us in Christ and through him and with him with his Spirit (*pneuma*) and his grace (*charis*), with faith (*pistis*), hope (*elpis*), and love (*agapē*), with insight (*gnōsis*) and wisdom (*sophia*), and with peace (*eirēnē*) (cf. Rom 15,13f.; Eph 6,23f.; Col 1,9). Still it is certain that "from his fullness we have all [already] received, grace upon grace" (John 1,16; cf. Eph 1,18–21).

Christology can show how this doctrine of the Church as the "mystical body of Christ" was decisively deepened in the Middle Ages through the doctrine of the *gratia capitis* with respect to Christ's humanity, which in turn is rooted in the *gratia unionis* with respect to his divine person. In this doctrine the mystery of Christ, of his nature and his work, of the God-man and the Redeemer, is seen from the point of view of the "gift of grace." It is a perspective that corresponds to the great history of salvation vision of "grace" found in Paul when he praises "the glory of grace [of God, *charis*] with which he has graced us in his beloved Son" (Eph 1,6) or when he praises "God, the Father of our Lord Jesus Christ, who has blessed us with every spiritual blessing [*eulogia*] through our communion with Christ in the heavens" (Eph 1,3), or when he concludes with the words: "Standing in the truth we want in every way to grow in love into him who is the head, Christ. From him the whole body is joined and held together through every bond of co-operation, corresponding to the energy given in each single member, and [from him] the growth of the body is thus brought about for its building up in love" (Eph 4,15–16). Paul's great christology in Col 1–3 and Eph 1–4 is the biblical foundation of these doctrines of *gratia capitis* and *gratia unionis* in Christ.

In the fight against Monophysitism and Monotheletism as well as Adoptianism, in the controversies about predestination and the struggles about the Eucharist, and finally in the resistance against the dialectical nominalism of Abelard and Gilbert of Poitiers, theologians such as Maximus the Confessor, and William of St. Thierry, Bernard of Clairvaux, and Anselm of Canterbury strove for that realism of faith which could grasp Christ's human nature as well as the hypostatic union in their importance for our Christian life. It was in the doctrines of *gratia capitis* and *gratia unionis* that they achieved this grasp. These terms were perhaps introduced by the school of Alexander of Hales (*Summa* IV, nr. 102–105). Bonaventure and Thomas Aquinas unfold the doctrine in detail (Bonaventure, *Sent.* III, d. 13, a. 2, q. 1–2; Thomas Aquinas, *Sent.* III, d. 13, q. 2–3; *Summa* III, q. 7, a. 8.13; q. 8, a. 1–6). "Grace" is here understood as coming from the "fullness" (*plērōma*) of the triune God as we encounter it in Christ (Eph 1,22f.; Col 1,19f.; 2,9; Eph 3,19; 4,13). In its real relation between Christ, the head, and the members of the Church this grace has simultaneously a personal, an ethical, and a mystical-real ontological character. It is at the same time the act of giving, a gift, and the demand or effect of this gift in us. In these two graces, *gratia capitis* and *gratia unionis*, all supernatural graces in creation are rooted: sanctifying grace and helping grace, the sacramental graces, the gifts of the Holy Spirit (cf. Isa 11,2), as well as the manifold fruit of the Holy Spirit (cf. Gal 5,22f.), and, at the end, the fulfillment of all graces in glory. Just as the five senses act for the whole body from the natural head, so the believing members of the body of Christ receive from their head the five inner senses (*sensus spirituales*, Origen) through which they find access to all that is supernatural and divine. Although each individual can receive only according to the measure determined by God, the whole fullness of grace and truth accrues to the Church through its head, because the Church as the body of Christ can never be without its head: "*Nos multi in illo uno unum, unus ergo homo Christus, caput et corpus* (We, though many, are one in him; Christ is thus one man, head and body)."[14]

Thus the New Testament (especially Pauline) image of the body again expresses the tension between divine giving and human receiving, divine action and human cooperation. It clarifies the personal relation of Christ to Christians and vice versa, and the Christians' being for each other, from each other, and with each other. At the same time, Christ's role as mediator, continued in the office of the Church, is stressed as in the image of the Church as a building. There is another image that takes up the basic idea of the body image, namely the parable in which Christ calls himself the *vine*. It closes with the words, "He who remains in me and I in him will bring much fruit; without me you can do nothing" (John 15,1–8).

d) The search for elements of an appropriate image of the Church cannot be concluded without discussing the biblical term that summarizes the doctrine of the Church in the dogmatics of the Orthodox by N. Trembelas,[15] "the Church as *the kingdom (or reign) of God on earth.*" In his *Dogmatics*[16] Androutsos proceeds in a similar way from the idea that the Church has been founded by Christ as the "pneumatic kingdom," because it is only through it that Christ's redemptive grace and salvation are borne and mediated in this world. The recent work by G. Karmiris, *L'insegnamento dogmatico orthodosso intorno alla chiesa* (Milan, 1972) develops the ecclesiology of the Orthodox Church by following the Greek Fathers of the fourth to the sixth centuries while using the Vatican II statement about the Church as sacrament as the point of departure and arrival.

Let us point briefly to the impressive ecclesiological attempts of Russian-Orthodox theologians: George Florovsky (1893–1979) attempts to understand the Church mainly on the basis of the Christology of the fifth century. In doing so he turns against the sophiological approach of Sergius Nicholas Bulgakov (1871–1944) as well as the pneumatological approach of Vladimir Lossky (1903–1958) and the eucharistic understanding of the Church in Nicolas Afanassieff (1893–1960).[17]

The following remarks will have to suffice on the subject of Church and kingdom of God. The biblical doctrine of the kingdom (or reign) of God cannot be subsumed under the doctrine of the Church. Still, one cannot speak of the Church without speaking about the kingdom of God, which has found the first form of its fulfillment on earth in Christ and his work of redemption. For this reason Jesus' preaching begins with the announcement that the reign of God is at hand (Mk 1,15: *ēngiken*) and in the context of an exorcism (Luke 11,20) it says that through this action the reign of God has become a present reality among human beings (*ephthasen;* cf. Luke 17,21). Of course, according to Jesus' own teaching the same reign is only in the process of coming. This is why Jesus' followers have to pray "Thy kingdom come!" (cf. Matt 6,10: *elthetō*). The reign of God is at the same time present and future, external and internal. The Church on earth and in this age displays primarily the outward eschatological aspect of the reign of God. This tension is expressed in Jesus' words to Peter, "You are the rock and upon this rock I will build my Church. . . . I will give you the keys of the kingdom of heaven" (Matt 16,18–19: *oikodomēsō, dōsō*). The visible Church must care for the invisible reign of God on earth. In the visible "kingdom of God" on earth there are wicked and weak persons beside the good (weeds beside the wheat; bad fish beside good fish: cf. Matt 13,24f.47f.). The good seed of the divine Word needs good soil on earth to grow (cf. Matt 13,3–9); and yet the seed grows by itself, it is a gift of God (like the growth of the mustard seed and the action of the leaven: cf. Matt 13,31f.33f.). Although complete commitment and self-abandonment are demanded from human beings (cf. Matt 13,44.45),. human activity will not bring about and create the future final reign, the heavenly kingdom; this kingdom remains a gift of God, which descends from God like the new heaven and the new earth, like the bride of the lamb, the new Jerusalem, in which God himself is temple and light (cf. Rev 21,1f.9f.22f.; 22,5). The Church is the final "array of God's forces" in this world.[18]

These short remarks on the topic of Church and kingdom of God will explain why the question of their relation will be discussed only at the end of the treatise on the Church, as a kind of conclusion and outlook (cf. below XVIII).[19]

V

The Church as a Sacramental Reality; The Use of Models; Ordering and Interpretation of the Structural Elements Drawn from Scripture

The structural elements for a theological concept of the Church, which have been drawn from the most important scriptural images, must be seen in their unity; they must be grasped in a comprehensive theological term that functions as a dogmatic "model concept." We will employ the idea that Vatican II repeats seven times (at least in substance), namely, the idea that the Church has sacramental character, that is, in fact, the *universale salutis sacramentum* (cf. LG 48; GS 45). Leonardo Boff made this idea the object of detailed research that has in many ways stimulated, furthered, and deepened the following discussion. We shall attempt to elucidate the idea in four steps: 1. the historical background of this new affirmation about the Church; 2. the transformation of the concept of sacrament; 3. the foundation of the idea of the Church as sacrament; 4. indications of the fruitfulness of this new concept of the Church and of sacrament.

1. HISTORICAL BACKGROUND

Drawing upon Leonardo Boff,[20] one can point to the following noteworthy aspects of the history of this theological concept of the Church. As the discussion of the image of the Church in the New Testament shows, the New Testament speaks about a reality which today we would call "sacramental." In Ephesians a mystical salvation-history perspective is dominant, while Colossians is characterized more by a cosmic perspective. Here, however, the dimension of ethics and grace is always linked with the ontic-mystical dimension. The earthly-historical and the mystical elements are seen in their unity when Paul and the author of Revelation speak of "the ancient people of God in a new aeon." The salvation-history perspective led to the view of the Church as *ecclesia ab Adam*, or *ab initio mundi*, i.e., the Church in its historical-cosmic dimension. On the other hand, Paul's "christocentric" perspective with his theological creation of the image of the "body of Christ" has taught us to see in a new way the unity of the Church's mystical and historical dimension, of the universal Church and the single communities, of the charismatic and institutional elements. At the same time this perspective made the historical and theological "mystery of Christ" (the God-man) the archetype for understanding the Church. This establishes the sacramental character of the Church, even if Scripture does not expressly use the word *mysterium-sacramentum* in regard to the Church.

Origen, the renowned founder of Eastern theology (d. 254), was the first to develop the idea of sacrament as a theological model in his biblical and Platonic-symbolic thinking. The hidden divine Logos reveals himself to us in the flesh (incarnation), in the word (Gospel), and in the Church (sacrament-office).—In the West, Cyprian, the famous bishop of the African Church (d. 258), experienced the distress of heresies and apostasies during the Decian persecution. Basing himself on Eph 5,32 and 4,4ff., he saw in the Church the *sacramentum unitatis*, the *una mater ecclesia*, which has been brought to earth as a heavenly Church and which has been entrusted to Peter and the apostles (Cf. *De unitate ecclesiae,* 5–7.)—Tyconius, in his hermeneutical treatise *Liber regularum* (ca. 380), takes up an idea of Origen and writes in the very first chapter (entitled *De Domino et de corpore eius*) that as head, Christ is one with his body, the Church. Therefore, everything said in Scripture about Christ can be referred to him as head or to the Church as his body (PL 18,15; cf. Augustine, *De doctr. chr.* III, 31,44).—Augustine (d. 431), who to a great extent determined the Western theology of the first millennium, often relies on this principle when he calls the Chuch *totus Christus* (the whole Christ, head and body) and when he sees this Church as a sacrament of salvation since the beginning of the world.—In the same way, Pope Leo I (d. 461) saw the Church as a *sacramentum salutis* in the history of humanity since its very beginning (Cf. *Sermo* 23,4; 307: PL. 54, 202; 230ff.). This understanding of the Church remained normative in the Western Church up to the High Middle Ages. It is an understanding that sees the unity of the divine and the human, the visible and the invisible, the historical and the metahistorical (cf. John Damascene, *De fide orth.*, III,1 = history of salvation; IV,3 = Church-Eucharist). It was not affected by the Neoplatonic idea of the Church as a hierarchically structured organization, which Denis the Areopagite presented in the sixth century and which was further developed in the East beginning with the legal reform of Justinian, and in the West beginning with Carolingian theology. Only the influence of Roman legal thought in the twelfth century and the adoption of Aristotelian metaphysics in the thirteenth century led to the increased disappearance of the terminology of the Church as sacrament.

Still, at least among the great Scholastics, the sacramental reality itself was still seen, in virtue of the christological point of departure, the doctrine of *gratia capitis* in Christ, and the development of the doctrine of the sacraments *in genere.* For Thomas Aquinas (d. 1274) the Church remains the body of Christ, an organ, the sacrament of

Christ on earth. The intrusion of nominalism in the theology of the fourteenth century suppressed Greek symbolic thought, so that even in the post-Tridentine ecclesiology of R. Bellarmine (d. 1621) no trace of this sacramental understanding of the Greek Fathers and the first millenium can be detected. The external aspect (*sacramentum tantum*) and the inner aspect of the Church (*res sacramenti*) had been overly separated in theological thought since the Reformation. Only the French school of P. Bérulle (d. 1629) brought about a change through its new view of the relation of the Christian to Christ, and of Christ's human nature to the divine Logos.[21] It is a view reminiscent of N. Kabasilas.[22] On the basis of this new view the Oratorian Louis de Thomassin (d. 1695) could again call Christ and his Church a sacrament: "Sacramentum universae ecclesiae circumgestebat Christus et in ipso demonstrabat." [Christ carried and revealed the entire Church as a sacrament in himself.][23] His profound understanding of the Church, however, was not able to have an impact during the Enlightenment.

Only Romanticism revitalized the symbolic thought that is the foundation of a sacramental understanding: e.g., J. W. Goethe (d. 1832).[24] This resurgence took place especially in the Tübingen school, which used symbolic thought to meet the challenge of Enlightenment rationalism as well as of the new German idealism. In 1835 H. Klee (d. 1840) called the Church, "a great sacrament . . . a fabric of sacraments . . . existence and life in the Church are on the whole sacramental."[25] Without using the term "sacrament," J. A. Möhler (d. 1838) portrayed the Church as the instrument of the Holy Spirit. In 1855 the Paderborn theologian J. H. Oswald (d. 1903) began his doctrine of the sacraments with an impressive introduction entitled "the sacrament in relation to the Church," in which he wrote that the Church "should be called not merely a sacrament, but *the* Christian sacrament. The Church *itself* is the sacrament as a means of salvation in the comprehensive sense of the word. Therefore, one could call the Church's entire activity . . . a sacramental activity."[26] In his *Mysterien des Christentums* (1865) M. Scheeben (d. 1888) elaborated in detail the nature of the Church as a mystery and its fundamental sacramental principle, without using the term "sacrament." For, despite his extensive use of the Greek Fathers, he was influenced in his thinking by members of the Roman school (C. Passaglia, J. B. Franzelin, C. Schrader), who attempted to interpret the Church in terms of the concept of *societas* together with the doctrine of redemption. This tendency is even clearer in L. Atzberger (d. 1918) and C. Feckes (d. 1958). Vatican I did not use the concept of sacrament for the Church, although it alludes to the same reality when it speaks of the Church as *"signum levatum in nationibus"* (a sign raised up for the nations) (cf. Isa 11,12; DS 3014) and when it develops the image of the Church that underlies the Council's Constitution on the Faith. The classical works of the major theologians between Vatican I and World War I although historically oriented, made no special contribution to this theme.

The spirit of the Liturgical movement, which was born in France after Vatican I, and of the Youth movement, which sprang up in Germany around World War I, gave rise to works of significant importance for the further development of the image of the Church as sacrament. Especially noteworthy are: Karl Adam, *Das Wesen des Katholizismus* (1924); Romano Guardini, *Der Gegensatz. Versuch einer Philosophie des Lebendig-Konkreten* (1925); and the numerous works of Odo Casel about the cultic mystery of the Church (collected in 1948 in *Das Kultmysterium der Kirche*), from which the "theology of mysteries" developed. Especially important was the encyclical on the Mystical Body of Christ (1943), which deepened the image of the Church beyond that of the Church as society. However, because of the influence of the old Roman school, the ontic and moral emphasis within the Church remained so separated that, despite the Pauline model of the body, the sacramental nature of the Church was insufficiently expressed. Nevertheless, despite the absence of the historicity of the Church, there are traces of the classical understanding of "sacrament." The encyclical even attempts to present the mystery of the Church in the exemplar of the mystery of Christ and his mother (Scheeben had repeatedly announced that he would use this exemplar as the image of the Church in his ecclesiology in vol. 3 of his *Dogmatics*). In continuation of, and dialogue with, the ideas of this encyclical Th. Soiron wrote his work about the "sacramental person" (1948). And in his work about the sacraments (1949), J. Fellermeier discusses "the sacramental cosmos, the sacramental existence of the Christian, and the Church as the universal sacrament."[27] In his essay about the Church as primordial sacrament, O. Semmelroth further developed these ideas.[28] The inner connection between the Church and the Eucharist, in which it builds itself up and is built up, is further deepened in the encyclical *Mediator Dei* (1950).

However, the breakthrough, prepared especially by H. de Lubac's "Meditations on the Church" (1952), happened only at Vatican II, where the idea of mystery and sacrament was again clearly expressed as a basic model for understanding the Church. Although it had been repeatedly called into question by the Church (esp. in 1947 in Lyon; cf. the encyclical *Humani generis* of August 12, 1950), the movement of *la nouvelle théologie* which formed around de Lubac was decisive for the new understanding of the Church at Vatican II. What de Lubac wrote in 1952 shaped the doctrine of the Council: "The Church, the whole Church, only the Church—the Church of today, of yesterday, and of tomorrow—is *the* sacrament of Jesus Christ!"[29] The Constitution on the Sacred Liturgy (SC 26) still called the Church (with Cyprian) *unitatis sacramentum*. The Dogmatic Constitution on the Church (LG 48) takes a step further in its meditation on the eschatological character of the Church and says that the exalted and risen Lord sent the Holy Spirit upon the apostles and thereby founded the Church as a universal sacrament of salvation (*et per eum corpus suum, quod est ecclesia, ut universale salutis sacramentum constituit*—cf. LG 1 and 59). The Decree on the Church's Missionary Activity (AG 1) quotes in its very beginning this new definition of the Church and points out that Christ established the Church before his ascension as "sacrament of salvation" (*ecclesiam suam ut sacramentum salutis condidit*) by communicating the mission he had received from his Father to the apostles (Matt 28,19f.). In the final work, Pastoral Constitution on the Church in the Modern World (GS 45) the Council again summarizes its doctrine as follows: "For every benefit which the People of God during its earthly pilgrimage can offer to the human family stems from the fact that the Church is the 'universal sacrament of salvation' [*universale salutis sacramentum*], simultaneously manifesting and realizing the mystery of God's love for human beings." This text clearly expresses the historicity of the Church and its universal saving mission by pointing to Christ, the head of the Church, who is also the goal of all human history, and "the focal point of the longings of history and culture" (GS 45).[30]

2. THE CONCEPT OF SACRAMENT

In order to understand correctly the new definition of the Church as sacrament, we must clarify the concept of sacrament. Not only the word, but also the reality "sacrament" has a long history.[31] In the present context let us point to the following aspects: Revelation speaks of *mysterion* (*sacramentum*) in two ways: First, it applies this term to the mystery of God's history of salvation, which has found its center and fulfillment in this human history in Christ (cf. John Damascene, *De fide orth.*, III,1; Col 1,26: "Christ in you, the hope of glory"). In a second sense, it uses this word to express the mysterious relationship between Christ and the Church, i.e., in a more general sense the idea of the covenant, for which the relationship between man and woman in marriage and love is used as an analogy (cf. Eph 5,32).

Augustine unfolds a new, third concept of sacrament on the basis of his Platonic Philosophy. He uses the term *signum* to refer to the visible reality of the sacrament as a sign of the invisible; and he uses the term *res* for its supernatural effect. In his doctrine of the sacramental character he brings to light the inner sacrament as *signum et res*. Augustine's concept achieves for the understanding of sacrament what had been gained at Chalcedon (451) for the understanding of Christ: the mystery of the sacrament consists in the interpenetration and convergence of outward sign and inner reality of grace, just as the mystery of Christ is to be seen in the personal unity of divine Logos and human nature. Hugh of St. Victor (d. 1141) summarizes these doctrines as follows: "Sacrament is a bodily or material element, presented in the visible world, which represents a certain invisible and spiritual grace by being an image, which signifies this grace through its institution [by Christ], and which contains this grace through its sanctification [by Christ]" (PL 176,415ff.).

A new, fourth form of understanding sacrament was developed in the thirteenth century with the help of Aristotelian metaphysics. In continuation of the Augustinian distinction between element and word, a distinction was made between, on the one hand, the visible outward sign (the pre-given reality) and the human action as a "material element" (*materia proxima, materia remota*) and, on the other hand, the spiritual word as the "efficient form" (*forma sacramenti*). Efficient causality for inner grace was attributed to this outward sign (the sign as a instrument of salvation, *instrumentum salutis*). Different schools gave different answers to the question of how the supernatural effect of the natural sign could be explained. Thomas and his followers spoke of a physical causality (the sacramental sign itself, because of its institution, contains this grace). Bonaventure, Scotus, and their followers spoke of a moral-intentional causality (God himself, because of his own promise, gives the gift of divine grace at the occasion of the free human performance of the sacramental sign).

A true deepening in the spirit of the biblical doctrine of *mysterion* was achieved by the fifth interpretation of sacrament, which was proposed, beginning in the 1930s, by Odo Casel's theology of mysteries in continuity with Cyril of Jerusalem and other Greek Fathers. He interpreted the sacrament and its effect (sometimes with less appropriate Platonic explanations) not so much in terms of Christ's person, but rather in terms of his saving deed. The sacramental sign appears as the "external sacrament," which contains the effectiveness of the divine saving deed in Christ as an "inner sacrament." Casel's perspective allows one to grasp historical reality as an essential structural element of sacrament.

In 1964 Karl Rahner proposed a sixth attempt of interpreting sacrament, probably influenced by the Lutheran theology of the Word: Sacrament is the most radical case of God's Word addressed to human beings, the exhibitive word of God.

In a seventh approach, E. Schillebeeckx, J. P. de Jong, and L. Boff have attempted to interpret sacrament in the context of a comprehensive symbolic thought as "real symbolic reality." The last two interpretations do not express the complex nature of sacrament as well as the earlier interpretations. For this reason, only these earlier interpretations were taken up in the introduction to the Constitution on the Church, where Vatican II says, "By its relationship with Christ, the Church is a kind of sacrament of intimate union with God and of the unity of all humankind, that is, it is a sign and an instrument of such union and unity" (LG 1; cf. GS 42). These interpretations also shaped the Constitution on the Liturgy: "The sacraments are ordered to the sanctification of human beings, to the building up of the body of Christ, and finally, to the worship owed to God; as signs they also have the task of instruction. They not only presuppose faith, but by words and objects they also nourish, strengthen, and express it; that is why they are called 'sacraments of faith.' They do indeed impart grace, but the very act of celebrating them disposes the faithful most effectively to receive this grace fruitfully, of worshipping God duly, and of practicing charity" (SC 59). The effect of the liturgy, the sacraments, and the sacramentals is thus the following: "If the faithful are duly prepared, almost every event in their lives is sanctified through the divine grace which flows from the paschal mystery of the passion, death, and resurrection of Christ, from which all sacraments and sacramentals draw their power [Casel's theology of mysteries!]. They also bring it about that there is hardly a proper use of material things which cannot thus be directed toward human sanctification and the praise of God" (SC 61). Especially since Augustine, Christ himself, who exercises his priestly office at the same time through his Spirit for us in the liturgy, has been seen as the supernatural ground of the sacramental event in the Church's liturgical action (cf. SC 7; PO 5; encyclical *Mystici Corporis*, AAS 35 [1943], p. 230).

3. FOUNDATION OF THE DEFINITION OF THE CHURCH AS SACRAMENT

In the doctrine of the Church's sacramentality, "sacrament" is used in a sense that differs from the seven single "sacraments" of the Church. Let us briefly clarify this new notion of sacrament.

a) The Church, like each single sacrament, is a sign of Christ in this world. The Council of Chalcedon (451) found a dialectical explanation of the mystery of Christ in the doctrine of the hypostatic union of the two natures in Christ. In the same way, the Church, as the Mystical Body of Christ, as both temple of God and people of God, must be understood dialectically. The complex and dialectical aspect of this mystery is expressed by the term "sacrament." Now, one must distinguish between Christ as the primordial sacrament (rooted in the hypostatic union of the two natures), the single sacraments (which are in every case a unity of outer and inner sacrament, *res et sacramentum*, of sacramental sign, *sacramentum tantum*, and sacramental grace, *res sacramenti*), and the Church as the "universal sacrament of salvation." Rahner and *Mysterium Salutis*[32] call the Church the "fundamental sacrament" (*sacramentum fundamentale, radicale*). However, it is better to reserve this expression for Christ as the "primordial sacrament," because Christ alone is the original source, root, and foundation for everything that is a sacrament or dispenses sacraments.

b) What, then, does the Council mean when it says that the Church is *universale salutis sacramentum* and *sacramentum unitatis*? Three assertions seem to be stressed in this doctrine.

(1) It is noteworthy that "salvation" always appears as the meaning and goal of the sacrament. The theology of the individual sacraments shows that every sacrament is intended to serve the salvation of human beings. Yet, this ministry of salvation is differentiated, corresponding to the number of the sacraments. Baptism and confirmation give to the Christian the supernatural life of a child of God, or sanctification; confession and anointing of the sick serve the process of healing from sin and its consequences in the individual Christian; holy orders and marriage are the great sacraments of the states of life, which order and bear the natural and supernatural life of the people of God. Only the Church in its totality can be called *sacramentum salutis* without qualification, because in it all realities implied in "salvation" are gathered. Not only the three groups of sacraments mentioned above are embedded in the whole of the Church; so is especially the central sacrament of the Church, which is at the same time its cult, the

center of its life, namely, the holy Eucharist as sacrifice and meal, as redemptive sacrifice of Christ and sacrificial meal of the community of Christ; and so is preaching, catechesis, and all efforts of pastoral care in the widest sense, which are intended to signify, mediate, and give God's salvation to human beings until the end of time, and which bring to God the adoration and worship of humanity. "Salvation as a whole" is meant when the Church is called *sacramentum salutis*. [The encyclical *Mystici Corporis* attempted to express the mysterious nature of this totality by pointing to the mystery of the fulfillment of salvation in the vision of God: *gratia-gloria*; cf. AAS 35 (1943), p. 232.]

(2) Repeatedly the Council texts speak of universal sacrament of salvation. The term *universal* is intended to express that the Church is a sacrament not only for those who are already known as members of the Church. The Church's mission of salvation extends to all human beings of all times and all places. The Church as sacrament embraces not only all saints and those who are on the path toward sanctity; it likewise embraces all sinners, all those who are morally and religiously weak, wounded, and sick, all the poor and all children;[33] and finally, as long as they live on earth, it also embraces all those who are far from God and at enmity with him, those whose path will with inner logic lead into eternal damnation unless they convert and receive healing and sanctification in the Church. "Universal" may also express that every action of the Church, its feasts and sacraments, its prayers and songs, its sacramentals, its laws and offices, its joys and sufferings, everything it is and has and does, bears this sacramental character and is thus a sign, a means, and a place of salvation for all. The Church militant, the suffering Church, and the Church triumphant are all together embraced by this *universale salutis sacramentum*. Later on we will develop these statements in more detail.

(3) The final mystery is expressed in the statement that

the Church is the sacrament of unity. As we will show, this statement does not merely intend to stress the unity of love in the Church as a moral demand and a sacramental-mystical gift; it points to the final ground of the Church in the triune God. The unity given in the Church, not only to all human beings of all times and places, but at the end of time even to the universe, the cosmos, is the unity that has its origin and final realization (cf. 1 Cor 15,20–28) in God, the creator of the universe (cf. 1 Tim 2,5), in Christ, the one mediator between God and human beings (Col 1,13–20), and in the Spirit of God as the Spirit of love and unity (cf. 1 John 4,7–16). We will deal extensively with this topic in Part Three. The essential thing is that when "sacrament" is chosen as a "model" or dogmatic concept for describing the Church, more is meant than a "structural-functional" view of the Church (cf. L. Boff). What is intended is a "categorical-ontological" view, and, at the deepest level, a "transcendental-theological" view of the Church (body of Christ).

(4) What we have just said will become clearer if we introduce a distinction that H. Plessner used in his anthropology to explain the position of humans among living beings. We can use his distinction to clarify the new form of "sacramentality." Plessner ascribes to plants a positionality of open form, to animals a positionality of closed form, and to human beings an excentric positionality.[34] Vatican II has given us new understanding for the distinction and inner unity of three related levels: the single sacraments in their importance for the life of individual Christians; the Eucharist in its importance for the community and life of the Church; and the Church as a whole in its importance as *universale salutis sacramentum* for people of all times and places. We can apply Plessner's distinction and say: The sacramentality of the single sacraments can be called "sacramentality of open form." In their particular character they open the way of salvation in the Church to every individual human being.

The sacramentality of the Eucharist, as the true sacrament of the cult of the Church community, understood both as an external (liturgical) community and as an internal community (body of Christ), could be called a "sacramentality of closed form." For the meaning of the Eucharist, in a way that differs from the other six sacraments, is to be sought in the self-enclosed ecclesial community. This is why the problem of intercommunion is also a problem of the unity of the Church. In this light we can grasp the importance and the limits of new attempts of a "eucharistic ecclesiology" which attempts to deduce the nature of the one Church exclusively from the life of the Church, from its eucharistic offering. Now, it is true that eating and drinking Christ's flesh and blood gives communion (*koinonia*) to the celebrating community (1 Cor 10,16f.) and thus confirms the Church as "body of Christ" (Eph 4,4–6; 1 Cor 12,14–26; Rom 12,4f.) whose head is the glorified Christ (Eph 1,22f.) and whose principle of life is the Holy Spirit (1 Cor 3,16f.; Rom 8,9–11). Yet, such a eucharistic ecclesiology presupposes the "unity of the Church," which was historically lost in the first centuries through division (schism) and separation (heresy or excommunication). There are, as a matter of fact, "many churches" today, without unity of communion.[35]

The Church itself, finally, possesses an "excentric sacramentality," inasmuch as its action, if it understands itself rightly, always points beyond itself: the Church's self-realization in its action is essentially "missionary," inasmuch as mission is not merely a certain task in history, but a structural feature of the Church's nature at every time and in each place. The Church's self-realization is thus essentially directed to those who do not yet belong to the Church and who are to find their way to it. The Church's role is not primarily to preserve itself, but to grow and to conquer the world according to Jesus' command: "Go into the whole world and proclaim the gospel to every creature" (Mark 16,15). It is not only in this spatially and temporally comprehensive sense that the Church's sacramentality is "excentric"; it is "excentric" also in the sense that even universal salvation is not the final goal. Universal salvation points beyond itself to the "glory of God the Father" as the final meaning of this salvation: "To him [God] be glory in the Church and in Christ Jesus through all generations from eternity to eternity, Amen" (Eph 3,21). "It is all for your sake, so that as grace extends to more and more people it may increase thanksgiving, to the glory of God" (2 Cor 4,15).

(5) To conclude, let us summarize the basic structure of what we call "sacrament." "Sacramental" does not refer to a certain pattern of thought in theology (Boff speaks of "sakramentell"); it refers rather to a certain reality in creation understood as a history of salvation. The origin and reason of this definite reality lies in "Christ," in whom God has become man (John 1,14; Phil 2,2–11) and whom God predestined from all eternity as the man who lives completely and exclusively for the all-comprehensive love of God. Because this man Jesus Christ gave rise to the possibility of radical salvation through his nature as the God-man; because he himself realized this radical salvation through his sacrificial death and resurrection; because he re-inserted the triune God into creation, which had lost salvation through the historical sin of man; because he thus created the Church as his bride and entrusted to it the way to his salvation through holy signs and rites—because of all this, the fundamental structure of Christianity in its concrete form in the space and time of this world is "sacramental." The immanent symbolic character which all particular reality has for human thought, which is capable of grasping the whole, can be the foundation of "sacramental thinking" in a general human sense, but it cannot give rise to "sacramental reality" in the Christian sense. This reality does not have its roots in a "transcendental christology" but only in the "historical Christ event." For those today who have a Kantian critical understanding of "hu-

man understanding" and a Hegelian dialectical ontology, "symbolic thinking," as it was newly established and unfolded by Ernst Cassirer (d. 1945) in continuity with Kant's critical understanding of the world,[36] may be a help for understanding the "sacramental as a phenomenon." "Sacramental reality," on the other hand, can be grasped only in the acceptance and celebration of faith; it cannot be founded in and adequately expressed by symbolic thinking.[37]

VI

The Christian, the Community, Particular Churches and the Church; The Sacramental Church in Space; Diversity in Unity

What was said above about the sacramentality of the Church shows that the first task of a theological understanding of the Church is to avoid both the Scylla of monism and the Charybdis of every form of dualism. This danger becomes especially clear in the basic orders of our image of the world, in the spatial image of reality, and in the temporal image of processes. In order to clarify and support what we said above and to concretize the idea of the sacramental structure that lies at the foundation of the Church, we will first turn to the order of space and reality by discussing the following questions: (1) the visibility of the Church; (2) membership of the individual in the Church; (3) the relationship of congregations and particular communities to the universal Church; (4) the relationship between its reality and its activity.

I. THE VISIBILITY OF THE CHURCH

What appeared as a "symbol" of a complex reality in Greek thought, based upon the logic of identity found in mythical thinking, is understood as a "sign" for a particular signified reality in Roman and medieval thought, based upon the logic of relation found in objective thinking. Whenever these different attempts of understanding the world are used by Christians of the East and the West in speaking of "sacrament," the essential thing is that the point of departure and the foundation of "sacrament" is a tangible aspect of our world of senses. Since Augustine and his Platonism we usually speak of a "visible sign" that points to an invisible reality and guarantees it. When we speak of the Church as the universal sacrament of salvation, this problem becomes especially clear. What do we mean when we say "visible Church"?

a) Historical Aspects

The Church is more than an organized community of human beings with a certain conviction and a certain goal and style of life (faith); it is more than a community visible to everybody and perceptible in its relationship to every other human community, such as the people and the state. This has been clear from the very beginning, when the creed of this Church made the Church itself an object of faith, like the historical Jesus of Nazareth. Dualism, which already appears in Platonism and even more so in the ethical perspective of Manicheism, and which was supported by various human power struggles, led in the course of the history of the Church to a repeated devaluation of the Church's visible reality. The true nature of the Church was seen only in the "invisible order of holy things" (communio sanctorum), in grace and predestination, which was then located exclusively on the side of the powerless and the poor of this world (although poverty and powerlessness often established themselves as a separate secular power). In their fight against the Constantinian state Church, the Donatists demanded and proclaimed a "Church of martyrs and saints." In the name of this Church they based ecclesiastical office and sacrament on the sanctity of the bearer of the office and minister of the sacrament, a sanctity that is subject to control. Against this view Augustine pointed out again and again that the Church is "the city on the hill" which cannot "remain hidden" (cf. Matt 5,14; Augustine, *Contr. Ep. Parm.*, III, cap. 5,27; *In Joh.* I,4 tr. 1,19: against the Manichees).

We encounter Manichean tendencies again in the anticlerical lay movements of the twelfth century, Peter of Bruys (d. 1126), Arnold of Brescia (d. 1155), the Cathari and Waldensians, against whom Dominic and his order struggled (cf. the work of Moneta of Cremona, 1260). Conversely, Bernard of Clairvaux wanted to help the papal Church not to become submerged in the new lifestyle of the bourgeiois age.[38] We meet the idea of an "invisible Church of the Spirit" in the Cistercian abbot Joachim of Fiore (d. 1202) and even more so among the Franciscan spirituals in the thirteenth and fourteenth centuries (e.g., Peter John Olivi, d. 1298). For Martin Luther the Church is founded completely on the "word of God." Also the sacrament becomes effective only in the word, which must be received by the individual in faith and confession. The Church (in his translation of the Bible, Luther uses only the word *Gemeinde,* congregation) is thus the congregation of those who believe in Christ, or, following the Apostles' Creed (e.g., in the catechisms), "the congregation of the saints on earth." Although word and sacrament are visible on earth, the Church itself always remains invisible, because faith and confession, as effects of the Holy Spirit in the human being, cannot be seen by the bodily eye.[39] Luther does not contradict this basic position when he writes in his *Concilien der Kirche* (1539) that the "holy Christian people" is recognized by seven main marks—namely, in addition to the word of God: baptism, and the sacrament of the altar, by the keys (Matt 18,15ff.), the ministers of the Church, the commandment, and the cross.[40]

Calvin (like Huss before him, cf. DS 1201) sees the Church at the beginning of his reform movement in a spir-

itualistic way as the community of the elect, the predestined; however, in the second edition of his *Institutiones*
(1543) he reaches a more concrete relationship to the reality of the Church in this world by reflecting on the Church
as necessary for salvation. Finally, in the last revision of
the *Institutiones* (1559) he stresses even more the necessity of the proclamation of the word, of dispensing the
sacraments, and of discipline in the Church. Nevertheless
it remains the "Church of faith" and God alone knows
who belongs to it. Baptism is a sign of Christ, a sign of
faith, and a sign of confession, but not a sign of the Church,
because the Church remains a spiritual reality. This view
manifests itself especially in the understanding of offices,
even if the final version speaks expressly of the visible
Church as the mother of the faithful (*Inst.* IV, can. 1–3). It
is mother in a moral, not a mystical sense.[41]

The most extreme spiritualism is found in Zwingli's
doctrine of the Church. On the one hand there is the universal Church of all believers, which has been acquired
and sanctified by Christ without spot or wrinkle (cf. Eph
5,27); on the other hand there is the single ecclesial congregation, which is a theocratic entity in this world and
has the right of excommunication over its members, even
its leaders. Everything is built exclusively on the spiritual
man, the "prophet" (in the sense of 1 Cor 14,3).[42] The
deeper reason for the spiritualism of the reformers lies in
the fact that they combine Augustinian-Platonic spiritualism with personalistic nominalism in which the model of
the sacrament no longer has any room.

The Church responded to this view with a new biblical
defense of its medieval doctrine of the sacraments and the
hierarchical priestly office in the Church. However, the
basic sacramental nature of the Church itself had not yet
been consciously reflected upon. It was only after the
above-mentioned development in the nineteenth century
that this doctrine came into view in the encyclical *Satis
cognitum* of Leo XIII. In continuity with the biblical doctrine of the body of Christ (1 Cor 12,12–27) he writes:

Just as the principle of life in living beings is invisible and completely hidden, but reveals itself in the movement and activity of their members, so also the principle of supernatural life in the Church clearly appears through its activity. Hence those who arbitrarily pretend that the Church is hidden and completely invisible are caught in a great and dangerous error, and so are those who look at it as if it were just any human institution with a sort of external discipline and external cult . . . , without the signs which show every day that it draws its life from God. (DS 3300–3301)

Since Leo XIII compares the two sides of the Church as body and soul, the sacramentality of the Church becomes clear only in its hierarchical offices. Only Vatican II, in continuity with the ideas of the encyclicals *Mystici Corporis*[43] and *Humani Generis*,[44] expresses the basic sacramental character of the whole Church and thus the new understanding of its "visibility."

b) Systematic Aspects

The Constitution on the Church (LG 8) says on this subject:

Christ, the one mediator, established and ceaselessly sustains here on earth his holy Church . . . as a visible structure. Through it he communicates truth and grace to all. But the society furnished with hierarchical agencies and the Mystical Body of Christ are not to be considered as two realities [*res*], nor are the visible assembly and the spiritual community, nor the earthly Church and the Church enriched with heavenly things. Rather they form one interlocked reality [*unam realitatem complexam efformant*] which is comprised of a human and a divine element [like the mystery of the *verbum incarnatum*] . . . so, in a similar way, does the communal structure of the Church serve Christ's Spirit who vivifies it by way of building up the body (cf. Eph 4,16).

This implies that all visibility in the Church is a "sacramental visibility": the visible wants to express and guarantee the invisible and, in turn, the visible receives its place and meaning in the Church only through the invisible.

2. MEMBERSHIP IN THE CHURCH

The sacramental reality of the Church must manifest itself also in its membership.

a) Historical Aspects

From the very beginning it has been the Church's practice that one becomes a Christian through baptism (cf. Acts 2,38.41). Through serious crimes, such as incest in Corinth (cf. 1 Cor 5,1–5), the Christian ceases to belong inwardly to the Church (cf. Heb 6,4–8) and is excluded from the community, at least as a punishment which should move one to repentance (*excommunicatio-reconciliatio*). The beginnings of the institution of penance, which arose especially during times of persecution, are connected with this. In the second century, at the latest, it became clear in the struggle against the first heresies (Gnosticism), that not only moral life but even more so unity of faith (*symbolum*) is a condition of membership in the Church. In the third-century controversy about baptism by heretics (cf. Cyprian, Ep. 69–75,265) it became clear that the proper administration of the sacraments is necessary for "valid and effective" membership in the Church. The Donatist controversy in the fourth century showed the same thing about free submission to the legitimate authority of the bishop or the synod of bishops. The complexity of the question is visible in the above-mentioned five conditions for external membership in the Church, which guarantees the inner relationship with Christ and his Spirit. It is also visible in the three forms of separation from this community: falling away by one's own choice (*apostasia*); excommunication by the community; and inner separation through heresy or schism (which are, in turn, externally and juridically acknowledged). Augustine (*Ad Bonifatium, Ep.* 98,1; PL 33,3590) speaks about the importance of baptism for the body of

Christ (*virtus in sancta compage corporis Christi*), and thus of the effect of membership beyond the effect of grace (cf. John 3,15). In his *Commentary on the Sentences* Thomas Aquinas makes a distinction between "incorporation in Christ," *merito*, which takes place already through the desire for baptism in the catechumens,[45] and "incorporation," *numero*, through the reception of baptism.[46] The Decretum Pro Armeniis of 1349 (DS 1314) teaches in a more juridical sense that through baptism we become "members of Christ and of the body of the Church." This doctrine was further confirmed by the decree of Innocent III (1201) according to which valid baptism always bestows the *character christianitatis* (cf. DS 781). Trent repeated this doctrine (cf. DS 1624) and in the code of canon law (can. 87) it is expressed as follows: "Through baptism a human being is constituted as a person with all the rights and duties of a Christian in the Church, unless a legal obstacle is present."

Beyond this limited legal perspective (from about the time of Boniface VIII) the full formulation reappeared in the work of Robert Bellarmine (1598): The Church is "the congregation of all those who confess the same Christian faith, who are united by participating in the same sacraments, and who stand under the leadership of the legitimate pastors, especially the one Vicar of Christ on earth, the Roman Pontiff."[47] This formulation was adopted in the proposal for Vatican I,[48] the encyclical *Mystici Corporis*,[49] and the first draft for the Vatican II Constitution on the Church.[50] In the new ecumenical climate after World War I the problem of this formulation became evident. This led to new formulations (gradated membership) at Vatican II.

b) Systematic Aspects

After the encyclical *Mystici Corporis* the theology of membership in the Church was further developed in order to include the membership of baptized Christians who do not submit to the supreme ecclesiastical authorities (e.g., the old Orthodox Churches) or who do not share the faith and the sacraments of the old Church (e.g., the Churches of the Reformation). A distinction was made between real (*reapse*) membership in the Church, and membership through a *votum ecclesiae*. However, this distinction is useful for non-Catholic Christians only if "Church" does not refer to the historical, present, Roman Church, but to a Church which is still to come and in which all believing Christian communities will find their home. For this reason Vatican II's Constitution on the Church expressly refrained from identifying "the Church" categorically-ontologically with the Roman Catholic Church.[51] Rather, it stated (LG 8) that this Church "possesses its concrete form of existence in the Catholic Church, *subsistit in ecclesia catholica*" (no longer called *romana*). In a similar way canon lawyers (following CIC, can. 87) attempted to distinguish between "constitutional" membership (through baptism) and active membership in the Church (through submission to the teaching, priestly, and pastoral office). In this way they wanted to stress that the effect of baptism is to constitute Church even among non-Catholic Christians.

The Constitution on the Church (LG 13) makes one further step when it speaks of membership on different levels. In order not to reduce the Church to an imperceptible Church of the Spirit, this gradation is explained in terms of human behavior: "All human beings are called [*vocantur*] to be part of this catholic unity of the people of God, a unity which expresses and promotes comprehensive peace in different ways. There belong to it or are ordered to it [*pertinent vel ordinantur*] the Catholic faithful as well as all who believe in Christ and indeed all human beings, called (*vocati*), as they are, to salvation by the grace of God." The Catholic faithful are mentioned first and the text says of them, "They are fully incoporated into the community of the Church [*plene ecclesiae societati incor-*

porantur] . . . through the bonds of the professed faith, the sacraments, the Church's government, and communion [*communio*]." Its catechumens are *ipso voto* joined (*coniunguntur;* LG 14) to the Church. For the first time in such an official document, the communities of other baptized Christians are expressly called *ecclesiae vel communitates ecclesiasticae.* The Church recognizes that in many ways it is linked (*coniunctam*) to them. The Constitution then enumerates the various values and benefits present also in these churches. This point is discussed in detail in the Decree on Ecumenism (UR 13). The Decree remarks that all of these churches are "separated [*seiunctae*] from the Roman apostolic see."

In the first place (UR 14) it mentions the Eastern Churches. They have the same origin as the Roman Church; for centuries they shared full communion of life and love; in many ways they have been an example for the faith and liturgy of the Western Church; finally, after the schism, they preserved the episcopal order, all of the sacraments, especially the celebration of the Eucharist as the center of the Church's worship, the veneration of Mary, and monastic life—in short, the great liturgical, theological, disciplinary, and spiritual heritage. The Decree expressly mentions those Eastern Churches that "already live in full communion [*in plena communione vivunt*] with their brothers who follow the Western tradition" (UR 17).

In the second place the Decree turns to "the churches and ecclesial communities in the West" since the late Middle Ages, especially those formed during the Reformation, which are linked with the Catholic Church through the bond of special affinity (*peculiari affinitate ac necessitudine coniunguntur;* UR 19). The Anglican communion is especially stressed (UR 13). These churches identify themselves as distinct from Rome not only historically, sociologically, psychologically, and in their worship but also "in the interpretation of the revealed truths." Still,

their commitment to Christ and to Scripture, their sacramental life and life with Christ offer many points of contact for dialogue that should lead to full *communio*.

As a third level after the Eastern Churches and the
Churches of the Reformation, the Constitution on the
Church (LG 16) mentions the non-Christian communities
that believe in God: in the first place the Jews, then the
Muslims. A fourth level, finally, consists of those who,
without their own fault, have not yet come to "the explicit
acknowledgment of (the revealed) God." They too, says
the Constitution, can come to salvation by God's grace, if
they lead a naturally good life (*recta vita*).

This discussion vividly shows the complexity of the
Church's sacramental nature. Objective validity and subjective effectiveness of the sacraments are seen in their
tension. Let us stress the following aspects:

It is fundamental for all reflection on the subject of
membership in the Church that the correct understanding
of sacramentality avoid both the rigorism of a phar-
isaically narrow belief in the Church and the indifference
of an uncommited liberal understanding of Christianity,
Church, and sacrament. The key is that sacramental reality (in the spirit of Casel's "theology of mysteries") becomes intelligible in Christ, the center of the world's history, not merely as a significant thing, but as a historical,
temporal event in the history of salvation. This insight has
several implications: (1) Not only must the form of membership (*incorporari, coniungi, ordinari*) be taken into account, but the Church itself must be understood as a
multi-level reality. This is a condition for understanding
how the one Church is necessary for salvation, and how it
mediates salvation to all human beings. "There is only one
God, and one mediator between God and human beings,
the man Jesus Christ, who gave himself as a ransom for
all" (1 Tim 2,5–6). (2) However, just as the reality of the
God-man Christ (who is the head of his body, the Church,
cf. Col 1,18) is accessible only through the historical Jesus

of Nazareth, so also membership in the Church can be determined only by visible elements (being joined to the teaching, priestly, and pastoral office). Still, one must acknowledge that Christ's salvation is possible even in a space outside these signs, according to the principle that Christ has not linked his grace exclusively to the sacraments.[52] Only in this way does it become possible and theologically intelligible that non-Christians who believe in God, and even those who do not yet acknowledge the revealed God, may belong to Christ, and thus to the Church.

The crucial elements for belonging to the visible Church are: baptism (as a rite of initiation that constitutes one as a member of Christ); the Eucharist as life resulting from being a member of Christ; the Eucharist, in turn, presupposes the legitimate office of the priest, *ordo;* and finally the acceptance of revelation in faith and life lived according to this faith. These three or four aspects are necessary for membership even though the individual aspects, except baptism, are viewed quite differently by the various Christian "churches." The fullness of Christian life, as it is present in the ancient churches of the East and West, includes in addition the seven sacraments and a hierarchically ordered leadership. At least since the Middle Ages, the concept of the Church and of "sacrament" has been shaped to such an extent in juridical terms that the dynamic nature of these realities and thus the multi-level reality of "membership in the Church" cannot, or cannot yet, be sufficiently grasped by theology. What can perhaps lead us to a more differentiated understanding of the Church is our Church's teaching that Christ instituted the "visible sign" in the sacraments not *in individuo,* but only *in specie.* This doctrine should apply also to the universal sacrament of salvation, the Church, and to its marks, and it raises anew the question of the criteria for membership in the Church.

3. THE RELATIONSHIP OF THE INDIVIDUAL CONGREGATION AND LOCAL CHURCH (OR PARTICULAR CHURCH) TO THE UNIVERSAL CHURCH

a) Historical Aspects

A glance at history can again show us a development that is significant for the understanding of the Church as the universal sacrament of salvation. At the beginning, as Scripture shows, there is the Christian "house community" (cf. Letter to Philemon) and the Christian "local community" (cf. the Pauline letters and Rev 2–3). Nevertheless, the New Testament use of *ekklēsia* shows that the universal Church was not understood as a sum of individual communities. From the very beginning the universal Church appeared in the individual community and the individual community recognized itself as an image of this universal Church, as responsible to it, and, in its innermost nature, supported and determined by it. At first, this particular community was a church with an *episkopos*, as it begins to appear around A.D. 110 in the letters of Ignatius of Antioch. At the end of the second century several communities, communities of Presbyters, formed in the larger cities (e.g., in Rome). They experienced their unity in the one bishop of the city and in the practice of liturgical stations.[53] Especially after the barbarian invasions "parishes" were formed in the sixth century which were grouped into "dioceses." Patriarchates came to be at the sites of the ancient "apostolic churches" (Rome, Alexandria, Antioch, Jerusalem) in the third century, and later at important political centers (Constantinople, Moscow). After the third century the Roman patriarchate gained special importance because it was the site of the tombs of Peter and Paul, because of Rome's political history, and because of the biblical Petrine office (Matt 16,18; Luke 22,32; John 22,15ff.). Constantinople also achieved special status, as the metropolis of the Eastern empire,[54] so that, after Rome, the patriarchates in their "ecclesial-political importance" were enumerated in the following order: Constantinople, Alexandria, Antioch, Jerusalem (cf. DS 661; *Const.* IV,870).

The understanding of the basic sacramental character of the Church can show that the diversity and transformation of the organization of the whole Church cannot change the inner relation of all member churches to the Church as a whole, even if new communities spring up today: personal communities (e.g., pastoral care of the military and of circuses, etc.), special parishes, associations of parishes, and special communities (such as the *"Integrierte Gemeinde"* in Munich). Just as the multiplication of masses does not multiply or alter the one sacrifice of Christ (even though they are of great importance for the pastoral order of the visible Church), so also the multitude and multiplicity of organization does not alter the inner unity of the Church as a whole. In all of these parts it appears as a unified reality. This is true even though the increase of the visible Church in this world, like its decrease, is without importance for its nature. Even though it has its eternal roots in Christ, it remains in this world in the need of "diaspora," as the very terms "parish" (*paroikia,* cf. Heb 11,9) and diocese (*dioikesis* means not only administration but also life in separation: Plato, *Timaeus,* 19b) show. In addition, one must not overlook that the Church, even though it is the universal sacrament of salvation for all of humanity, remains always "the little flock" (Luke 12,32), not in the sense of an elite Church or even a ghetto Church, but because the one who is far from the universal Church *spiritualiter* may belong to it *sacramentaliter* (through baptism: nominal Christianity), and the unbaptized (not only the catechumens, but also non-Christians) may belong to it *spiritualiter.* The understanding of the Church's sacramentality should help to dispel both the idea of an elite Church or a ghetto Church and the idea of a state Church or a Church that is purely a cultural phenomenon.

b) Systematic Aspects

While the individual sacraments may be conceived in terms of human beings, the Church as the universal sacrament must be understood primarily in terms of Christ, the primordial sacrament. Here the same point holds for the individual community and for the universal Church: the gate to the Church is baptism; and the main pillars for the community as well as for the Church are the truths of Christian revelation as grasped in faith, the eucharistic worship as the center of life, and the hierarchically ordered priesthood as the first bearer of proclamation and worship in the community and in the Church. Closely associated with the hierarchically ordered priesthood is the priesthood in which all Christians share through baptism, the priesthood of living in this world out of the Spirit of Christ and for the exalted Lord. In the missionary spirit of the Church and borne by the community in the universal Church, this basic Christian attitude becomes effective and fruitful for the fullness of Christian life and of the Church. Nevertheless, the particular community, the Church, and the sacraments are determined by a pre-given inner structure which cannot be grasped in the concepts "people's Church" or "voluntary Church. "The Church's inner unity (one, holy Church) manifests itself in faith and sacrament, while its visible organization (the twelve apostles with Peter as spokesman and vicar of Christ) rests on office (catholic, apostolic Church). It is somewhat misleading to call the members formed in this organization "particular churches" since the relation of parts to a whole differs from the relation of members to a body. In addition, unity in the Church is not only a unity of being but even more so a unity of life better understood as sacramental unity in the primordial sacrament, Christ.

4. THE RELATIONSHIP BETWEEN REALITY AND ACTIVITY (CONSTITUTION AND REALIZATION) IN THE CHURCH

a) Historical Aspects

The history of mission in the Church offers an especially good example for this final reflection. A sociological, cultural, or political science of history may give various reasons for the greater or lesser growth of the Church in various times and places. The theological meditation of faith, on the other hand, can recognize the effects of the sacramental structure of the Church in this growth. After all, the "little flock" of the time of the first love (cf. Rev 2,4), despite its lack of power in the world and despite the persecutions inflicted on it by the power of this world, conquered precisely this powerful and educated world of antiquity with the folly of the word of the Cross (cf. 1 Cor 1,18.21). And this conquest took place despite the quarrels and divisions and all other forms of human weakness at work in the Church itself from its very beginning to dissolve and impede it. (Cf. 1 Cor 5–8 and the history of heresies from the very beginning: Irenaeus, Hippolytus, Epiphanius, etc.) Although there were more effective gains in the Constantinian era, there was also more division and apostasy. In the difficult times after the barbarian invasions, when the old empires and cultures of the Greeks and Romans collapsed, the Church gained the great world of the Germanic peoples. The politically and culturally powerful Church of the Middle Ages led to the divisions of the late Middle Ages. The visible sign in the sacrament is not the sign of someting visible, but of an invisible reality which flows from the Cross of Christ.

b) Systematic Aspects

Parts Three and Four will show how the Church's sacramental structure acts. At this point, let us emphasize only the following aspects: (1) Just as human activity in a sacrament does not mean human *achievement* (it serves only as the conditional preparation for the reception of grace), so also in the case of the Church: The goal of all activity in the Church is God's gift of salvation, which can only be received.[55] When this is forgotten, one's own greatness and power turns into a path that leads down, not up. (2) Effectiveness does not correspond to the reality from which it proceeds, inasmuch as this reality is subject to our control and knowledge only as a visible sign, while the effect is the signified, the inner, the invisible essential reality, which can only be received as a gift. Activity in the Church, we could say, is reciprocal activity ordered to reception. Christian activity must always understand itself as a sign (cf. ". . . I believe, Lord, help my unbelief!" Mark 9,24) just as genuine love always knows that it is completely a gift, even when it gives itself (cf. 1 Cor 4,7). (3) Of course, the inner reality of the sacraments does not exist without the realization of the outward sign through a free human activity. At the same time, the gift of grace in the sacrament is the gift of access to a new existence, "an existence whose binding and obligation . . . , expressed in one word, is engagement through and in Christ, the essential engagement, filled by the Spirit and the gift of grace."[56] Sacrament becomes real only in the paradox of "action out of grace." (Cf. Phil 2,12: "Work your salvation in fear and trembling, *because* God is the one who is at work in you, both to will and to work. . . .") It is an activity carried out in the full freedom of love and obedience. This implies obligation for the sacramental Church as well as for every Christian, who becomes a member of the Church only through the sacraments. (4) The sacramental character of the Church is clearest if we look at the activity of the "mystical body of Christ." The glorified Lord, who is incapable of suffering, suffers in his suffering (and sinful) members on earth (Gal 2,19f.); and in grace the suffering members on earth already share in the power and glory of the exalted Lord, their head (1 Cor 6,17.19; Col 1,24; 2,18).

VII

The Church from the Foundation of the World, since Christ and until the End of Time; The Sacramental Church in Time

Space and time, as I. Kant showed, are the basic forms of pure intuition in human knowledge. Thus the concept of the Church's sacramentality must express itself first of all in these forms. In this section, let us attempt to grasp the specific character of the Church's sacramentality from the perspective of activity in time by indicating some historical and systematic aspects of the following topics: the sacramentality of time; the temporal framework of the Church; the eschatological character of the Church in this world; the relationship of the Church militant, the Church suffering and the Church triumphant; the transient character of the Church's form but the intransient character of its content; finally, a brief look at the question of the membership of the angels in the Church, to clarify one again the concept of its sacramentality.

I. SACRAMENTAL ASPECTS OF THE UNDERSTANDING OF TIME

Time has been interpreted in many ways: as objective succession in the movement of the heavens (Greek cosmic time), or as subjective succession in the sequence of our inner experiences through memory and anticipation (Augustine). Israel, on the other hand, developed a truly "sacramental" consciousness of time, especially after the Exile. It developed this consciousness above all in the liturgy, in the "remembrance" (*sakar*) of a saving event such as the Passover. In celebrating the memorial of a historically past event, this event became present; liturgical action functioned as a sign that allowed a historical event to become a present event, and by grace the past event allowed itself to be attained in the existential present through the action of celebration. The sign, performed in the present of the celebration, effected the grace of the presence of the event that had long been concluded in an objective past.[57]

2. THE CHURCH'S EXTENSION IN TIME

This "presence in the mystery," however one may understand it, sheds new light on the question of the Church's temporal extension in this world.

a) First, the Church, as the space of the New Covenant, the Covenant of redemption, and as the "body of Christ," begins with Christ. It begins with the historical Jesus, the incarnate Son of God, who alone is the primordial sacrament and thus the origin and bearer of the universal sacrament Church. Below (VIII) we will discuss the events in the life of Jesus through which the Church was founded and instituted. Already at this point, however, we can understand the following point: If the Church must be understood in terms of the historical Jesus, then the completely different temporal space into which the historical Jesus entered through his death and Resurrection and exaltation belongs to it too. The Church comprises thus first of all the Church in this world, from Pentecost to the end of time. Jesus' final words in Matthew's account point to this space of time: "See, I am with you always, until the end of the world" (Matt 28,20). Jesus undergirds this statement by saying that the Gospel must be preached to all nations before the end of the world (Mark 13,10; Matt 24,14). According to the image of the judgment all peoples appear before the throne of the judge, and he judges according to the law of the mercy with which they treated "the least of his brothers," in whom he himself is present (cf. Matt 25,31–45). From the very beginning, the Church has lived from this faith in the "presence of the exalted Lord in his Church." This faith is the basis of its worship and of the whole new "Christian morality." The Pauline letters (and the New Testament letters in general) are filled with this conviction. This historical space of the Church is sacramental, inasmuch as the invisible exalted Lord is present in the being and activity of the visible Church.

b) Paul especially extended this temporal space of the Church beyond the historical Jesus into the past: he does so, first of all, by reflecting on the inner connection between the people of God in the Old Testament and in the New Testament. For, every Christian reality stands solidly on the ground of Christ and his apostles. It is a ground that stems entirely from the history and culture of the old Israel and it must be understood in this light. Through their faith, Christians appear as the true children of Abraham (cf. Gal 3,7.14; Rom 9,7f.). The New Covenant has replaced the Old Covenant (cf. Matt 5,21f.27f.33f.38f.43f.; Heb 8,13) and the Last Supper of Christ is the institution of the *"New Covenant"* (cr. 1 Cor 11,25; Luke 22,20), because Christ has become the "new passover" (1 Cor 5,7). What we said previously about the basis and development of the idea of the "people of God" explains why one can say that the Church reaches back into the space of the Old Covenant, and even to Adam, the first human being mentioned in revelation. In the *Shepherd of Hermas* (around 150) the Church is depicted as the "old woman" for whose sake the world was created (PG 2,897). The Second Letter to the Corinthians of Ps.-Clement (around 150) interprets Adam and Eve allegorically as Christ and his Church and says that for this reason the Church existed "not only in this time, but from the very beginning."[58] Origen (d. 254) writes in his commentary on the Canticle, "Do not think that the bride or the Church has existed only since the coming of the redeemer in the flesh; she has existed since the beginning of the human race, indeed since the beginning of the world, or even since before the creation of the world. For the apostle said, 'God has chosen us in Christ before the foundation of the world' (Eph 1,4)."[59] Ps.-Epiphanius (d. 403) stresses that "the bride of Christ, the holy Church, which has really existed since the beginning of the world, but has been revealed only in the course of time through the manifestation of Christ in the flesh . . ." is the foundation of truth and saving doctrine.[60] Augustine summarizes these doctrines when he writes, "The body of this head (Christ) is the Church . . . not only the Church that exists only now, but the Church of those who constitute the entire people of saints, beginning from Abel to those who will be born until the end of the world and who believe in Christ. All of them belong to the one *civitas* which is the body of Christ with Christ as head."[61] While Ps.-Clement speaks in his allegorical manner of the "spiritual Church from the beginning," today we should speak more correctly of the Church's sacramental temporality, inasmuch as the historical Christ is the source of the salvation of all human beings of all time, "those who have lived since Adam and those who will be born as long as the world exists who profess the true faith and thereby belong to this Church" (*Ca. Rom.*, I,9,17; cf. Thomas Aquinas, *Summa Theol.*, III, q.8, a.3, c: on belonging actually and potentially to the Mystical Body of Christ and to its head). The meaning of the Church is the salvation of the world, and this salvation is to be found only in the primordial sacrament of this world, in Christ. It becomes historical reality for the individual through a present relationship to the Church, the *universale salutis sacramentum*.[62]

3. THE ESCHATOLOGICAL CHARACTER
OF THE CHURCH IN THIS AGE

What we have just said brings us to consider the Church's sacramentality which recent theology often calls "eschatological."[63] The Church's sacramentality in the order of time becomes especially clear in its "eschatological existence." Above we said that the Church, seen in space, is not the sum of all its communities; the whole Church expresses itself in each community. Now we must likewise say: The Church, seen in time, is not the sum of *ecclesia ante legem, sub lege,* and *sub gratia;* the reality that can be called "Church" in the true sense is in every time completely present in its actuality and effectiveness (as the space of the mediation of salvation), although it appears differently to us human beings at different times. Because signs are of a visible order, the signs of this sacramentality in the different phases of salvation history are different: before the Law the sign was the moral and religious order of nature; under the Law it was the Law of Moses; under grace it is Christ's saving mystery, the presence of the historical Lord, who has become transtemporal through his exaltation. Still, the Church has always remained an effective sign of salvation, and the one salvation becomes effective through it in every time according to the mode of that time. This dialectic between *visible* and *invisible* contains the other dialectic between *already present* and *still to come,* which implies, in turn, the dialectic between God's gift of grace and human activity in grace, the dialectic that constitutes the sacramental character of "Christian existence from the mystery of Christ."

Through its faith in Jesus, the Messiah, the community of Christ (the Church) knows that it stands in the time of salvation promised by the prophets; it knows that it has crossed the threshold of eschatological salvation, even though this salvation has not revealed itself in universal and cosmic terms, . . . and even though this fulfillment gives rise to new promises. . . . The present is a certain anticipation of the future; the future is the manifestation and full realization of the present.[64]

This eschatological nature of the Church reveals the sacramental meaning of its "pilgrimage."

4. THE CHURCH MILITANT, THE CHURCH SUFFERING, AND THE CHURCH TRIUMPHANT

What we have just said brings to light a new dimension of the Church as *universale salutis sacramentum*, a dimension that has been expressed since the Counter-Reformation in the somewhat unfortunate terms "the Church militant, the Church suffering, and the Church triumphant." The original meaning of the idea of the Church's threefold form was heavily distorted in iconography: See the images of the Church militant after the reform of Cluny; of the Church suffering in the images of the poor souls in purgatory; and of the Church triumphant in the Church's "triumphal chariot" (cf. Otto van Veen, 1580) or, after the discovery of America, in its "triumph over the peoples" (P. P. Rubens, 1623) or over its enemies (Memmingen, 1700), especially over Satan, through the word and the Cross of Christ (Melk, 1726). The basic meaning of this idea is not the peculiar character of the Church's three forms but their deep inner unity in the one Church. It is the realization that the whole people of God is a sacramental unity. The Christians who are still pilgrims in this age and those who have died (those who need purification as well as those who are in the glory of the divine light) are so united that the prayer of the Church on earth, especially in its eucharistic sacrifice, helps those who have died; likewise, in the celebration of martyrs and saints the same Church can effectively request the prayer of the Church in heaven for the Church on earth. The community of prayer is a "sacramental" community, because its prayer has its center and source in Christ, the crucified Lord: "Whatever you ask the Father in my name, I will give it to you . . . he will give it to you. . . . Ask, and you will receive, so that your joy may be complete" (John 14,13; 16,23–24). "Whatever you ask for in prayer, believe that you have received it, and it will be yours" (Mark 11,24; cf. 11,23). At least since the third century, this faith in the unity of the earthly and the trans-earthly Church has been alive in prayer for the dead and in the remembrance of martyrs. In his doctrine of the *civitas coelestis*, Augustine gave theological expression to this faith. The feast of All Saints, which had been celebrated since the fifth century (Chrysostom) on the first Sunday after Pentecost, was moved at the end of the ninth century to November 1. The feast of All Souls was later introduced by Odilo of Cluny (d. 1045) on November 2. The *Divine Comedy* of Dante (d. 1321) presents a rather independent Church of the beyond; similarly the twelfth century, which was dominated by the Crusades and by antiheretical struggles, introduced the term "Church militant" (John of Salisbury, d. 1180) as a more worldly version of the old idea of *militia Christi*. In the Counter-Reformation this idea was made narrower and given Counter-Reformation meaning. The correct understanding of these three modes in which the one Church appears is to view them in the perspective of the *universale salutis sacramentum* in their mutual activity. In 1700, the Oratorian Gaspar Juenin defined the Church's nature in terms of this threefold division as follows: "The nature of the Church must correspond to the Church militant on earth, to the Church triumphant in heaven, and to the Church suffering in purgatory; for indeed, the believers who struggle on earth, the blessed who triumph in heaven, and the souls who suffer in purgatory, all of them belong to the Church."[65]

5. THE CHURCH'S TRANSIENT FORM
AND ITS PERMANENT CONTENT

The Church shows its sacramental character especially in the fact that its visible face changes and passes away, as does "the form of this world" (cf. 1 Cor 7,31). Just as the mortal body of Christ was subject to the laws of development and aging, so also the Mystical Body of Christ is subject to this law of corruptibility in its earthly appearance. At the end of the Old Testament, there was the "remnant." According to the image given by the Apocalypse, a small Church will stand in this world at the end of time. However, this transient character of the sign is at the same time the sign of imperishability, just as the cross of Christ as a sign of death is at the same time the sign of the gift of redemption and eternal life. Augustine once interpreted Jesus' words "I am the way, the truth, and the life" in the sense that Christ wanted to say, "Through me (as way) you come, to me (as truth) you come, in me (as life) you remain." Then he explains: "One can see from this that nothing must tie us to the way, since even the Lord himself, inasmuch as he deigned to be our way, did not want to tie us to the way, but wanted us to go on (with him). *Nec . . . tenere nos voluit sed transire*" (*De doctr. christ.*, I,38; PL 34,33).

Of this outward form of the Church one must say: "Human beings do not exist for the sake of the Church, but the Church exists for the sake of human beings" (Pius XI, Feb. 28, 1927). In its historical form, this appearance is not a goal, but a means. Still, although the outward sign may change, it must be present as a sign which is necessary for salvation: *civitas in terra peregrina in coelo fundata* (Augustine, *Sermo* 105,9; PL 38,622). "In faith," says the Letter to the Hebrews, "Abraham already searched as a pilgrim on this earth for the firmly founded city, whose builder and creator is God" (cf. Heb 11,8–10) and "in the same faith you have already come to Mount Zion, to the

city of the living God, to the heavenly Jerusalem, to innumerable angels, to the feast of joy" (Heb 12,22). The fulfillment in God's presence will lift all that is earthly beyond
its transient and perishable character. Nevertheless, only
the transient and perishable is the place and basis of the
fulfillment given by God. To pass away is a characteristic
of the sacramental sign; and inasmuch as the priestly office of the Church on earth shares in the nature of the
earthly Church as service, it too will pass away. The Lord's
promise, "You will sit on twelve thrones and judge the
twelve tribes of Israel" (Matt 19,27–30), as well as
the announcement of the apostle, "Do you not know that
the saints will judge the world? Do you not know that you
will judge angels?" (1 Cor 6,2f.), cannot be projected into
the world of fulfillment in terms that stem from the world
of space and time. The Church of fulfillment no longer
needs office and the temple, as the Apocalypse of John says
(Rev 21,22). Again and again our human thinking takes
refuge in monism or in a dualism that attempts to break
apart the whole into autonomous and independent parts.
The basic mystery of the understanding of the Church as
universale salutis sacramentum is that it attempts over
and over again to avoid these erroneous paths of natural
understanding by grasping the revealed image of the
Church in faith.[66]

In this light we can understand that everything in the
Church that is a sign is characterized not only by "tradition" but also by "innovation." Every organism (and the
Church is the body of Christ) is characterized by identity
in growth, by change in the growth of form in an identity
of essence. This is why tradition cannot merely mean
"passing on the unchangeable"; it must also mean "maturing of an identical reality in its life." Conversely, "innovation" cannot merely mean "getting something new"; it
must be understood as "renewal of the pre-given, which
remains identical with itself, according to the law of life."

6. ARE THE ANGELS PART OF THE CHURCH?

Augustine once wrote in the *Ciy of God*, "It is quite right to speak of a community between angels and human beings. Accordingly . . . one can only speak of two cities or associations, one of good angels and human beings, and the other of evil angels and human beings" (*Civ. Dei*, XII,1). Likewise in the *Enchiridion* he says that God's temple, "the Church, is as a whole in heaven and on earth" (*Enchiridion*, 15,56). The Letter to the Hebrews tells Christians that they have come "to the heavenly Jerusalem, to innumerable angels" (Heb 12,22). And the author of 1 Timothy implores his reader in the name of "God, Jesus Christ, and the elect angels" (1 Tim 5,21). Thomas Aquinas writes, *"Boni angeli et homines ad unam ecclesiam pertinent.* The good angels and human beings belong to the one Church" (*Summa theol.*, III, q.98, a.4, c.).

Still, on the basis of what we have said about the Church's sacramental nature, the following truth must be preserved: The Church's sacramental nature presupposes a visible side which, according to revelation, cannot be attributed to angels. In addition, the meaning of the sacraments is mediation of salvation. According to the image of angels presented in revelation, the fallen angels have not been redeemed. Hence one must conclude that the Church is "a Church for human beings" and as such a Church it is *universale salutis sacramentum*, the offer and space of salvation for all human beings of all time. In its human transient character this Church is the eternally enduring salvation for all human beings: "Where a garden blooms today, a wilderness spreads tomorrow. Where a people dwells in the morning, decay crouches in the evening.— You, Church, are the only sign of the eternal over this world. Everything not transformed by you is transfixed by death."[67] Nevertheless, since Christ is the Lord of the whole cosmos (cf. Col 1,9–23), the whole cosmos (i.e., all of creation and thus also the good angels) is included in the body of Christ. In opposition to an exaggerated and erroneous veneration of angels today (cf. *Opus Angelorum*), which is similar to the practice of early Judaism and the Kabbalah, one must point out that even Scripture says, "It was not to angels that God subjected the world to come." "He put everything under the feet" of human beings (Heb 2,5.8). "The reality is Christ. Let no one despise you by insisting in apparent humility on the veneration of angels, by bragging with visions and puffing himself up without reason in an earthly manner. He does not hold fast to the head from which the whole body, nourished and knit together through its joints and ligaments, grows through God's action" (Col 2,17–19).

Part Three

Manifestations of the Church's Being, Life, and Activity in the Light of Its Sacramental Structure

One can look at the Church from a sociological and political viewpoint as a social phenomenon of this world like other societies in this world; one can abstract from it certain psychological aspects, or aspects of the history of culture or the history of ideas. This is often done today, not only by persons outside the Church but also by theologians. Such a way of looking at the Church may help to correct a certain theological monism that always threatens theological thinking due to its object. Still, dogmatic reflection must over and over again attempt to rise above this inner-worldly mode of thinking, in order to display the true mystery of the Church, its sacramental nature, especially as this nature expresses itself in the manifestations of the Church's being, life, and activity in this world. In Part Three we will make this attempt. We will first discuss the questions of the founding, the basis, and the genesis of the Church (VIII); then we will investigate (critically and from the point of view of faith) the contemporary reflections about the Church's structure, orders, and organization (IX), look at the results gained in this investigation from the perspective of the biblical statements about vocation, mission, and office in the missionary Church (X), and finally discuss the most impor-

tant offices in their historical genesis and their function in the Church according to the Church's own teaching (*XI*). Reflections about the "marks" of the Church (*XII*) will conclude this Part and form a bridge to Part Four about the Church's tasks in this world.

VIII

The Founding, the Basis, the Genesis of the Church; The Beginning (archē) of the Sacramental Church

The triple division (founding, basis, and genesis) that underlies our discussion is not arbitrary. As we will show, these three dimensions are necessary in their complementarity if the Church's coming to be, as our faith sees it, is to be understood correctly. A brief glance at the history of the question will illustrate this. Just as the essential structure of the individual sacraments consists of three elements: institution by Christ, outward sign, and inner effect of grace, so the beginning (archē) of the Church as universal sacrament can be clarified under three aspects: the "founding" of the Church (corresponding to the institution of the sacraments by Christ); its "genesis" as "coming to be in history" (corresponding to the "sacramental sign"); and its "basis or foundation in the saving mysteries of Christ" (corresponding to the "inner effect of grace").

I. HISTORY OF THE QUESTION

The Church's coming to be appears in the writings of the New Testament, not as the answer to a theological question, but as the simple description of a complex self-understanding of the Church in faith.

a) The Book of Acts, the first *apologia* for the Church, portrays the Church as it grew from the event of Pentecost and the activity of the apostles in the Spirit of Pentecost. Peter, as the leading apostle of the first Christian community, and Paul, as the successful missionary and apostle of the Gentiles, are presented as the main forces involved in the Church's genesis. Conversion to faith in Christ, baptism in the name of Jesus, the gift of Pentecost for every baptized person, the celebration of the Eucharist and active social love: these are the vital requirements for being a Christian, for membership in this first community of Christ. The synoptic Gospels supplement this narrative with their account of the person of Christ (as the first Christians understood him in their faith), of his proclamation of the kingdom of God, of the election and mission of his disciples and apostles, and of the great events during his death on the cross and his subsequent Resurrection. Paul, finally, constructs his image of Christ on the basis of the theological understanding of the events of Christ's death and Resurrection and his exaltation and lordship. And he proposes this understanding as the criterion for the new Christian self-understanding and the new understanding of the world which the Church proclaims and exemplifies to the world. The Pastoral Letters show a first fixed organization in the communities.

b) The only real problem with which the young Christian community had to wrestle theologically and existentially was its relationship to the community of God's chosen people of the Old Testament (gathered around the Temple and the synagogues). This problem seems to have been already a problem for Christ himself (especially in Mark's account). He appears as the one who "offers the eschatological reign of God" (Mark 1–6). When Israel rejected this offer (Galilean crisis) "the rejection of his offer was the rejection of his person" (F. Mussner; cf. Mark 7–16). This rejection also transformed the role of the disciples whom Jesus had gathered around himself from the very beginning (cf. Mark 1,16–21; 2,14f.18; 3,13–19). Those who extended his activity and who were the core of his future "messianic community of salvation" became "the first bearers of the Jesus tradition" that was preserved in the Church after Easter. The tension between the community of Christ and the people of Israel entered into a critical phase after the stoning of Stephen (Acts 7,58) and the execution of James in A.D. 44 (Acts 12,2). The "Church" finally emerges as distinct from the "Synagogue" after the destruction of Jerusalem and its Temple by Titus (A.D. 70).

c) At the same time (under Nero, A.D. 66) the young community of Christ began its struggle with the pagan Roman power. The question of the Church's origin leaves thus the first phase, "the description of its own self-understanding in faith," and enters the second phase, of raising the theological question of the "basis or foundation of the Church." This phase lasted up to the Enlightenment or to the Modernist controversy at the beginning of the twentieth century. From the time of the great Fathers (Ambrose, Augustine, etc.) to the Middle Ages (cf. Council of Vienne, 1312; DS 901) the Church's coming to be was described in the image of the birth of the Church from the open side of the crucified Lord.[1] The subsequent power struggles in the Church and juridical thinking added a further theological foundation, the election and mission of the apostles, especially Peter, as bearers of the Church's hierarchy. The Counter-Reformation stressed in a special way the office of Peter and the papacy. However, the question of the Church's coming to be always remained the question of the "theological foundation" of the Church, and each period understood this question in its own way.

d) It was only after the Enlightenment and the Modernist controversy that the critical question of the "unique act whereby the historical Jesus founded the Church" was raised. Vatican I had already stated in its Dogmatic Constitution *Pastor aeternus* that Christ, the eternal shepherd and bishop of our souls (cf. 1 Pet 2,25), decided to build the Church (*sanctam aedificare ecclesiam decrevit*) and that he called the apostles, and first among them Peter, for this purpose. A. Loisy, in his dialogue with A. Harnack's *Wesen des Christentums,* and on the basis of his historical-critical method for interpreting Scripture, reached the following conclusion: "Christ did not formally found the Church; he did not give a form of government to this Church, although his proclamation of the kingdom of God and the transfer of this message to the disciples gave rise to the Church in such a way that it was still the result of Jesus' action and will."[2] When *L'évangile et l'église* was condemned by Cardinal Richard in 1903, Loisy again declared, "One appears not to notice that the divine institution of the Church is an object of faith, not a fact which can be historically proven, and that apostolic tradition, rightly understood, implies the Church as founded upon Jesus, rather than by him; or if this tradition attributes the founding of the Church to him, it attributes it to the risen Christ, not to the redeemer who preached the Kingdom of God."[3] Loisy seeks the historical origin of the Church only in the "faith of the Church." The crucial objection against Loisy's position is that it raises the first Christian communities, and thus the Church as a whole, in an exaggerated way as a creative and normative beginning above the Gospel.[4] The decree *Lamentabili* of 1907 (DS 3652) and the encyclical *Pascendi* of the same year (DS 3692) condemned the doctrine of Loisy and other Modernist authors of that time; the oath against Modernism of 1910 obliged all priests and teachers to the statement: "The Church, the guardian and teacher of the revealed word, has been directly and immediately instituted by the true and historical Christ himself, and she has been built upon Peter, the leader of the apostolic hierarchy, and upon his successors through time" (DS 3540).

e) The increasing use of the historical-critical method in Catholic exegesis since World War I, especially since 1943 (encyclical *Divino Afflante Spiritu*) and after Vatican II, intensified the question of the words and deeds of the historical Jesus (*ipsissima verba et facta*) and Bultmann's demand of demythologizing has led to formulations that resemble those of Loisy's first book. Hans Küng summarized this position in his book *Die Kirche* (1967) in the following propositions: (1) The pre-Easter Jesus did not found a Church during his lifetime; (2) through his preaching and activity the pre-Easter Jesus created the foundations for the appearance of a post-Easter Church; (3) the Church has existed since the beginning of faith in the Resurrection; (4) the origin of the Church lies thus not simply in the intention and mission of the pre-Easter Jesus, but in the whole Christ-event, i.e., in God's activity in Jesus, beginning from the birth of Jesus, his activity and the call of the disciples, to his death and resurrection and the gift of the Spirit to the witnesses of the risen Lord. By these propositions Küng intends to clarify the text of Vatican II's Constitution on the Church (LG 5), which says:

The Lord Jesus inaugurated his Church by preaching the good news, that is, the coming of the reign of God. . . . In Christ's word, in his works, and in his presence this kingdom reveals itself to human beings. . . . When Jesus rose again . . . he manifested himself as Lord, Messiah, and as the Priest appointed for ever, and he poured out on his disciples the Spirit promised by the Father. It is from this source that the Church, equipped with the gifts of her founder and faithfully guarding his precepts of love, humility, and self-sacrifice, receives the mission to announce the kingdom of God and to establish it among all peoples.

However, in this text the Constitution speaks only of foundation (*fundatio*); only in LG 18f. does it deal with the institution of the hierarchy, basing itself on Vatican I; and it adopts in their entirety the authorities on which Vatican I bases its doctrine (cf. below XI). A more general remark is pertinent here: The critical distinction between the activity of Christ before and after Easter is a way of posing the question that stems from the Enlightenment; it is not based upon the text of the Gospels (esp. Mark) which was formed long after the sending of the Spirit. Rather, it must be brought to the text from the outside, which is why so many different and even contradictory answers are given to it.

Let us turn, then, to the three perspectives mentioned above. An approach from all these perspectives at the same time will show the complexity of the question, but also the possibility of a valid answer.

2. THE FOUNDING OF THE CHURCH

The question of the founding of the Church by the historical Jesus is intimately connected with the questions of the person and self-awareness of Jesus, which must be treated in christology. At this point it suffices to indicate that it would not correspond to the biblical narratives, and that it would, therefore, be false, to understand Jesus in the manner of antiquity as a god who took on human form but who acts completely with the knowledge and will of his divine nature, i.e., who acts and lives from the very beginning with a clearly conscious knowledge of the entire future (Monophysitism). It would be equally false to see Jesus as a merely earthly human being who works with a merely prophetic consciousness of mission for the final establishment of the messianic reign that had long been promised in Israel and who reacts to the behavior of others towards him and his message in a merely human way (Arianism). We human beings cannot penetrate and comprehend the person and self-awareness of Jesus. They always remain a mystery (essentially more so than a mere human being's awareness). However, the following statements can be drawn from the Gospel accounts.

a) From the very beginning, Jesus gathered disciples around himself. They did not follow this rabbi through personal inclination, but they were expressly called by him in quite specific situations that demanded a difficult existential decision (cf. Mark 1,16–20; 2,13–17; Matt

4,18–22; John 1,35–51). From the number of his first followers Jesus selected seventy-two disciples (only according to Luke 10,1; they recall the seventy elders who were
co-workers of Moses (cf. Num 11,24–30) and the Twelve
whom he called apostles according to the unanimous testimony of Scripture (corresponding to the twelve sons of
Jacob as the forefathers of ancient Israel, cf. Gen 35,23–26;
Exod 24,4). It seems that before the multiplication of
loaves and the Galilean crisis, Jesus sent out in his name
and like him the Twelve and the Seventy-Two, to proclaim the reign of God and to confirm their preaching
through cures and exorcisms (cf. Mark 6,7–13.30–44; Luke
9,1–17). After the Galilean crisis many admonitions and
parables appear in Jesus' preaching that can be interpreted
in a special way as instructions given to the Twelve, who
are to continue his cause after the suffering he had predicted to them three times. The symbolical number
twelve of the apostles, the later instruction of the disciples, the new content of his preaching of the reign of God,
as well as Jesus' messianic awareness, which is expressed
at least in the cry of exultation after the disciples' return
(cf. Luke 10,21–24; Matt 11,25–30), suggest that from the
very beginning Jesus wanted to raise up the "new kingdom
of God," even if this could be understood at first as an offer
to the whole of Israel and took on its specific form only
after the rejection of this offer, the specific form which
does not intend an eschatological Jewish sect, as the
Qumran sect, but "the whole new Israel" (Rom 4,1f.12;
Gal 3,29; Jas 2,21f.).

b) Consequently, no break in Jesus' self-awareness (a
break of which there is not even a hint in Scripture) is
implied when Jesus, before his suffering, promises the
Spirit as a consolation and power for the proclamation of
the gospel to the Twelve (cf. John 14,16.26; 15,26; 16,13;
Acts 1,8; Luke 24,46).

c) He institutes and commissions the memorial of his
death on the cross as a new Passover for the New Cove-

nant (Mark 14,22–25; Luke 22,15–20; Matt 26,26–29; 1 Cor 11,23–25; cf. John 13,1–3).

d) In this light one can also understand the missionary command of the risen Lord (Matt 28,18–20; cf. Mark 16,15–18).

e) One can understand in this light as well the command to forgive sins (cf. John 20,21–23; Luke 24,47f.; 2 Cor 5,19f.), although the language of the first community of disciples may be very much reflected in the last two commands. The separation between the pre-Easter and the post-Easter Christ was part of the consciousness of the disciples, probably only for a short while; it does not affect the person of Christ and it is soon replaced in the community by a relation in faith to the one exalted Lord. In addition, the accounts of the life of the historical Jesus in the Gospels need not always imply the formation of new material; they can also be a deeper understanding of historical reality. It is often true of human experience, especially deeper experience, that the right understanding of reality manifests itself only after the fact as a reconstruction in memory. The modern concept of "historical" is very complex, even in the natural sphere; all the more so in the case of the mystery of Christ's person and work.

f) K. Weiss, and especially W. Wrede and A. Schweitzer (consequent eschatology, 1901), understood the Gospel narratives of the vocation and mission of the apostles and all texts that point to a "founding of the Church by the historical Jesus" as a later interpretation of the Christian community, because Christ himself, according to their view, expected the imminent end of history and therefore did not think of founding a "Church in this world." They based themselves on the following texts from the eschatological discourses already found in Mark: "Amen, I tell you, among those standing here there are some who will not taste death before seeing the reign of God having come in power" (Mark 9,1; of course, this text could refer to the event of Pentecost!). "Amen, I tell you, this generation will not pass away until all of this happens" (Mark 13,3; one must ask whether "this generation" is really meant historically!). "Amen, I tell you (in your flight from one city to the other) you will not have gone through all the towns of Israel before the Son of Man comes" (Matt 10,23; "Israel" is used in this text because the logion is from the period before the "Galilean crisis," cf. Matt 10,5f.!). In the spirit of the Enlightenment, which has no access to the Christian mystery, Wrede understands everything in Jesus' person and work as either consistently eschatological or as entirely non-eschatological and historical, just as Holzmann and the Tübingen circle wanted to understand everything as either Synoptic or Johannine, and as David Friedrich Strauss wanted to see everything as either historical or supernatural-mythical.[5] The appropriate principle, corresponding to the archetype of the God-man Jesus Christ, is not the exclusive principle of "either A or B," but the inclusive principle of "A as well as B."[6]

3. THE BASIS OF THE CHURCH

One cannot understand the Church's beginning unless one reflects about the much deeper question of the "basis or foundation of the Church." What we have said so far about the "founding or institution" of the Church is only an externally visible aspect. Only meditation on the Church's "basis or foundation" shows the meaning of this external aspect as a true sacramental sign for the *universale salutis sacramentum*. This foundation is to be sought no longer in Jesus' action, but in his person and his personal destiny. The first two chapters of Ephesians develop this perspective in an impressive view of salvation-history which ends as follows: "So then you are no longer strangers and sojourners, but you are fellow citizens with the saints and members of the household of God, built upon the foundation of the apostles and prophets, Christ Jesus himself being the cornerstone in whom the whole structure is joined together and grows into a holy temple in the Lord, in whom you too are built up into a dwelling place of God in the Spirit" (Eph 2,19–22). Christ is the cornerstone of the Church's foundation (cf. Eph 2,20; 1 Pet 2,6), he is the head of his body, the Church (cf. Eph 1,22; 4,15; 5,23; Col 1,18; 2,10.19). The Church is "the fullness of Christ, of him who fills all in all" (cf. Eph 1,23; Col 1,19f.). How has Christ become the head and fullness of the Church? We can attempt to give three answers to this question; together they constitute a single answer.

a) The first aspect of the Church's foundation or basis can be seen in the statement of the Prologue of John, "The word became flesh" (John 1,14). In his "incarnation" Christ laid the "physical-supernatural" foundation of his Church. The Son of God, co-eternal with the Father, took on human nature in space and time through his second birth, in time, from the virgin Mary and thus united this human nature with the divine nature in the unity of his divine hypostasis (cf. Phil 2,5–11; Heb 2,11.14–28; cf. KKD IV, *Christology*). In this way he became the second Adam, the progenitor of a "new humanity" (cf. Rom 5,12.15)[7] and created a new order of salvation and being, the "sacramental order." This sacramental order is analogous to his own nature as the God-man by implying a convergence of outer and inner, of creaturely and divine being, of divine gift (as cause) and human task (as condition). This is the eschatological mode of existence of the kingdom of God (cf. KKD IX, *Eschatology*). The fulfillment will be realized only after the final judgment, when God creates a new heaven and a new earth (cf. Rev 21,1) and when Christ hands over everything, including all human beings as his brothers and sisters, to the Father, so that God is "all in all" (cf. 1 Cor 15,28).[8] This sacramental mystery of Christ became manifest in his Resurrection and so Paul writes, "This (Son of God) came according to the flesh from the seed of David, but according to the Spirit of sanctification he was powerfully manifested as the Son of God through his Resurrection: Jesus Christ, our Lord" (Rom 1,3f.).

b) The second event in the life of Jesus that provides the Church's foundation is his death and Resurrection. In this redemptive action and passion Jesus laid the foundation of grace and the moral foundation of his Church. Through his "obedience unto death, even death on the cross" (Phil 2,8) he atoned for the disobedience of Adam and his descendants. "For as by the disobedience of the one man (Adam) the many were made sinners, so by the obedience of the one the many are made just" (Rom 5,19). Through his sacrifice on the cross, Christ made atonement beyond all human measure, and beyond all measure he merited grace for us. "The law came in to increae the transgression; but where sin increased, grace abounded all the more, so that, as sin reigned in death, grace also might reign through the justice (of God) for eternal life through Jesus Christ our Lord" (Rom 5,20–21). "For God decreed to let all fullness dwell in him and through him to reconcile everything to himself. . . . And you too . . . he reconciled through the death in the body of his flesh, in order to let you come holy and spotless and blameless before his face" (Col 1,19–22; cf. 2 Cor 5,18f.). For all who believe in him and "let themselves be reconciled" (2 Cor 5,20), Christ, the head of his Church, has become the cause of salvation by being "handed over for our sins" (cf. Isa 53,4) and by being "raised for our justification" (cf. Rom 4,25). The doctrine of redemption (cf. KKD IV) must unfold this truth of faith. In the present context it is enough to indicate that the Church's second foundation lies in Jesus' cross and Resurrection: "Take care of yourselves and of the whole flock, in which the Holy Spirit has appointed you as overseers, so that as shepherds you may care for the Church of God, which he has obtained through his own blood [!]" (Acts 20,28).

Redemption, and thus the Church, is a work of the "triune God," not only of the incarnate Son. As Eve was born from the side of Adam, so the Church was born from the side of Christ on the cross, and every Christian is born from the water of baptism. Baptism itself is the mystical

entering into the death and Resurrection of Christ (cf. Rom
6,2–11; Col 2,12: "You were buried with him in baptism in
which you were also raised to life with him"). It is only
through these events in the life of Jesus that the Church,
which he built upon the rock of Peter's faith (cf. Matt
16,18), became the *universale salutis sacramentum* for the
whole world and for all time. This foundation of the
Church, in turn, demands that all Christians enter and join
themselves to the foundation by following Christ in the
mystery of the cross: "And he [Jesus] called to him the
multitude and his disciples and said to them, 'If anyone
wants to follow me, let him deny himself and take up his
cross and follow me. For whoever wants to save his life
will lose it, but whoever loses his life for my sake and the
Gospel's will save it'" (Mark 8,34–35). And Paul could
write, "Now I rejoice in my sufferings for your sake, and in
my flesh I complete what is lacking in the sufferings of
Christ for his body, the Church" (Col 1,24). "He [Christ]
died for all so that the living might live no longer for themselves, but for him who died and was raised to life for
them" (2 Cor 5,15).

c) The third event in Jesus' life that gives to the Church
its foundation is the "sending of the Holy Spirit." This
event is part of the life of Jesus and part of the foundation
of the Church. Christ was conceived in the Spirit of God
(cf. Luke 1,35; Matt 1,18). Through the appearance of the
Holy Spirit he is revealed in John's baptism as the Son of
God and as the messiah (cf. Isa 11,1–5; Christ-messiah-
anointed) anointed by God's Spirit (cf. Luke 3,21f.; Matt
3,16f.). Through all his life he is led by the Spirit (cf. Luke
4,1; 10,21; Matt 12,28; Heb 9,14; etc.) so that Paul can say,
"The Lord is the Spirit" (2 Cor 3,17). For this reason, God's
Spirit in the Spirit of Christ acts as the Holy Spirit in the
Church. Before his ascension, Christ commanded his dis-
ciples, "Do not leave Jerusalem, but wait for the promise
of the Father . . . you will be baptized in Holy Spirit"
(Acts 1,4–5). The author of Acts describes in detail the

descent of the Holy Spirit at Pentecost and the foundation
of the Church through the activity of the apostles on that
feast day (Acts 2). The Spirit of God is fundamental for the
whole life of the Church. We can say: the mission and
indwelling of the Spirit is the "personal-mystical" foundation of the Church. H. Schlier once summarized this truth
as follows:

Holy Spirit is God's Spirit in the Spirit of Jesus Christ. He opens
God's salvation in Jesus Christ and makes this salvation experience. This is the reason why his gift is given to the world (cf. Luke
11,13). He gave himself radically into the word of the apostolic
Gospel (cf. Gal 1,11f.15f.; 2 Cor 2,6; John 15,26: the Gospel is
fruit, form, and instrument of the Spirit), into the sign of baptism
(cf. Tit 3,5) and of the Lord's Supper (cf. 1 Cor 10,1–4) and he
administers these means of salvation through the official ministry which receives him as a gift (cf. 2 Tim 1,6f.). He thereby opens
up a new dimension of the Spirit's and Jesus Christ's rule and
claim, and constructs the body of Christ, the Church. Its members, those who are baptized and who believe, realize and experience through his illumination (cf. Heb 6,1–6) the truth of salvation and the situation of the world (cf. Rom 8,2–11). He liberates
them from the supposed way of salvation through the Law, from
sin as fundamental egotism and from its death, from the overpow-
ering force of the world and its goods, and from the promise of
human beings (cf. 2 Cor 3,18; Gal 5,16–26). He bestows upon
them God's peace, which is beyond all understanding, and God's
unshakeable joy, and even nights of suffering (cf. Col 2,14).
Through him and his wordless voice they can pray in their heart
to God the Father (cf. Rom 8,15; Gal 4,6). Already they are transformed by him, who is a first gift and foreshadowing of the future
(cf. Rom 5,2; 8,18–30; Col 1,27).[9]

One could compare this threefold foundation of the
Church to the threefold testimony of our faith in Christ
summarized in the Johannine Comma: "There are three
who witness to our faith, the Spirit, the water, and the
blood; and these three are one" (1 John 5,7f.), and see in
these three things an indication of the three sacraments of

initiation in the Church: baptism (water), the Eucharist (blood), and confirmation (consecration with the Spirit). The decisive thing in this fourth century addition is the phrase, "and these three are one."

d) These are the three mysteries of salvation through which the Church is in a special way the Church of the living triune God. If the mystery of the triune God is not to be obscured by the danger of tritheism, the incarnation of God must be seen as a work of the triune God, and in a more differentiated thinking, as the Gospel of John states, as a "mission from the Father" (*ho pempsas me*, the one who sent me; 26 of the 33 texts with *pempō*, to send, have this meaning).[10] In the same way, the cross must be understood as the work of the triune God (cf. John 3,5; Matt 20,28; Heb 9,14), and in a more differentiated thinking as the work of Jesus Christ (cf. John 10,18: "I have the power to give my life, and I have the power to take it up again"; cf. Isa 53,7: the sacrifice is voluntary; cf. Eph 5,2). Likewise the sending of the Holy Spirit is the work of the triune God (cf. John 14,16: the Father sends; 15,26: whom Jesus sends from the Father and who proceeds from the Father), and in a more differentiated thinking the Spirit's own work (cf. John 16,13f.), while Christ's Spirit is always "the Spirit of God." The reflections on the Church's task and mission in this world will show how much the mystery of the triune God continues beyond the mission of the Son and the Spirit in the missions that take effect in the offices of the Church and that continue the work of the triune God in an innermost work of the Church.[11] This continuation of the trinitarian missions becomes intelligible only if we go beyond the founding of the Church and its foundation to the question of the Church's "genesis."

4. THE GENESIS OF THE CHURCH

The Church's ultimate ground lies in the activity of the triune God. Its ground lies in the three most important events of salvation: the incarnation, the redemptive work of Christ, and the sending of the Holy Spirit. However, the entire work of God through the historical Jesus of Nazareth in the Holy Spirit unfolds itself in this world only through the human beings who allow themselves to become instruments of Christ and his mission, just as Christ made himself the instrument of his Father's will.

a) The Gospel of John introduces a clear distinction in speaking of the mission of Jesus. When "mission" applies to the person of Jesus, the word used is *pempō*. On the other hand, "when the issue is the foundation of [Jesus'] authority in the authority of God, inasmuch as God is ultimately responsible for the words and actions of Jesus and guarantees their validity and truth," the word *apostellein* is used.[12] It is as if the Evangelist wanted somehow to distinguish the mission of the Son by the Father from the mission of Jesus of Nazareth (cf. John 20,17) even though this Jesus is always the God-man (cf. John 1,14). In addition, one should note John's statement that the Spirit of God, whom the Father and the Son will send forth after Christ's exaltation, will not speak of himself, but will speak what he hears and will take from what belongs to the Son, in order to proclaim it to the apostles and the future Church (cf. John 16,13–15).

b) The Church's "genesis" as distinct from its founding and basis becomes even clearer if we look at the cooperation of human beings. The Church came to be, and still comes to be, when human beings place themselves with their powers and their innermost freedom at the disposal of the triune God to serve as his instruments: when they receive their mission from Christ, accept it and carry it out; when they attempt to fulfill the task that lies in this mission in the power of the Spirit of God, which is the Spirit of Christ. Vatican II alluded to this question in many ways without dissolving the mystery that lies behind it. In the Constitution on Divine Revelation (*Dei Verbum*) it provided access to the question in the following words:

"The obedience of faith must be given to the revealer God, an obedience by which one freely entrusts one's entire self to God" (DV 5). On this foundation the Council introduces the concept of "apostolic tradition" in its whole breadth and depth: "This tradition which comes from the apostles develops in the Church with the help of the Holy Spirit. For there is a growth in the understanding of the realities and the words which have been handed down. This happens through contemplation and study made by believers . . . through inner insight which comes from spiritual experience, and through the preaching of those who have received through episcopal succession the sure gift of truth" (DV 8). The text goes on to an extensive discussion of the unity of Scripture, tradition, the Church, and the Magisterium, and after briefly explaining the inspiration of Scripture it returns extensively to the laborious human task of the exegete in the interpretation of Scripture (DV 12). The *Introduction to Dogmatic Theology* (KKD I) must discuss the problems of the development of dogma, a development that displays the particular nature of human cooperation in this unfolding of divine revelation within the space of the Church through all time.

c) A still more comprehensive view of human cooperation through faith in Christ will be gained in the discussion of the orders and offices in the Church (cf. below IX and X). All of these aspects, which are indicated only briefly at this point, show the importance of human cooperation: besides the Church's being founded by the historical Jesus and its foundation in the three great salvation events in the life of Jesus, an important role is played by human activity in the Church in the obedience of faith, in the surrender of love, and in human effort (the kingdom of God suffers violence, and only those who use violence will take it: cf. Matt 11,12). This role is being played right now, it has been present in the Church's genesis from the beginning, and it will be at work through all time. The fundamental mystery of the doctrine of grace about the cooperation of "grace and freedom" (cf. KKD V,239–256) comes into play here. It is a cooperation that can be called "sacramental," in the wider sense of that term as we developed it above, inasmuch as human activity is a guarantee of the divine activity. The condition for being such a guarantee is that human activity understand itself as a sign of God's activity and not isolate itself in the self-glorification, autonomy, and pride stemming from original sin, thereby severing itself from the source from which alone God's kingdom can grow in this world, namely, from the activity of the triune God through Christ in the Holy Spirit in his Church. Thus Paul writes, "I planted, Apollos watered, but God gave the growth. So that neither he who plants nor he who waters is anything, but only God who gives the growth . . . for we are God's fellow workers, you are God's field, God's building" (1 Cor 3,6–9).

IX

The Structures of the Church's Being; Orders and Organization in the Church; The Constitution of the Sacramental Church

Our meditation on the biblical images of the Church has shown that various structures are used by Scripture as paradigms for the Church. Each of the different images, the image of the building, that of the body of Christ, and finally that of the people of God, expresses a different basic structure with a number of different structural elements. The model of the Church especially stressed by Vatican II is the biblical image of the "people of God" in the period of salvation-history constituted by the New Covenant. The Old Covenant was characterized by a strong distinction and tension between the fundamental theocratic order of the covenant law, and prophetic proclamation or the interpretation and application of the Torah by the Sanhedrin. In the New Covenant, in the Church which is rooted in Christ and his work, this tension is taken up into a higher unity (the body and its head) which can be understood as a sacramental unity.

In the light of the new understanding of the Church as *universale salutis sacramentum* we must acquire a new understanding of those aspects we usually call "constitution" by analogy to other forms of human community. The main focus should not be the external constitution but rather the basic law of the inner order that shapes the various forms of external constitution. For this reason we will first take up the question of the Church's ontological structure or inner constitution (basic law); then we will deal with the most important orders that bear this basic structure, the orders in which this structure becomes transparent; finally, we will turn to the present form of the Church's organization as a whole, inasmuch as its basic structure (as an immanent principle) is at work in it. These three aspects of the Church's "constitution" must again be seen in terms of the three structural elements of "sacrament": the Church's "organization" is rooted in the "institution by Christ"; the Church's "orders," as the "sacramental signs," are more subject to the developments of time; and the Church's "ontological structures" manifest something of the transtemporal ground of the "effect of grace" in the Church as the universal sacrament of salvation.

The Church's Inner Constitution or Ontological Structure; Its Basic Law

As we showed above, the word "Church" has referred from the very beginning to a reality that comprises the house community as well as the community of a larger city and the entire Church as the people of God. But this fact suggests that the Church's constitution will contain various forms according to its natural foundation (in the family, local communities, and the entire people) and according to the self-understanding of these natural communities with their different dimensions. Still, in the Church itself, independently from its natural surroundings, there develops a constitution that manifests an inner ontological structure that cannot be equated with any of the known forms of community in the world. This is not contradicted by the fact that beginning in the fourth century

(after Constantine) the Eastern churches developed a pre-
dominantly patriarchal-synodal structure, while the Western church developed the papal and episcopal order. The
events that came to expression in our Church during Vatican I and Vatican II show that the Church's ontological
structure cannot be expressed with full validity and eternal duration in a natural constitution (which is necessarily
affected by original sin and thus subject to the cross). The
following points will make this clear.

1. In the Gospel of Christ, which is actually the
Church's "basic law," there are indications of certain basic
and inalienable structures (visible in all aspects of the
apostolic office). Nevertheless the Gospel does not contain
a comprehensive "basic law" of the Church that could be
viewed as a "constitution" in a legal sense. In general, one
could at most say that because of the Church's foundation
in the transcendent, exalted Lord, who is present in it and
its activity as "head of the body" and in the "Holy Spirit,"
the Spirit of Christ, there is an order "from above downward" which expresses itself in the human realm according to the example of the Lord as an order not of lordship
but of service, without losing its character of authority.
Since Gregory I, 580–604 popes have called themselves
"servus servorum dei" according to Matt 20,22. However,
inasmuch as the Church on earth is the "body of Christ"
without which the "head," Christ, does not want to exist,
there is also a true order of life "from below upward,"
inasmuch as Christ has in fact (not necessarily) linked his
activity to the activity of the body and its members.

2. One reason why we find no "constitution" of the
Church in the Gospel is that in our natural way of thinking a constitution is a "legal" entity (rooted in the Roman
understanding of law) formally quite distinct from a moral
or religious order. The Gospel does not know this distinction. "The legal aspect is not as distinguishable from the
remaining reality and activity of the Church as in the case
of a profane society or a state" (Kl. Mörsdorf). For the "le-

gal" aspect of the Church is not rooted only in the natural-human realm. It cannot be separated from natural-moral and natural-religious reality; it has its root and meaning in God and his revelation, in nature, in history, and in Christ. For this reason it can be grasped only in the complexity of the "sacramental," a complexity that is understood only by faith.[13]

3. One aspect of the Church as the people of God is the "pilgrim state" (Cf. 1 Peter 2,11; Heb 11,13; Ps 38,13: pilgrims and sojourners on earth). This state implies that the order that was fixed at a certain time always develops and must allow itself to be developed toward the future through the work of the Holy Spirit (John 16,13); as the order of the "missionary Church" it must always be open to the manifold human order of the peoples to whom the message of Christ must be brought in a new way; and as order in a limited understanding of the *ecclesia semper reformanda* it can also be developed in an ecumenical spirit without losing its identity. For it is an identity that cannot be completely measured with a human measure. "The absence of a really closed and self-sufficient written constitution of the Church is an expression of the fact that it does not live from the letter, but from the spirit, that it is not the law, but the Gospel" (Kl. Mörsdorf).

4. All earthly forms of constitution must serve not only the individual human being, but also (and in all forms of absolutistic rule of the state or of the party in a particular or exclusive way) the constituted community as a "political power." The Church cannot understand itself as a "political power" vis-à-vis its members in this world, even if it must necessarily practice "ecclesiastical politics" and behave politically in relation to political powers. The purpose of its existence and its action is the individual human being as person and child of God. This is why in the Church's sacramental law there appears an "internal forum" unknown in secular constitutional law, and why the goal, e.g., in the tribunal of penance, is not the preserva-

tion of the law but the pardon of grace. This is also the reason why, as we will show below, the Church's offices are not defined through the exercise of an order of right and power, but rather through the service of human beings. They have a fundamentally personal character, because the "kingdom," the only kingdom the Church must serve, is the "kingdom of God," while God is not a trans-personal power or order but the personal triune God. Still, inasmuch as God is the "creator of the world" and thus also the Lord of its inner orders, and inasmuch as in Christ Jesus "God has become man," the earthly and objective aspect of these orders must find visible expression. This is why the Church has developed Canon Law. Therefore, Church law, like the Church itself, possesses a sacramental character.

5. The problems that underlie the question of a possible constitution of the Church became especially clear in the proposal for a *lex fundamentalis* of the Church following Vatican II's Constitution on the Church[14] and in the discussion surrounding this proposal[15] which led in 1976 to a terser formulation of this basic law.[16] In these attempts the necessary bipolarity of sacramental reality (visible sign for something invisible that is still guaranteed by the believing realization of the sign) appears over and over again reduced to the level of a comprehensive law that wants to secure grace legally and fix the free action of the Spirit of God in the static order of a legal structure. The dynamic, eschatological, and pneumatological-charismatic character of the Church, which is emphatically stressed in Vatican II's Constitution on the Church, is somewhat neglected or even pressed into the service of this static institution, in the name of the law. This does not imply that the Church's constitution with which dogmatic theology must deal should not be set down in an ecclesiastical legal code or in some other legally binding document (*lex fundamentalis*). Again the main point is to avoid a one-dimensional reduction as well as a dualistic separation of

the two orders (the natural and the supernatural) present and comprehended in the sacramental understanding. This demand will be understood and realized only after a period of intensive further reflection on the sacramental character of all aspects of the Church and on the new broader understanding of "sacramental."

Orders in the Church

Because of the Church's basic sacramentality, its inner structures must manifest themselves in orders that can be compared to human orders while still being essentially different from them. Let us point out only the most important orders.

I

The first thing to be clarified is what is meant by "order." Every order implies at least three elements: first, the "reality" that appears as ordered or that must be ordered; second, one or more "principles of order" rooted in that reality as well as in its goal or meaning, i.e., in a greater complex of meaning that can be grasped in human thought; and finally, a "structure" of order determined and realized through the application of the principles of order to the ordered reality. The type of order under discussion is the order for human beings and communities, which cannot limit itself to material and ideal elements of order but must take account of the personal freedom of human beings.[17] And thus Augustine, in his great meditation about peace, defines order as follows: "*Ordo est parium dispariumque rerum sua cuique loca tribuens dispositio.* Order is the disposition of equal and unequal things that gives to each its place" (*City of God*, XIX,13; cf. the two books *De Ordine* of 386). Thomas Aquinas stresses that "*Sicut ordo rationis rectae est ab homine, sic ordo naturae est a deo;* as the order of right reason is from man, so the order of nature is from God" (*Summa Theol.* II–II, q.154, a.12, ad 1). He also stresses that there are as many orders as there are principles of order (cf. *Summa Theol.* I, q.21, a.3, c; q.42, a.3, c). Since the Copernican revolution brought about by Kant, the basic problem of all order has come to be understood as the question, Who or what creates orders and what is the foundation of such orders? Kant sees ordering power only in "an activity of reason" (*Critique of Pure Reason,* B 134f.). Beyond Kant's limitation, theology, as the attempt to understand Christian revelation, must still reflect on the question of a personal (creative) authority (God) above human beings as the cause and ground of order in the material, spiritual, and personal world. On the basis of these reflections, let us turn to the most important structures of order in the Church and their problematic character.

2. PAPAL AND EPISCOPAL-CONCILIAR ORDER

Shortly before the beginning of Vatican II, Hans Küng expressed the opinion, based on the decree *Haec sancta synodus* of the fifth session of the Council of Constance (1415), that an ecumenical council stands above the pope and functions as check upon the pope.[18] In his lecture "Episcopal Council or Church Parliament?" H. Jedin replied that even conciliar decrees must be interpreted historically and that therefore the binding character postulated by Küng is questionable.[19] Pope Pius XII expressly stated that the teaching of the bull *Unam Sanctam* of Boniface VIII, which demands "papal power also over earthly power," was not binding. While it is true that a conciliar definition becomes binding when it is confirmed by the pope (cf. DS 686; 1235), the following statement of Vatican II's Constitution on Divine Revelation remains normative: "It is clear, therefore, that sacred tradition, sacred Scripture, and the teaching authority of the Church are so linked and joined together that one cannot stand without the others, and that all together and each in its own way under the action of the one Holy Spirit contribute effectively to the salvation of souls" (DV 10).[20] Conciliarism in its long history from the canonists of the twelfth century (Huguccio, etc.) down to the Council of Trent[21] may have some importance as an ultimate challenge in confrontation with the extreme papalism of a Boniface VIII, but it cannot annul the jurisdictional hierarchy of the Church (and its biblical foundation, cf. below XI). Vatican II can be an example of the coordination of the two modes of authority: in the deliberations of the Council, the pope had only one vote, like any other council Father (cf. his additions to the Constitution *Dei Verbum*), and yet it was only his recognition that gave to the decrees their final binding character for the Church. With regard to the sacramental character of these orders, one can point out that the council of all bishops and prelates does in fact "represent" the Church (cf. *Senatus populusque Romanus*) but that it cannot be a sacramental sign for the unity of the Church without the pope as head and apex of the college of bishops (not only as *primus inter pares*). Western conciliarism understood the councils as "authoritative representation of the Church." In a similar way the Eastern idea of "sobornost," which had been at work since the eleventh century and was elaborated in nineteenth-century Russia (A. St. Khomiakov), sees ecumenical councils as the only representation of the Church, understood, however, as a community of love in the Holy Spirit.[22]

3. HIERARCHY, CONSISTORY, SYNODS, AND ADVISORY BODIES

The original hierarchical system of the Church, based upon the college of bishops, which was the point of departure for the Roman papacy (esp. after Leo I, d. 430) and the Eastern patriarchal sees, was increasingly given external support as the Church grew. These supports did not change the Church's inner system of order, and yet, as the development of the Church of Rome during Vatican II shows, they must be taken into account, if the Church's concrete order is to be understood. Beginning at the time of Pope John VIII (872–882) the papal consistory was developed. The consistory was constituted by the presbytery of the city, presided over by the bishop of Rome, which met regularly to assist in deliberating and deciding important questions. This *"Curia"* of the pope was very important from the twelfth to the sixteenth century, when it was more and more replaced by the college of cardinals. At present there are three types of consistories in the Church (secret, semi-public, and public), with different participants and different tasks.[23]

The Churches of the Reformation, which do not have a distinct consecrated priesthood, though they have different ecclesiastical offices (especially Calvin's Reformed Church), developed a "Synodal Constitution" which was combined in the course of time with the episcopal and presbyteral system (cf. the Anglican Church) or with a consistory constitution (cf. the German Lutherans). At the beginning it was understood as an assembly of the Reformed ecclesiastical offices. Since the nineteenth century, however, it was transformed (especially among Lutherans) into a "parliamentary ecclesiastical body" with lay participation. When the ecclesiastical rule of territorial princes ended in 1918, the synods became the highest ecclesiastical organs. This form of constitution took on a special form in the "Holy Synod" of the Russian Church from 1721 to 1917, which was headed by a procurator (a layman) of the czar and which had become an organ of the state for directing the Russian Church. The other Eastern Churches (at least after the twelfth century) had introduced a synod of bishops with legislative, judicial, and executive power as a support for the patriarch (cf. the Roman consistory). Since the nineteenth century this "permanent Synod," headed by the patriarch and including in part lay members, has been the executive organ in that church.

Vatican II gave an impetus to related developments in the Roman Catholic Church. Let us take a brief look at them. In general, the various forms of synods and councils introduced after the Council do not intend to change the inner structure of the Church, even if they have introduced externally more "democracy" into the Church. Rather, as an answer to the changes in the understanding of authority and obedience in human society since the Renaissance and especially in modern times since the French Revolution, they are intended "to make it possible for ecclesial orders and decrees to be received in a genuine and inner meaning according to the principle: *Quod omnes tangit, ab omnibus tractari et approbari debet.* What concerns all must be dealt with and approved by all."[24] Although the new institutions have an active voice, the authority to make decisions still rests as before with the various hierarchical instances.

The following bodies may be mentioned: (a) The Synod of bishops, which serves to inform and advise the pope and to further communication among bishops all over the world, was established through the *Motu proprio "Apostolica sollicitudo"* of September 15, 1965. It received its statutes through the directive *"Ut generales normae"* (Dec. 8, 1966; AAS 59 (1967) 91–103) of the papal Secretariat of State and was for the first time convened for September 29, 1967, as an assembly of two hundred bishops of the world Church. The Synod is convened by the pope, usually every two years. (b) At the same time the *Motu proprio "Catholicam Christi ecclesiam"* (Jan. 6, 1967; AAS 59 (1967) 25–28) established a lay council and the study commission *Justitia et Pax* to advise the pope in political and economic questions of today's world. (c) Vatican II's decree *Christus Dominus* (CD 38) made episcopal conferences an important element of the Church's constitution (collegiality!).[25] Such conferences had been formed in Germany after the revolution of 1848 and they had been recognized in CIC canon 292. The Church's hierarchical structure remained intact. The decisions of the episcopal conferences attain legal force in the various dioceses only when promulgated by the local bishop. (d) Through the Decree on the Apostolate of the Laity (AA 26) pastoral synods were organized in each country. Their members are taken from various professions and states of life, differing in each country, and they are to a great extent elected democratically. In addition, they themselves draw up lists of questions by written consultation with the entire Christian people. The democratic principle was applied in quite different ways in different countries (with questionable power in Holland, with theological acumen in Austria). The legal binding force of these synods is always linked to the confirmation on the part of the bishops.[26] Since 1969 such pastoral synods of various length have been held in different countries. Holland has set up a permanent "pastoral council." (e) Vatican II's Decree on Bishops (Oct. 28, 1965) initiated the formation of diocesan pastoral councils: "It is highly desirable that in each diocese a pastoral council [consilium pastorale] be established over which the diocesan bishop himself will preside and in which specially chosen clergy, religious and lay people will participate. The function of this council will be to investigate and to weigh matters which bear on pastoral activity, and to formulate practical conclusions regarding them" (CD 27). In the various dioceses of West Germany such pastoral councils have been established since 1968. (f) The Decree on the Ministry and Life of Priests (Dec. 7, 1965) recommends that the bishops set up a senate of priests [coetus seu senatus sacerdotum]: "The bishops should gladly listen to their priests, indeed consult them and have discussions with them about those matters which concern the necessities of pastoral work and the welfare of the diocese. In order to put these ideals into effect, a group or senate of priests representing the presbytery should be established. It is to operate in a manner adapted to modern circumstances and needs and have a form and norms to be determined by law. By its counsel, this body will be able to give effective assistance to the bishop in his government of the diocese" (PO 7). Also the cathedral chapter is called *senatus seu consilium* in canon law, canon 391. The similarity of the term has raised questions about the distinct areas of competence of these two bodies. The chapter with its "permanent members" as the bishop's collaborators has precedence. (g) Finally, the Council texts contain numerous references to parish councils. Thus the Decree on the Apostolate of the Laity (Nov. 11, 1965) writes:

In dioceses, as far as possible, there should be councils which assist the apostolic work of the Church either in the field of proclamation or sanctification, or in the charitable, social, or other spheres. To this end, clergy and religious should appropriately cooperate with the laity. While preserving the proper character and autonomy of the various lay associations and works, these councils will be able to promote mutual coordination. Councils of this type should be established as far as possible also on the parochial, interparochial, and interdiocesan level as well as in the national or international sphere. (AA 26)

These parish councils are headed by lay people, even if their decisions become legally binding only when promulgated by the pastor. The Constitution on the Church says about the importance of lay people in these councils, "Let sacred pastors recognize and promote the dignity as well as the responsibility of lay people in the Church. Let them willingly make use of their prudent advice. Let them confidently assign duties to them in the service of the Church, allowing them freedom and room for action" (LG 37). And the Decree on the Apostolate of the Laity says, "The laity should unfold their charisms for the Church and discuss their insights with their brothers in Christ, especially with their pastors who have the authority to judge the genuineness and ordered realization of these gifts. Pastors do not have this right to extinguish the Spirit, but to test all things and keep what is good (cf. 1 Thess, 5,12.19.21)" (AA 3). Beginning in 1968 the local bishops had statutes and election procedures drawn up for these pastoral councils and the councils themselves were established. W. Bayerlein took stock of the work of the lay councils in parishes, regions, dioceses, and inter-diocesan areas and pointed to practical difficulties which arise from the questions of chairmanship, the representation of various states of life, the division of labor, and the right relation between power and service.[27]

The Organization of the Church; Hierarchy and Democracy

The hidden basic structures of the Church mentioned in the first section of IX are made transparent by what has just been said in the second section. The question of organization, the subject of the present section, concerns the concrete order of the historical Church. The basic problem that arises in this context can be expressed in the following terms: 1. hierarchy; 2. democracy; 3. hierarchy and subsidiarity; 4. authority and obedience.

I. HIERARCHY

a) The Church's basic order is called "hierarchical." The Council of Trent, in its discussion of Holy Orders, calls the Church "*hierarchica*" (DS 1767) and Chapter Three of Vatican II's Constitution on the Church has the title: *De constitutione hierarchica ecclesiae.* The word "hierarchy" occurs for the first time in Denis the Areopagite, the unknown author of the works *On the Heavenly Hierarchy* and *On the Ecclesiastical Hierarchy* (PG 3) which were discussed in A.D. 533 at a meeting in Constan-

tinople where they were subjected to criticism.[28] It is difficult to decide to what extent the creation of this word was
influenced by Neoplatonic thought (Proclus: cf. Stigl-
meier, Koch) or by Gnostic thought (cf. H. Ball). Both
forms of thought played a role in the contemporary monastic theology against which Denis turns in his works. It is
certain that the term "hierarchy" (= holy rule) was not in
use before Denis and that it became an important theological term through him. Through Dun Scotus Erigena's (d.
877) translation of Denis (after 845) and his own main
work *De divisione naturae* (866), which originates in the
same thought, the word entered Western theology. The
school of St. Victor pointed to Denis's writings[29] and the
great Scholastics Albert the Great and Thomas Aquinas
wrote extensive commentaries on his works.

b) An important problem connected with this word appeared in High Scholasticism. M. Kaiser formulated the
problem as follows: "Hierarchical community is not
equivalent to subordination under the pope, but it means
legally fixed union with the whole Church which is represented in the many episcopal churches."[30] Bonaventure,
over against Denis's three definitions of the hierarchy of
angels, gives the following *definitio magistralis: "Hierarchia est rerum sacrarum et rationabilium ordinata potestas, in subditis debitum retinens principatum."*[31] His
concern is inner unity in all order, as is clear from the
following statement: *"Et quemadmodum in hominibus
sunt gradus et ordines et quoad naturalia et quoad officia
commissa sive dignitates et quoad gratuita, salva tamen
unitate speciei."*[32] "Hierarchy is an ordered power among
holy and rational beings which retains its due rule among
those subject to it . . . just as there are degrees and orders
among human beings with respect to their natural condition and the offices given to them or the dignity of their
state as well as with respect to their gratuitous gifts, while
the unity of species (of human beings or of services) is
retained." Denis' definition (cf. De cael. hier., cap. 3, par.

1; PG 3,163f.) is reproduced somewhat differently by Thomas Aquinas: *"Hierarchia dicitur quasi sacer principatus.* Hierarchy is, as it were, a holy rule" (*Sent.* II, d.9, q.1, a.1, c). He then explains: *"In definitione hierarchiae ponitur ordo in quo exprimitur gradus potestatis.* Order is part of the definition of hierarchy, and order expresses a certain degree of power" (ibid.). Immediately after this text (ad 3) he insists that in this definition *ordo* is equivalent to *ordinatio "secundum quod nominat relationem, quae est inter diversos gradus,* inasmuch as it means a relation which exists between different degrees." This Thomistic conception is probably the reason why until today in our Thomistically oriented Catholic thought the idea of order (pre-eminence and subordination) was dominant in the concept of hierarchy. *"In nomine autem principatus duo intelliguntur, scilicet ipse princeps et multitudo ordinata sub principe.* The term *principatus* (rule, authority) expresses two things: the *princeps* (ruler) himself and an ordered multitude which stands under him" (*Summa Theol.* I, q.108, a.1, c).

c) Bonaventure's position and the definition formulated by M. Kaiser is more correct and more consonant with the thought of antiquity as well as Scripture. J. Colson[33] points out that the reality meant by "hierarchy" is defined by the "liturgical ministry" of the priest (cf. Rom 12,1; 15,16; Rev 5,10). In all its external differentiation, this ministry is a single reality ordered and ordained by God. "Hierarchy" is thus characterized as a participation in the consecration and task of the hierarch, the highest high-priest, who has received this power from God and who must use it for God for the salvation of human beings. All Scholastics point to this connection, following Denis who writes, "Hierarchy is a holy order, knowledge, and activity; its goal is to lead one as far as possible to likeness with the Godhead, and in an appropriate proportion [*secundum modum recipientis,* according to the mode of the recipient!] its goal is to raise one to become an image of God according to the illuminations bestowed by God" (*Cael. hier.*, cap. 3, par. 1). One could thus say that hierarchy is the institution that comprises all specific means of salvation, an institution in which the divine hierarch first of all reaches perfection and participates in that most sacred reality which belongs to his office . . . , and its goal is to lead all human beings to divinization through his office, in which others participate (*Eccl. hier.*, cap. 1, par. 3). The point that is seen in the Neoplatonic understanding of the "sacred" as a transforming power can be seen from the Christian perspective as follows: Hierarchy is the one organized "office" in the Church that serves the representation of the invisible Lord according to the structural principle of the unity of body and head. More specifically, in an "objective" sense, "hierarchy" refers to the treasures of this organized office (the Gospel, the sacraments, offices), and in a "personal" sense to the bearers of this holy power.[34] The present formula used for the ordination of priests expresses this perspective, as we will show below (XI).

d) This definition helps to clarify a distinction that has been brought to our attention in a new way by Vatican II: the distinction between *hierarchia ordinis* (the hierarchy of orders, which is transmitted through consecration and cannot be lost), which is found in the bishops, priests, and deacons, and *hierarchia jurisdictionis* (the hierarchy of jurisdiction, which is transmitted through mission or, as in the case of the pope, through election, and which can in principle be terminated), which is found in the pope and the bishops and the orders immediately subordinated to them. Vatican II pointed to three aspects that relate these two orders to each other in a way that had not been sufficiently taken into account after the development of Western canon law in the Middle Ages.

(1) Concerning the bishops' power of jurisdiction, Vatican II expressly declared, "This power [*potestas*], which they personally exercise in Christ's name, belongs to them as their own, ordinary, and immediate power, although

its exercise is regulated by the highest authority of the Church (the Pope) and can be circumscribed by certain limits, for the advantage of the Church or of the faithful" (LG 27).

(2) The teaching that considers sacramental consecration to be the only source of *potestas ordinis* of the bishops which had been current since the Middle Ages and especially since Vatican I, was complemented decisively by the following statement: The bishops' tasks "are by their very nature carried out only in hierarchical communion [*hierarchica communione*] with the head and the members of the college of bishops" (LG 21,2). Therefore, "one is constituted as a member of the episcopal body [*corporis episcopalis*] by virtue of sacramental consecration *and* by hierarchical communion with the head and members of the college" (LG 22,1). The text continues to state expressly that "the order of bishops is the successor to the college of the apostles . . . or, rather, in the episcopal order the apostolic body [*corpus apostolicum*] continues without a break. Together with its head, the Roman Pontiff, and never without this head, the episcopal order is the subject of supreme and full power over the universal Church." This can also be understood in the sense that the Church's unity is sacramentally signified and guaranteed not only through the college of bishops, but also through communion with the successor of Peter (except in the case of a vacancy of the see: election of the pope by the college of cardinals).

(3) The newness of this understanding of hierarchical office in the Church becomes especially clear when Vatican II speaks about the participation of the laity as baptized Christians in the threefold offices of Jesus Christ (cf. LG 34–36) and then goes on to speak about the ordained pastors (*sacri pastores*) as exclusive bearers of the hierarchy as distinct from the laity (LG 37). Although the Council stresses over and over again that the laity should develop and contribute their experience and their own initiative for the good of the Church, indeed, that "the right

and duty to exercise the apostolate is common to all the faithful, both clergy and laity" (AA 25), there remains a fundamental distinction (which was weakened or abandoned by the churches of the Reformation), namely the distinction between the ordained bearers of the office (the clergy) and the baptized faithful (as laity). This distinction goes back to the office of the apostles, which was instituted by Christ, and it is founded upon the special form of mission into the ministry of the Church through the sacramental sign of the imposition of hands, which is clearly visible in Acts and in the Pastoral Epistles.[35]

Many reasons, both justifiable and false, contributed at different times to different models and understandings of this relationship between clergy and laity in the Church. For example, the Church's missionary activity during the transition from antiquity to the world of the Germanic peoples gave rise to medieval "clericalism" in the feudal system of the Middle Ages, occasioned by differences in education, possessions, and the civil state. In a theologically quite unjustifiable way, this clericalism extended and often misused, in the sense of a secular distinction of states, the distinction between clergy and laity. This misuse may have been one of the occasions for the misunderstanding of the Reformation, which grew out of the Renaissance and humanism and which eliminated the distinction. Further misinterpretation of this distinction on the basis of a supranaturalist ontology, furthered by the Neoplatonic form of thought in Denis, may have given additional strength to the medieval abuses. However, none of these facts of secular history can eliminate the distinction itself. For, it is a distinction inserted forever in a binding way into the Church's foundation through the election, mission, and activity of Christ and through the formation of the college of apostles during his lifetime. In theological-dogmatic and legal terms it is still expressed by the distinction between hierarchy (and clergy in the more narrow sense) and laity.

This distinction is in no way opposed to the biblical

teaching of the priesthood of all the baptized in the sense of 1 Pet 2,9 (cf. Rev 5,10; 1,6; Exod 19,6), as we showed when we treated the sacrament of baptism.[36] Vatican II sought to eliminate the misunderstanding of the distinction as a "difference with regard to power and rights" by continually and emphatically stressing that Scripture and the early Church sees office as a "service and ministry" (*munus* and *ministerium*, not *officium* and *potestas*; cf. below X). In clear and incisive terms the Decree on the Church's Missionary Activity describes the distinction and cooperation of clergy in the common missionary activity of the Church: "While pastors and the laity retain each their own due functions and their own responsibilities, the whole young Church should render one vital and firm witness to Christ, and thus become a shining beacon of the salvation which comes to us in Christ" (AG 21).[37] In this context we must now turn to the problem raised by the modern demand for "the democratization of the Church."

2. CHURCH AND DEMOCRACY

a) In a well-known classification Aristotle confronts three acceptable systems: monarchy, aristocracy, and the constitutional state, with three aberrations: tyranny, oligarchy, and democracy. According to Aristotle, democracy is relatively speaking the most tolerable aberration.[38] The root of this classification lies in his conviction that a good system must be anchored in transcendent realities, such as God, ideas, and the good. When human beings make arbitrary decisions, any system turns evil. A genuine democracy with equal voting power of everyone may well be the lesser evil in a situation with many parties, but it remains an evil, since truth and virtue are no longer the ultimate standard.

The decisive point is that no earthly constitutional system can be applied immediately to the Church, not even one classified as good by Aristotle. The reason is that all these secular systems are suited only to earthly states, as the following four points of contrast indicate: (1) Earthly states must care for and administer secular goods and values. (2) To carry out this task they must use principles and orders primarily founded in human reflection on earthly experience. (3) They must see the common good as their final goal and the individual, his right and welfare, as subordinated to it. (4) For this reason the state or the community is itself in a special way the object of its concern for preservation, development and security.

In contrast one must say about the Church: (1) It is, taken as a whole, not its own sovereign as a state is, but lives from the gifts it has received and continues to receive from God in Jesus Christ. (2) Its first and only task is to serve the individual human being as a child of God and to lead every individual to God, to whom are due all human service, adoration, and surrender. (3) It must take the principles of its service, which is its power (*deo servire regnare est*, to serve God is to rule),[39] from the Gospel of Christ and from the entirety of God's revelation. Although these principles correspond to the innermost depth of human nature, they contradict over and over again the actual desire of the perverse human heart. (4) In its external appearance the Church can never be an end to itself, even though for the sake of Christ and as the sign and space of the redemption in this world which has been won and given by Christ, it must care for itself as a distinct body, as the body of Christ, which is always one with its head.[40]

b) This specific nature of the Church comes to light in a new and more differentiated way if we compare its system with the system of a democracy. The word *democracy* often means not only a political or social system of a constitutionally governed community with certain economic ramifications. At times it serves as a catchword to express the desire of breaking through a pre-given political or social system.[41] Still, the following points hold for democracy, which seems valuable to us today because of a certain transparency of the relationship of power and rights: (1) The power of rule exercised in this form of government is derived from, and controlled and guaranteed by, the people, even if this power is exercised more indirectly by a representation of the people that is elected for a certain period. (2) The practice of general, secret, and free elections safeguards the freedom of every citizen and the equality of all citizens before the law. (3) Nevertheless, despite the principle of majority in elections, the protection of certain minorities must be ensured by law. (4) Finally, and this is the real problem of every democracy, the "freedom and equality" of every individual can exist in the long run in this world only if the spirit of "brotherhood" (cf. the catchword of the French Revolution) realizes the four absolute ethical demands: "unselfishness, honesty, love of neighbor, and sense of community."

In contrast the following points hold for the Church: (1) The foundation and guarantee of power and right in the Church is the threefold image given us by revelation: the image of God, the creator and Lord: of Jesus Christ, the redeemer of his Church; and of the action of the Holy Spirit in the Church. The fundamental orders of human life and community are certainly contained in this law given to us by revelation. However, they are contained in it not as human statutes but as creaturely orders given in advance to human beings and must be accepted by them. They must again and again be embraced by faith and carried out in the obedience of faith. Spiritual and existential growth in this order is possible only if one allows oneself to be formed by it and actively participates in this formation. (2) The freedom of the individual as well as of the community is thus freedom in the divine order, a freedom that is a grace, a gift of Christ and his Gospel, for human beings whose nature is disordered by original sin (cf. John 8,32.36: "the truth . . . the Son will make you free"). In this way Christian freedom is always opposed to every form of human self-glorification and arbitrariness. (3) In the same way the equality of all human beings before God is not a right to the same claims, which would make human beings equal also among themselves; it is, rather, the expression of the fact that all live by the grace of God. But God gives his gifts in his freedom (cf. Matt 20,15: the parable of unequal pay), which is his love. It is a love that finds its limits only in the freedom of receiving human beings, a freedom it respects with reverence. Of course, God is ever greater than the guilt we know and confess (cf. 1 John 3,20). (4) The brotherhood that, if understood correctly, is not a prerogative of democracy, but an innermost expression of humanity, is indeed part of the Church's foundation and constitution. It is here that the demand for "more democracy in the Church" must find its access to the realization of its ideal.[42]

c) In his reflections about "democracy in the Church" Ratzinger points to four aspects and demands especially stressed in Vatican II's understanding of the Church. They can and should serve the properly understood wish for "more democracy in the Church."

(1) The first aspect to be mentioned is the "spiritual character of office" which takes its sacramental character seriously and which thus subordinates secular interests and needs to the concern for God's kingdom and justice in this world. This principle can and should lead to the right cooperation of the various interest groups in the service of the Church's single goal; thus it can overcome splits and polarizations in the Church.

(2) The second aspect is the correct "understanding of community," which Ratzinger describes as the "subject character of the community." The community is not the sum of its members but a communion of life in which respect for each other, patience with each other, and especially interest in each other are recognized and practiced as the rules of the community and as principles of Christian brotherhood. They must be realized especially in appoint-

ments to the various offices, apppointments that should
do justice both to the basic hierarchical structure and to
the rules of brotherly communion. The history of the
Church shows good and bad examples of this. Exclusive
election by the community would introduce a false understanding of democracy into the Church. Appointment
from above without regard for the community misses the
communitarian character of the Church as a whole. The
best form of appointment in each case will be reached only
if the right understanding of the Church is alive in parishes, dioceses, and the universal Church as "the community of Christ." Today the Church stands in the middle of
a clash between the traditional medieval feudal structure
and the modern liberal structure of society. Hence what is
needed especially for today is the formation of a new consciousness from top to bottom. Only in this way will it be
possible to recognize and realize the reforms our time demands from us and from our Church.[43]

(3) The Church's third path into modern society was
shown and described by the Council in the rediscovered
principle of collegiality. This early Christian concept is
endangered through the democratic thinking of our time
and so the *Nota explicativa* on *Lumen Gentium* expressly
declared, "*Collegium* is not understood in a *strictly juridical* sense as a group of equals who entrust their power to
their president, but as a fixed group whose structure and
authority is to be deduced from revelation." Yet collegiality is a fundamental principle of the Church. This was
explicitly stated not only by the Constitution on the
Church, but also by Paul VI at the end of the Council's
third session when the Constitution was promulgated.
The biblical meaning in this new understanding of the
Church's structure is expressed in the term "collaboration" (which occurs fifteen times in the New Testament).
Like no other this term dominates the different Council texts. What is demanded is a *"fraterna collaboratio
fidelium"* (GS 21), a *"parochialis et interparochialis, dio-*

ecesana et interdioecesana, nationalis et internationalis collaboratio" (AA 10), a liturgical, missionary, economic, social, and political collaboration, and especially a collaboration of the faithful, priests, and bishops among one another and with one another, a collaboration from below up and from above down. Collaboration is demanded with non-Christians and atheists also where such collaboration serves the gospel and the salvation of human beings. Of course, it is a long way from idea to reality. Still, the recognition of the right idea is of fundamental importance, which is shown by the contrary experience with the dissemination of false ideas and ideologies.

(4) The fourth way to be mentioned is "the voice of the people" as a factor in the Church. The Constitution on the Church speaks of the charisms and the "supernatural sense of faith of the whole Christian people" (LG 10); Ratzinger points out how in the great doctrinal controversies the Church relied, not on the mighty and the learned, but on the faith of the people, according to the saying of the apostle, "God chose what is foolish in the world to shame the wise, God chose what is weak in the world to shame the strong, God chose what is low and despised in the world, even things that are not, to bring to nothing things that are" (1 Cor 1,27). This way is especially important for carrying out the "reform of the liturgy" in the Church.[44]

(5) As a further reason for and way toward "more democracy in the Church" one should probably add what Y. Congar has developed in his essay "Reception as an Ecclesiological Reality."[45] The goal of Christian proclamation is reached only when the truth of faith and the order of God is received with something more than mere silent obedience. The Gospel demands a free acceptance by human beings and it demands loving abandonment to God. It is this acceptance that makes possible collegiality and collaboration in all areas. The way towards such a "reception" is to be sought in the following directions: in the "translation" of the message of Christ from its historical

time into our present; in the clarification of the saving
meaning of this message for all human beings of all times;
in leading all toward the fundamental reality of revelation,
namely, the fact that God is love. These pastoral efforts
have always been, and still are, the foundation of an order
in the Church that can be experienced by each individual
as "more democracy."

(6) One way in which the Church, from its very beginning, has attempted and nowadays once again is continuing to attempt to make each individual aware of "brotherhood" as a basic communitarian principle and thus of its
particular mode of "democracy" is the liturgy, particularly
the eucharistic celebration. The thorough reform of this
aspect of the Church's life (especially the introduction of
the vernacular) is intended to serve this experience of
brotherhood in the community. Of course, the development also shows that there can be a danger of "democratic
levelling" even in the highest realities; there can be so
much freedom in a worldly sense that the larger unity of
the whole is endangered by arbitrariness, and so much
equality of all that the directedness of the liturgy towards
the unique depth of the human heart and the greatness of
the divine reality are hindered through mass appeal and
can no longer be sufficiently realized and experienced.

(7) A final way in which the Church has always approached "more democracy," even if at times with inappropriate means, is the way of "brotherhood" in social
work (cf. the history of charity in the Church). Vatican II
dealt extensively with this aspect in its final weighty document, the Pastoral Constitution on the Church in the
Modern World. In many countries (e.g., those of South
America) great obstacles dating back to feudal times are
present. The materialistic principle of equality proclaimed
by Marxism cannot be the solution to these obstacles,
which is shown by the results of this system in various
countries. Still, it must be stressed that personal love of
one individual for another, on which Christian thought

insists so strongly, can solve the great social and economic problems only if it is integrated into a social and economic system determined by "justice," by the justice objectively required in each case. It is true that the human person is highest; but since the person is a member of communities, personal freedom and power are borne and shaped by the goods and values of these communities in the world. At least since the nineteenth century, Christian social teaching has attempted to develop these ideas.[46] Teilhard de Chardin in his evolutionary thought sees the possibility of a breakthrough of the democratic idea in the unification of the various opposite tendencies "to a single coherent planetary system." Freedom is to be expected from "trans-humanization," equality through "living coextensively with humankind," and brotherhood through the realization "that all of us together are the front line, the spearhead of an evolutionary wave which is in full course." Is this conception not too biological in its application to human freedom?[47]

To conclude, let us reflect on the relationship of all of these aspects to the sacramental nature of the Church. The response to the problems raised in this section must be found in the interaction of person and community, of community and universal Church, of natural and supernatural order, of human effort and divine grace. And the final basis for this interaction lies in the Church's sacramental nature. This intuition into the Church's nature also illumines a tension that is significant for every human community, namely, the tension between personal order of love, the cultural and social order of society, and the political order of law and power.[48]

3. HIERARCHY AND SUBSIDIARITY

G. Gundlach (d. 1963) developed the theory for the principle of subsidiarity and Pius XI introduced it in his social encyclical *Quadragesimo Anno* (1931) along with the principle of solidarity as binding for Catholic social teaching. The principle of subsidiarity asserts that the higher and larger social or political units in the life of a community may intervene with active help and may absorb the functions of lower and smaller units only when the power of these units does not suffice to reach their social and human goals. Since then the Church has often appealed to this principle to ward off the increasingly extensive intrusions of the state into Christian society, especially into family life in questions of education and formation. The principle was also used to show the limits of the work of associations in the Church. In the words of *Quadragesimo Anno:* "It is against justice to absorb the tasks which can be fulfilled and brought to a good end by smaller and subordinate social institutions into more comprehensive and superior institutions. At the same time it is quite disadvantageous and confuses the whole order of society. For, every social activity is in its essence and concept subsidiary; it must aid the members of the social body, but it must never smash them together or absorb them" (no. 79).

The demand is often made today that this principle of social philosophy should be applied not only to the disposition of the whole people, which is administered and ordered in different ways by the two communities, the state and the Church, but also to the Church taken by itself. In order for this demand to be met correctly, the general meaning and the limits of this principle have to be clarified; already in the general public social order it must be thought through in every particular case (e.g., retirement insurance, welfare payments, family subsidies, social security, etc.).

a) What is at issue in the public social sphere of the state and the Church is primarily the distribution of common goods and the realization of general welfare for partial communities and individuals as members of the larger community. Material, ethical, and personal perspectives usually overlap in such a way that economic and institutional powers are the primary and essential factors in the realization of the principle of subsidiarity. In the specifically inner-ecclesial sphere, on the other hand, the goal and meaning of this activity is the kingdom of God ("Seek first the kingdom of God!" Luke 12,31; cf. 12,22–34; Wis 7). This kingdom is in this world, but not of this world (cf. John 18,36); it obeys the laws of the Sermon on the Mount, which contradicts the spirit of this world (Matt 13); although all ethical strength must be committed to its realization (cf. Matt 11,12), it is first of all and essentially a grace for which one must pray (cf. Matt 6,10; Rev. 22,17); and, unlike the public social order, it is not anchored in social institution and economic order, but most deeply and primarily in the free, loving and sacrificial self-giving of the person (the individual human being).

b) Common goods and the general welfare constructed on their basis are primarily grounded in the particular pre-given goods of this earth and in the natural dispositions and forms of behavior of human beings in this world; they are the goal and the result of a correct constitution of the various communities and of a correct distribution of the rights and duties of individuals and partial communities in the whole of society and the state. The reign of God, on the other hand, lies primarily in the interior of human beings (cf. Luke 17,21). It is a participation in the eschatological reign of Christ (cf. Mark 25,34) and a downpayment of the eternal fulfillment of the human person in God, the creator. For the human person is created in the image and likeness of God (Gen 2,16) in order to be a child of God in this world (Matt 18,1–3) and to be for all eternity an heir of God and co-heir of Christ in God's eternal kingdom (Matt 13,13; 18,3; Rom 8,17).

c) The principle of subsidiarity, which cannot be maintained without the principle of solidarity (all are responsible for all), finds visible expression in this world above all in the validity of general "human rights" as they were worked out in 1948 by UNESCO and legally established on

the international level by the Human Rights Convention
of 1965. The Church has been founded by Christ; it is
determined by him in its fundamental structure; and his
Spirit dwells in it. Hence, in addition to human "rights
and duties," it must take its awareness of the following
aspects seriously: the "gratuitous" character of the world
as a creature; the law of love; the nature of "office" as a
ministry; and voluntary sacrifice as a way towards an active ordering of this world. Only on this basis can the
principle of subsidiarity be applied "objectively" in particular cases.[49]

d) While the doctrine of human rights, according to
which the few must be taken care of by the many, stems
from natural human self-understanding, the hierarchical
principle is a law of God's salvation history (biblical revelation). In this law the many must again and again be saved
and guided by the few (persons who have been chosen and
sent by God: patriarchs, Moses, judges, kings, prophets,
apostles, saints). This hierarchical principle does not abol-
ish human rights, but it integrates them into higher ethical and human order of love so that they partially lose their
one-sided "legal" character.

On the basis of these general reflections one must ask in
each case whether and how the principle of subsidiarity
can and must be applied within the Church. In general one
can say that next to the hierarchical principle the freedom
of human and Christian conscience is completely and
fully preserved in the Church. Of course, the extreme case
of this preservation is the possibility that an individual, by
leaving the Church and its hierarchical principle, loses its
gifts of salvation and fails to achieve his or her eternal
fulfillment. One must also recognize that the bearers of
ecclesiastical office can fail to act in accordance with the
ministerial character of their office and thus become a
scandal for the faithful. Many recent publications point to
this possibility, even if they frequently fail to achieve the
correct understanding of the Church and the *"sentire cum
ecclesia"* rooted in this understanding.[50]

4. AUTHORITY AND OBEDIENCE

The Church's special "organization" does not stem from the human desire to "organize" or some other social desire, but it manifests itself as a permanent divine mission (can 108 § 3). Hence we must achieve a new understanding of the following three realities: (a) The authority of the Church is not rooted in some common goal or a creative personality but in the mission of Christ. It is, therefore, an authority of representation and service (cf. 1 Cor 4,1; 12,7; Eph 4,12ff.). By the same token, its origin in God and its final goal, the glory of God and the salvation of human beings, increase its binding character.[51]

b) Obedience to the Church's authority is not primarily a sociological demand but, on the deepest level, a religious demand. It is the attitude of listening to the witness of the one sent by God, and its witness (*hypakouein, martyrein, apostellein*) is the full unfolding of its own Christian nature. This is why Christ judges the refusal to listen, disobedience, as the despising and rejection of himself and God (Luke 10,16) and says, "If someone fails to obey [*parakousēi*] even the Church, count him as a sinner and a gentile" (Matt 18,17).[52] Human failing, the human desire to dominate, may endanger "representative authority," and creaturely pride may endanger "serving obedience." Nevertheless, it would be "donatism" to ignore divine mission because of human weakness. Still, since the Church's authority is an authority of representation and service, it cannot replace the immediate relationship of every individual human being to God, and it cannot relieve the faithful of self-confidence, of their own initiative for the kingdom of God. The Church's authority is a great grace for the one who sees its sacramental nature with the eyes of faith, and who is able to perceive God's mission and inaudible command in its visible authority. A way opens for him or her to an authentic *sentire cum ecclesia* which helps him or her to find the faith that overcomes the world (cf. 1 John 5,4).[53]

c) Catholic Action, which was established in 1925 by Pius XI (*Duas primas*, Dec. 21, 1925), was intended to correct laicism, which fails to understand the Church's supernatural hierarchical structure.[54] It gave to the faithful a more explicit share in the hierarchical apostolate, but not in the hierarchy, i.e., in the power of mission, not the power of holy orders; it clarified the importance of the laity in the Church, which had at times not been recognized in the period after Trent in virtue of an overly rigid preservation of the Middle Ages, and thus it made this source of life again available to the Church.[55] Vatican II took a step further by stating that the "participation in the apostolate of the Church" is already given as a task to every Christian through baptism: "The apostolate of the laity is a participation in the Church's saving mission itself" (LG 33,34,37); it is not a concession of the hierarchy.

d) The Church as a sacramental organization in human hands raises the problem of the individual as a spiritual, free, and responsible personality. For every human being there is a sphere of spiritual-moral life that is subject only to the individual's responsibility and thus is withdrawn from the grasp of authority, even that of the Church, although this sphere cannot be defined in general terms. It is the place of moral-ascetical principles like *epieikeia, aequitas, discretio spirituum,* etc. It remains the task of the individual Christian not to become restricted to the narrow sphere of social obligations in the Church (such as Sunday Mass, fasting, receiving the Eucharist at Easter), but to unfold as broad and deep as possible a space of personal religious life and to put it as fruitfully as possible at the disposal of the Church. Only in this way can one resist the danger of a loss of individuality in a mass through misunderstood organization. The fundamental Christian law of love remains always to some extent private and personal; it remains in some sense charismatic, until it finds its fulfillment in the coming aeon.[56]

X

Vocations or Charisms, Ministries, Offices or Commissionings in the Missionary Church as Universal Sacrament of Salvation

HISTORICAL ASPECTS

The question of office in the New Testament was raised particularly by Protestant theology at the turn of the century after the dialogue between Catholic and Protestant theology had started anew around 1850 (A. Möhler, Thiersch, Denzinger). The Protestant side took as its point of departure a social-critical point of view based on Enlightenment thought, but it was soon confronted with the underlying question of the nature of the Church. Harnack, in his important investigations about the genesis and development of the Church's constitution in ecclesiastical law in the first two centuries,[57] distinguished two organizations in the early Church: a charismatic-religious organization in the individual communities and an administrative-economic organization of the universal Church as it developed in early Catholicism. In contrast, in 1892 R. Sohm defended the thesis, "Ecclesiastical law contradicts the nature of the Church." He drew a clear distinction between a Church of love in early Christianity and a Church of law in early Catholicism. P. Battifold, H. Bruders and other Catholic theologians attempted to

show against this claim that already in the New Testament true offices are present side by side with charisms,
that charism and office do not contradict but complement
each other, and that there is an interior unity between
them. Post–World War II exegesis increasingly introduced
the tradition-critical idea of "development" into the question of office.[58]

An objective dogmatic treatment cannot take its point
of departure in the oldest reconstructed literary strata of
the New Testament, which are then interpreted, as
already in the case of Harnack, in terms of the social structures of Judaism and antiquity. Rather, it should begin
with the seam between the New Testament and the first
post–New Testament writings, i.e., around the year 100,
the time in which the Pastoral Letters, 1 Clement, and the
Didache prove themselves as a preliminary conclusion of a
genuine development, not as a break with a completely
different past. Only in this way can one gain a view of the
whole of the New Testament doctrine, which serves as a
foundation of all further development. Early Catholicism
is present already in the New Testament.[59]

APPROACH TO THE SUBJECT

Our reflections about the Church's constitution showed
some of the tensions between the individual and the
many, the members or aspects of organization and the
whole. In natural thought, "office" has to do with
"power," and thus with something that affects human beings as a whole, beyond mere spiritual "authority." In the
context of "office," therefore, the question of the above-
mentioned tensions, and thus the question of the deeper
ground and meaning of "sacramental" reality in the
Church, takes on an increasing urgency.

As a point of departure let us take the extremely relevant and dense text, Ephesians 4,1–16. Whether one considers it authentically Pauline (e.g., Schlier and the Catho-

lic tradition) or pseudepigraphical (e.g., Brox, Schmid, Klauck, Käsemann), one thing is certain: it portrays the early Christian problem of the structure of office in the Church in a unique way, but completely in the spirit of Romans 12 and 1 Corinthians 12. It begins with the exhortation to "the unity of the Spirit in the bond of peace" (Eph 4,3), the origin of which it sees in the Church's sacramental ground: "One body and one spirit, just as you were called to the one hope that belongs to your call, one Lord, one faith, one baptism, one God and Father of us all, who is above all and through all and in all" (Eph 4,4–6). The goal and meaning of this unity is "to equip the saints for the work of ministry, for building up the body of Christ" (Eph 4,12). "Offices and ministries" are introduced as a help for this unity. In particular, some are called to be "apostles, some prophets, some evangelists, some pastors and teachers" (Eph 4,11). The text expresses the specific task of these ministries, in which every member of the community participates according to a particular call, as follows: "Speaking the truth in love, we are to grow up in every way into him who is the head, into Christ, from whom the whole body, joined and knit together by every joint with which it is supplied when each part is working properly, makes bodily growth and upbuilds itself in love" (Eph 4,15–16). The text clearly characterizes the ministries as "gifts" (*charismata*) that come from God and as "human services" (*diakoniai*) through which the community of those joined in faith and love grows into the body of Christ whose head is Christ, the exalted Lord, who sits already at the right hand of the father.

We can recognize three processes in this text which, in turn, give rise to three groups in the community. Each of these groups has its proper task, although it bears full fruit only in mutual cooperation. (a) In the first place there is each and every individual as a believing and baptized Christian, called by God to sanctification in Christ and in his Church.

(b) For many (and at first probably for all) this call implies an inner obligation for various "ministries" in the community. The terms "prophets, evangelists, pastors, teachers" probably refer to these different ministries in the Church.

(c) These ministries (taking into account the special terminology of the New Testament) are preceded by a particular "office" of leadership and guidance that belongs to the "apostle." According to the unanimous testimony of the Gospels, the apostle has been called in a specific "call and mission" by Christ himself.

The text suggests thus that we should look at "office" in the Church under the three aspects of "calls" (charisms), "ministries," and "offices" (missions). According to the "structures, orders, and organizations" discussed in the preceding chapter (IX), we will discuss only this general structural aspect of "ministerial office." Again, the three aspects of the "structure" of office" point to the three necessary and intertwined structural factors of sacrament: "charisms" are related to the "institution by Christ," the various "ministries" to the "outward signs," and the "inner effect of grace" is rooted in the "offices" in the narrower sense which are transmitted through sacramental signs. The true "offices" in particular will be the subject of the next chapter (XI). The themes of the present chapter (X) are: the unity of the three tasks; the ministries and their multiplicity; the understanding of office and the most important offices; the offices and the charisms; the Christian layperson and the Church.

I. THE UNITY OF THE THREE TASKS

"To equip the saints for the work of ministry, for building up the body of Christ" (Eph 4,12). In this text Paul is guided completely by his concern for the unity (*henotēs*, Eph 4,3) of the Church. Thus he sees the three goals proposed in the text just quoted in terms of this unity. The one who has been called (Eph 4,1) as a Christian must bring about these three things. Nevertheless, there is a differentiation that is also mirrored in the fivefold division (apostles, prophets, evangelists, pastors, teachers) of the ministerial offices. The text is not a sufficient reason, but a point of departure, for the threefold division to be discussed here: calls, ministries, offices.

A first task of every baptized Christian is to grow "to mature manhood, to the measure of the stature of the fullness of Christ" (Eph 4,13). This cannot happen without the work of ministries in the Church and without the building up of the body of Christ through the apostolic office. Nevertheless, the office and the ministries remain ineffective if the individual does not allow himself to be grasped, to be prepared, and to be formed. The formation of the individual Christian is a gift of God mediated through the offices and ministries in the Church; but it is also a proper task that must be accepted and carried out by the individual. As we will show, this formation is the gift and task of the "baptismal priesthood" that belongs to every Christian.

This preparation of the saints is mediated by a number of "ministries" that are like joints in the body. "The whole body, joined and knit together by every joint with which it is supplied, when each part is working properly, makes bodily growth and upbuilds itself in love" (Eph 4,16).

The guiding apostolic office is assisted by such powers, which in some way participate in the "office of the apostle" without themselves being an apostolic office. The apostle explains their difference as follows: "But grace was given to each of us according to the measure of Christ's gift" (Eph 4,7). "Prophets," who are explicitly mentioned together with apostles in Ephesians 2,20 and 3,5, probably occupied a special position as charismatics next to the apostles, as indicated also by 1 Corinthians 14 and *Didache* 10,6; 11,3–12. Perhaps at the beginning they even led the liturgy of the community on certain occasions. But they do not have the office of apostles.

It is to the apostles that the text seems to attribute in a special way the "building up of the whole body, the Church," i.e., the responsibility for the whole of the Church, for the body of Christ on earth. Although the concept of apostle is still unclear in Paul, Luke says about the "twelve" found in Matthew and Mark that Christ himself called them apostles (cf. Luke 6,13; Mark 3,13–19; Matt 10,1–4). Their ministry must be called "office" in the strict sense, as we will show. This is why they were "sent." But also their action is effective only in union with the ministries and the saints who let themselves be built up into the body of Christ, the Church.

2. THE MINISTRIES AND THEIR MULTIPLICITY

In Judeo-Christian thought, "ministry" or "service" was not considered demeaning as in Greco-Roman thought, even though it includes a "being tied to the Lord." It simply belonged to the human social order. In fact, the greatness of a lord makes service particularly honorable. This is clear whenever human beings stand in the service of God as a "servant of God" after David especially in the piety of the Psalms: cf. Psalm 19,11; 116,16; cf. Rom 1,1; Jas 1,1; etc.). In this light, serving appears as an honorable task and the "master-slave" relation in the civil sense is often inverted in the Christian understanding of the world (cf. 1 Cor 7,22; Phlm). Through Christ, "service," which was a special form of the love of God in the Old Testament (cf. Psalm 100,2; Deut 10,12; 11,13ff.) became also an excellent form of the love of neighbor: "to dedicate oneself to the service of the saints" (1 Cor 16,15) in the provision of aid (2 Cor 9,1) and especially the service of the word (2 Cor 3,8) or the service of reconciliation (2 Cor 5,18) or in general in "apostolic service" (Acts 1,25; Eph 4,12.16). To serve is the highest distinction of every Christian since Christ said of himself, "I have not come to be served, but to serve" (Matt 20,28; Mark 10,45). He sanctified the example of serving when he washed the feet of his disciples during the Last Supper (John 13,1–17) and said, "If any one serves me, the Father will honor him" (John 12,26).

It is in this service that the Spirit's gifts of grace (charisms) take effect in the Church. The apostle describes their multiplicity when he speaks of the gift of "the utterance of wisdom . . . the utterance of knowledge . . . faith . . . gifts of healing . . . the working of miracles . . . prophecy . . . the ability to distinguish between spirits . . . various kinds of tongues . . . the interpretation of tongues" (1 Cor 12,8–10). The unity of all these gifts lies in the one Spirit, in the one Lord, and the one God (cf. 1 Cor 12,4–11). Every service is borne by the basic attitudes of "lowliness and meekness, with patience, bearing with one another in love" (Eph 4,2; cf. Col 3,12f.).[60]

3. THE UNDERSTANDING OF OFFICE AND THE MOST IMPORTANT OFFICES

What we today call "office" is also called "service" or "ministry" (*diakonia*) in Scripture (cf. 1 Cor 12,5; Acts 1,17.25). The New Testament has no separate word yet for "office." Nevertheless what we today call "office" is clearly present. Of course, there is a deep difference between the secular and the ecclesial understanding of office, even if in the course of history secular offices, above all higher offices, such as kingship, attributed a divine aura to themselves.

Secular offices are organs in human society. They are formed by society itself for the preservation and administration of systems of order that transcend the individual. One finds such orders in the moral, legal, economic, and political spheres. From society and from the sphere of reality they serve, these offices receive a certain "authority and power." The transfer of these secular offices happens through election or appointment, or they are usurped by their bearer or inherited from the preceding bearer. In contrast, the offices in the Church are essentially a gift of God and they are founded in the person and work of Christ: they are in some way "Christ-offices." They must thus be understood as participations in the offices Christ has as teacher (prophet), king (son of David), and priest (according to the order of Melchizedek: Heb 5,8ff.).

The immediate relationship of New Testament offices to God and Christ becomes clear in the concept of "mission." This concept expresses a reality that may be comparable in formal terms to the transfer of power, rights and duties to an "emissary" in a secular power, as the representative of that power outside its own sphere of power, or within its own sphere in places in which the true bearer of power cannot always be present. In terms of content, however, there is the deep difference that office in the Church is not primarily the representation of a "power" but the channel of "the mercy and grace of God and Christ." In addition, the reason for "representation" is not that God, the true bearer of power, cannot be present, but only that the infinite God wants to enounter finite created human beings in a finite created way when he manifests the signs of his grace so that human beings can truly understand them, grasp them, and respond to them as deeds of grace and not as deeds of power. This is why God brought about the gift of redemption not through a deed of power, but in the mystery of Christ—through his incarnation, through his death and resurrection, and through the sending of the Holy Spirit. The special form of the transfer of office in the Church is linked to this point: it does not happen through heredity or election, and it cannot be usurped (Heb 5,1–4). Rather is is brought about by a sign-action (the imposition of hands, *ordinatio*). This sign expresses that what is transferred is not a power proper to its bearer. Rather, God gives a foreign, borrowed, and entrusted power as a gift and task. Both the one who ordains and the one who is ordained stand in the same way before him as "representatives and responsible stewards." While all secular offices are in some way rights and duties immediately located in the human sphere of being, office in the Church implies clearly and exclusively rights and duties that come immediately from God, lead immediately to God, and are given exclusively for the sake of salvation. Ecclesial power is a *sacra potestas*, a "spiritual authority" (P. Krämer). In fact, what is ultimately involved is not rights and duties but "God himself."

This is clear, for example, in the Old Testament where the one "messenger or emissary of God" (*maleach Yahweh*) is not really an intermediary being sent by God which stands between God and human beings (as in the angelology of later Judaism). He is God's form of appearance, a representation of God himself (cf. Gen 16,7–13; 21,17–21, Hagar; 22,11–18, Abraham; 31,11–13, Jacob). The same point is even clearer in the New Testament in the mission sayings in Luke and John (cf. Luke 9,1f.48; 10,3.16; John 5,23; 13,20; 15,21), which see the origin of the mission of the disciples and apostles in the Father, since their mission is a "participation in the mission of Christ." Also the nature of the Spirit, the source of charisms, is interpreted by means of the terminology of mission (John 14,26; 15,26; 16,7). The New Testament expressions for "mission" offer no formal criteria for positing a material distinction between the mission of the Son and the Spirit from God and the mission of the apostles and disciples by Christ.

These observations point to the foundation of the structure of New Testament office; they point to its "personal" nature, its nature as a participation in the office of Christ. Secular office, on the other hand, is defined by impersonal orders, even if these orders are related to human persons. Of course, the personal nature of office is not "individually" maintained in the Church for the single bearers of the office; but it lies as the "office of Christ" in this historical succession of offices in the Church through the ages.

Inasmuch as the Church's offices, like secular offices,

serve human beings who stand in space and time and in the orders of this world, they take on various forms: first of all the threefold form of "teaching office, priestly office, and pastoral office" as exemplified in Christ; further, the one apostolic office was differentiated in its subordinate aspects through the presbytery and the diaconate; finally, as we will see below, a distinct Petrine office developed quite early in the Church as an office of the unity of the Twelve.

The Catholic understanding of office becomes clearer still if we look at the more impersonal foundation of office in the churches of the Reformation.

The Reformation doctrine of office follows from, and asserts itself as, a conscious opposition to the Catholic priesthood (we will speak about this priesthood in the following) and it follows from the priority of the Gospel, i.e., of the doctrine of justification, over the Church. In Lutheran terms (according to the Confessio Augustana, art. 5) only one office has divine right, namely, the office of preaching or the pastoral office. The Reformed Church has two theological offices, pastor and teacher, and two lay offices, elder and deacon. The congregations of a certain area unite in a presbyterial and synodal constitution.[61]

Beginning in World War II the confessing church developed "ministries" in the Christian sense and the VELKD re-introduced the episcopal office according to the Scandinavian paradigm. In the common ecumenical search of the present day (cf. below XIII) the reformed churches (especially the Anglican Church) are striving for an understanding of succession and ordination that would be compatible with the Catholic and Orthodox faith.

4. THE OFFICES AND THE CHARISMS

Our reflections about "calls, ministries, and offices" have already brought to light the great unity of life and activity in the manifoldness of gifts and tasks. In the discussions that went on during Vatican II, this unity appeared in the tension between "charisms and offices." Several council fathers (e.g., Cardinal Suenens) argued that the charisms of the early Church, as one sees them in the Pauline letters, seem to have been neglected or left to die in the Church. These discussions deepened the awareness of the importance of the Holy Spirit for the Church and its life and action (cf. Heribert Mühlen).

It would, of course, be wrong to play out charisms and offices against each other or to style office simply as a charism and to see the Church one-sidedly as a "charismatic community" (a tendency seen at times in Küng and Hasenhüttl). Thus the Vatican II Constitution on the Church writes,

These charismatic gifts, whether they be the most outstanding or the more simple and widely diffused, are to be received with thanksgiving and consolation, for they are exceedingly suitable and useful for the needs of the Church. Still, extraordinary gifts are not to be rashly sought after, nor are the fruits of apostolic labor to be presumptuously expected from them. In any case, judgment as to their genuineness and proper use belongs to those who preside over the Church, and to whose special competence it belongs, not indeed to extinguish the Spirit, but to test all things and hold fast to that which is good (cf. 1 Thess 5,12.19–21). (LG 12)

The text suggests that one should clarify above all the concept of "charism." It distinguishes clearly between "simple and widely diffused" gifts of grace to which the word of the apostle applies, "grace [charis] was given to each of us according to the measure of Christ's gift" (Eph 4,7; cf. 1 Cor 12,11) and "outstanding" gifts which can probably be linked to what we have just called "ministries." Paul enumerates the following gifts (charismata) (cf. 1 Cor 12,8–10): Wisdom for practical truths (sophia), knowledge for speculative truths (gnōsis), faith (pistis) for the mysteries of divine revelation, power of healing (hia-

mata, cf. Acts 4,30; 1 Cor 12,28,30), power of miracles
(*dynameis,* 1 Cor 12,28.30), prophecy (*prophēteia,* 1 Cor
14,3; Acts 11,27) for the edification, exhortation, and consolation of the community, the power to distinguish between spirits (*diakriseis pneumatōn,* 1 Cor 14,21; 1 Tim
4,1) in order to distinguish false prophets from true
prophets, speaking in tongues (*glōssai*) in ecstasy with incomprehensible words to the glory of God, and interpretation of tongues (*hermēneia glōssōn,* 1 Cor 12,28.30). The
decisive thing in all these gifts is that they are given for the
"upbuilding, encouragement, and consolation" (1 Cor
14,3) of the community. This is why the highest of all
charisms is "love" (*agapē,* 1 Cor 13). Thus Paul has great
reservations about a speaking in tongues that no longer
fulfills this service, although he expressly wants to recognize the genuine gift of speaking in tongues and of prophecy (1 Cor 14,1–40). As a Jew with a Greek education he
does not want to release the gifts of the Spirit from the
control of the mind. And so he says, "I will pray with the
spirit and I will pray with the mind also, I will sing with
the spirit and I will sing with the mind also" (1 Cor 14,15).

In Ephesians 4 Paul introduces the charisms as special
"gifts of the Spirit." In 1 Corinthians 12,28 he unites them
with various ministries and offices as "positions (*etheto*)"
of God: "Apostles, prophets, teachers, workers or miracles, healers, helpers, administrators, speakers in various
kinds of tongues." This shows that charisms must not be
played out against offices, and vice versa. Everything is
God's gift and decision, and everything must serve the
unity and the peace and the edification, the exhortation
and consolation of the whole community. Although Ephesians 4,7 calls the charisms "grace (*charis*)," they must be
distinguished as capacities for the service of the community from the graces given to someone for his or her personal healing and sancitification. They must also be distinguished from offices in the proper sense, inasmuch as
offices derive their authority from the mission (perhaps

one could even say from participation in the mission of Christ). The importance of charisms, on the other hand, lies more in an objective service for the community, and their origin lies in the spirit. For this reason charismatics who participated in the leadership of the community (cf. 1 Thess 5,12ff.; Rom 12,6ff.: prophecy, service, teaching, exhortation, giving in liberality) could not claim the same authority as apostles and presbyters (cf. Matt 28,16; Mark 16,19; Luke 10,16; 24,9.33; Acts 1,26; 20,28; 1 Cor 4,14–17). However, the apostles or their representatives often officially appointed charismatics to the leadership of the community (cf. 2 Cor 8,23; Phil 2,25; Rom 16,1–16) so that their charism would become fruitful for their office. Rightly understood, offices are also charisms in the Church (cf. 2 Tim 1,6), which is not to say that all charisms are as such offices. For this reason one cannot call the offices "special charisms" (W. Beinert). "All members of the community should freely obey (2 Cor 2,9; 1 Thess 5,12f.) the official leaders of the Church. Despite the fullness of the Spirit granted precisely to them, these leaders have recourse to their office and its infallible character (Gal 1,8ff.; Acts 15,22ff.) in the proclamation of the Gospel (Acts 5,42) and in the selection of charismatics for official functions (Acts 13,1ff.)"[62] While calling, mission, and commissioning are decisive for offices, charisms are determined by God's free gift and the need of the community.

5. THE CHRISTIAN LAYPERSON AND THE CHURCH

Long before Vatican II, Y. Congar published his great systematic *Outline of a Theology of the Laity* (1952), which provided the foundation for the new view of the laity in the Vatican II understanding of the Church. It provided a new foundation for grasping the specific nature and the specific place of the laity as a state and form of life in the Church. It also provided a foundation for understanding the deep cooperation of hierarchy and laity to the glory of God and the salvation of humanity, in the name of the world's own value, and for the sake of the building of God's kingdom in this sinful world.

Congar shows that the reality that has, at least since Clement (cf. 1 Clem 40,5; written 95–97), been called "laity (*laikos*)" as distinct from the hierarchical office, began in the second and third centuries (Cyprian, Tertullian, Clement of Alexandria, Origen) to constitute a particular state or form of life in the church distinct from the clerical or religious state of life. However, what we today call the "laity" arose only in the High Middle Ages, especially through the theological shift brought about by Thomas Aquinas (d. 1274). The reason for this shift was that, due to the Aristotelian manner of thinking, the things of the "world" were for the first time seen and accepted in their own value and being, while early Christianity up to the Middle Ages had seen them almost exclusively in terms of God, due to a strong Neoplatonic influence on its world view. It is only in this new positive understanding of the world that the modern Christian concept of the laity has been developed.

Within the order of states of life in the Church the specific task of the laity lies in the Christian care for the things of this world. The Consitution on the Church has this to say about it: "The term laity is here understood to mean all the faithful except those in holy orders and those who belong to a religious state approved by the Church, that is, the faithful who by baptism are incorporated into Christ, are placed in the people of God and in their own way share the priestly, prophetic, and kingly office of Christ, and to the best of their ability carry on the mission of the whole Christian people in the Church and in the world. Their secular character is proper and peculiar to the laity" (LG 31). The Council also speaks about the collaboration of the three states of life, the priesthood, the religious state, and the laity:

Although those in holy orders may sometimes be engaged in secular activities, or even practice a secular profession, yet by reason of their particular vocation, they are principally and expressly ordained to the sacred ministry. At the same time, religious give outstanding and striking testimony that the world cannot be transfigured and offered to God without the spirit of the beatitudes. But by reason of their special vocation it belongs to the laity to seek the kingdom of God by engaging in temporal affairs and by ordering them according to God's will. They live in the world, that is, they are engaged in each and every work and business of the earth and in the ordinary circumstances of social and family life which, as it were, constitute their very existence. There they are called by God so that, being led by the spirit to the Gospel, they may contribute to the sanctification of the world, as from within like leaven, by fulfilling their own particular duties. Thus, especially by the witness of their life, resplendent in faith, hope and charity they must manifest Christ to others. It pertains to them in a special way to illuminate and order all temporal things with which they are so closely associated that these may be effected and grow according to Christ and may be to the glory of the Creator and Redeemer. (LG 31)

These teachings are extensively unfolded in the Decree on the Apostolate of the Laity. However, their newness and importance can be understood only when one sees them against the background of the Catholic Action[63] which had been understood since 1925 (Pius XI) as the organization of those who have been called to "a collaboration and participation of the laity in the hierarchical apostolate of the Church." In this view, the laity is understood in terms of the hierarchical apostolate. In Vatican II the laity is understood more correctly in terms of the sacramental nature of the Church as a whole. The apostolate of the laity is no longer seen as a participation in the apostolate of the hierarchy (viewed in juridical terms), but rather as a participation in the apostolate that belongs to the very essence of the Church as a whole and to every member according to its special graces (Eph 4,7) in virtue of its membership in the Church. For this reason the Council, following Y. Congar, discussed the participation of all the laity in the offices of Jesus Christ: teacher, priest, and pastor.[64]

The inner distinction of the mission of the laity "from those who, by reason of their office, represent the person of Christ" (LG 37) in no way compromises the laity's unique mission to be witnesses for the faith in the family and in their professions, in those places of the world difficult for a priest to reach (LG 35). It also does not compromise the status of the world as God's creation, as well as its value and ordination to God's praise (LG 36). In the spirit of the Pauline (Stoic) model of the body (1 Cor 12,12–31; Rom 12,4f.) the Council speaks about a mutual fraternal cooperation (LG 32) in the services the hierarchy, religious, and laity provide for each other and for the whole Church.

One could raise the question whether this teaching allows one to speak of a separate "world office" of the laity. The Council texts do not use this term. However, its use could lead to an increased awareness of the world as God's creation. For, even in theology, today's world has become a "secular world" to an extent no longer in harmony with the biblical message. We human beings grasp and understand realities of religion and of faith only inasmuch as we gain an existential relation to them in realizing their values. In this way the awareness of a specific "world office" of the laity could contribute to an increased awareness and realization of Christian responsibility for creation, even in this secular world.[65]

XI

The Hierarchical Offices of the Apostolic Church

Our point of departure must be, as above, the insight and demand that all manifoldness of appearances and forms of life, of effects of grace and factors of power in the Church, be reduced to a unity. They must be led back to unity in Jesus Christ, the head of the body who is the first priest and himself the sacrifice in the eucharistic and sacramental life of the Church. For this reason it is very important not to see the offices in the Church as a mere juxtaposition of functions, functions which developed, early perhaps, but still one after another.

We must first speak about the one office of Christ in the Church because the various functional offices in the Church live and operate by participation in, and for the sake of, Christ's office.

Christ's office, which unfolds itself in the threefold form of teacher, priest, and pastor, has found its unified, always living and effective expression in a single functional office, in the office of the twelve apostles and their successors. For a long period of time (at least from the Middle Ages to Vatican II) this truth has not sufficiently been seen.

The other offices must be understood in the light of this central apostolic office. In particular, the office of Peter or the papacy constituted itself as a visible form of the unity of the college of the Twelve, with different forms of understanding in the history of the Church.

The office of the presbyter or priest is, from a pastoral

point of view, intimately connected to the office of apostle or bishop. From the point of view of ecclesial order, it is a subordinate office.

The office of the deacon had already appeared in apostolic times. Even more than the office of the presbyter it was subject to transformations in the course of the Church's history.

The differentiation of the one apostolic office can be understood as follows: In an upward direction it found a real expression of its unity in the office of Peter or the papacy. In a downward direction, in serving the life of the Church, it created a number of differentiations in the presbyterate and the diaconate. Let us take a brief look at these offices, one by one.

The Office of Christ and Its Threefold Form

1. In terms of natural descent, Christ did not belong to a priestly family of the Old Testament, such as Aaron or Levi. From an Old Testament perspective he must be called a "layman." Thus the letter to the Hebrews says, "For it is evident that our Lord was descended from Judah, and in connection with that tribe Moses said nothing about priests. This becomes even more evident when another priest arises in the likeness of Melchizedech, who has become priest, not according to a legal requirement concerning bodily descent but by the power of an indestructible life" (Heb 7,14–16). All the greater does Christ's priesthood appear to the author of Hebrews. It is an eternal priesthood (Heb 7,21–24; cf. Psalm 110,4) and absolutely unique because of its perfection. "For it was fitting that we should have such a high priest, holy, blameless, unstained, separated from sinners, exalted above the heavens. He has no need, like those high priests, to offer sacrifices daily, first for his own sins and then for those of the people; he

did this once for all when he offered up himself. Indeed, the law appoints men in their weakness as high priests, but the word of the oath, which came later than the law, appoints a Son who has been made perfect for ever" (Heb 7,26–28). In the following chapters (Heb 8–10) the letter to the Hebrews deals extensively with the uniqueness of the high priest Jesus Christ and with the uniqueness of his sacrifice in the New Covenant established by him.

2. This one priesthood of Jesus Christ gathers into itself all the great tasks that the Old Testament distributed to various offices: the office of the priest as well as those of the prophet and of the king. In the theocratic system of the Old Covenant, these offices belonged more to the sphere of the world. In the New Covenant they are spiritualized and interiorized by Christ, the Son of God made man, and they receive a new, sacramental form.

a) Since Joseph, Jesus' father by adoption, was of David's family (cf. Luke 1,27), Jesus was counted as a descendant of David. A Messiah, an anointed one, a definitive ruler had been promised to Israel and this Messiah was to be a "son of David" (2 Sam 7,12–16; Matt 9,27; 12,23; 21,9) or even "David brought back to life" (Jer 30,9; Ezek 34,23–31; 37,24–28). Like David he was to be shepherd and king over Israel, and like David he was to give a new organization to the people (David built up the capital, Jerusalem, and prepared the construction of the temple). The decisive event was that Christ established an interior kingdom of God, as the parables of the kingdom show (cf. above II.3.d.); that he replaces the temple cult with a new cult, a cult centered around his own sacrifice of himself; that he was to construct a new hierarchy on the foundation of the apostles; and, above all, that he himself was to stand in the history of the Church as the recipient of this new cult of God's people and as its mediator before God. In accordance with the inner nature of his kingdom, his kingship is an interior kingship: "My kingship is not of this world" (John 18,36).

b) Christ is also the new Moses. This is clear in the

antitheses of the Sermon on the Mount, "You have heard that it was said (by Moses) to the men of old . . . But I say to you . . ." (Matt 5,21–48). Moses had been promised, "I will raise up for them a prophet like you from among their brethren; and I will put my words in his mouth, and he shall speak to them all that I command him" (Deut 18,18). The first disciples thought that in Christ they had found the prophet "of whom Moses wrote" (John 1,45). Christ called himself the only "teacher" (Matt 23,11; John 14,16) and teaching was the main activity of this rabbi in the years of his public life. To his apostles he left the command to teach as a testament, "Go therefore and make disciples of all nations . . . teaching them to observe all that I have commanded you" (Matt 28,19–20). The apostles carried out this command, as we see from the testimony and activity of Paul (cf. Gal 1,6–9.12; 1 Cor 1,17; 9,16: "Woe to me if I do not preach the gospel!"; Eph 4,11–14; 1 Tim 4,13.16; 2 Tim 2,8f.; 4,5) and also of Peter (cf. Acts 2,14–40; 3,12–26; 4,19f. etc.). The interiorizing of this office in the New Testament is visible above all in the identity between "the truth" and the person of Christ (cf. John 14,6; 8,32).

c) Christ's highest and most mysterious office is his priesthood. In this office the fulfillment has grown especially far beyond the Old Testament type. Prayer, holy rites, and sacrifices belonged to the Old Testament priesthood in the mediation between God and humanity. This is true in a special way also of Christ. Since his youth he had probably taken part in the liturgy of the temple and the synagogue. He sang the Psalms with his disciples. Beyond this, he taught them to pray in a new way to God, his Father and their Father (John 20,17). The Gospels tell that he prayed before all great events of his life: during his baptism (Luke 3,21), before choosing the apostles (Luke 6,12), after the multiplication of loaves and the promise of the Eucharist (Mark 6,46), before the promise of primacy (Luke 9,18; Matt 16,17), during the transfiguration (Luke 9,29), after the return of his disciples in his great jubilation

(Luke 10,21; Matt 11,25), at the raising of Lazarus (John 11,41), in his high priestly prayer (John 17), and finally in the garden of Gethsemane (Matt 26,39) and when dying on the cross (Luke 23,46). Often the disciples find him praying alone (Mark 1,35; Luke 5,16) or on the mountain (Matt 6,46; Luke 6,12; 9,29); it is told that he spent a whole night in prayer (Luke 6,12). He prays for the glorification of the Father and his own glorification (John 12,28; 17,1–5), for his apostles (John 17,6–19), for Peter (Luke 22,31), for all believers (John 17,20–26), and for his enemies (Luke 22,31). The early Church was convinced that also the glorified Christ prays for us in heaven (John 14,13; Rom 8,34; Heb 7,25; 1 John 2,1).

Also the rites he teaches his disciples point far beyond the rites of the Old Testament. He commanded his apostles to baptize (Matt 28,19), in a different way than the baptism of John the Baptist (Mark 1,8). He commanded them to forgive sins as no human being had ever done (John 20,21). He commanded them, finally and above all, to celebrate in a completely new way the Passover meal, Israel's holiest rite (Luke 22,20; 1 Cor 11,24–25).

The greatest event, however, is his sacrifice on the cross which fulfills the sacrifices of the Old Testament and thus abrogates them. As the sacrificial priest he offered himself as a sacrifice on the cross (Heb 9,14.28; 1 Peter 1,18f.; Isa 53,4–12). This is why the author of Hebrews extensively discusses, for the first time, the priesthood of Christ (cf. Heb 8,6; 9,15: Christ, the founder and mediator of the New Covenant) and his sacrifice as a unique and absolutely definitive sacrifice (Heb 9,15–28) which is completely effective (Heb 10,1–18). The new form of his priesthood is to be "a priest forever according to the order of Melchizedech" (Psalm 109,4; Heb 5,6; 7,17). And so "he holds his priesthood permanently, because he continues forever" (Heb 7,24).

Now, the decisive point is this: Christ received these offices from his Father in his mission. And they do not stop with his death, but are passed on to his disciples (John

20,21). This point is already stressed in the letter of Clement (written between 95 and 97).

Jesus the Christ was sent from God. The Christ therefore is from God and the apostles from the Christ. In both ways, then, they were in accordance with the appointed order of God's will. Having therefore received their commands, and being fully assured by the resurrection of our Lord Jesus Christ, and with faith confirmed by the word of God, they went forth in the assurance of the Holy Spirit preaching the good news that the Kingdom of God is coming. They preached from district to district, and from city to city, and they appointed their first converts, testing them by the Spirit, to be bishops and deacons of the future believers. And this was no new method, for many years before had bishops and deacons been written of; for the scripture says thus in one place "I will establish their bishops in righteousness, and their deacons in faith." (Num 12.7; *1 Clem* 42,2–5; Loeb, 79–81)

We will discuss below the above-mentioned questions about succession. Let us take a look now at the most important offices.

The Apostolic Office as the Central Office of the New Covenant, and the Bishops as the Successors of the Apostles

To approach a correct understanding of the apostolic office we will first speak about Christ's disciples, among whom the twelve apostles form a special group. The office of these Twelve continues to live in the bishops. This fact must be made intelligible by a discussion of apostolic succession.

I. THE DISCIPLES OF CHRIST

From the very beginning Jesus had disciples (*mathētai*) as did the old prophets before him (cf. 1 Sam 19,20; Elias and his school) and above all John the Baptist (Matt 9,14; 11,2) as well as the Pharisees (Matt 22,16; Mark 2,18). Of course, the relation between Jesus and his disciples differed from that between the Pharisees and their students. Christ himself chose his disciples (John 15,16), not vice versa. What determined and maintained the group of disciples was not Jesus' teaching but his person. Luke once mentions seventy (or rather seventy–two) such disciples (Luke 10,1–24), a number that probably recalls the seventy elders (*zekenim, presbyteroi*) of Moses (Num 11,16.24). Perhaps it also contains an allusion to the institution of the presbyterate in the early Church. The early Church called Christians "the disciples of Christ (cf. Acts 6,1.7, etc). In Ignatius of Antioch, finally, the title is reserved for those who proved themselves as followers and students of Christ in martyrdom, in accord with Jesus' command, "If anyone would come after me, let him deny himself and take up his cross daily and follow me" (Luke 9,23; Ign. Rom. 4,2; 5,3). The apostles were probably a special group among the disciples. According to the Gospels they were called as the first disciples, partly while they were still disciples of John (cf. John 1,35–51) partly as fishermen on the Sea of Galilee (Mark 1,16–20; par.).

2. THE TWELVE APOSTLES

The three synoptics tell that Jesus selected a group of twelve men from among the disciples. They are mentioned by name and were of the greatest importance probably already during Jesus' public life and certainly in the early Church. Luke gives the following account: "In these days he went out to the mountain to pray; and all night he continued in prayer to God. And when it was day, he called his disciples [*mathētai*], and chose from them twelve [*dōdeka*], whom he named apostles [*apostoloi*]; Simon, whom he named Peter, and Andrew his brother, and James and John, and Philip, and Bartholomew, and Matthew, and

Thomas, and James the son of Alphaeus, and Simon who was called the Zealot, and Judas the Son of James, and Judas Iscariot, who became a traitor" (Luke 6,12–16). Mark, who does not yet call the twelve "apostles," explains their task in the following words, "And he appointed [*epoiēsen*] twelve, to be with him, and to be sent out [*apostellē*] to preach and have authority to cast out demons" (Mark 3,14–15).

This text, which is the oldest together with 1 Corinthians 15,8–11, indicates that "apostle" means "the one sent by God as his messenger." In Israel's monarchy the term was used for the prophet (1 Kgs 14,6, Septuagint). In the post-exilic period it was used for teachers of the law who were sent by the king (2 Chron 17,7–9). In the early Church the title was first used in general for missionaries in the community (Rom 16,7; 1 Cor 12,28; Gal 1,1). Beginning at least with Luke (cf. Luke 6,12) it was limited to the Twelve and the general use disappeared. Matthew says, "And he called to him his twelve disciples and gave them authority over unclean spirits, to cast them out, and to heal every disease and every infirmity" (Matt 10,1).

According to Matthew 10,5–15 (cf. Luke 9,1–6) these Twelve received their own preliminary mission. "These Twelve Jesus sent out, charging them, 'Go nowhere among the Gentiles, and enter no town of the Samaritans, but go rather to the lost sheep of the house of Israel. And preach as you go, saying, The kingdom of heaven is at hand. Heal the sick, raise the dead, cleanse lepers, cast out demons. You received without paying, give without pay'" (Matt 10,5–8). According to Matthew 28,18–20 (cf. Mark 16,14–18) the risen Jesus before his ascension (cf. Luke 24,47–49) gave to the Eleven (*hendeka*) their definitive mission into the world. "All authority [*exousia*] in heaven and on earth has been given to me. Go therefore and make disciples [*mathēteusate*] of all nations, baptizing them in the name of the Father and of the Son and of the Holy Spirit, teaching [*didaskontes*] them to observe all that I have commanded

you; and lo, I am with you always, to the close of the age."
These texts describe the communication of a mission.
They show that the title "apostle," which had not been
used in such a way in Israel, developed from a term expressing a certain function into the title for an office.

The Twelve are, simply speaking, "those sent by
Christ." Thus he says to them, "He who receives you receives me, and he who receives me receives him who sent
me" (Matt 10,40) and "He who hears you hears me, and he
who rejects you rejects me, and he who rejects me rejects
him who sent me" (Luke 10,16) and "As the Father has
sent me, even so I send you" (John 20,21). The term "the
Twelve" itself underwent a certain development (cf. 1 Cor
15,5 as opposed to Matt 19,28). The names of the twelve
apostles, who were personally chosen and appointed by
Christ, probably preceded the use of this term (Mark 3,13–
19).[66] The role of the twelve sons of Israel as progenitors of
the Old Testament people of God resembles the role of
these Twelve for the new people of God, the Church. It is
upon them that the Church is built (cf. Matt 16,18; Eph
2,20; Rev 21,14). This is why Jesus especially prays for
them in his high-priestly prayer (John 17,6–19) after having taught them in a unique way in the years of his public
life. To them "it has been given to know the secrets of the
kingdom of heaven" (Matt 13,11). Jesus cleared up their
misunderstandings (about true purity: Matt 15,12ff.; about
the indissolubility of marriage: Matt 19,10ff.). With much
patience he answered their questions (Matt 18,21). He prepared them for his passion by repeatedly predicting it
(Matt 16,21ff.; 17,22; 20,17ff.). And he taught them about
the fall of Jerusalem and the end of the world (Matt 24–25).

In addition to his teaching Jesus transmitted authority
to his disciples and to the apostles as shown already by the
great chapter on instruction (Matt 18). This transmission
of authority is expressed with particular clarity in the missionary command with the instruction for baptism (Matt
28,19), in the instruction for the new paschal celebration

(Luke 22,19), and in the preparation of the Twelve for the forgiveness of sins (John 20,21; 2 Cor 5,19f.). In this way the apostle stands above the Church, above its choice (Gal 1,1: "apostle, not from man or through men, but through Jesus Christ and God the Father"; cf. *1 Clem* 42 and 44) and above its judgment (1 Cor 4,3f.). He must not proclaim his own teaching, but pass on the message he received (Mark 3,14; 2 Cor 2,17: "For we are not, like so many, peddlers of God's word; but as men of sincerity, as commissioned by God, in the sight of God we speak in Christ"). This is why the apostle's word must be taken as God's word (2 Cor 5,20; 1 Thess 2,13: "And we also thank God constantly for this, that when you received the word of God which you heard from us, you accepted it not as the word of men but as what it really is, the word of God, which is at work in you believers").

The apostles founded and directed new communities (Acts 8,14f., 15,2; Rom 15,15; 2 Cor 10,13–16; 2 Thess 3,4; etc.), they enforced ecclesial discipline (1 Cor 5,3–5; 1 Tim 1,20; Acts 5: Ananias and Sapphira), and they appointed co-workers and successors by the imposition of hands (Acts 6,6; 1 Tim 4,14; 5,22; 2 Tim 1,6). Yet they are not lords but servants of their community (Mark 10, 44–45; Matt 24,45–51; Rom 12,7.13; 2 Cor 1,24; 4,5) and its shepherds like Christ (John 21,15–17; Acts 20, 28; 1 Peter 5,2–5). The foundation of their office is the love of Christ (John 21,15ff.). Their activity manifests a teaching office, a pastoral office, and a priestly office. They are bearers of the deposit of faith (1 Tim 6,20), bearers of the tradition (1 Cor 11,23; 15,3) and of succession to their office in the apostolic Church in appointing their successors (Acts 1,17.22–26).

3. APOSTOLIC SUCCESSION

The articles published in *Concilium* 4 (1968) show that the constitution of ecclesial office through the succession of the bearers of this office, which appeared to be clear and certain in Vatican I, has become questionable today in several respects. Küng's eight theses (ibid., pp. 248–251) demand, quite justifiably, that succession and tradition be seen as a unity. In addition, however, they demand that the concept of succession be severed from that of the office in particular and joined to the whole apostolic Church. The historical succession of bearers of the apostolic office, the bishops, and of the Petrine office, the popes, is not the only mode of succession. For the sake of a "charismatic structure of ecclesial office" one must see the possibility of another mode of succession (e.g., in Communist countries) without historical succession through the transmission of offices in the rite of the imposition of hands. There can be a presbyteral in addition to an apostolic succession (in addition to Küng, Finkenzeller and W. Kasper hold this view for ecumenical reasons).

a) The Legitimating Basis of Succession

What is the origin of the doctrine that ecclesial office depends on succession? What are the inner reasons for this doctrine? In the Old Testament, succession in the central priestly office was given simply by membership in the tribe of Levi or the family of Aaron and through a ritual assignment to the exercise of priestly functions. Christ did not belong to a priestly family and had no descendants. According to the unanimous testimony of Scripture, he based his activity for the salvation of humanity, and thus his priesthood, on the mission and command of the Father. He entrusted this office to those whom he had chosen as his "servants and stewards of the mysteries of God" (1 Cor 4,1). And he did so by passing on to them his own mission. "As the Father has sent me, even so I send you" (John 20,21). About himself he said that he had been sent to preach the message of the reign of God (cf. Luke 4,43). In the same way, after the resurrection, he sent his apostles into the world to preach this gospel of the reign of God so that "repentance and forgiveness of sins should be preached in his name to all nations" (Luke 24,47) and "to the whole creation" (Mark 16,15). He characterized this sending as an expression and effect of the authority in heaven and on earth given to him by his Father. "All authority in heaven and on earth has been given to me. Go therefore and make disciples of all nations, baptizing them in the name of the Father and of the Son and of the Holy Spirit, teaching them to observe all that I have commanded you; and lo, I am with you always, to the close of the age" (Matt 28,18–20). This great missionary command, which (according to Matthew) was Christ's testament to the Eleven (Twelve), is the root of the apostolic office in the Church and of all succession in this office which bears the Church in the authority of Christ until the end of time.

b) The Principal Aspects of Succession

The missionary command, whose formulation in Matthew 28,18 may be a theological unfolding of Christ's words in the understanding of Matthew and the early Church, brings out four aspects. These aspects have been decisive for succession and thus for ecclesial office. The first aspect is personal mission, of which we spoke above in the context of the apostolic office. The first task contained in this mission is to make disciples of "all peoples," of all human beings of all times and places. The full form of being a Christian is and remains being a disciple, following Christ. However, this task is not realized in a simple interplay of word and response; it must be realized by God.

For this reason there is a second aspect, that of sacramental action. For no one can become a Christian in the full sense without baptism in the name, the death, and the resurrection of Jesus Christ, who represents the triune God. Personal discipleship is realized only through the rite of baptism as instituted by Christ. This rite signifies "dying with Christ" and in this signification it communicates "life with Christ" in the grace-giving activity of the triune God (cf. Rom 6,8; Col 3,3f.). Baptism can be taken as a sign for the encompassing sacramental activity of the apostle.

The third aspect is likewise sacramental. Matthew presents it in a rather Jewish-Christian way as "teaching them to observe all that I have commanded you" (Matt 28,20). Mark calls the content of the proclamation "the gospel," "Go into all the world and preach the gospel to the whole creation" (Mark 16,15). Luke characterizes the content of the gospel when he says, "repentance and forgiveness of sins should be preached in his name to all nations" (Luke 24,47) because in repentance and forgiveness the reign of God realizes itself in this world, as Jesus said in his first proclamation (Mark 1,15) and Peter in his pentecostal sermon, the introductory sermon on the Church's birthday (Acts 2,38).

This third aspect contains the element of tradition, an element that had been a matter of course already in the proclamation of the Old Testament message. The truth of God's gift of salvation to humanity is ever new and, corresponding to new circumstances, it is "passed on in the living word" (Eusebius, *HE* III,39; Papias: "by the living and abiding voice"). And yet, having once been given in Christ, it must always remain identical with itself. For this reason Paul explicitly based the fundamental truths of Christian life, Christ's resurrection (1 Cor 15,1–3) and the commission for the eucharistic celebration (1 Cor 11,23), on this principle of tradition. "For I received from the Lord what I also delivered to you" (1 Cor 11,23). The word of proclamation is tied to the witness, and the witness is in turn tied to the word of proclamation, although these two bonds do not have the same inner form.

The fourth aspect of office which is at work in succession is expressed as follows in the missionary command,

"And lo [be certain] I am with you always, to the close of the age" (Matt 28,20). This is probably not a word of consolation for the apostles. The Jewish eschatological world view had already been overcome when Matthew wrote down these words. What stands behind them is probably already the image of the Church found in Ephesians and Colossians, where the Church cannot exist without Christ, the body without its transfigured head. A later period is quite justified to read in this sentence that Christ himself is at work when someone acts as an apostle of Christ, when he acts sacramentally in the Church as a "servant of Christ and steward of the mysteries of God" (1 Cor 4,1).

Recent studies (W. Selb; J. Fellermayr) attempt to derive this (Jewish) understanding of succession in the Church from Roman views on inheritance. I think it more correct, however, to suppose merely that the same structural elements are at work both in the ecclesial understanding of succession and in the Roman understanding of inheritance. These structural elements lie in the complicated interplay between nonpersonal aspects (the inheritance or the authority of the office) and personal aspects (rights of possession). Further research will have to clarify this issue. At any rate, the differences between these two historically significant events, succession in ecclesial office and inheritance of certain goods, are at least as great as their analogous external similarities in general structure.

The mission of the Son (succession) and the mission of the Spirit (tradition) belong together in the apostles and their successors. Historically the apostles are clearly distinct from their successors. One aspect of this distinction is that only the apostles are bearers of revelation, while their successors are proclaimers of the revealed truth. In addition, only the apostles are sent "into the whole world" (Mark 16,15); their successors were soon appointed only for a certain area (diocese: Gregory IX., c 34,35 X1,3). Still, it would certainly be too little to see the office of the successors only as an "analogy to the apostolic office."[67]

c) *The Historical Development of the Idea of Succession*

The Church was not always as conscious of the ideas we just developed out of the great missionary command. They had to develop slowly and come to consciousness in the Church's thinking and acting. It can be shown, however, that the historical development of the idea of succession was not a deviation, even when it was partly triggered and directed by external secular stimuli. Above all, the hierarchical order in succession, according to which only bishops are the true successors of the apostles (which has been generally taught since the second century), has good historical grounds.

In recounting the apostolic council (Acts 15) Luke still mentions "apostles and elders [presbyters]" five times next to each other. The account of Paul's farewell at Miletus mentions that Paul called "the elders [presbyters] of the church" (Acts 20,17) and that he addressed them as *"episkopoi* (bishops, overseers)" (Acts 20,28). In these texts "presbyter" and "apostle" still seem to refer to the same office. The Jewish-Christian communities of the early period probably followed Jewish tradition and had a "college of presbyters" at the head of the community, while in the gentile Christian communities, especially those of Paul, "bishops and deacons" (Phil 1,1) are mentioned as the leadership. The Pastoral Epistles already speak about a single bishop at the head of the community (cf. 1 Tim 3,2; Tit 1,7).

Scripture already makes clear that succession in an office or appointment to an office was done with the old Jewish rite of the imposition of hands (deacons: Acts 6,6; Barnabas and Paul: Acts 13,3; esp. in the Pastoral Epistles: 1 Tim 4,14; 5,22; 2 Tim 1,6; Titus 1,5; cf. Num 27,18ff.; Deut 34,9; *Did.* 15,1f; KKD VII §4–5).

The first letter of Clement (written in 95 to 97) lays down a clear sequence: "Christ was sent from God, and the apostles from Christ. In both ways, then, they are in accordance with the appointed order of God's will" (*1 Clem.* 42,2). Clement adds, "They appointed their first converts, testing them by the Spirit, to be bishops and deacons of the future believers" (*1 Clem.* 42,4). He explicitly stresses that this was "nothing new" (*1 Clem.* 42,5). Clement introduces this teaching as a divine order, but he goes on to argue for it from Roman administrative prudence and from the necessity of a human order. "Our apostles also know through our Lord Jesus Christ that there would be strife for the title of bishop. For this cause, therefore, . . . they appointed those who have been already mentioned, and afterwards added the codicil that if they should fall asleep, other approved men should succeed to their ministry" (*1 Clem.* 44,1–2).

According to the letters of Ignatius of Antioch the communities of Asia Minor at the end of the first century were headed by single bishops, aided by a college of presbyters and deacons. Thus he writes, "Be zealous to do all things in harmony with God, with the bishop presiding in the place of God and the presbyters in the place of the council of the Apostles, and the deacons . . . entrusted with the service of Jesus Christ" (*Ign. Magn.* 6,1; cf. *Phld.* 4; *Smyrn.* 8). The inner connection between tradition of teaching (*paradosis*) and succession in office (*diadochē*) are stressed by Papias (ca. 130) and Hegesippus (ca. 180; Eusebius, *H.E.* 4,22).

Irenaeus of Lyons (140–202) recalls for us this catholic understanding of succession in opposition to heretical Gnosis. Against Gnostic claims, he appeals to the "tradition which originates from the apostles, and which is preserved by the succession of presbyters in the Church" (*Adv. Haer.* III,2,2). "It is within the power of all, therefore, in every Church, who may wish to see the truth, to contemplate clearly the tradition of the apostles manifested throughout the whole world; and we are in a position to reckon up those who were by the apostles instituted bishops in the Churches, and (to demonstrate) the succession of these men to our own times" (*Adv. Haer.* III,3,1). As an example for this apostolic succession, which is for him a guarantee for the true tradition of the apostolic message, he gives the list of Roman bishops. During his own time Eleutherius sat as the twelfth successor on the "chair (*cathedra*)" of Peter (*Adv. Haer.* III,3,3; cf. III,24; V,2; DS 3057: Vatican I).

Similarly Tertullian (d. ca. 220) writes, "Let them [the heretics] point out the origins of their churches, unfold the sequence [*ordinem*] of their bishops which comes down by succession [*per successionem decurrentem*] in such a way that the first bishop has as his origin and predecessor [*auctorem et antecessorem*] one among the apostles or one among apostolic men who remained with the apostles. For, this is the manner in which the apostolic churches [*ecclesiae apostolicae*] prove their origin" (*De praescript.* 32; cf. *Adv. Marc.* IV,5,2 where he speaks first of "the authority of the apostolic Churches [*auctoritas ecclesiarum apostolicarum*]."

In Cyprian (d. 258) this succession in the apostolic office is acknowledged and confirmed through the recognition of neighboring bishops. This recognition expresses the collegiality of the true bishops; it shows the unity of these true bishops against the various heresies of the time for the sake of securing the truth of apostolic teaching (cf. *Ep.* 45,3 to Pope Cornelius; *Ep.* 68,3f. to bishop Stephen of Arles). The bishops are portrayed as "vicars and successors of the apostles" (*Ep.* 66,4). Cyprian explicitly teaches that "the power to forgive sins has been given to the apostles and to the Churches which they established as commissioned by Christ [cf. James 5,16], as well as to the bishops who succeed them in virtue of being appointed as their vicars" (*Ep.* 75,16 to Firmilian).

Hippolytus (ca. 222) writes in the introduction to this refutation of heresies, "The Spirit himself convicts the heretics of their error, the Spirit who has been given to the apostles; since we as their successors [*diadochoi*] share in the same grace, high-priestly dignity [*archtherateia*] and doctrine [*didaskalia*] and belong to the guardians [*phrouroi*] of the Church, we keep our eyes open and do not keep silent [*oude siōpōmen*] about the true teaching" (Wendland III, p.3,1.3–6). About the heretics, on the other hand, he says, "They have embarked on inventing [*epicheirēmata*] because they have accepted nothing from the holy Scriptures and have not kept the succession of a saint [*tinos hagiou diadochēn*]" (ibid. 3,16–18). Chrysotom (d. 407) speaks at a later date about the "successors of Peter," by which he means the bishops (*De sac.* II,1).

The following general conclusions can be drawn from this survey. Since the beginning of the third century the hierarchically ordered clergy has been seen as constitutive for the Church. This perspective was so strong that the focus of attention shifted away from the fact that ecclesial office derived from and developed from the apostolic office. This shift is clear already in the various prayers for ordination extant in Hippolytus' *traditio apostolica* (ca. 220), with different versions for the ordinations of bishops, presbyters, and deacons. The bishop was ordained by all the bishops who were present. In this way he was received into their college. The presbyter, as a priest of second order, was ordained only by a single bishop and stood under his authority. In his list of the Roman clergy, Pope Cornelius (251–253) already mentions eight levels of ordination (the subdeacon and five lower orders in addition to those mentioned in Hippolytus). Except for brief interruptions in Rome, these were preserved in the Western Church up to Vatican II (cf. KKD VII,V,2).

The clear distinction between the bishop as a successor of the apostles and the presbyter as a secondary office, a distinction that appears as tradition already in the ordination prayers in Hippolytus, forbids the positing of a presbyterial succession in addition to an apostolic succession of bishops. This point will be taken up again in the discussion of the presbytery. In this period (second century) only the bishop was understood as a legitimate successor of the apostles. This doctrine has become quite clear again since Vatican II. Although it had not been doubted throughout the centuries, it had been somewhat obscured in the medieval understanding of holy orders. Holy orders were seen primarily in the ordination of priests and not in episcopal ordination, because the office was understood primarily in terms of its powers and tasks, symbolized in the instruments handed to the candidate, not in terms of succession and the cathedra. The lack of precision in the terms *episkopos* and *presbyteros* up to the early second century cannot be used as an argument against the more than 1900 years of tradition about apostolic succession in the bishops.

d) Magisterial Teaching and the Systematic Place of Succession in Office

Let us first point to the principal ecclesiastical declarations on this subject. Up to Vatican I, apostolic succession was mentioned in pronouncements of the Magisterium only when the issue was the presbyteral arrogation of episcopal rights: Synod of Sens (1140) against Abelard (DS 732); Council of Florence (1431) Decretum pro Armeniis: only bishops can dispense the sacrament of confirmation (DS 1318).

Luther was the first to teach that the apostles are unique historical figures who have no successors but only, at best, vicars. Leo X (DS 1476) and the Council of Trent (DS 1768) opposed this teaching. Trent also stressed the difference between bishops and priests in the power to ordain and confirm (DS 1777). Although it focused one-sidedly on papal power, Vatican I taught "the ordinary and immediate power of jurisdiction" of bishops in their dioceses (DS 3061), a point repeated by Leo XIII in 1896 (DS 3307). Pius XII went back to *1 Clement* when he stressed that the bishops are "by divine institution successors of the apostles" (DS 3804). It is remarkable that neither canon law (since the eleventh century) nor the fundamental theology and dogmatics of the nineteenth century (cf. Ehrlich and Scheeben, VI §334) dealt with the question of the apostolic succession of bishops. The Church's first systematic code of canon law, the Codex Iuris Canonici of 1917, merely says in Canon 329, "The bishops are the successors of the apostles and in virtue of divine institution they are placed at the head of greater areas of the Church, which they lead with ordinary authority under the authority of the Roman Pontiff."

Vatican II clearly emphasized the dignity of the bishops after a period of almost a thousand years in which this point had been obscured. It did so by declaring that the consecration of bishops is the true sacrament of orders in the Church. It also dealt extensively with the episcopal office (LG 20–24). Even in this text, however, one cannot find a special theological treatment of apostolic succession. The reason is that the doctrine of the apostolic succession of bishops has been such a matter of course in the consciousness and life of the whole Church since the third century that its theological discussion appeared unnecessary.

In the light of this historical survey, let us attempt to determine the systematic place of apostolic succession in ecclesiology. As suggested above, when we took the great missionary command as the point of departure, the general place of this doctrine is the understanding of the Church as a whole. It would be misleading to see apostolic succession only in the individual transfer of official powers from the one who ordains to the one who is ordained.

The specific place of this doctrine, however, must be seen in the connection between the apostolic office and the episcopacy alone. For it is here that we must look for the life setting (*cathedra*) in which the identity of word and sacrament and office is preserved and guaranteed in the Church through all times and places.

The normative character of the form "apostles-bishops" is indicated by three teachings that have been maintained since the second century: the important difference in grade between episcopate and presbyterate; the ordination of bishops by several or all bishops present, which signifies that the bishops form an episcopal college; only bishops possess the fullness of ordination and only the bishop ordains for his diocese as coworkers in the kingdom of God presbyters who are subject to his authority. The few exceptions in which individual abbots were granted the power to ordain cannot prove the contrary, as is proven elsewhere (KKD VII, p. 359). Only bishops, through the power to ordain, possess that spiritual generative power which keeps the apostolic office alive throughout all times and places. This life-giving function is the proper theological place of apostolic succession in the Church.

4. THE BISHOPS

a) Fundamentals

As we will show again in the discussion of the office of Peter and the popes, the apostolic office, already in the fundamental data of Scripture, really contains two offices: the office of the Twelve and the office of Peter. The inner unity of these offices lies in the commission to serve the whole Church. From the Church's perspective this commission remains always the same. From the perspective of the number of those who serve, however, it differs in its concrete realization according to the unicity of Peter and the multiplicity of apostles and bishops. The Vatican II Constitution on the Church expresses this teaching as follows: "The Roman Pontiff . . . has full, supreme, and universal power [*plenam, supremam et universalem potestatem*] over the whole Church. . . . Together with their head, the Supreme Pontiff, and never apart from him [bishops] also have supreme and full authority over the universal Church" [*subjectum quoque supremae ac plenae potestatis in universam ecclesiam*; notice the distinction between *universalis potestas* and *universa ecclesia*] (LG 22). The problems connected with this doctrine and the theological attempts to solve them will be discussed in the following section on the office of Peter and the pope. At this point, leaving aside these problems, let us present the basic truths about the Catholic episcopal office.

b) The Bishops as Successors of the Apostles Are Symbol and Guarantee for the Unity of the Churches in the Church

As indicated above, it has been a matter of course in the Church's teaching since the second century that bishops are the legitimate successors in the office of the apostles. The transition from the apostles, who were sent into the whole world, to the bishops, who were clearly appointed for a certain limited area (in geographical and personal terms) points to the problem of the relation between multiplicity and unity in the understanding of the Church and of ecclesial office. Let us get a clear grasp of this problem, because it is fundamental for all further reflection about offices in the Church. In general terms we have already addressed the question above (VI).

The Church is not a mere external society (*societas*) with certain goals and purposes. It is, rather, an inner community (*communitas*) of persons that has its root in a third common person, in Christ. For this reason the Church cannot be understood as the sum or addition of individual communities or associations of communities, of dioceses. The Church is always a unity in itself. In an individual parish, just as in a diocese and in the Church as a whole, it is always "the whole Church." This unity and wholeness is not to be understood merely in terms of the philosophical doctrine of universals, as if the Church were merely present in each parish or diocese in the way in which "human being" is present in each individual human being. The Church's unity is not a natural fact. It is, rather, a gift and task that stems from Christ. It is a gift and task for all who belong to him, who are members of his body, so that he might be their head. The Church's unity and wholeness is also misunderstood, however, if it is understood exclusively in terms of the image of the body in its organic dimensions alone. Human unity in the community or family of Jesus is only a sacramental sign and guarantee for inner unity and wholeness in Christ. The Church's nature is unique and cannot be explained by any natural analogy.

The Church, as Christ's work, is built upon the apostles (Eph 2,20). Since the second century the universal Church has, accordingly, been understood primarily in terms of its organization into episcopal Churches. Now, although each diocese is wholly and completely Church, no diocese is called universal Church. The universal Church exists, rather, in episcopal Churches and is formed out of episcopal churches which are united under the pope as head, just as the twelve apostles had their "spokesman" in Peter. This is why Christ said to this Peter (pope), "On this rock I will build my Church" (Matt 16,18), just as the apostle says that the Church is "built upon the foundation of the apostles and prophets, Christ Jesus himself being the cornerstone" (Eph 2,20). The bishop, then, is a sign and guarantee of the Church entrusted to him.

For this reason Ignatius of Antioch (d. 116) stresses again and again that everyone who wants to belong to the Church must have unity and communion with the bishop, "joined together in one subjection, subject to the bishop and to the presbytery" (Eph. 2,2). "Let us then be careful not to oppose the bishop, that we may be subject to God" (Eph. 5,3; cf. 20,2). In Magn. 3, obedience to the bishop is compared with obedience to Christ as the bishop of all (cf. 1 Pet 2,25). And thus Ignatius says, "Be zealous to do all things in harmony with God, with the bishop presiding in the place of God" (*Magn.* 6,1). "As then the Lord was united to the Father and did nothing without him . . . so do you nothing without the bishop and the presbyters" (*Magn.* 7,1; cf. *Trall.* 3,1; *Phld.* intr.; 7,2; *Smyrn.* 8,1; *Pol.* 6,1).

Cyprian (251) goes a step further when he stresses that the episcopal office is one office. "The episcopate [*episcopatus*] is only one, and the individual bishops share in it only in the preservation of the [one] whole [*episcopatus unus est, cuius a singulis in solidum pars tenetur*]" (*De cat. eccl. un.* 5). This is why since the second century the episcopal office has been seen as the guarantee of unity among the Churches against heresies and schisms. Tertullian called enmity against the bishop the "mother of all schisms" (*De bapt.* 17).

In his own way Denis the Areopagite (ca. 500) expresses the importance of the bishop in the Church when he writes, "The divine state of the hierarch (i.e., the bishop) is the first among the states that contemplate God. It is also the highest and the last, because in it the whole institution of our hierarchy is completed and concluded" (*Hier. eccl.* V,5).

The Vatican II Constitution on the Church says on this point: "The individual bishops are the visible source and foundation of unity in their own particular churches, which are constituted after the model of the universal Church; it is in these and formed out of them that the one and unique Catholic Church exists" (LG 23; cf. Cyprian, *Ep.* 55,24; 36,4).

c) The College of Bishops and Individual Bishops

The individual bishop is the sign and guarantee of the Church's unity for the Church of his territory (diocese) and the representative of the one universal Church. This fact is the basis of the idea that all bishops together form a college of bishops. The Constitution on the Church also uses the expressions "order (*ordo*)" or "body (*corpus*)" or "communion of bishops (*communio episcoporum*)" (LG 22). The unity of this college is to mirror the unity of the living Church.

The second session of Vatican II (October 11–16) already recognized the concept "college" as a key concept for understanding the episcopate and discussed it extensively.[68] This discussion clearly showed that this concept has its origin in the apostolic college of the Twelve, and its basis in the commission given by Jesus to these twelve (cf. Matt 18,18; 28,19; John 20,21; Acts 2,42f.; 4,33ff.; 6,1f.; 8,14; 15,1–29; Gal 1,17.19; 1 Cor 9,1–5; 15,7–9; Eph 2,20; 3,5; etc.). The discussion unfolded the great tradition for this teaching without overlooking that the East understood the idea of the college more personally in terms of the common task of all bishops in the one Church, while the West understood it more juridically as the unity of equal bearers of an office.[69]

The history of the Church shows how the demand for a collegial unity of all bishops in the universal Church was realized: In the second century it was realized especially in the name of the struggle for the one revealed truth against all heresies; in the third century it was realized through the numerous regional synods; and in the fourth century, after Constantine, through the ecumenical councils. Cyprian wrote, "We must securely maintain and defend this unity [of the Church], especially we bishops, who preside in the Church, in order also to prove the episcopal office as a single and undivided office. . . . The episcopal office is only one, and individual bishops share in it only in the preservation of the [one] whole" (*De cat. eccl. un.* 5). Further expressions of episcopal collegiality at that time were the *litterae commentatitiae* written for believers by bishops to other bishops. The rite of episcopal ordination clearly expresses that the newly ordained becomes bishop by being received into the "communion of bishops."

In the fourth century there arose the problem of the

inner differentiation of this collegial unity. The Church, which had grown and had been furnished since 312 with external power, was organized into metropolitan sees (corresponding to the state's administrative districts) and patriarchates (deriving from the old apostolic Churches). A further differentiation was brought about by the rise of the Roman pope as the bearer of the one Petrine office. Such differentiations are expressed in the "Pentarchy" of Justinian (527–565) by the use of different terms for the power of individual patriarchates: Antioch spoke of its *"exousia"*; Jerusalem of its *"akoloutheia timēs"*; Constantinople (after 381) of its *"presbeia tēs timēs,"* of its importance as the new Rome (can. 3); and Rome, finally, appealed more and more (especially after Leo the Great, 430) to the office of Peter as founded on Scripture (Matt 16,18), an office now held by the bishop of Rome as the occupant of the *cathedra* (chair) of Peter (cf. DS 811, Innocentius III). The original meaning of collegiality had been that each individual bishop integrated his personal faith commitment in the synod into the anonymity of the faith commitment of all. In the course of the development of power, however, collegiality became increasingly an external community in which everyone wanted to bring to bear his faith commitment as a conviction of conscience. The effect of this development can be felt in the great doctrinal disputes of the third to the sixth centuries, in the question of heresy, and in the power struggles after the Carolingean period in the questions raised by the East-West schism.[70]

The Western Church consciously addressed the problem of episcopal collegiality, at least after the turn of the millennium. A certain strain was caused at times by the question of the relation of individual bishops to the bishop of Rome, the pope of the universal Church. This strain became especially clear in the periods of the papal exile in Avignon (1305–1378) and of the Western schism (1378–1417), in which esteem for the papacy suffered greatly. The general development of Western individualism after the end of the Middle Ages contributed its part to this development. The integration of the papacy into episcopal collegiality still presented repeated difficulties in Vatican II. The *"Nota praevia explicitativa"* for Chapter Three of the Constitution on the Church (Nov. 16, 1964) and its interpretation makes these difficulties particularly clear.[71]

According to the teaching of Vatican II (LG 22), the collegiality of bishops is visible in ecumenical councils, which are convened and confirmed by the pope and in which he presides. Every collegial act of the bishops requires either the initiative or at least the later approbation of the pope.

Collegiate unity is also apparent in the mutual relations of each bishop to individual dioceses and with the universal Church . . . each bishop represents his own Church, whereas all, together with the pope, represent the whole Church in a bond of peace, love and unity . . . in so far as they are members of the episcopal college and legitimate successors of the apostles, by Christ's arrangement and decree, each is bound to have such care and solicitude for the whole Church. (LG 23)

In particular, they have the task of world mission. The manifoldness of liturgical and spiritual traditions only shows "the catholicity of the undivided Church" (LG 23). Episcopal conferences serve the realization of this common task of the episcopate in the whole Church.

Again, the collegiality of bishops is not a natural community of all bishops, given as an encompassing natural bond in the manner in which the family encompasses father, mother, and children. It is also not created by the free association of bishops. It is, rather, a supernatural community founded upon Christ, his mission, the commission he gave to the Twelve and, finally, upon the very person of Christ who is "the pastor and bishop of our souls" (1 Pet 2,25). Hence it remains for every bishop and for all times a grace and a task.

d) *Powers and Tasks of the Bishop*

Secular thinking and secular powers often prevented the correct supernatural understanding of episcopal powers. This becomes clear already in the institution of chorbishops (rural bishops as opposed to city bishops) which arose in the East in the fourth to the seventh centuries and in the West in the eighth and ninth centuries. These difficulties took their effect especially in the fourteenth to the sixteenth centuries. Due to the weakening of the papacy mentioned above, two parties formed themselves, that of an episcopal conciliar system and that of an integrally papal system. While the first practically denied the specific character of the Petrine and papal office, the other wanted to make the bishops mere vicars and delegates of the pope. Even in Thomas Aquinas the bishops are compared to the proconsuls and to royal officials (*Sent.* IV d20, q4, a3, ad3; II d44, q2). The reform councils of Constance (1414–1418), Basel, Ferrara, and Florence (1431–1445) wanted to strengthen episcopal power at the expense of papal power. The Pragmatic Sanction of Bourges (1438) accepted the decrees of Basel for France; the German princes accepted them for Germany at Frankfurt and Mainz (1438/39). The popes attempted to secure their rights through the Concordat of Frankfurt (1447) and the Concordat of Vienna (1448) and through the concordat of Leo X with Francis I of France (1516). The Council of Trent reestablished a certain equilibrium and stressed the bishops as legitimate successors of the apostles (DS 1768). Even the bishops appointed by the pope are legitimate and true bishops in this sense (DS 1778). This means that the bishops receive the power of ordination and jurisdiction immediately through episcopal ordination. Through this ordination they are received into the college of bishops and become true successors of the apostles. "Together with their head, the Supreme Pontiff, and never apart from him, they have supreme and full authority over the universal Church; but this power cannot be exercised without the agreement [*consentiente*] of the Roman Pontiff" (LG 22; CD 4).

Having spoken about the tasks of the bishops in the universal Church, let us briefly look at their tasks in their local churches, in the diocese for which a bishop is consecrated. Christ's office has the threefold form of teaching, priestly, and pastoral office. Similarly the bishop has the obligation to maintain the purity of doctrine and of instructing the faithful people.

He has a priestly task, especially in caring for the clergy of the diocese and for all ecclesial institutions of the believing people. He carries out this task by ordaining priests, which is the bishop's prerogative, by dispensing the sacrament of confirmation, through which the universal baptismal priesthood of all believers is brought to its completion, by consecrating the holy chrisms for baptism, confirmation, anointing of the sick and priestly ordination, and by consecrating churches.

The third element of the episcopal office is the exercise of the pastoral office in the bishop's diocese by legislation, jurisdiction, and administration, by organizing the diocese, and by administering its finances. Especially important in this respect is the establishing and maintaining of personnel for carrying out these comprehensive tasks. Vatican II dealt extensively with this aspect in a separate Decree on the Pastoral Office of Bishops in the Church (*Christus Dominus*); the directorium *"De pastorali ministerio episcoporum"* (June 20, 1973) added details of implementation for this decree. In its various parts, the code of canon law spells out the rights and duties of bishops.

e) *The Image of the Bishop*

The teaching of the above-mentioned documents on bishops must be seen, in the light of Scripture, as mystery. It must be seen in terms of the mission of Jesus Christ and the Spirit. The concretizing of this supernatural reality in this world, however, must not be lost sight of; otherwise the dogmatic truths run the danger of becoming ideological assertions. Let us concentrate at this point on ruling bishops. The institution of auxiliary bishops is difficult to grasp in dogmatic terms. It appears to be primarily a legal reality, which needs to be submitted to a thorough, new reflection, especially after Vatican II, which led to a sharp increase in the number of auxiliary bishops. Here are a few thoughts from the Church's history on the election of bishops, on canonical aptitude and thus on the image of the bishop.

(1) The central importance of the bishop for the Church as a community and society, as Christian mystery and secular institution, explains why the question of episcopal appointments has always occupied the interest of the Church itself, as well as the interest of the powerful of this world.[72] In the second and third centuries the communities of believers, together with the clergy, and with the cooperation of the neighboring bishops, chose a bishop, who was then ordained by the imposition of hands by all bishops present (cf. Cyprian, Hippolytus). The First Council of Nicaea (325) gave the right of confirming ordinations to the metropolitan bishops (can. 4). It also demanded the presence of at least three bishops at episcopal ordinations and the consent of the other bishops of a province. The rise of canon law influenced by state law after Constantine transformed the people's and the clergy's right of election into a right of suggestion. The clergy and special laypersons suggested suitable men from among whom the metropolitan bishop chose the new bishop. To resist the interference of secular powers the Second Council of Nicaea (787) declared episcopal appointments by secular powers to be null (can. 3). Since this time the Eastern Church has granted the right of suggestion to the bishops (since the Middle Ages, not without the involvement of a synod) while the metropolitan bishop selects and ordains his candidate.

The development in the Western Church was somewhat parallel. Beginning in the Carolingian period, there was a strong involvement of kings and other potentates of the empire, especially because of the secular fiefs and benefices connected with the episcopal sees. The appointment to a spiritual office and the secular entitlement by the king (e.g., Henry II) were no longer distinguishable. This is why reform movements after the turn of the millenium had to struggle for the legal independence of the Church. It was only in the investiture struggles (Concordat of Worms, 1122) that free election of bishops could be regained by the Church.

At the end of the twelfth century the powerful cathedral chapters had gained the right of election. Innocent III granted them this privilege to exclude the lower clergy and the laity from episcopal elections (Const. 24: Mansi XXII 1611). Already in the ninth century Rome had attempted to gain the right of decision in controversial cases. In 1080 a synod under Gregory VII decreed that the power of decision rests with the apostolic see and the metropolitan bishops. The primary purpose of this decision was not to establish power, but to serve order. After Urban V (1363) Rome, by "reservations," had increasingly gained the power of decision, so that it took appointments for the whole West into its own hands. When the Council of Basel abrogated these reservations, the concordat between Pope Nicholas V and Emperor Frederick III (1448) placed the power of decision again into the hands of the cathedral chapters, at least in even numbered (!) months. With papal support the kings of France (concordat of 1516) soon regained the right of nomination. The Spanish crown had the right of presentation and partly also that of nomination, both in the mother country and overseas. In many cases the so-called Irish mode of election prevailed, which gave to rulers the right to exclude unacceptable candidates from elections. Following the secularization of 1803 a new order for episcopal elections was established in various states (in

Bavaria the kings had the right of nomination; in Prussia and the Rhine province there were free elections by the cathedral chapter). After the revolution of 1918 and the demise of the European ruling houses Rome regained the right of decision (cf. CIC can. 329 §2; can. 332 §1). The procedure of lists proposed to Rome partly limits this right. The papal nuncios became more and more important in this process. Due to the new understanding of the Church as the people of God, there were demands for a participation of the clergy and the believing people after Vatican II.[73] On March 25, 1972 (cf. *Osserv. Rom.* of May 12 and 13, 1972) new "directives for episcopal appointments in the Latin Church" were published which applied past practices to the new situation created by the Council (cf. KKD VII p. 367).

(2) From the very beginning the Church concentrated not only on the procedure of appointment but on the "canonical aptitude" of the person who was to be burdened and entrusted with this office. Already the Pastoral Epistles lay down in detail what is required of a bishop (Tit 1,5–9; 1 Tim 3,1–7). The canons of the early councils and canon law, which arose in the Middle Ages, extensively addressed this question. The new guidelines of 1972 have this to say in section 6:

The candidates are to be examined [by the episcopal conference] in such a way that a decision is reached whether they possess the qualifications required for a good pastor and proclaimer of the faith. In particular, whether they have a good reputation, whether they live an exemplary life, whether they possess mature judgment and prudence, whether their character is balanced and stable, whether they are solidly rooted in the authentic faith and are faithfully devoted to the apostolic see and the magisterium of the Church, whether they have good knowledge of faith and moral doctrine and canon law as well, whether they distinguish themselves by piety, a spirit of sacrifice and pastoral zeal and are suited to an office of leadership. Special attention should be paid to intellectual capacity, education, social attitude, readiness for dialogue and cooperation, understanding for the signs of the time, the praiseworthy striving for impartiality in conflicts between various factions, family background, health, age, and hereditary characteristics.

(3) A history of the image of the bishop exists only for the bishop of Rome (cf. the numerous histories of the popes, Döllinger, Haller, Seppelt, Ranke, Pastor, etc.). There are also histories of individual dioceses and local churches. Only a comprehensive view of episcopal churches and local churches could produce a living history of the Church. For every century and every spiritual epoch it would give space, next to the mighty and the important of this world, to the great pastors and penitents, next to the men of great deeds, to those who pray and endure in suffering, next to the great, to the many little ones who carried on the kingdom of God in circumstances where the only thing that counts is work in little details, endurance and sacrifice and where the great breath of missionary work can be felt. Such a history of the Church as an episcopal history of the churches could show to our time of uniformity and mass culture something of the necessary and beneficial pluralism of the living Church. It could help the Church today to find cures for the ills of our time in concrete examples and thus to serve the life and growth of the kingdom of God.

The Apostolic Office and the Office of Peter: The Papal Office

As we have shown above, Scripture presents from the very beginning twelve men, listed by name, whom Jesus of Nazareth chose, taught and sent in a special way, and to whom he gave the title "apostles." Only six of them are portrayed in greater historical detail: Judas, the betrayer; James the elder, a relative of Jesus and the first martyr of the college of Twelve; John, son of Zebedee, who presents himself in his writings as the beloved disciple; Matthew-Levi, the Evangelist, whose call is reported by the three Synoptics (Mark 2,14 par.); and Peter with his brother Andrew. They are later joined by Saul-Paul, the apostle uniquely called by the exalted Lord (Acts 9ff.). From the very beginning, Paul's authority in the Church was different from that of Peter. He made his impact above all through his human and missionary personality as it appears in his numerous letters. The book of Acts, which can be called the first history of the Church (although not in a modern sense; it is primarily the first apology in behalf of the Church), deals only with the activity of Peter and Paul.

If one takes the testimony of Scripture as a whole, Peter stands out among the apostles. In the college of the Twelve and in the early Church up to the year 42 and in the apostolic council in 49/50 he played a special role. We must analyze this role because it is in it that we can find the foundation for a special Petrine office. The following outline suggests itself. We will: look at the position of Peter in the college of Twelve; show the importance of Peter for the early Church according to Christ's words and the book of Acts; clarify the problem of succession in this Petrine office; sketch the dogmatic development of the papal office in the history of the Church; and, finally, bring out the importance of the papal office for leadership in the Church (primacy of jurisdiction), as well as its importance as the column and foundation of truth (infallibility). The last section will clarify the relation of the papacy to the universal episcopal office within the Church in the light of historical development.

I. PETER AND THE COLLEGE OF THE TWELVE

Peter is mentioned 114 times in the Gospels alone, and 57 times in the Acts of the Apostles. For comparison, John is mentioned 38 times in the Gospels and 8 times in Acts.[74]

The Gospels unanimously report that Jesus himself distinguished Peter among the Twelve. Although the pericopes dealing with Peter's call (Mark 1,16–20; Matt 4,18–22; Luke 5,1–11; John 1,41f.) differ greatly, all evangelists agree that Christ gave to Peter alone among the Twelve a special name that functions as a title: the name "Peter" which means "rock." According to John 1,42, Christ gave Peter this name when he first called him; according to Matthew 16,16, after Peter's great messianic confession; according to Mark 3,16, when the college of the Twelve was established. It is untenable to claim that Peter received this title only from the risen Lord (1 Cor 15,5; Mark 16,7).[75] The meaning "kēpha = measuring stone" (R. Pesch) has been sufficiently substantiated exegetically. Peter was called as the first (Mark 1,16) or as one among the first (John 1,41: after Andrew and John). Perhaps he was called together with James and John on the occasion of the miraculous catch of fish (Luke 5,1–11), where he appeared as the spokesman in all his humility. His house at Capernaum was Jesus' lodging during his public life (Mark 1,29ff. par.; 2,1; 3,20; 9,33); his boat was the one from which Jesus preached to the people (Luke 5,3); together with John and James he was a witness of the raising of Jairus' daughter (Mark 5,37 par.), of the transfiguration on Tabor (Mark 9,2 par.), and of the agony in the garden (Mark 14,33 par.). In order to pay for his and Peter's temple tax, Jesus performed a special miracle (Matt 17,24–27) and, together with John, Peter was given the task of preparing the paschal meal (Luke 22,8). Jesus began the washing of the feet with Peter (John 13,6ff.). It was to Peter that the women were sent to proclaim the resurrection first (Mark 16,7). The risen Christ distinguished Peter by a special appearance, the first to the apostles (Luke 24,36; 1 Cor 15,5). When Jesus reprimanded Peter for "little faith" (Mark 14,28ff.) or his sleeping (Mark 14,37ff.) or his earthly thinking (Mark 8,33), he showed that he expected something special from Peter.

In the most important events Peter was the spokesman

of the twelve apostles. He expressed their astonishment after the miraculous catch of fish (Luke 5,8); he answered the Lord's question about the disciples' faith in the Messiah (Mark 8,27 par.); in their name he attested their firm faith in the word of the Lord after the eucharistic discourse (John 6,68); and he expressed the scandal felt by the disciples after Jesus predicted his passion (Mark 8,32 par.). In general, he expressed the disciples' burning questions and doubts to the Lord (cf. Luke 12,41; Matt 15,15; Mark 10,28ff. par.; Matt 18,21). Thus it is certainly no accident that Peter's name is first in the lists of apostles (Mark 3,16; Matt 10,2; Luke 6,14; Acts 1,13), and that the college of apostles seems in some places like Peter's following (Mark 1,36; Luke 8,45; 9,32: Simon Peter and those who were with him; Acts 2,14; 2,37: Peter together with the Eleven).

We must especially mention three events in which Jesus uniquely distinguished Peter: Peter was called to be the rock-foundation of the Church and the keeper of the keys of the kingdom (Matt 16,16–19); Jesus assured Peter of special prayer for his faith, so that Peter would strengthen his brothers after his repentance (Luke 22,32; cf. John 6,68f.); the risen Lord handed his whole flock over to Peter as the first shepherd (John 21,15–17). The particular exegetical difficulties presented by these three passages cannot obscure the fact that they somehow belong together. According to these texts, the foundation of Peter's external authority, that very authority which, according to the account of Acts, became visible in the early Church after Pentecost, goes back to the earthly life of Jesus.[76]

2. PETER'S POSITION IN THE EARLY COMMUNITY

The whole first part of Acts shows that Peter occupied the first place in the early Church. He initiated and carried out the election of Matthias so that the college of Twelve would be preserved after the departure of Judas (Acts

1,15ff.). After Pentecost he delivered the first catechetical sermon, whereupon three thousand let themselves be baptized and Christ's community began (Acts 2,14–36.37–42). In support of his preaching he worked the first miracles (Acts 3; 9,31–41). When the Jewish temple administration took steps against the apostles, Peter was the spokesman in defense of the Gospel (Acts 4,8; 5,29). He judged the purity of motives in the case of Ananias and Sapphira (Acts 5,1–11) and in his anathema against Simon Magus (Acts 8,21). He made the first missionary journeys to Lydda, Joppa (Acts 9,32ff.36ff.) and to Caesaraea (Acts 10,1.24). Instructed by an apparition he decided to receive the first gentiles, Cornelius and his house, into the Church (Acts 10,47; 11,2ff.; 15,7). He was miraculously liberated a second time from prison (Acts 12,3–17; cf. 5,19). He guided the discussion and the definition of the first dogmatic pronouncement of the Church at the Apostolic Council (Acts 15,6–11). According to tradition (we will discuss this below) he worked before Paul and together with him as a missionary in Rome, the capital of the world of that time, where he died as a martyr under Nero.

Quite independently of this Roman question, Scripture is unanimous in ascribing to Peter a leading position unlike that of any other apostle in the early Church. Acts expresses this fact with great simplicity in its account of Pentecost. "But Peter, standing with the Eleven, lifted up his voice and addressed them, Men of Judea and all who dwell in Jerusalem, let his be known to you, and give ear to my words" (Acts 2,14). Peter is not outside of the Eleven. But he is not merely one of the Twelve. He is their leader. And he is their leader not because of his own charismatic power but because he was commissioned and sent by the Lord. Above we derived the apostolic office from the election, guidance, and mission of the Twelve. In the same way we may and must derive a specific Petrine office from the special election, guidance, and mission of Peter. This office has a special place in the Church and its organization, not above, but next to, the apostolic office, in which Peter shares like the other Eleven.

Paul clearly testifies to this office when he writes, "Then after three years I went up to Jerusalem to visit Cephas (cf. Gal 2,9.11.14), and remained with him fifteen days. But I saw none of the other apostles except James, the Lord's brother" (Gal 1,18–19). This universally acknowledged position of Peter is also the reason why Paul opposes him so decisively and publicly in the question of gentile Christians (Gal 2,11–21). The same conclusion is suggested by the replacement of Peter's secular name "Simon" with Cephas or Peter.

Just as the apostolic office is continued and further unfolded in the episcopal office, so the office of Peter can be seen and encountered in a new way in the papal office. Before unfolding this point we must clarify the problem of succession in the Petrine office.

3. THE QUESTION OF SUCCESSION IN THE PETRINE OFFICE

The chain of succession between apostles and bishops can only be understood as a historical development, as a development, however, that has the whole power and binding force attributed to historical reality in the Christian world view, which is built upon creation, the incarnation of God and the transfiguration of the world. The same point holds for the chain of succession between the office of Peter and the papacy. As the episcopal office was grasped only after considerable time, so also the idea of succession in the office of Peter became conscious only at a later time. This is not surprising if we consider that the basic mysteries of christology and the trinitarian understanding of God were clarified only in the fourth century. The following facts support faith in the succession of the papacy to the office of Peter.

a) The fundamental point that applies to apostolic succession applies here too: The basic structure Christ gave to the Church founded by him must be preserved through all time. If, as we have shown, there is a Petrine office in this basic structure, then it must continue to exist in the Church, although its external understanding will have to adapt itself to each historical period.

b) Since *1 Clement*, and especially since Irenaeus and Tertullian, the succession of bishops based on the apostles has been tied to an episcopal see (*cathedra*). In the same way, succession in the office of Peter must be defined by a *cathedra*, because it is also an episcopal succession, although an episcopal succession of a special kind.

c) If succession in the office of Peter is to be connected with the *cathedra* of Peter in Rome, then a historical connection between Peter and this Roman episcopal see must be shown. The question we must ask is this: Was Peter in Rome? How and when did he get there and what role did he play in the Church of Rome?

When was Peter in Rome? If one combines the reports of Acts with Paul's autobiographical notes in Galatians, one can piece together the following data of Peter's life. After the death of Jesus (A.D. 30), Peter was the head of the college of Twelve in Jerusalem, not in the sense of the monarchic episcopate, which we clearly encounter only around 100 in the letters of Ignatius of Antioch, but because of the personal authority given to him by Christ. Around 32 Paul was converted by the intervention of the risen Lord before Damascus (Acts 9). Three years later (i.e., 35) Paul "went up to Jerusalem to visit Cephas, and remained with him fifteen days" (Gal 1,18). This passage indicates, as we noted above, that Paul knows about the special position of Peter (he always calls him "Cephas," never by his secular name "Simon"), and that Peter occupied this position also in Jerusalem, which is why the newly converted Paul looks only for him, Cephas, and stays with him. In connection with the activity and martyrdom of Stephen (before 32), the Christians, especially gentile Christians, were expelled from Jerusalem. Only the apostles were able to remain (Acts 8,1; 11,19). This expulsion led to the founding of new Christian communities outside of Jerusalem. The gentile Christian community of Antioch, the capital of Syria, became the most important such community. The apostles sent Barnabas as organizer and missionary to Antioch (Acts 11,22). Barnabas, in turn, brought Paul there as a collaborator (Acts 11,25). Due to the activity of these two missionaries to the gentiles, "the disciples were for the first time called Christians" (Acts 11,26). Under the leadership of Barnabas and Paul, Antioch thus became the center of gentile mission, just as Jerusalem with the apostles remained the center of Jewish mission. The inner unity of the two fundamentally different missionary branches was expressed in the economic support by gentile Christians, who lived in rich cities, for the poor Jewish Christians in Jerusalem (cf. Acts 11,29f.; 1 Cor 16,1; Gal 2,10; Rom 15,25–38; 2 Cor 8,1–9.15).

King Herod Agrippa (41–44) had James the Younger, brother of John, put to death and Peter imprisoned. But Peter was miraculously freed by an angel (Acts 12,1–17). Two details of the report of Peter's liberation are especially important: First, Peter sent reports of his miraculous liberation to "James and the brethren" (Acts 12,17), which shows that at this time James the Elder, the brother of the Lord, had either become or was about to become the leader of the Jerusalem community. Second, as its initiator, Peter still intended to be a leader of the great gentile mission. James the Elder was the spiritual head of the Jewish Christians, which is clear at the council of Jerusalem (Acts 15,13.20). In addition, the text reports that Peter "went to another place" (Acts 12,17). When Paul came to Jerusalem after his first missionary journey (around 49), fourteen years after his first visit, he reports that "James and Cephas and John, who were reputed to be pillars, gave to me and Barnabas the right hand of fellowship" (Gal 2,9). This text shows, first, that Peter was present in Jerusalem again (the apostolic council belongs in this context; Acts 15), but that he no longer had the position of leadership, which is why James is mentioned before him. It is uncertain where Peter went in 42. The most likely place is Antioch, since Paul speaks of Peter's arrival in Antioch and of a controversy about Jewish laws concerning table fellowship (Gal 2,11–16). It is unlikely that this event took place in 49, shortly before the apostolic council. At the apostolic council Peter clearly acted as the spokesman for the gentile mission (Acts 15,7–11).

This is the last direct scriptural testimony for Peter. An exception is perhaps 1 Peter. The letter is directed "to the exiles of the Dispersion in Pontus, Galatia, Cappadocia, Asia and Bithynia" (1 Pet 1,1), i.e., to the communities of Asia Minor. The letter's final greeting says, "She who is at Babylon, who is likewise chosen, sends you greetings" (1 Pet 5,13). "Babylon" probably refers to Rome (cf. 2 *Apoc. Bar* 11,1; 67,7 which was written at about the same time). If there are no convincing reasons to consider 1 Peter pseudepigraphical, two conclusions can be drawn from it. First, Peter was in Rome at the time of the letter's composition. Second, he sends this letter to the communities of Asia Minor with authority, which neither proves nor excludes that he visited these communities after 42. Also the construction of the narrative in Acts might suggest that Peter went to Rome after 42. The narrative of Paul's missionary activity ends with his stay in Rome (Acts 28, 30f.). By analogy, when Acts says that Peter "went to another place" (Acts 12,17), Rome might be meant, although the statement, for reasons no longer known to us, is rather cryptic. Perhaps the author, who wrote in Rome, wanted to conceal Peter's presence in Rome, which would make sense during the persecution of Christians under Nero (64–68).

Peter's presence and martyrdom in Rome were not called into question in antiquity and the Middle Ages, nor even during the Reformation. It was only in the nineteenth century that the validity of the tradition, and even the mere fact of Peter's presence in Rome, were questioned by an absolutely sceptical criticism, especially on the part of Protestants.[77] Since 1936 K. Heussi has repeatedly and in numerous writings attempted to prove that Peter's stay in Rome is a mere legend. He was opposed by the Protestant theologians H. Lietzmann and K. Aland. Aland wrote in 1959, "What other option, in terms of historical method, is open to us except that of accepting Peter's martyrdom in Rome as a fact? This result is, in my opinion, inescapable, if one uses the methods and perspectives which apply to historical critical research on the first and the second centuries."[78]

Let us take a brief look at the oldest testimonies for the presence of Peter in Rome. *First Clement* (written in 95–97) speaks about Peter's and Paul's martyrdom (*1 Clem.* 5, 2–7). In summary it points to "a great multitude of the chosen" who by their martyrdom "offered among us [*en hēmin*] the fairest example in their endurance" (*1 Clem.* 6,1), which can only refer to the martyrs under Nero. In his letter to the Romans, Ignatius of Antioch (d. 107) appeals to these two apostles, Peter and Paul, who died there as martyrs, "I do not order you as did Peter and Paul" (*Ign. Rom.* 4,3). Bishop Dionysius of Corinth wrote around 170 in his letter to the Roman community, "Both apostles, after beginning the planting in our Corinth, have taught in the same way. Then they acted as missionaries [*phoitē-santes*] in Italy and suffered martyrdom there at the same time" (Eusebius, *HE* 2,25,8). Under Pope Zephyrinus (198–217), the Roman presbyter Gaius wrote to the Montanist Proclus of Hierapolis, who had pointed to the grave of Philip and his prophetic daughters, "I can show you the signs of victory [*tropaia*, tombs] of the apostles. For if you go to the Vatican hill or to the road to Ostia, you will see the signs of victory of those who founded [*hidrysamenōn*] this church [in Rome]" (Eusebius, *HE* 2,27,7). Around 200, Irenaeus of Lyons refers to "the very great, the very an-

cient, and universally known Church founded and organized [*fundata et constituta*] at Rome by the two most
glorious apostles, Peter and Paul" (*Adv. Haer.* 3,3,1). From
this point on there is a unanimous tradition about the
Roman activity and martyrdom of Peter and Paul, the two
princes of the apostles. The earliest testimonies to these
facts were not challenged until the middle of the nineteenth century.

In recent times three very important archeological discoveries have joined these literary witnesses. (1) A festal
calendar assembled in A.D. 354 by Philokalus, of which
parts are quoted in corrected form in the so-called *Mar-
tyrologium Hieronomynianum* (ca. 450), contains the following passage, "June 29, memorial of the apostles Peter
and Paul, of Peter in the Vatican, of Paul on the road to
Ostia, and of both *ad catacumbas* under the consulship of
Tuscus and Bassus [i.e., 258]."

(2) The text just quoted mentions a common place of
veneration *ad catacumbas* in addition to the two graves on
the Vatican hill and the road to Ostia. According to an old
tradition (cf. PL 13,347–424) Pope Damasus had the following inscription affixed *ad catacumbas:* "You shall
know that saints have dwelt here before, and everyone can
ascertain that their names were Peter and Paul" (*EH* 589).
Ancient tradition identifies this place *ad catacumbas*
with the *Platoma Apostolorum* under San Sebastiano on
the Via Appia. It was found during excavations conducted
in 1892 and 1915. The eastern wall of this room is covered
with grafitti consisting of invocations of the two princes of
the apostles. It is possible that during the Valerian persecution in 258 the bones of the apostles were kept here until
they could be returned to their places in the Vatican and by
the road to Ostia.

(3) Still more important is the third archeological testimony unearthed in the excavations under the Vatican basilica since 1939. Under the *confessio,* the papal altar in
the center of the basilica, Peter's *tropaion* was found as

mentioned by Gaius. As the excavations show, Constantine's architects had to overcome considerable difficulties in the sloping terrain in the midst of a large pagan graveyard in order to situate the new basilica of Peter in such a way that the present day *confessio*, the papal high altar, came to lie exactly over this *tropaion*, i.e., over Peter's grave.[79] If M. Garducci's research is correct, the bones found in a little marble shrine in the red grafitti wall behind the *tropaion* are the remains of Peter, placed there in 258.[80]

Peter's presence in Rome is thus well established, even in historical-critical terms. The question remains, however, what role in the Roman church should be attributed to him. At least since the presbyter Gaius and Irenaeus of Lyons, tradition affirms that Peter "founded" the church of Rome. This statement means that on the basis of the authority given to him by Christ and universally recognized in the early community, Peter is considered to be the first leader of the Christian community in Rome. It should be added that such a role cannot be identified immediately with the monarchical episcopate attested by Ignatius of Antioch. It is certain that Paul was not the founder of the Christian community in Rome and that the simultaneous mention of his name is to be explained by his personal authority as missionary to the gentiles and by his martyrdom with Peter in Rome.

4. THE DEVELOPMENT OF THE PAPACY IN THE HISTORY OF THE CHURCH

Focused on the question of the succession of the papal office to the office of Peter, let us give a brief sketch of the development of the idea of the papacy in the history of the Church. The meaning of the question to be discussed here can be expressed as follows: How did it come about in the history of the Church that the bishop of Rome claimed the leadership, not only of his Roman diocese, but of the whole Church of Christ, and that this office was not only so claimed but acknowledged by others as the office of the leadership exercised by Peter in the college of apostles, as the office of the first spokesman, the office given by Christ to Peter according to the three passages already mentioned (Matt 16,16f.; Luke 22,32; John 21,15–17)? One can distinguish three dimensions of this office: First, the office of the shepherd who has primary responsibility for the whole flock of Christ; second, the office of the keeper of the keys of God's house; third, the office of truth which is to guarantee and preserve the purity of the message of Christ in the Church of Christ.

In discussing this question, we will: a) comment on the three Scripture passages that deal with the Petrine office; b) show the increasingly important position occupied by the patriarchate of Rome among the patriarchates formed in the first four centuries; and, finally, c) analyze how this office of Peter unfolded and defined itself as the papal office in the history of the Church.

a) Christ's Three Distinguishing Words to Peter and the Papacy

(1) First a few remarks on the order of the three texts, all of which are texts without parallels, found only in their respective Gospels. In order to understand the texts of sacred Scripture correctly, we must understand them in terms of their authors, their audience, and their own mentality. The authors of the New Testament writings composed their own accounts of historical events as personalities with their own background and for a certain audience or readers in a particular situation. In this perspective the following points concerning the Petrine texts must be kept in mind.

(i) Mark, Peter's companion and the reporter of Peter's preaching (cf. Papias in Eusebius, *HE* 3,39,15), clearly portrays Peter as the spokesman of the Twelve. He mentions his failure, but he does not have a specific text for the unique distinction given to Peter. Perhaps this absence reflects Peter's own self-effacing manner in not speaking about his distinction in the circle of the Twelve.

(ii) On the other hand, Matthew, the educated Jew and tax collector Levi, wrote his Gospel for Jewish Christians, largely independently from Mark. This may be the reason why, among various elements of the tradition, he stressed precisely this distinction of Peter, who understood himself as the apostle to the gentiles (Acts 10, 1–11.18; 15,7–11), and why he clarified Peter's special position in the Church in terms of the organization of the Jews and their piety in the temple of Jerusalem (Matt 16,16–19).

(iii) Luke, the educated doctor from Antioch on the Orontos in Syria, was himself a gentile Christian and wrote his Gospel, probably in Rome, for gentile Christians. Perhaps due to the influence of Stoic philosophy, he is especially interested in the historicity and the truth of the teaching (Luke 1,1–4) which is to be passed on by an authority. For this reason he alone gives an account of how Jesus appointed Peter to keep and preserve the truth of faith (Luke 22,32).

(iv) The Gospel of John, which extensively presents Jesus' self-portrayal as the good shepherd (John 10,1–16), reports in an appended chapter how Peter, despite the betrayal, of which he must be conscious and which must make him humble, is appointed by the risen Lord as the unique shepherd of the whole flock of Christ (John 21,15–17). One cannot overlook that this account fits the beloved disciple and the situation around 100, when heresies already threatened to tear apart the flock of Christ (cf. 2 Tim 3,1–17).

(v) In Luke's Acts, Peter already appears as the one who uniquely fulfills these special tasks in the circle of the Twelve (cf. Acts 2,14ff.; 3,12ff.; 4,8ff.; 5,3ff.; 10,1–48; 12,11ff.; cf. above, section 3).

(2) Let us turn first to the passage Matthew 16,16ff., because much has already been written about it.[81] When Christ asked the apostles, his closest companions, who they thought he was, Peter confessed, "You are the Christ [= Messiah, Mark 8,29; Luke 9,20], the Son of the living God" (Matt 16,16). Christ answered, "Blessed are you, Simon Bar-Jona! For flesh and blood has not revealed this to you, but my Father who is in heaven. And I tell you, you are Peter [petros], and on this rock [petra] I will build my church, and the powers of death shall not prevail against it. I will give you the keys of the kingdom of heaven, and whatever you bind on earth shall be bound in heaven, and whatever you loose on earth shall be loosed in heaven" (Matt 16,17–19). The last phrase about the power to bind and to loose (without the keys saying) appears also in Matthew 18,18 spoken by Christ to his disciples (mathētai probably refers to the twelve disciples in the narrower sense) in response to a question by Peter. Matthew 16,16ff. is a pericope found only in Matthew.

Because of its importance for understanding Peter and the papacy, this text has raised many exegetical questions. The following brief remarks must be kept in mind when addressing these questions. An explanation of the text as a theologoumenon of the early community adopted by Matthew cannot be maintained due to the Gospel's date of composition, the clear meaning of the text and the convergence of this text with the texts Luke 22,32 and John 21,15–17, which likewise show that Christ gave to Peter a unique position in his Church.

The question has been raised whether Jesus really spoke these words after Peter's confession, which occurred, according to Mark 8 and Luke 9, shortly after the second multiplication of loaves in Caesarea Philippi (cf. John 6,68). Cullmann assumes a separate oral tradition used by Matthew according to which the risen Jesus spoke these words when he appeared to Peter before all the other apostles (cf. Luke 24,34; 1 Cor 15,3). E. Stauffer and others suppose that Matthew 16,16ff. should be seen as of a piece with the call of Peter to be the highest shepherd (John 21,15). These hypotheses were suggested by form criticism, according to which Peter's messianic confession in Mark still betrays a false, political understanding of the Messiah. The three synoptic accounts show that immediately after the first prediction of the passion, Peter decidedly opposed the idea of a suffering Messiah. Jesus sharply reprimanded him ("Get behind me, Satan!" Mark 8,33; Matt 16,23) for thinking not God's thoughts but human thoughts. Perhaps this form-critical perspective overlooks Peter's impetuous character, which makes it quite conceivable that he would respond to the miracle of the multiplication of loaves with a convinced messianic confession and that soon afterwards he would resist the new image of the Messiah.

Another objection against this text is based on the phrase "building my church [ekklēsia]." This expression is unique in the Gospels: it does not even occur in Paul. In response to this difficulty one can point to the contribution of the learned Jewish rabbi Leo Baeck, who investigated this passage in the light of his understanding of the "logic of Jewish images." He reaches the conclusion that the images of the rock (kēfa) and the construction of the temple, the saying about the keys (keys for the treasury of the temple preserved in the kippa, cf. Isa 22,22) and of the power to bind and to loose (to unlock, in Aramaic kafat, and lock the treasury) correspond in their sequence completely to the logic of the Jewish imagination.[82]

How one understands Christ himself is of fundamental importance for the understanding of this passage. Only if one acknowledges that the earthly Jesus of the Gospels possessed a messianic consciousness can one understand why he would speak about "his church." Only on this basis can one understand, further, that he would promise the office of universal shepherd and the power to bind and to loose to the apostle Peter, the apostle who was so distinguished by him, and that he actually fulfilled this promise after his resurrection when he bestowed pastoral authority on Peter (John 21,15ff.).

The phrase "heaven and earth" makes it clear that the Church to be founded is a Church in this aeon, in our aeon, in this world. It is for this Church that Peter is the rock and foundation, the keeper of the keys. According to Jesus' words in John 21 about the transfer of the pastoral office over "the sheep of Jesus" he had, therefore, the following functions: In some way he represents the heavenly and exalted Christ for the entire visible Church as the people of God on earth. We will deal with some further exegetical questions when discussing the images contained in this saying.

(3) Let us now turn to the other texts, although we will deal with them in more detail in the context of the questions of infallibility and the primacy of jurisdiction. Luke 22,31ff. is part of the Lord's farewell sayings to his disciples, spoken in the Cenacle after Judas, the betrayer, had left the Twelve. The text must be read in the whole Lucan context. Jesus tells his apostles that they "have continued with me in my trials" (Luke 22,28) and he promises to them an eschatological reward in the kingdom of his father. "Trials" must be understood in terms of the imminent catastrophe of the crucifixion. Christ cannot fulfill the expectations of the "political Messiah" maintained by some Jews, an expectation by which also the disciples, as children of their time, are affected. Perhaps Judas's downfall has its roots here. By his betrayal he perhaps wanted to force Jesus to manifest himself and his political messianic power publicly. For this reason Christ says, "Satan demanded to have you [plural, i.e., the apostles] that he might sift you like wheat" (Luke 22,31). What is special about these texts is that Christ links this statement with a double personal address to Simon Peter (from chapter 6 on, Luke had used only the name Peter). "Simon, Simon . . . but I have prayed for you (singular, i.e., Simon)

that your faith may not fail [*eklipēi*]." To understand this saying, one must see it together with Jesus' demand that they buy a sword (Luke 22,36) and his prediction of Peter's threefold betrayal (Luke 22,36) just after Peter's attempt to raise himself above the other apostles: "Even though they all fall away, I will not" (Mark 14,29; Matt 26,33; Luke does not include these words). The saying about Jesus' prayer for Peter's faith is intelligible in this context only if it is taken together with the second phrase reported by Luke: "And you, turn to your brethren [*epistrephas*, in an active sense] and strengthen them" (Luke 22,32). In view of Peter's betrayal, this saying is usually translated in the sense of repentance "when you have turned again." This translation is not supported by the original text.[83] The important point in this saying is that Peter receives from Christ the commission "to strengthen [*stērison*] his brethren." "This accords to Peter a position and task in the circle of the Twelve which establishes him as their head and leader."[84] If one combines this text with Matthew 16,17–19, one sees that it refers not only to Peter but to his office, which continues to live in the Church founded upon him. We will return to this point.

(4) The third text to be discussed is John 21,15–19. It is found in the supplementary chapter of the Gospel, which is found in all manuscripts and which has always been quoted like the rest of the Gospel. Perhaps it was added by John himself (with the exception of the last two verses) or by one of his students. At any rate, it is quite Johannine in thought and remains biblical revealed truth. It is perhaps difficult to decide whether the narrative of the miraculous catch of fish as reported in John 21,1–14 belongs into the post-Easter period or, as in Luke 5,1–11, into the period of Jesus' public ministry. It is also difficult to decide whether John 21,1–14 constitutes a second miraculous catch in addition to John 6,16–21 (the two multiplications of loaves reported by Mark and Matthew are a similar case). Peter's confession of his guilt as reported in Luke 5,8 belongs per-

haps in the context of John 21,1–14 (John does not mention this confession, just as he says nothing about Peter's repentance, cf. Luke 23,62). If this is the case, Jesus' threefold question "Simon, son of John, do you love me, more than these?" would be better motivated as corresponding to Peter's threefold denial. A particularly important feature of this text is that Christ, only here as in Matthew 16,17, calls Simon "the son of John." The decisive point is that after Peter's threefold assurance of love Christ gives to this "son of John" the commission, "Feed my lambs, tend my sheep, feed my sheep [*boske-poimaine ta arnia-probatiamou*] (John 21,15.16.17).

If one sees that the mystery of grace is the core of the message and the redemptive deed of Jesus Christ, one can see this mystery of grace at work when Christ promises the office of leadership to Peter in response to his messianic confession (Matt 16,16ff.) and when the risen Lord actually gives this office of leadership to Peter after Peter's deep fall and repentance (John 21,15–17). Since the flock of Christ does not cease to be the flock of Christ after Peter's death, the saying in John 21 should not be seen as addressed only to Peter personally; it should be seen as addressed to his office. There are, of course, other interpretations in recent exegesis, but they should be judged in terms of their starting points.

b) The Development of the Roman Patriarchate during the First Four Centuries

How have these three sayings addressed to Peter been understood by the tradition? When the Gnostics attempted to downplay Peter and his authority by recourse to Galatians 2,11, Tertullian stressed in all clarity that one can hardly suppose that "anything remained hidden from Peter, who was called rock for the building of the Church, who received the keys of the kingdom of heaven and the power to bind and to loose in heaven and on earth" (*Adv. Haer.* 22; composed around 200). Tertullian probably did not think that the power of the keys was given to the whole Church or to a successor of Peter in Rome. In fact, he expresses the contrary opinion in a later work of his Montanist peroid, *De Pudicitia* 21,9 (composed 219–21). Bishop Agrippinus of Carthage (cf. Cyprian, *Ep.* 7,14; not Pope Callixtus I, as is often assumed on the basis of Hippolytus *Phil.* 9,12) had appealed to Matthew 16,18 as a basis for his right to allow all sinners to reenter the Church by repentance. Tertullian responds that the promise in Matthew 16 was given "to Peter personally [*personaliter hoc Petro conferentem*]," not to the whole Church or to its bishops. Only a pneumatic, not a psychic, person could be considered as a successor of Peter.

Cyprian (d. 258) once interprets this passage as a promise given by Christ to all bishops (*Ep.* 31,1). He also stresses that Peter, on whom Christ built the Church, "is the origin of the Church's unity" (*Ep.* 72,6; *De Cath. Eccl. Un.* 4 and 6).

Pope Stephen I (254–57) seems to have been the first to claim Matthew 16,18 for the bishop of Rome as the successor of the apostle Peter. Bishop Firmilian of Caesaraea in Cappadocia once wrote to Cyprian (*Ep. Cypr.* 75,16f.) that "Stephen glories in the place of his episcopacy (Rome) and claims to stand in the succession of Peter."

In a definitive way this claim has been made by the Roman bishops only since Pope Damasus I (366–84) (cf. the Roman Synod in 382; Mirbt, *Quellen*, 142f., n.314). Pope Damasus appealed to Matthew 16,18 to substantiate the precedence of Rome over the other patriarchates— Alexandria, Antioch, and Jerusalem. His appeal was repeated in the *Decretum Gelasianum* (DS 350f.). According to this decree, the order Rome-Alexandria-Antioch is founded upon the fact that Peter was in Rome and was buried there, that Peter's first disciple Mark was bishop in Alexandria, and that Peter temporarily held the episcopal office in Antioch.

After Damasus the idea of primacy was further extended. Jerome (347–420) writes, "The primacy was entrusted to Peter, in such a way, however, that each apostle occupies his proper rank" (*In Is.* 6,1,7; *Anecdota mared-solana* III 3, Paris). "Peter is the prince of the apostles upon whom, as upon a firm foundation, the Church of the Lord is founded" (*Contra Pelag.* I,14b).

According to Augustine (d. 431) "Peter represents the Church in symbolical universality because of the primacy of his apostleship." Christ is the *petra* upon which Peter is built; but Peter too is the *petra* upon which the Church is built (*In Joh.* 21, *Sermo* 124,5). In his *Retractationes* (I 21,1) the later Augustine stresses that earlier he had understood Peter as the rock, but that later (perhaps after the catastrophe of 410, cf. *Sermo* 296,5) he understood Christ as the *petra* while Peter merely shares the name. He adds that the reader may decide which of these opinions is more probable.

Bishop Optatus of Mileve (Mauretania, 365–85), like Augustine, wrote against the heresy of the Donatists in his two books on the Church, but with greater clarity: "You cannot deny knowing that in the city of Rome the episcopal see was given first [*primo*] to Peter, so that the head of the apostles would occupy this see. He is called *kephas* in order that through this one see [*una kathedra*] the unity of all others might be preserved. The other apostles were not to defend individually their own see, so that he who sets up another see against this singular see [*singularem cathedram*] is shown to be schismatic and a sinner" (Mirbt, *Quellen*, 131, n.287f.).Optatus continues to enumerate the successors of Peter up to his own time (i.e., up to Pope Siricus, the successor of Damasus), thirty-eight names in all (with three omissions).

One should also mention the Edict of the Three Emperors (Gratian, Valentinian and Theodosius) (Feb. 28, 380), in which they demand that all peoples remain "in the religion which the divine apostle Peter passed on to the Romans" and which has flowered to this day of Damasus (Mirbt, *Quellen*, 141, n.310).

The teaching that Peter is the foundation of the whole

Church is not restricted to the Western Church but can be found equally in the Eastern Church. In his homily (54) on Matthew 16,13–23 John Chrysostom (354–407) extensively deals with the two promises of Christ to Peter: because of his faith Peter will be the rock of the whole Church of Christ; and because of his confession of Christ as Son of God and Messiah he was given the power of the keys. In a similar way Augustine stresses again and again (cf. *Sermo* 76,1; 149,7; 232,3; 270,2; 295; 296) that Peter received this unique office "because of his faith and his confession." This probably means that Peter's faith is the reason for the distinction given to him, not that the faith of Peter is itself the rock-foundation of the visible Church, as Luther repeatedly claimed.[85]

Perhaps in response to the controversy between Rome and Constantinople after 451 (can. 28) the Syrian Jacob of Batnae, also known as Jacob of Sarug (451–521), wrote his great hymnic poem about Matthew 16,16f. in which he stresses that Peter received the gift of faith for his confession: "You are worthy of it and revelation as well as confession will be unshakeable, not exposed to uncertainty." "You I want to fit as the first into my building, for you are truthful. You shall be the foundation for the holy temple which I construct on it for myself." "To you I entrust the bedchamber of the Father's daughter [i.e., the Church], upon you I want to found it, for your construction prevails against all division." "When he [Christ] began the construction of the house he chose Kephas, laid him down as the foundation and gave him as a wedding gift the charisma to defeat death and Satan" (BKV *Syr. Dichter*, 317–32).

In the Church of Rome itself it was Pope Leo I (440–61) who stressed with final decidedness the primacy of the Roman bishop as the successor of the see of Peter. Perhaps the controversy with the newly established patriarchate of Constantinople (Synod of Chalcedon, 450) had some influence on this development. Leo explicitly rejected canon 28 of that Synod in which 150 Eastern bishops attributed to Constantinople (Roma junior, as they called it) "the same greatness [*magnificam esse, megalunestai*] in matters of the Church as to Rome," even though they called this "primacy [*primatum, presbeian*] of the holy Church of Constantinople" "second [*deuteran*] after Rome." Yet, since primacy, as in the case of Rome, was determined by the unique office of Peter (not by a decision of the fathers, as in canon 28) one should not speak of a second primacy.[86] Leo writes, "Through the blessed Peter, prince of the apostles, the holy Roman Church possesses ruling authority [*principatus*] over all Churches of the whole world" (*Ep.* 65,2). "The power and authority given to the apostle Peter is active and continues to live in his see [*in sede sua*, i.e., *romana*] and his dignity is not curtailed even in an unworthy successor" (*Sermo* 3,3). Peter is "the forefather of this see [Rome] and the *primas* among all bishops" (ibid. 4). "Only Peter is chosen to be the head of all peoples called [by Christ], of all apostles and all fathers of the Church, . . . the leader of all those ruled, above all, by Christ" (*Sermo* 4,2). "For this reason he is the head of the whole Church" (ibid. 4; cf. *Sermo* 73,2; 82,3; *Ep.* 11; etc.). In this teaching the doctrine that the pope as the successor of Peter is the head of the whole Church has come to a certain conclusion. One should point out that the Roman bishops never appealed for this doctrine to the political position of the earthly Rome, but always and only to the presence of Peter and Paul in Rome, to their graves in the city, and to the biblical words of Christ to Peter.

c) Outlines of the Development of the Idea of Roman Primacy up to the Present

Let us draw only some of the most important lines through the history of the Church that can serve to clarify some principles for the understanding and evaluation of the idea of primacy. The true mystery of the entire Christian event, and thus also of the office of Peter and the papacy, is that it is in this world and for this world but not of this world. As a result of this dilemma, outward progress often contains the germ of an inner regress, and every outward destruction can be source for interior renewal.

(1) It is a historical fact that the Church of Rome (Rome was the capital of the world-empire of that time) has the greatest number of martyrs (catacombs), the oldest baptismal creed (*Symbolum Apostolorum*), the oldest list of bishops (Irenaeus recorded it around 190 with thirteen names), as well as the oldest list of canonical books (the Muratorian Canon of the second century). Thus Irenaeus was able to present Rome as the paradigm of the preservation of the apostolic tradition. He writes, "It is the greatest and oldest and universally known Church founded and built by the two glorious apostles Peter and Paul at Rome" and "because of its special preeminence every church must agree with it." "The apostles, after founding and furnishing the Church, transferred to Linus (the successor of Peter) the episcopacy for the administration of the Church [*episcopatum administrandae ecclesiae*]" (*Adv. Haer.*, III,3,1–3).

When the eastern Rome (Constantinople) was founded by Constantine and when he gave external freedom to the Church in the Roman empire, the patriarchates Alexandria, Antioch, Jerusalem, and Constantinople began to develop alongside Rome. This situation gave to the Church's doctrinal controversies of the second to the fifth centuries a political impact in the empire. It was thus also for the sake of the Christian teaching that the Roman popes became more and more political authorities. This development can be observed even in the protracted christological controversies from the Council of Nicaea in 325 to the Second Council of Constantinople in 680.

(2) The dilemma between spiritual and secular power, which began with the "Constantinian turning point," became especially clear after the fifth century when the in-

flux of the Germanic peoples dissolved the unity of the Roman empire. As a result the Western Church (Church of Rome) had to constitute itself as a political power, especially because the last Western emperors had (after 402) taken up residence in Ravenna. After the division of the Roman empire in 395 into the Eastern and the Western empires, Pope Innocent I (401–417) gave new weight to the papal office as a leading power in the West by giving aid to Rome after it was sacked and burned in 410 by the Visigoths under Alaric, and by intervening in the doctrinal controversies in Africa where, together with Augustine, he struggled for a correct understanding of the Church against the Donatists. At the Council of Chalcedon (451), Leo I (440–461) gave a powerful and clear defense of the Church's teaching on Christ. Through his courageous bearing at Mantua in 452 he persuaded Attila, king of the Huns, to withdraw from Italy, and in 455 he prevented the Vandal king Gaiseric from sacking and burning Rome.

Completely new demands were placed upon the popes when the last Western emperor, Romulus Augustus, was deposed in 476 and the Germanic mercenary leader Ottokar was recognized by the Eastern empire as emperor of the West. Under the rule of the Ostrogoth Theodoric (493–526) and the Byzantinian emperor Justinian (527–565) the popes maintained their possessions and preserved the Church's peace. In 529 St. Benedict (480–543) founded Monte Cassino near Naples as the mother abbey of his great order. A new age for the Church was brought about by the first Benedictine on the papal throne, Gregory the Great (590–604), who was a man of great religious-ascetical depth and high intellectual and political preparation.

(3) Gregory's pastoral rule became for many centuries the basis for the education of the clergy. His liturgical books (*sacramentarium* and Gregorian chant), his sermons and scriptural commentaries, and not least his worldwide activity through letters to all the great leaders of that time

brought to the papacy in the West a completely new historical importance and built the bridge to the new Western Middle Ages. With great foresight he initiated the Anglo-Saxon missions, and the new Christians of this area in turn provided the great missionaries for the Germanic peoples of the continent in the seventh and eighth centuries. The decisive task of the Western Church was first of all to preserve that freedom from political power that had given it the strength in the great persecutions of the first three centuries to overcome even the political Rome from within.

(4) Of course, the rise of the Roman patriarchate and the blossoming of the Christian West gave a new acuteness to the tensions between the Eastern and the Western Church. An additional factor in this development was Islam, the new power that beset the Church especially in the East and in Africa through its conquests after 632. In addition, the Langobard empire in northern Italy sought and found recognition by the Roman popes, in contrast to the politics of the East. The split between the Eastern and the Western Church was further widened by the Monothelite controversy, which was resolved in 680 at the Sixth Ecumenical Council at Constantinople. A number of popes of Eastern origin (Greeks and Syrians, from John V, 685, to Zacharias, 752) increasingly appeared as strangers in the Western Church. The dilemma of this estrangement between East and West becomes especially clear if one considers that up to the fifth century the Eastern patriarchates bore the main burden of doctrinal decisions. Now they were pressed from the south by Islam and from the north by the Russians and the Normans. Due to the inner estrangement from the West they received little help from the Western Church against these dangers, so that problems of power were able to aggravate the problem of inner spiritual distance.

(5) The Western Church and its papacy increased its power and deepened its specifically Western spirit through the agreement between the popes and the Franks under

Pippin and Pope Stephen II (752–757), then through the
defeat of the Langobards at the hand of Charlemagne during the reign of Pope Hadrian (772–795), and especially
through the coronation of Charlemagne under Pope Leo
III in the year 800. Through his military-political and
cultural-spiritual impact, Charlemagne became the father
of the Christian West. Roman spirit, the education of antiquity, and Germanic vitality entered into a new union and
produced the new world of Western Christendom. This
new culture radiated especially from the Benedictine monasteries, with full support from Charlemagne. It was from
these monasteries that the great missionizing of the Germanic north (Ansgar 801–865) as well as of the east of the
empire (Bohemia, Hungary, Bulgaria) was begun, parallel
to the great missionary effort launched in the ninth century by Byzantium into Russia (Vladimir and Olga). German emperors such as Otto I (936–973) and Henry III
(1039–1056) in some way completed the work begun by
Charlemagne. However, this development of the Western
Church led to an ever-deeper distancing from the Eastern
Church. This distance became apparent under the patriarch Photius in 837; under Pope Leo IX and the patriarch
Michael Cerularius (1054) it led to a definitive break and
mutual excommunication (cf. Mirbt, *Quellen*, 277f.).

(6) The set of problems mentioned at the beginning became especially acute in the history of the papacy of the
High Middle Ages (eleventh to thirteenth centuries). It
was a period in which the fundamental Christian ideas and
values had tremendous influence on the development of
human culture in general. This influence proceeded from
the Church. It was also a period in which the temptation
and danger of secular goods and powers for these ideas and
values was strongly felt. Even the great inner spiritual reform initiated by the Benedictine order in the eleventh
century (Cluny; Bernard of Clairvaux and the Cistercians)
showed the degree to which spiritual powers in this world
are succeptible to secular temptation (eg. Gregory VII, *dic-*

tatus papae). This problem became particularly clear under Gregory VII (1073–1085) and the fifty years of investiture controversy initiated by him (a solution was found in the Concordat of Worms in 1122). The defense of the holy places of Christianity against the powerful advance of Islam, a defense attempted in the crusades (1096–1270), showed the deeply problematic nature of the use of earthly means of power for the defense of spiritual values.

The development of a specific inner law of the Church in Bologna (after Gratian, twelfth/thirteenth century: *Corpus iuris canonici*) was hindered by the unfolding of the old pagan Roman law in the service of a Germanic concept of the state. This concept not only gave rise to the struggle between the pope and the emperor, it also led to the unfolding of the modern idea of the state since the Renaissance. Great developments took place in the Church's educational system through the founding of the universities (Paris around 1200). The excellence of medieval education is especially visible in the towering theological *summas* of the thirteenth century. Yet it did not escape the tendencies towards dissolution at the beginning of the fourteenth century (nominalism, William of Ockham). The new pastoral orders of the Dominicans and Franciscans (Augustinians and Carmelites) were of fundamental importance for ecclesial reforms, especially in the newly formed large cities, which were decisive for the great economic upturn of the Middle Ages. Yet they could not in the long run protect themselves against the secularizing influence of these cities.

The first four general Western Councils (the Lateran Councils from 1123–1215) laid the spiritual foundation for the beginning Christian age of High Scholasticism. The most comprehensive intellecutal achievement of antiquity, the work of Aristotle, was received in the newly formed universities, first in the faculty of arts, then, beginning with Albert the Great, also in the faculty of theology, and this reception gave to the Christian education of this period a uniquely broad basis. Yet this reception at the same time allowed the erroneous ideas that had already led to the downfall of antiquity to enter into the Christian world. The high Christian culture was able to maintain itself for no more than two generations (1215–1295). The struggles of the pious and powerful Pope Boniface VIII (1294–1303) were an especially clear sign of the limits set to a union between the Christian missionary task and earthly power.

The popes were thus the initiators of both the Church's rise and its decline in the West. Decline became especially clear in the exile of the Roman popes in Avignon (from Clement V to Gregory XI, 1305–1378). This period was frequently marred by fiscalism, simony, and nepotism. It also became clear in the following Western schism (1378–1417) where a Roman pope reigned in addition to a pope in Avignon, joined temporarily by two or three other "Popes." This spiritual and political division entered deeply into individual churches and ecclesial spheres as well as into the overall politics of the empire.

(7) In this time of great need two erroneous ideas were able to gain strength. They were to determine the next three centuries of the Church's history, and the papacy had to define its role in the universal Church in opposition to them. The first was the idea of a "purely spiritual Church" as developed out of nominalist thought by the Oxford theologian John Wycliffe (d. 1384). The natural consequence of this idea was a laicism that deeply contradicted the Church's inner nature, as well as the nationalism propagated by John Huss (d. 1415) in Prague (Bohemia). In union with the apocalyptic-socialist ideas of Abbot Joachim of Fiore (d. 1202) these currents led to the destruction of the image of the Church of Christ in this world as conceived by faith, to the destruction of the universalism inherent in this image. The destruction of the correct image of the Church brought about by these errors affected above all the thinking of the simple people.

More highly educated circles, on the other hand, were affected by the ideas of the new humanism, which they received with enthusiasm. In the case of Petrarch (d. 1374) these ideas remained anchored in faith as a sort of higher self-reflection. Soon, however, they increasingly cultivated and spread the spirit of pagan antiquity itself. This development was fostered by the immigration of Greek scholars into Italy and Germany after the Muslim conquest of Constantinople in 1453. After a few excellent popes (e.g., Nicholas V, 1447–1455) who stimulated the Church to new cultural achievements, the spirit of humanism spawned that series of "Renaissance popes" (Sixtus IV, 1471–1484; Innocent VIII, 1484–1492; Alexander VI, 1492–1503; Leo X, 1513–1521; Clement VII, 1523–1534) who inflicted great damage on the Church, not political damage, but spiritual damage. This damage became clear in the breaking forth of new religious movements initiated by Martin Luther (1483–1546) in Wittenberg (Germany), and by Huldrych Zwingli (d. 1531) and John Calvin (d. 1564) in Switzerland. In the name of a "reformation" of the Church, these movements led to a second great schism in the one Church of Christ and to a falling away of great areas from the papal Church of Rome in matters of doctrine and discipline.

(8) The internal and external importance of the papacy for the Church became especially clear in this period of confusions in which Luther maligned the pope as the "antichrist." The papacy became the bearer of a true new reform of the Church. The origins of this reform lie in the eleventh century (Cluny, cf. above point 6), transformed after Avignon and the schism through the reform and new organization of the Benedictine monasteries (Melk, Kastl, Bursfeld) after the provincial chapter of Petershausen (1417)[87] it gained new inner strength in confrontation with the Lutheran Reformation.

The reform Council of Constance (1414–1418) had succeeded in overcoming the papal schism. However, there was a marked gain in the strength of conciliarist ideas that wanted to place the council composed of bishops and secular powers over the decisions of the popes. The reason for these difficulties was that the understanding of the Church as a whole was still insufficiently unfolded. The development of conciliarism led to a new schism at the reform Council of Basle (1431–39).[88] Still, the pious although weak Pope Eugenius IV was able to strengthen papal power and remove the schism through his negotiations with the Greeks and because the secular powers were willing to give in. Without taking account of the immediately preceding councils, and in opposition to the illegal Council of Pisa, the Fifth Lateran Council (1512–17) continued the tradition of the medieval Roman councils. It decreed a few practical reforms but did not reach the great reform that would have been necessary.

In the same year 1517 Martin Luther published his 95 theses in Wittenberg, which marked the beginning of the so-called Reformation. He demanded a council without the pope, on German soil, principally convened by the secular guilds and powers. This council was to achieve a reform, not in the first place of the Church's life, but of its doctrine. The power of the old conciliarism and Luther's conciliarist understanding, in addition to the difficult political situation in Europe and the new political power of Lutheranism in the Smalcaldic League of 1531, were the reasons why the Church's new reform Council of Trent could begin only in 1545 (it lasted until 1564). Despite the continuing inner damage of the Renaissance, this Council showed the great interior importance and power of the papacy. The Church's doctrinal traditions could be clarified and confirmed by the newly acquired knowledge of Scripture and essential reforms of ecclesial and Christian life were realized. The spirit of the Baroque was born, beginning in Italy and Spain under the leadership of the Jesuit order, founded by Ignatius of Loyola (d. 1556). It was an expression of joy in the Church's faith, of the power of its faith, and it gave new strength to all aspects of the culture of the Catholic West.

However, the secular lay culture of the Renaissance, the individualism of humanism, and the power and wealth of the growing cities with their bourgeoisie had succeeded in definitively dissolving the unified culture of the Middle Ages. Even the Christian humanism of the seventeenth century (Francis de Sales, and Vincent de Paul) was unable to lead the Church, burdened as it was by the politics and wealth of the ecclesiastical state, to become again the leading spiritual power.

(9) The time of great transitions between the Council of Trent and Vatican I is characterized by tremendous spiritual battles, which we must sketch at least by certain key phrases, in order to give some idea of the work and life of the popes and thus of the form of the idea of the papacy in this time. The political life of this period was determined by the development of absolute rule and nationalism. Its economic life was shaped by the various forms of capitalism and mercantilism, of economic liberalism and socialism. The spiritual force, however, that carried the seventeenth and eighteenth centuries of the West consists of tendencies usually summarized by the term "Enlightenment." The fundamental element of the Enlightenment worldview is the isolation and absolutizing of single powers, values and realities which should be seen and lived as a unity in order for the human person, as seen in the Christian understanding of the world, to find a true place and orientation in the world. What became thus determinant for the human understanding and relation to the world, was a series of "isms": rationalism and sensualism, individualism and socialism, liberalism and determinism, positivism and skepticism, naturalism and deism, pietism and atheism. In this sketch we cannot unfold the fragmentary and erroneous nature of these "isms." The end of this spiritual development is the historical event of the French Revolution (1789). It signaled the collapse of these spiritual confusions as well as the end of the

remnants of the medieval system of the world and thus the necessity of a new orientation and foundation of social and economic relations.

Napoleon was the first to call the preceding attempts at mastering reality "ideologies" estranged from reality. Through the extension of his power and the annexation of large territories he brought about the so-called "secularization" of the German countries. For the Church this secularization was the greatest loss of political and economic power. It destroyed great spiritual goods of old monastic libraries and works of ecclesiastical art. Nevertheless, it also freed the Church from secular baggage and thus aided the great new religious and social initiatives of the nineteenth century.

In the spiritual battles of the Enlightenment, the Roman Church had remained on the defensive, partly because of its own political and economic entanglement in this world. This entanglement was visible especially in Italy, where the Church and the ecclesiastical state stood in the way of the formation of the new Italian national state. Yet precisely the power and the difficulties of the ecclesiastical state helped the Church to focus more clearly on the papacy in its importance for the Church universal in the spiritual battles of the time. This development led to the Vatican I definitions of the pope's primacy of jurisdiction and of his infallibility in matters of faith and morals. Pope Pius IX (1846–1878), who was pious but weak in character, had to, and was able to, confirm these fundamental doctrines about the papacy and to sustain the loss of the ecclesiastical state in 1870. In this way he opened the way for the Church into a completely new time and development. Thus the turn of events in 1870 brought the fundamental mystery of Christianity to expression in the papacy and in the Church. The loss of the ecclesiastical state, which had been built up and fought for through 1200 years, opened a new period for the inner Church, a period shaped by great popes.

(10) The Church had become powerless in this world

and the pope a prisoner in his Vatican palace. Yet under Pope Leo XIII (1878–1903), who was open to the world and decisive in his actions, the Church could dedicate itself in a new way to the burning social questions by developing and proclaiming the Christian social teaching vis-à-vis the liberalism and socialism of that period. It was able to take the first steps towards a theology that could take the offensive against opposed ideas of the modern age. His pious successor Pius X (1903–1914) worked for the inner renewal of the Church and the world through his decrees on communion and the renewal of canon law as well as Church music. His motto was *omnia instaurare in Christo.*

The highly educated Benedict XV (1914–1922) attempted in vain to act as a peacemaker in the confusions of World War I (1914–1918). Through his noble character he could at least defuse the Italian situation. The prudent and energetic Pius XI (1922–1939) negotiated the Lateran treaties, which clarified the political position of the popes in the new ecclesiastical state and integrated them in appropriate fashion in the great concert of world powers. The *"Reichskonkordat"* of 1933, of which Hitler made a farce, allowed significant operations of personal assistance and prevented much of the destructive activity of politicians in this time of extreme lawlessness.

In the years of World War II (1939–1945), which shook the whole world and brought Europe to the edge of a precipice, and in the first few years of reconstruction, the Church was led by a pope of extraordinary greatness of spirit and heart, Pius XII (Eugenio Pacelli, the *pastor angelicus*, 1939–1958). Like no one before him he knew how to make the Church respected and heard on the international spiritual scene. The ascendancy of the Church as a spiritual power in this world, which began in 1870, reached in some way its peak in his pontificate. The Church was acknowledged in a new way as a "power," but the inner estrangement of the people, for whom this Church exists, could not be prevented. Not even five years later, many accused the Church, probably not with full justification, of triumphalism, a triumphalism that was no longer able to proclaim in a credible way the path of the crucified Lord in this world.

(11) In this time God sent his Church a pope of quite different style (in the conclave his election appeared to be the attempt to avoid an impasse), John XXIII (1958–1963), of humblest origin and almost childlike piety, who wanted to gain the new world for the Church more through goodness than through the truth. Although no one had dared to hope it would happen, he proclaimed and convened a new Council, the Second Vatican Council (1962–1965). In his opening speech to the Council, which for the first time in the history of the Church brought together all bishops and prelates of the Church (2300), he charged the Church not merely to preserve the truth of the Christian tradition, but to proclaim it in the new world in such a way that the questions of the present would be taken into account (*aggiornamento*) and that it would be understood by people of our time. The Council should "make a step ahead towards a penetration of doctrine and the formation of conscience" by distinguishing "the substance of the old doctrine of the treasure of faith from its formulation in a certain linguistic dress." In addition he charged the Church, understood as the "mother of all," to speak in the spirit of the Bible, with pastoral intent and in an ecumenical spirit that takes into account the other Christian churches and the other religions.

The Council attempted to fulfill these tasks under Pope Paul VI (1963–1978), and the Church has taken on a new face. The reform of the liturgy, the newly formed councils and commissions, the new openness in missionary methods, openness in relation to science and the world, the abrogation of the bans of excommunication of 1054 in the historic meeting with the patriarch Athenagoras, the trips of the pope in his service of peace and dialogue, his ecumenical activity, and his hotly debated encyclicals formed merciful and prudent bridges in the ruptures and confusions connected with every council and with every new beginning.

The new pope, John Paul II (since 1978), who had for decades lived and worked as a bishop under Communist rule (the first Pole on the papal throne), has attempted to realize the spirit of the Council in this world, especially the spirit of the final Constitution on the Church in the Modern World. He has done so through his "pilgrimages" into all areas of the universal Church, through his numerous great speeches, which always aim at the Christian person and the Christian world belonging to that person. May the attempt on his life, ordered as it was by a regime opposed to God and the Church, not end his activity, which he began like a conquest of the world. May it perhaps also show more clearly that, besides activity, suffering is a basic power for all effectiveness in the kingdom of Christ.

This brief sketch of the transformation of the idea of the papacy in the course of the centuries has perhaps made us sense something of the importance of the office of Peter and the pope. We must now take a closer look at the two tasks of the papacy stressed by Vatican I, the task of ruling the universal Church and the task of preserving the one message of Christ (the primacy of jurisdiction and infallibility), as well as the relation between primacy and episcopacy. In this way we will see the papacy in the framework of the totality of the Church in a way that it can be understood today.

5. THE PRIMACY OF JURISDICTION

In the preceding sections we have laid out the foundations of the papal office in Scripture and tradition and the development of the papacy in the first five centuries. Now we must draw the conclusions from these premises for the specific doctrine of the pope's primacy of jurisdiction. We will first look at the pope's characteristic titles, at their foundation and their history, then analyze the images found in the history of the papacy, the images that characterize the pope's special position as the successor of Peter, and finally approach a clearer understanding of the fundamental biblical words of Christ to Peter by following the history of theology, including the teaching of Vatican I and concluding with the aspects added by Vatican II.

a) Titles of the Office

Titles often have a long history and thus point to changes in the understanding of an office. Let us look only at the most important of the pope's titles in their dogmatic importance.

(1) In the Roman sphere the most important title is *summus pontifex*. It derives from the ancient Roman title *pontifex maximus* which referred (after about the third century B.C.) to the *pontifex* highest in rank, the president and representative of the college of *pontifices* (i.e., those who prepare the way in religious matters), who had to take care of the public and the private cult (the cult of the gods and of the dead). The most noble citizens of the state strove for this honorable office until the emperor Augustus took it for himself, from which point on, it remained linked with the emperor. It was only in A.D. 383 that the emperor Gratian gave up this title, urged by Pope Damasus and Bishop Ambrose of Milan. It was a sign of the disappearance of the spirit of pagan Rome. The title was transferred to the popes and this transfer was formalized in the course of the fifth century. Still, other bishops held the title too until it was reserved for the popes in the Renaissance.[89]

(2) Also the title *vicarius Christi* was generally applied to bishops in the patristic age, with preference, however, for Peter because Christ had given to him the universal pastoral office (John 21,15–17). Since the High Middle

Ages it has been taken exclusively as a papal title, at times with the variations *vicarius Petri* or *vicarius Dei.*[90]

(3) Already at an early period, clerics, bishops, and popes (Damasus, Leo I) called themselves *servus Dei* (following Rom 1,1; Phil 1,1; 2 Pet 1,1). Augustine once called himself *servus Christi servorumque Christi,* a servant of Christ and of the servants of Christ (PL 33,494). The formula *servus servorum Christi* was introduced into the papal titles by Gregory I (d. 604). Gregory probably wanted to respond to the title "ecumenical patriarch" claimed by Constantinople.[91]

(4) Despite Matthew 23,9 ("call no man your father on earth") "papa" (Greek *pappas*) became, at least after Constantine, a title for bishops, abbots, and patriarchs in the East (following probably 1 Cor 4,15 and Phlm 11). In the fourth century this title appeared for the first time in the West (*sub Liberio papa*) and since the fifth century it has been given more and more exclusively to the pope.

(5) As the Church grew, its organization had to be worked out in more detail. (a) Episcopal sees tied to a specific place were formed in the second century, at which point one can speak of a monarchical episcopate (cf. Ignatius of Antioch and the lists of bishops compiled at the end of the century). (b) Several episcopal sees (cities) were united under one archbishop or exarch. The exarch's see was chosen on the basis of the see's status due to its foundation by an apostle or an apostle's disciple, or due to the missionary, and in certain cases the political, importance of the city. (c) Following Constantine's division of the empire into administrative provinces, the Church was subdivided into provinces or metropolises, each of them comprising a certain number of exarchs (cf. Council of Nicaea, A.D. 325, canons 6 and 7). (d) Corresponding to the Palestinian institutions of the patriarchate (after A.D. 70 under the Davidide Gamaliel II and his son until the abolition of the institution by the Romans in 415) the idea of apostolic fatherhood gave rise to the patriarchates of Alexandria,

Rome, and Antioch, all of them founded by Peter or his disciple Mark (cf. Mirbt, *Quellen*, 142f., no. 314). Jerusalem—the place of Golgotha, the Church of the Holy Sepulchre, and the Cenacle—was also a scene of Peter's activity. In 336 Constantinople transferred the relics of Andrew from Achaia (Church of the Apostles!) as well as the relics of Paul's disciple Luke, since Andrew had probably worked in the area in which Constantinople was built in 312.[92]

In terms of these titles, the pope is "patriarch of the West, metropolitan and bishop of Rome." However, these titles are secondary in comparison with his primacy over the whole Church.

b) *The Pope's Primacy over the Whole Church*

The pope's primacy over the whole Church, as we showed above, is founded upon the succession of Peter. It is a unique primacy, just as there was only one Peter in the college of apostles. In order to make the pope's claim to primacy theologically intelligible we must analyze the images which speak about this primacy. Let us look at the four images present in Christ's words of promise and call addressed to Peter.

(I) THE IMAGE OF THE ROCK "You are Peter and on this rock I will build my Church." As indicated by the context of this saying in Matthew 16,18, and as stressed by the fathers, especially Chrysostom, Ambrose, and Augustine, Peter receives this promise as a response to the faith given to him by the Father and his confession of this faith in Jesus the Messiah. "You are the Christ [the Messiah, the anointed], the Son of the living God" (Matt 16,16; Mark 8,29; Luke 9,20). The reason for the promise lies thus in the special revelation Peter received from the Father in heaven (Matt 16,17: "For flesh and blood has not revealed this to you, but my Father who is in heaven") and in the fact that Peter publicly confesses this faith as the spokesman of the college of apostles. "The revelation as well as its confession will be unshakeable. They will not fall into uncertainty" (Jacob of Batnae, d. 521).[93] The content of the promise is likewise twofold: Peter shall be the rock-foundation of God's temple in which God's community (*Qahal, ekklēsia*) gathers, and this rock-foundation shall assure the Churches solidity and endurance ("and the powers of death shall not prevail against it" Matt 16,18). These words of Jesus guarantee "that the Church, which Jesus will build upon Peter as the foundation, will never succumb to the power of death, i.e., it is promised imperishable permanence as long as the time of this world lasts. As one can conclude from the logical connection among the various parts of the promise, this imperishability and indestructibility has its reason in the fact that Simon Peter is its foundation."[94]

In the interest of a clear dogmatic position, let us say a few words about the numerous questions that have been raised about this text especially since the Enlightenment and also in recent times in the name of ecumenical dialogue. First, a merely verbal interpretation of the definitions of 1870 is today often simply placed alongside the confused pluralism of exegetical and theological opinions. Two paths are then often suggested to mediate between these extremes: a "theological" path, which is supposed to reconcile the word of revelation, modern exegesis, the experience of faith, and the personal experience of life; and a "pastoral" path, which seeks a solution in an open dialogue between the teaching Church and the listening Church. The following must be said concerning these suggestions: They are useless if one does not clearly distinguish between faith and knowledge, and if one leaves aside the hierarchical Church with its magisterium and pastoral office in order to find the truths of faith in a free democratic space, under the supposition that these truths will create and carry forward a new understanding of the Church.

Second, in terms of literary analysis and redaction criticism, the Matthean text may appear at this point as an "amplification" of the Marcan text. However, this assertion does not justify the judgment that the amplification is a mere work of the evangelist or a creation of the developing theology of the early community. Not only the first version in Mark, but also the text of the other Synoptics and evangelists, is, according to the Church's understanding of Scripture, revelation. The above judgment on the Matthean "amplification" would be mere Enlightenment thinking with a fixation on facticity which has lost a sense that spiritual growth takes place through the "remembering" of truths and realities, a remembering that becomes possible only by understanding them more deeply. Enlightenment thinking is unable to do justice even to secular historiography. Much less can it achieve an appropriate grasp of truths like the truths of faith, which have a certain fullness of content and value.

Third, in terms of source criticism and form criticism, the following aspects of this text can be stressed: The macarism Matthew 16,17 ("Blessed are you, Simon Bar Jona!") addressed to Peter corresponds to Jesus' cry of praise "I thank thee, Father, Lord of heaven and earth, that thou hast hidden these things from the wise and understanding and revealed them to babes" (Matt 11,25–27; cf. Luke 10,21f.), which refers to the apostles in general. The apostles, and Peter in a special way as their spokesman, appear as the privileged witnesses of Christ, the Messiah, on the basis of a special revelation by the Father, who alone knows the Son and can reveal the Son to us.

The whole context of Matthew 16,16–20 suggests that Simon Bar Jona received the symbolical name (and title) *Kepha* = Peter (*Petros*). Jesus does not use this name at any other point in the Gospels, while Matthew uses it from the very beginning (4,18; 8,14; 10,2 in contrast to Mark 1,16) as does Luke. John reports in 1,42 that Jesus promised Peter this name at their first meeting. According to J.

Blank, one can conclude from the connection between the name and its interpretation in Matthew 16,18 that both were formed in the post-Easter Jewish Christian community, because Peter, according to Galatians 2,7 belongs to that community, not to the pagan Christian community as suggested by Acts. This hypothesis, however, is without any proof.

By "my Church" Jesus probably means the Church as a whole (Matt 16,18), not a local Church as in Matthew 18,17 (cf. Rom 16,16). The image of the permanence of the Church due to its rock foundation fits Matthew 7,24–27 (the prudent man who builds his house on rock). The saying about the "gates of Hades" (Matt 16,18; cf. Qumran 1QH6,24: "the gates of death") probably does not refer to "the wicked powers" (H. von Campenhausen; J. Jeremias, *ThW* 6, 923–27) that dwell in Hades, but to the place of perdition and death itself. Some fathers thought "the gates of Hades" referred to heresies. Thus Epiphanius (d. 403) writes, "The gates of Hades signify the heresies and the heresiarchs. For in every way faith has been made secure in him [Peter], who received the keys of the kingdom of heaven and who loosens on earth and binds in heaven. In him all the subtle questions of our faith are clarified" (*Ankyratus*, 9). The saying of Peter as the Church's rock-foundation has been clearly maintained in the tradition at least since the third century. Cyprian (d. 258) already writes, "For to Peter, upon whom the Lord built the Church, and to whom her unity goes back" he gave first the power to bind and to loose (*Ep.* 73,7). In his poem on Matthew 16,16ff. Jacob of Batnae (d. 521) says on this point, "When he began the construction of the house, he [Christ] chose Kephas, laid him down as a foundation and gave him as a wedding gift the *charisma* to defeat death and Satan." Although Augustine repeatedly mentions Christ himself as the rock-foundation when discussing Matthew 16,18 (cf. *In Jo Sermo* 124,5) he never excludes Peter as the rock-foundation.[95]

(2) THE IMAGE OF THE KEEPER OF THE KEYS Matthew 16,18–20 forms a unity of meaning with respect to the question of the "primacy of Peter" (the pope). This unity should not be a hindrance but a stimulus for meditating on and explaining the specific meaning of the three images individually and in their interconnection. The first phrase, that of the rock-foundation, is quite clear in its essentials. However, the second and the third phrase contain considerable difficulties, already in the question whether each of them has a distinct meaning or whether they mean the same thing. At least since the studies of K. Adam[96] it is advisable, also from a Catholic perspective, to look at the two phrases separately.

Let us first analyze the second phrase, "I will give you the keys of the kingdom of heaven" (Matt 16,19a). Apart from the apocryphal Greek Apocalypse of Baruch (11), which seems to have undergone a Christian redaction at this point, there is no place in the Old Testament that speaks about "keys of the kingdom of heaven." In the New Testament, the term "keys" is generally used in a metaphorical sense. The passages about keys of heaven (Luke 4,25; Rev 11,6) or about the "keys of the underworld" as the dungeon of the evil spirits (Rev 9,1; 20, 1–3) or "the keys of death and Hades" (Rev 1,18; Christ has the power to lead the dead to resurrection) are all not relevant to our passage. Somewhat closer is the reprimand addressed to the scribes and Pharisees that they "shut the kingdom of heaven against men" (Matt 23,13). According to Luke 11,52 they do so by usurping the scriptural message of the kingdom of God for themselves alone or by disfiguring it in their preaching, thus preventing others from entering the true kingdom of God. Even closer to our text is the idea of the eschatological "key of David" possessed by the exalted Christ (Rev 3,7; cf. Isa 22,22). In the light of this passage, the saying about the keys given to Peter would mean that Christ wanted to give to him, and through and in him to the Church built upon him, the key to God's eschatologi-

cal royal rule. Handing over the keys is thus the appointment to a fullness of authority. The keeper of the keys
possesses, on the one hand, the power to dispose of things
(e.g., of the contents of a treasury; "Every scribe who has
been trained for the kingdom of heaven is like a house-
holder who brings out of his treasure what is new and what
is old," Matt 13,52). On the other hand, he has authority to
permit or deny entry (cf. Rev. 3,7: "who opens and no one
shall shut, who shuts and no one opens").

What is the object of this authority? What is at issue is
the communication of God's gifts of grace in Christ and
the judgment about the acceptance or refusal of these divine favors by members of the Church of Christ (cf. John
20,23). The offer of grace is made in the proclamation of
the effective word of God (Isa 55,10f.; 1 Thess 2,13), in the
effective signs of the sacraments, and in the special form of
the forgiveness of sins. In Christian art since the fifth century, Peter has been identified exclusively by the attribute
of the keys.

(3) THE IMAGE OF THE POWER TO BIND AND TO
LOOSE "And [this word is missing in some manuscripts]
whatever [hoean] you bind on earth shall [in the sense of
"ought," the meaning of the Aramaic future] be bound in
heaven, and whatever you loose on earth shall be loosed in
heaven"(Matt 16,19b.). The first question is what is meant
by binding and loosing.

Lightfoot and Wünsche, in fact even Zahn and Wellhausen, interpret this phrase in the light of the narrow rabbinical exegesis of
binding and loosing (declaring as permitted or forbidden by doctrinal decision, laying an obligation on a person or removing it).
Köhler and Heitmüller even interpret Matthew's binding and
loosing in terms of ancient magical practice. They overlook that
Matthew 16,19 belongs in the context, neither of rabbinical nor of
hellenistic, but of Christian thinking.[97]

Adam sees in this passage a clearly anti-pharisaic tendency
(similar to that in the cry of praise, Matt 11,25). "The anti-

pharisaic tendency of the Lord's message of salvation cul-
minates in Jesus' handing authority over to Peter."[98] "Peter's new authority with regard to salvation will 'bind and
loose' differently than the old authority of the scribes and
Pharisees. It will 'loose' from superfluous human norms
and 'bind' into the right spirit of the law which is the Spirit
of Christ."[99]

The concepts 'heaven' (Matt 16,19b) and 'kingdom of heaven'
(Matt 16,19a) differ only inasmuch as 'heaven' means God and his
heavenly world as such, while 'reign of heaven' refers to God's
heavenly glory which grasps the human person. The image of the
keys of heaven as well as the formula of binding and loosing in
heaven do not express 'earthly' decisions by Peter, but 'heavenly'
decisions. They express his importance for every believer with
respect to the kingdom of heaven. . . . The believers, therefore,
have an obligation to submit to his decrees as they submit to the
commandments of God himself. They are the path into the kingdom of heaven.[100]

In this light one can see the inner connection between
these words of Jesus in Matthew 16,18ff. and his words to
the apostles in Matthew 18,18 (cf. Matt 18,1; ThW 3,751)
and in a wider sense with his words to the apostles in John
20,23. Peter is addressed, not personally as an individual
apostle, but as the Church's foundation, as the first of the
apostles upon whom the Church is founded (Eph 2,20; Rev
21,14).

Also the salvation of individual Christians is contained
in their membership in the Church. Consequently, this
"binding and loosing" in connection with the "power of
the keys" is in a special way related to the salvation of the
individual in the Church, partly with respect to sin and
grace in the power to "forgive sins" (John 20,23). Sin is
here seen above all in its relation to fellow Christians (fellow man: commandments four to ten) (Matt 18,15–18).
These sins, which are committed against a brother or sister and through them against God (cf. Matt 19,40–42;
5,23f), are subject to the Palestinian-Syrian procedure of

exclusion from the community, which is preceded by a threefold disciplinary process. The first step is a private, one-to-one reprimand, the second a reprimand in the presence of witnesses, and the third a reprimand before the whole community with its leader. Only then should the step of exclusion be taken, a step that can be reversed as soon as the sinner repents (cf. Tit 3,10; *ThW* 3, 752). Since Tertullian (*Pud.* 21) and Origen (*Comm. in Matt.* 12,14), there has been a unanimous interpretation of the power "to bind and to loose" as applying also to the forgiveness of sins by excommunication and reconciliation (cf. Büchsel, *ThW* 2, 60).

In this way the three phrases of Christ's promise in Matthew 16,18f. produce a clear image of the importance of the Petrine primacy for the whole of the Church and for each individual Christian.

(4) THE IMAGE OF THE SHEPHERD Among the images that clarify the primacy of Peter (and the pope) there is also the image used by Christ in John 21,15–19. This text can be seen as a further interpretation and fulfillment of Christ's saying in Matthew 16,18f. (We have already introduced it above.) Peter is not directly called shepherd, as he is called "rock" in Matthew 16,18. Yet the threefold exhortation, "Feed my sheep (lambs)" clearly projects the image of the shepherd.

This image has a great history in Scripture. Let us look at some elements of ths history. In the Old Testament, God himself is the "shepherd of Israel" (Psalm 23,1–4; Ezek 34,11.22). The Old Testament promises call the Davidic king of the end times "shepherd" (Ezek 34,23f.; 37,24). Jesus applies this image to himself and to his messianic task (John 10,1–18; cf. Luke 15,1–7; Matt 18,12f.; Mark 14,27). Heb 13,20 calls him "the great shepherd of the sheep." Paul himself does not use this image for Jesus. 1 Peter, on the other hand, speaks of Christ as "the shepherd and guardian of your souls" (1 Pet 2,25) and as "the chief shepherd" (1 Pet 5,4), and with certain echoes of Ezek

34,1–22 it develops the image of the elders of the Church as shepherds. The "pastors [shepherds] and teachers" mentioned in Eph 4,11 next to apostles, prophets, and evangelists are probably of subordinate rank.

The pastoral commission given to Peter in John 21,15–19 is quite special. The whole flock, the totality of sheep (and lambs), is entrusted to him. This totality expresses the unity of the flock as well as the prominent position of Peter in it (in comparison with the other apostles). For this reason Cyprian (d. 258) writes, "He builds his Church on him, and although he gave to all the apostles the same power after his resurrection [John 20,22f.], nevertheless, by the word of his power, he ordained that the origin of this unity would derive from him [Peter]. Certainly, the other apostles too were what Peter was, furnished with the same share in honor and power [a reference to the episcopal system?]. But the beginning proceeds from unity, in order that the Church of Christ be proven as one" (*De Unit. Eccl.*, 4). This statement is especially significant because in early Judaism the earthly shepherds "were seen as notorious robbers and deceivers" (*TWNT* 6,487f.). It also becomes obvious that the New Testament uses the title of shepherd only in an extended sense.

The author of John 21 connects Peter's appointment as the unique shepherd of the whole flock with the prediction of Peter's death, in contrast to the prediction of long life for the beloved disciple. The connection is expressed in Christ's command, "Follow me!" (John 21,19.22). Perhaps the author points to Peter's martyrdom as an accomplished fact. Still, the text expresses an awareness that the higher pastoral office demands also a stricter following of Christ. In his commentary on this passage, Augustine unfolds the selfless love of the highest shepherd for the flock entrusted to him in a contrast with 1 Timothy 1,7 and 2 Timothy 3,1–9 (vices of the end times).

This [martyrdom] was the end of that betrayer and lover, presumptuous in reliance on himself, fallen by denying his Lord, purified by weeping, tried in profession, crowned by suffering. This was his end when he died in perfect love of his Lord, having claimed earlier with inappropriate haste that he would die for him. Strengthened by Christ's resurrection he did what he promised hastily. . . . Those who shepherd Christ's sheep and consider them their own rather than Christ's prove that they love themselves, not Christ. They are led by the desire of glory, rule or gain [1 Pet 5,2–4], not by the love of obeying, of helping, and of pleasing God.

Augustine mentions the love of self as the root of all the vices of the evil shepherds and continues:

Especially those who lead Christ's flock must guard themselves from this vice, so that they do not seek what is their own, but rather what is Christ's, and do not misuse those for whom Christ's blood has been poured out to serve their own desires. In him who pastures Christ's sheep, love must increase to such spiritual ardour that it overcomes even the natural fear of death which leads us to resist death even though we want to live with Christ [Phil 1,25]. . . . The good shepherd gave his life for his sheep [John 10,11.18] and he prepared for himself many martyrs among his sheep. Those to whom he entrusted his sheep to be pastured, i.e., to be taught and guided, must they not, therefore, all the more fight for truth to the point of death and the shedding of blood? Since he himself went before us with the example of his suffering, who would not see that the shepherds must join him, all the more because so many sheep even did so? For also the shepherds are sheep in the one flock under the one shepherd. All of us he made his sheep. because he too, in order to suffer for us, has become a sheep [cf. John 1,29; 1 Pet 1,18f.]. (In Joh. sermo 123)

The Jewish image of the shepherd originally contained primarily the element of care for body and life (cf. "shepherd of souls" 1 Pet 2,25). In the second century, beginning with the struggles against Gnosticism, the Hellenistic element of instruction became more pronounced (cf. Aberkios Inscription, Z 3–6). The decisive element of the image, however, is the following: Although the New Testament image of the shepherd does not mean a powerful

ruler, in contrast to the secular use of this image in antiquity, it still expresses great authority and responsibility.
This is clear, for example, in the words addressed by Paul
to the bishops (episkopoi) of Asia Minor during his farewell in Miletus. "Take heed to yourselves and to all the
flock, in which the Holy Spirit has made you overseers
[episkopoi], to care for the church of God which he obtained with his own blood" (Acts 20,28). The same thing is
expressed in the exhortation 1 Pet 5,2–4, "Tend the flock
of God that is your charge . . . not as domineering over
those in your charge but being examples to the flock."
What is here said of the bishops in relation to their
churches applies in a special way to Peter in relation to the
one entire community of Christ and of God.

(5) PETER'S UNIQUE POSITION IN THE CHURCH
The four images used by Christ in addressing Peter show
his special position in the Church as a whole and thereby,
not personally, but due to his office, his special position in
the college of apostles. In the subsequent period this special position was clarified more and more through the
phrases "rock of the Church" and "head of the apostles."
Cyprian (d. 258) stressed that Peter, "who was the first to
be chosen by the Lord, and upon whom he built his
Church" (Ep. 71,4; 73,7; De Pat. 9) did not insist on his
preeminence (Gal 2,11–21) but let himself be corrected in
all patience by Paul. Origen (d. 254) calls Peter, the rock,
"the first fruit [aparchē, cf. Rom 16,5; 1 Cor 15,5] of the
apostles" (Contr. Cels. II, 65). Cyril of Jerusalem (d. 386)
speaks of Peter as "the preeminent head and the first
leader of the apostles [koryphaiōtatos kai prōtostates tōn
apostolōn]" (Cat. II,19; XI,3; XVII,27). Epiphanius of Salamis (d. 403) calls him again and again "the prince, the
first of the apostles [archēgos, koryphaiōtatos]" (Ancyr.
9,11,34; Haer. 51,17; 59,7). Similarly Chrysostom (d. 407)
calls him "the first [koryphaios] of the choir, the rock
[kephas] of the apostles, the head [kephalē] of this brother-

hood and the prince [*koryphaios*] of the whole inhabited world" (*In illud Hoc scitote*, 4). Augustine (d. 430) speaks of Peter as "the representative of the unity of the college of apostles [*tamquam personam gerens ipsius unitatis*]" (*In Joh.* 118,4). He uses the term "primacy," as in the following text. "The Church, which is founded upon Christ, received from him the keys of the kingdom of heaven, i.e., the power to bind and to loose sins. For what the Church is in a proper sense in Christ, Peter is in a symbolical sense in the *petra*. In this symbolical meaning the *petra* signifies Christ and Peter signifies the Church." "Because of the primacy of his apostleship, Peter represents this Church (which forgives sins) in symbolical universality [*Cuius ecclesiae Petrus Apostolus propter apostolatus sui primatum gerebat figurata generalitate personam*]. As for himself, he was by nature a human being, by grace he was a Christian, by more abundant grace an apostle, in fact the first apostle. But when he was told, 'I will give you the keys of the kingdom of heaven' . . . he symbolically represented the whole Church [*universam significabat ecclesiam*]" (*In Joh.* 124,5).

A theological highpoint which could only be disfigured or clarified was reached by such assertions when the great spiritual and political personality of Leo I (440–461) succeeded to the see of Peter. His image of the papacy is not theory but the image of his own life and activity. He unfolds this image above all in the four sermons given at the anniversary of his installation on the chair of Peter (*Sermo* 2–5, summarized in *Sermo* 83). Let us summarize the most important statements contained in these sermons. "He [Christ] . . . gave us helpful support in the apostle Peter and this support will never be absent from his work. The solidity of this foundation on which the huge building of the Church is built remains unshaken, however great the burden of the temple that rests on it may be. For this strength of faith which was recognized in the prince of apostles propagates itself. Just as what Peter believed

about Christ remains for ever, so also what Christ instituted in Peter will stand for ever" (*Sermo* 3,2). "In this way
the Lord calls him [Peter] rock and foundation, he appoints
him keeper of the gate of heaven, and judge about the
remission or nonremission of sins, so that his judgment
will be valid also in heaven. In these mysterious titles we
should recognize how intimately he is linked with Christ.
He thus performs his office now with even greater perfection and success. He fulfills all his duties and all his cares
and tasks in him and with him [Christ] who so distinguished him" (*Sermo* 3,3). "Most beloved, one celebrates
today's feast with true devotion as one sees and honors in
my lowly person the one who for ever unites in himself the
cares of all shepherds with the care for the sheep entrusted
to him and who loses nothing of his dignity, even in an
unworthy successor." This is an anti-Donatist statement.
Leo continues, "[Peter] is not only the ancestor of this see,
but also the *primas* of all bishops" (*Sermo* 3,4; cf. *"Petrus
princeps apostolici ordinis,"* Sermo 82,3; *"princeps est
episcopalis coronae,"* Ep. 11). "In the whole world only
Peter is chosen to be the head of all peoples called [by
Christ], of all apostles and all fathers of the Church. And
so, despite the many priests and despite the many shepherds in the people of God, only Peter is the true leader of
all who have, in the first place, Christ as their leader. A
great and admirable share in its power, most beloved, did
divine grace give to this man. And although according to
the will [of that grace] the other heads of the Church share
many things with him, it is always through him that grace
bestows everything on others. . . . Thus he who holds
the first rank among the apostles is the first to confess his
faith" (Matt 16,17f.). Leo interprets Jesus' response as follows: "Just as my father manifested my divinity to you, so
I will proclaim to you your privilege, for you are Peter.
Although I am the unshakeable rock [Matt 7,24f.], the cornerstone [Eph 2,20] who unites the two into one [Eph 2,14],
the foundation apart from which one can lay no other [1

Cor 3,11], still, you too are a rock, because you have been made strong through my strength and because through this communion you have come to share in my personal power. . . . The noble building of my Church, which will reach all the way to heaven, will rise on the foundation of this faith" (*Sermo* 4,2). On the keeping of keys Leo says, "This power is given to Peter in particular [in Matt 18,18 it is given to all the apostles] because above all leaders of the Church there stands the person of Peter. Peter's privilege holds also for his successors whenever they pronounce a judgment, filled with his sense of justice. . . . In Peter all are strengthened [Luke 22,31f.] and the assistance of divine grace is regulated in such a way that the strength which Christ gives to Peter passes through Peter to the apostles . . . because he gave such authority to him whom he chose as head of the whole Church" (*Sermo* 4,3–4).

Leo's statements can and must still be understood in a theologically correct way. One can see this in a theologically and humanly great letter that Gregory I (d. 604) wrote to John, the bishop of Constantinople, who had taken the title "ecumenical bishop." "Has not the venerable Council of Chalcedon, as your brotherhood knows, honored the bishops of this [Roman] see, which I serve in God's providence, with the title 'ecumenical bishop'? Not one, however, wanted to be called by this name, not one used this name, so that it would not seem as if he wanted to deny all his brothers the honor by claiming it only for himself" (Ewald-Hartmann, V,44). Still, "the care for the whole Church and the leadership is committed [to Peter]; *cura totius ecclesiae et principatus committitur*" (V,20).

c) The Development of the Doctrine of the Pope's Primacy of Jurisdiction from the Sixth Century to Vatican II

Several points become clear in the light of the above. (1) Christ entrusted the building up of his Church to the twelve apostles (Matt 28,20: the missionary command and Matt 18,18: the power to bind and to loose). (2) Among these apostles he uniquely distinguished Peter so that his Church might endure. He made him the rock-foundation of the Church (Matt 16,18); to him he entrusted the power of the keys (Matt 16,19); and him alone he appointed as the shepherd of his whole Church (John 21,15–19). (3) Since earliest times this Petrine office has been connected by tradition with the Roman episcopal see. In addition, Peter's grave is in Rome, which signifies the permanent presence and effectiveness of the prince of the apostles in the Roman see. Since earlies times (1 Clement, Pope Stephen, Tertullian, Cyprian, Pope Victor), the words of Jesus to Peter have for this reason been claimed also for the bishops who succeeded Peter on the see of Rome. (4) Concerning Peter's relation to his fellow apostles, the tradition contains only Jesus' saying in Luke 22,32 ("turn to your brothers and strengthen them"). As we will show in the context of the discussion of infallibility, this exhortation applies to faith.

For this reason, the development of the doctrine of primacy, especially since the early Middle Ages, focused on the question of Peter's relation to his fellow apostles, of the pope's relation to the bishops. Let us sketch this development a little, since an understanding of the doctrines defined at the First Vatican Council depends upon an understanding of this development. Of great importance was the political and the related economic and social development of the Roman episcopal see after Constantine. This development was occasioned by the development of the Western Roman empire: by the absence of the Western Roman emperor from Rome (his residence was in Ravenna); by the weakness of the last Western Roman emperors and their eventual downfall; and by the advance of the Germanic peoples and their rule in Italy. For the bishops of Rome, whose Church had grown above all from the blood of martyrs, these developments were not only an occasion but a call, the call of a historic moment to political action in the world in the service of the Church.

This action culminated in two events. (1) The coronation of Charlemagne in 800 by Leo III (795–816) constituted a new Western Rome" in the "Holy Roman Empire of German Nation." (2) The development of this new empire under successive imperial houses necessarily led to conflicts between the papacy and the emperor. For in this arrangement neither the Church nor the empire was absolute. They were supported by regional relations of power and possession (after Gregory the Great even the *patrimonium Petri* developed step by step into the ecclesiastical state). The emperor, as signified in his coronation by the Church, derived his power from God, just as the Church argued for its worldly power on the basis of the mission and authority given by Christ. Beginning with Pope Gelasius I (d. 496) the doctrine of the "two swords" (Luke 22,35–38) was interpreted in the sense of an equal side by side existence of worldly and spiritual power (*auctoritas sacra pontificum et regalis potestas: Decretum Gratiani*, c.10 D. 96; cf. *LThK* 10 (1965) 1429f.). This was still the teaching of Peter Damian (d. 1082).

According to Pope Gregory VII (1073–1085) the pope alone holds these two swords, even when he hands one of them to the emperor (cf. his *Dictatus Papae*; Mirbt, *Quellen*, no. 547: 27 propositions). This doctrine led to the investiture controversy with the emperor Henry IV, which was resolved only in the Concordat of Worms in 1122. Pope Innocent III (1198–1216) again stressed the superiority of the papacy by comparing the Church's power to the sun and secular power to the moon, which derives all its brilliance from the sun (*Ep.* I,401; Mirbt n 599). Pope Boniface VIII (1294–1303), finally, proclaimed the "worldwide monarchy of the Church under the popes" as a doctrine of the Church ("Furthermore we declare, state and define that it is absolutely necessary for the salvation of all men that they submit to the Roman Pontiff"; bull *Unam Sanctam*, DS 875).

Great catastrophes followed: the imprisonment of the popes in Avignon (1309–1377) and the great schism (1378–1417); the controversies with conciliarism; and the deep disturbance caused by the "Reformation," which opposed the visible papal universal Church by an invisible "spiritual Church" and individual local churches. These catastrophes were certainly able to eliminate the political aberrations of Boniface VIII, but they were unable to overcome the narrow juridical-personal perspective in the understanding of the papacy. Robert Bellarmine (d. 1621) still used the terms "*Monarchia Petri*" (*De Rom. Pont.* I,ii). He did so even though he stressed quite rightly that not only Peter but also the other apostles could be called *fundamentum ecclesiae* (cf. Eph 2,20) because all of them together (not only Peter) founded the individual churches in the world and received the totality of revelation from Christ. But only Peter is "the ordinary and universal shepherd and the head, upon whom the other apostles depend, namely, as delegates." For it was only to Peter that Christ said, "Upon this rock I will build my Church." According to Cajetan (Thomas de Vio; d. 1534) the other apostles were given their authority only personally, not for their successors (*De compar. auct. papae et concilii*, c. 3, n. 39).

Such views fail to see the college of apostles and thus the apostolic (not merely Petrine) Church. At the other extreme, the later ecclesiological experiments of Gallicanism, Febronianism, and episcopalism failed to see the correct doctrine of papal primacy in their more "democratic" perspective on the Church. They failed to see the true *plenitudo potestatis* of the pope in the Church as a whole (the whole is more than the sum of its parts).

It was only in the nineteenth century that the deeper theological vision of the Church appeared again. The stimulus for this vision came probably from Romanticism, which possessed a more profound sense of the historical and mystical dimensions of existence (Tübingen school, J. A. Möhler). Another important stimulus was the great political conflict between the idea of the absolute ruler and

state (F. W. Hegel) and democratic revolution (beginning
with the French Revolution in 1789), which again pushed
the more political aspect into the foreground. These spiritual conflicts led to the first dogmatic definitions about
the Church at the First Vatican Council (1870). However,
due to the unfortunate historical events of that time, only
a partial aspect could be worked out. The important Roman school [involving mainly Jesuits: Giovanni Perrone
(d. 1876); Carlo Passaglia (d. 1887); J. B. Franzelin (d. 1876)
and especially Clemens Schrader (d. 1875)] did the preparatory work for the drafts on the Church and the papacy (*De
Ecclesia*, 10 chapters; *De Romano Pontifice*, 2 chapters). A
commission of theologians convoked by Pius IX (1846–78)
added the question of infallibility to these drafts. Transformed and merged into the document *Supremi Pastoris*,
the drafts were distributed to the Council fathers on January 21, 1870 (15 chapters, 21 canons). The Council had to
be dissolved after the fourth session because of the Franco-
Prussian War. It was able to promulgate only the *Constitu-
tio Dogmatica I De Ecclesia Christi* with the title *"Pastor
Aeternus"* (July 18, 1870), which defined in four chapters
the decisive doctrines concerning the pope's primacy of
jurisdiction and his infallibility. Let us look at some of the
important parts of this decree (cf. DS 3050–3064):

(Introduction) . . . In order that the episcopate itself might be
one and undivided, and that the whole multitude of believers
might be preserved in unity of faith and communion [*fidei et
communionis*] by means of a closely united priesthood, He
(Christ) placed St. Peter at the head [*praeponens*] of the other
apostles, and established in him a perpetual principle and visible
foundation of this twofold unity, in order that on his strength
[*fortitudo*] an everlasting temple might be erected. . . .

(Chapter 1: The Establishment of Primacy) We, therefore, teach
and declare, according to the testimony of the Gospel, that the
primacy of jurisdiction over the whole Church was immediately
and directly promised to and conferred upon the blessed apostle
Peter by Christ the Lord. . . . Therefore, if anyone says that the

blessed apostle Peter was not constituted by Christ the Lord as the Prince of all the apostles and the visible head of the whole Church militant, or that he received immediately and directly from Jesus Christ our Lord only a primacy of honor and not a true and proper primacy of jurisdiction, *anathema sit.*

(Chapter 2: The Continuation of the Petrine Primacy in the Roman Popes) Now, what Christ, the Lord, the Prince of Shepherds and the great Shepherd of the flock, established in the person of the blessed apostle Peter for the perpetual safety and everlasting good of the Church must, by the will of the same, endure without interruption in the Church, which was founded on the rock and which will remain firm until the end of the world . . . even to this time and forever he [Peter] lives and governs and exercises judgment in his successors, the bishops of the holy Roman See, which he established and consecrated with his blood. Therefore, whoever succeeds Peter in this Chair, according to the institution of Christ himself, holds Peter's primacy over the whole Church. . . .

(Chapter 3: The Power and Meaning of Primacy) After an appeal to the Council of Florence (1439; DS 1307) the text continues) . . . And so We teach and declare that, in the disposition of God, the Roman Church holds the pre-eminence of ordinary power [*ordinariae potestatis principatum*] over all the other Churches; and that this power of jurisdiction of the Roman Pontiff, which is truly episcopal, is immediate. Regarding this jurisdiction, the shepherds of whatever rite or jurisdiction and the faithful, individually and collectively, are bound by a duty of hierarchical subjection and of sincere obedience; and this not only in matters that pertain to faith and morals, but also in matters that pertain to the discipline and government [*disciplinam et regimen*] of the Church throughout the whole world. . . . This power [*potestas*] of the Supreme Pontiff is far from standing in the way of the power of ordinary and immediate episcopal jurisdiction by which the bishops who, under appointment of the Holy Spirit [cf. Acts 20,28], succeeded in the place of the apostles, feed and rule individually, as true shepherds, the particular flock assigned to them. Rather this latter power is asserted, confirmed and vindicated by this same supreme and universal shepherd. . . . Furthermore, from his supreme power of governing [*gubernandi*] the whole Church, the Roman Pontiff has the right of freely communicating with the shepherds and flocks of the whole Church in the exercise of his office. . . . [W]e also teach and declare that he [the Pope] is the supreme judge of the faithful; and that one can have recourse to his judgment in all cases pertaining to ecclesiastical jurisdiction. We declare that the judgment of the apostolic See, whose authority is unsurpassed, is not subject to review by anyone; nor is anyone allowed to pass judgment on its decision [thus no appeal to an ecumenical Council]. . . .

(Chapter 4 deals with papal infallibility, which we will discuss later.) (Cf. DS 3050–3064).

If we see the Holy Spirit at work in the Church's doctrinal developments, we may recognize that the historical moment for the dogmatic definition of the special primacy of the pope in the Church of Christ was a divine *kairos*, in view of the strong democratic tendencies of the following period.

The defect of the definition lies above all in what it could not discuss and clarify due to historical circumstances. What is lacking is a concrete comprehensive image of the Church within which primacy can be understood. Although the Pauline image of the Church as the "mystical body of Christ" was still understood in all its breadth, the document discusses only those who hold a specific office in the Church, not the Church as a people. The "laity" are only those who hear, receive, and obey. What is also lacking is a correct view of the episcopal office as an office that must be seen not merely in terms of the papacy but in terms of the college of apostles and in terms of its fundamental importance for the universal Church, not just the diocesan local church. But what is especially lacking is the perspective of the ecumenical question, the relation of the Roman Church to the other Christian churches, and the proper understanding of the fundamental, worldwide task of the Church, not only in the sphere of world mission, but also in the sphere of world culture, i.e., of all human dimensions of this world. The human person, as the true addressee of God's saving action in this world, had not yet become *the* problem by which all of the Church's activities must orient themselves.

Subsequent popes deepened and clarified some of the teachings of Vatican I. In places where they attempted to respond to the real questions of the time they also prepared the way for a new image of the Church. However, this image was unfolded more by spiritual movements arising out of the people of the Church and the world.

In his encyclicals, which are animated by the newly revived Thomism, Leo XIII (1878–1903) deals above all with the unicity and organic unity of the Church. He offers a new view of the Holy Spirit as the soul (Augustine) and the heart (Thomas Aquinas) of the Church. Through his openness to the new workers' questions (social encyclical), he also improved the Church's relation to the simple people of the Church. In addition he achieved friendlier terms between the Church and secular powers, especially Germany.

The solution of the difficult "Roman question" (the loss of the old and powerful ecclesiastical state, which had been annexed by the newly formed Italian national state) was the work of the learned and sober Pius XI (1922–1939). Through his *Azione Cattolica* he overcame the often unfortunate struggle of earlier times against a misunderstood "laicalism" and impressed the Church's worldwide missionary task upon the consciousness of the time.

In the meantime, especially after World War I, spiritual movements had arisen among the Church's people: the youth movement, the biblical movement, the liturgical movement, and the ecumenical movement. In his numerous pronouncements Pius XII (1939–58) relied heavily on the earlier Roman school. Still, in his encyclical *Mystici Corporis* (1943), which showed the Church to be the haven of salvation during the most bitter sufferings of the war, he began a completely new discussion about belonging to the Church through the phrase *ordinari ad* (being ordained to).

The Second Vatican Council used this discussion as a point of departure. The plan for a Council arose, by divine providence, through the "first and unexpected budding forth of the word Ecumenical Council" in the heart and on the lips of the childlike, pious Pope John XXIII (1958–63). Its theme was the self-understanding of the Catholic Church in our time. It developed a comprehensive image of the Church in which, besides ecclesiastical offices, the people of God came into view in the first place as the true body of this hierarchically organized community. It achieved a new understanding of the episcopal office in terms of the apostolic office and the college of apostles, out of which, according to Christ's will, the office of Peter and the pope arises as member and head. The new understanding of the Church overcame, above all, the one-sidedly juridical way of looking at all offices, including the papacy. All offices were shown in their hierarchical order and organic unity, in their service for each other and for the whole people of God as well as the whole world of human persons, in which the true area of the Church's task is to be sought. In all its internal and external unity and unicity, the Church is not a closed societal block but an organism. The whole of the universal world-Church is present and alive in the small local churches. In the same way, the authority and dignity of the papal office is effective and alive in the bishops and their organs, not on the basis of juridical delegation, but because the Church is a whole, unified as the body of Christ and as the bearer of his Spirit in this world, unified, that is, as the *universale sacramentum salutis*.

In order to clarify and deepen the new vision of Vatican II, one must penetrate ever more deeply into the convergence of various aspects: the political and societal, the juridical and sociological aspects, spirit and charity, sacrament and eschaton. The image of primacy that developed in Vatican I appears in a new depth and breadth in Vatican II, because it is inserted anew into the whole of the world-

Church. Nevertheless, the specific element of the papal office, its inner reality, cannot be deduced from the whole of the Church, not even by an ever-so-perfect sociology. It can be understood only in terms of the internal and external structure of the Church, which is given by Christ and clearly portrayed in the revealed word of the New Testament. In this structure, a single historical person stands at the beginning and at the end as the bearer of this Petrine papal office. The situation of our understanding of Christ is the same. All our knowledge and understanding engendered by faith in the mystical, eucharistic, and eschatological Lord of the Church must always orient itself by the historical Jesus. Again and again we must seek and seek to understand this historical Jesus. The papacy, like the Church as a whole, is a sacramental reality in which the external historical sign (successor on the chair of Peter) must be seen as united with the inner reality (vicar of Christ), which can only be grasped by faith, and with the institution by Christ, which is guaranteed by the scriptural passage about the Petrine office for the Church as a whole and by the biblical image of the Church.

In this light let us say a few things on primacy in the ecumenical perspective.[101] It is no longer possible today to join Cyprian in seeing the Petrine succession in the bishop of each local Church (cf. Meyendorff, I., 117). Schmemann is probably correct (II., 146ff.) when he sees in the Eastern churches a certain one-sided development of the institution of the Council in the direction of the "Holy Synod," and a similar one-sidedness in a "mysticism of highest authority" (in the Church's sphere, corresponding to the emperor in the secular sphere) connected with the patriarch and his rule, a one-sidedness that stems perhaps from a certain religious nationalism. In addition, following the new approaches of Vatican II, one must stress not only the Church's catholicity but also the ministry of service and collegiality of the papacy as well as of all offices in the Church, with due regard for hierarchical order (cf. Stir-

288 Sacramental Structure of the Church

nimann II., 262–288). What has to be clarified vis-à-vis the churches of the Reformation is the concept of "office."

What is the content of the authority and task contained in the pope's primacy? The Church's documents express it as follows: "visible head of the whole Church [*totius eccle-siae visibile caput*]" (LG 18); "shepherd of the whole Church [*totius ecclesiae pastor*]" (LEF, c. 29, par. 2); "su-preme shepherd of the Church [*supremus ecclesiae pas-tor*]" (ibid. c. 31, par. 2); "head of the college of bishops [*collegii episcoporum caput*]" (LG 22). Canon law unfolds the various social, juridical, economic, cultural, and politi-cal aspects of this primacy in detail. Nevertheless, it is important not to allow the term "primacy of jurisdiction" to mislead one into a view of the Petrine and papal office that places the emphasis too much on legislation, juris-diction, and administration in the various areas of the Church's life. Rather, primacy should be seen as contain-ing the fullness of the apostolic office, of which Paul says "servants of Christ and stewards of the mysteries of God" (1 Cor 4,1). On the basis of John 20,21 ("as the Father has sent me, even so I send you"), Cyril of Alexandria (d. 444) once gave the following theologically deep and spiritual admonition: "The Lord explained to us the manner of his mission in many ways: once he said, 'I came not to call the righteous, but sinners' [Matt 9,13]; in another place he says, 'For I have come down from heaven not to do my own will, but the will of him who sent me' [John 6,38]; and again, 'For God sent the Son into the world, not to con-demn the world, but that the world might be saved through him' [John 3,17]" (PG 74,719f.). Christ was the first to serve in this total way and he called the apostles, in the first place Peter, into this service. Yet in all the love that this total service involves, it contains also a challenge for decision in struggle and suffering (Luke 12,49–53), the rejection of all falsehood (Matt 12,30; 5,37), and reproof as well as punishment of evil (Matt 23; rev 5). All these as-pects, however, must serve life, growth, conversion, and renewal.[102]

Vatican II summarizes the pope's primacy of jurisdiction as follows: "The Roman Pontiff, by reason of his office [*munus*] as Vicar of Christ, namely, and as pastor of the enire [*tota*] Church, has full, supreme and universal power [*potestatem*] over the whole Church, a power which he can always exercise unhindered" (LG 22,2). This means that on the basis of his office the pope in his own person possesses full priestly authority (to sanctify as priest, to proclaim as teacher, and to lead as shepherd) over the whole Church and that he does not need to be empowered or confirmed in the exercise of this authority by a synod of bishops or the people of the Church.

However, Vatican II adds something to this teaching: "The order [*ordo*] of bishops is the successor to the college of the apostles in their role as teachers and pastors, and in it the apostolic college is perpetuated. Together with their head (*una cum capite suo*), the Supreme Pontiff, and never apart from him, they have supreme and full authority over the universal [*universam*] Church." The exact meaning of this text will be discussed below in the section on the relationship between the pope and the bishops.[103]

6. INFALLIBILITY (OF THE CHURCH—OF THE POPE)

The dogma of infallibility is concerned with the question of truth. Three preparatory reflections may help to prepare the ground for discussing it.

a) Concerning the *critical* side of the truth of faith: The Vatican I teaching about infallibility stands in the context of the discussion of primacy. Thus, at the beginning of the chapter on infallibility the Council says, "[T]he supreme power of teaching [*suprema magisterii potestas*] is also included in this apostolic primacy which the Roman Pontiff, as the successor of St. Peter, the Prince of the apostles, holds over the whole Church" (DS 3065). This statement is based on the twofold distinction of power as power of

ordination and power of jurisdiction. The power of jurisdiction is linked with the magisterium and the pastoral
office, while the power of ordination is linked with the
priestly office. These connections show that what is entrusted to the Church's magisterium is not truth as such,
as it is present, for example, in the revelation of Scripture
prior to our human understanding, but the decision over
truth and falsity in assertions which the believer draws by
research and reflection from this revelation.

It is significant that Vatican II showed the unified root of
the two powers in a single *sacra potestas*, a single spiritual
authority, just as it integrated the various theological interpretations of revelation in the one "self-revelation of
God" (DV 1).[104] This *sacra potestas* is immediately rooted
in the Lord and his Spirit, who are present in the Church.
Canon law, of course, continues to maintain the "two
levels" (K. Mörsdorf) of this one ecclesiastical power, that
of sacramental ordination (which is irrevocable) and that
of canonical *missio* (which is revocable). This distinction
between what is permanent and what is historical and
changeable (between metaphysical and physical aspects)
will continue to occupy us.

b) The *truth of faith as a living reality:* In contrast to
Vatican I, Vatican II's Constitution on the Church raises
the question of infallibility as the question of the infallibility of the Church as such, where the Church is seen as
the people of God. On the basis of baptism and the other
sacraments, the whole people of God shares in the priesthood of Christ (LG 10). In the same way, it shares in
Christ's teaching office.

The holy People of God shares also in Christ's prophetic office: it
spreads abroad a living witness to him, especially by a life of faith
and love and by offering to God a sacrifice of praise, the fruit of
lips praising his name (cf. Heb 13,15). The whole body of the
faithful who have an anointing that comes from the holy one (cf. 1
John 2,20.27) cannot err in matters of belief. This characteristic

[*peculiaris proprietas*] is shown in the supernatural appreciation of the faith [*sensus fidei*] of the whole people, when, "from the bishops to the last of the faithful" [Augustine], they manifest a universal consent in matters of faith and morals. By this appreciation of the faith, aroused and sustained by the Spirit of truth, the People of God, guided by the sacred teaching authority [*magisterium*], and obeying it, receives not the mere word of men, but truly the word of God (cf. 1 Thess 2,13), the faith once for all delivered to the saints (cf. Jude 3). The people unfailingly [*indefectibiliter*] adheres to this faith, penetrates it more deeply with right judgment, and applies it more fully in daily life. (LG 12)

It is clear that this text does not speak about truth and error, about which inerrant decisions are to be made, but about the living truth itself, in which the whole people of God shares through its supernatural appreciation of faith (*supernaturalis sensus fidei totius populi*) and which grows in this believing people according to the rules unfolded in the Dogmatic Constitution on Divine Revelation (DV 2–10). It is against this background that one can understand the claim to the inerrancy of the whole body of the faithful in its correct transcendental sense (individual believers, whole groups, and even majorities can err). The truth about which this text speaks cannot be discovered by majority decision of the people of God as expressed in polls, etc. It can be reached and preserved only in obedience to the sacred magisterium of the Church.

c) The truth of faith as a *supernatural gift of grace:* The point just discussed shows the special nature of this truth of faith: The magisterium must reach decisions about it and it can be found and preserved only in obedience to this magisterium. God gives this truth as his gratuitous gift, as a supernatural truth. Mere natural human research and judgment cannot find it, nor can mere human power preserve it and keep it pure. Nevertheless, once human beings receive it and reflect on it in the power of the Holy Spirit, they can grasp its inner correctness and its fruitfulness for understanding, and relating to, themselves and the world.

They can maintain and unfold it further in the obedience of faith and in prayer. For this reason, Vatican II demands,

> The faithful, for their part, are obliged to submit to their bishops' teaching, made in the name of Christ, in matters of faith and morals, and to adhere to it with a ready and respectful allegiance of mind. This loyal submission of the will and intellect must be given, in a special way, to the authentic teaching authority of the Roman Pontiff, even when he does not speak *ex cathedra* in such wise, indeed, that his supreme teaching authority be acknowledged with respect, and that one sincerely adhere to decisions made by him, conformably with his manifest mind and intention, which is made known principally either by the character of the document in question, or by the frequency with which a certain doctrine is proposed, or by the manner in which the doctrine is formulated. (LG 25)

After these preliminary remarks, let us unfold the doctrine of infallibility. The first section will give a brief historical introduction. The second section will present the foundations and first outlines of this doctrine in Scripture and tradition. The last three sections will unfold the content and meaning of the Church's charisma of infallibility by discussing its subject and bearer, its object, and its conditions.

Historical Aspects

a) For a correct understanding of the development of the doctrine of infallibility in the faith of the Church, one must clearly grasp the contemporary concept of infallibility. Infallibility, at least since Vatican I, has been understood in the sense that "the bearers of ecclesiastical offices, who are called by Christ to the faithful preservation and infallible interpretation of his revealed doctrine, are preserved by the assistance of Christ and the Holy Spirit (in a charismatic way: here and now) from proclaiming a false doctrine" (J. Pohle). This charisma does thus not reveal any new truth. It only interprets the pre-given reve-

lation. It is not an internal grace of inspiration, but it presupposes human search, the openness to the whole of the
Church, and various endeavors that are generally necessary for finding the truth. The result of such endeavors, of
course, is not the mere result of human activity, but a gift
of God. This gift remains independent from the natural
intellectual and moral qualities of the bearer of the office.[105]

b) As we will show below, this doctrine can be seen in
Scripture and the whole course of tradition, if the inner
growth of the Church's understanding is taken into account. The understanding of infallibility must be included
in the transformations implied in this growth. The conviction that revelation has found its external conclusion with
Christ's ascension and his sending of the Spirit, and more
specifically with the death of the last apostle, as well as
the insight that this revelation is necessary for the understanding and reality of human salvation, has from the very
beginning led to the conviction that the Lord and his
Spirit, whose living presence is a gift given to the Church
for all time, would preserve this revelation in the Church
without falsification and unfold it in it in a living way
(inerrancy of the Church). The unfolding of the understanding of the Church's nature was accompanied by an
unfolding of the understanding of its inerrancy.

c) In opposition to the various Gnostic tendencies of the
second and third centuries, which stressed the deeper "understanding of revelation" by individuals, especially charismatic interpreters, the Church realized the importance
of the tradition and the magisterium of the Church, especially the magisterium of its bishops (Tertullian;
Irenaeus). When Constantine granted political freedom to
the Church, the bishops of the whole Church could work
together in the councils convened by the emperor. The
Church's inerrancy was seen above all in these "ecumenical Councils" and their common decisions.

d) Since the fifth century (Pope Leo I and Chalcedon) the

Church has seen more clearly the special importance of the Roman Church and its bishop for the preservation of the revelation passed on to the Church. Up to the twelfth century (and in the East to this day) the main emphasis was placed on the doctrine of the inerrancy of the whole Church and the connected doctrine of the stability of this inerrancy (the Church's indefectibility) in all the transformations of history.

e) The controversies between the emperor and the pope (Gregory VII and the investiture controversy) after the schism between the Eastern and the Western Church (1054); the spirit of the mendicant orders, whose members not only gave up their possessions but submitted their obedience of faith in a special way to the Roman episcopal see; the fact that the councils of the Western Church were convened no longer by the emperor but by the pope (the Lateran Councils)—all these may be reasons why the Church's inerrancy was understood more and more as a "papal inerrancy" (Thomas Aquinas). In the Counter-Reformation, especially in Jesuit theology, this papal inerrancy became the principal theme of ecclesiology in response to Luther, who reviled the pope as the "antichrist."

f) Up to the eighteenth century, the decline of the papacy through the captivity of the popes in Avignon and through the conciliarism occasioned by the long Western schism acted as a certain restraint against this doctrine of the inerrancy of the pope. Conciliarism saw inerrancy only in the decrees of ecumenical councils, which were conceived of as standing above the pope. In the spirit of humanism ("back to the sources") and as a reaction against the dialectic of nominalism, which continued to exert its influence in the Reformation, the theology of the fifteenth century (especially Spanish Dominican theology, e.g. Francis of Vitoria, d. 1546) returned to the spirit of High Scholasticism, especially to Thomas Aquinas (cf. the many commentaries on the *Summa* composed at that time). In this spirit,

Melchior Cano (d. 1560) wrote his *Loci theologici* (published in 1563). Following certain leads of *De inventione dialectica* by the humanist Rudolph Agricola (d. 1485) he sought the grounds for theological truth not in aspects of content (as Melanchthon did in his *Loci theologici* of 1521 and 1559) but in the fact that particular doctrines are attested by revelation, tradition, the Church, the ecumenical councils approved by the popes, and by the popes themselves.[106] This approach still stresses the unity of witnesses instituted by God for inerrant truth in the Church.

g) Due to the conflict with the Reformation in the sixteenth century, the inerrancy of the pope was stressd more and more, especially by the school of Louvain, where Jansenism was soon to find its home.[107] It was perhaps Jansenism that introduced the stronger expression *infallibilis-infallibilitas* (cf. DS 2329 of the year 1690) in the place of the traditional phrase *"errare non posse"* (cf. *Catechismus Romanus* of 1566, I,10,n.18). As early as 1682 Pope Innocent XI wanted to define the doctrine of the pope's *infallibilitas*. In 1664 Versant distinguished the pope's active infallibility from the passive infallibility of the Church of believers.[108] In his *Institutiones Theologicae* (Vol. I, Ludguni 1700) Gaspar Juenin (1650–1713) adopts the *Loci* of Melchior Cano in the formulation, *De ecclesiae infallibilitate* (Q4 cp5 a3) and calls the pope's decrees *ineluctabilia ac infallibilia*, with the erroneous qualification, *"ubi ecclesiarum consensus accessit* (where the consent of the churches is added)" (ibid. Q5 cp2). Towards the end of his life the Father General of the Jesuits Tirso Gonzales (d. 1705) published a treatise, *De infallibilitate Romani Pontificis*, and in 1741, two volumes of that title were published by A. Ossi in Rome. In 1756 the AugustinianIgnatius Kranabiter published a summary of Melchior Cano's *Loci theologici*. While Cano himself did not use the term "infallible," Kranabiter summarizes Cano's extensive discussions in the terse formulation,

In the doctrine of faith and the precepts of morality, the Church is infallible. (Q3 n23)

Only the Roman pontiff, when he speaks *ex cathedra* . . . and teaches the whole Church, is infallible in his dogmatic decisions. . . . We assert that these pontifical decisions and definitions are infallible and worthy of being used in dogmatic argumentation, provided that, having taken mature counsel, even without a council (not from private opinion or any fortuitous hastiness of the mind), having implored the divine presence, and drawing (his decisions and definitions) from the word of God as it is written down or passed on by tradition, [the pope] as the successor of Peter and the vicar of Christ on earth makes them and proposes them to be believed and observed for the due instruction of the universal Church in matters of faith and morals." (Q4 n40)

A general council confirmed by the Roman pontiff is infallible in declaring matters of faith and morals, and it calls for full faith on the part of theologians. (Q5 n51)

h) Stimulated by the Roman restauration (the struggle for the ecclesiastical state) as well as by Neoscholasticism and the Jesuit theology that contributed to it, a movement arose at the beginning of the nineteenth century that under Pius IX led to the dogmatic definition of the pope's infallibility at Vatican I. Vatican II confirmed this definition.

Foundations of the Doctrine of the Inerrancy (Infallibility) of the Church in Scripture and Tradition

a) Scripture presents three areas in which this inerrancy is rooted, but it does not yet completely clarify their connection and relation. One such area is the college of the twelve apostles, whom Christ commands to missionize the whole world (Matt 28,19f.). At the same time he promises them that he will be with them until the end of the world. He assures them that their word will be counted as his own word or that of his Father: "He who hears you hears me . . ." (Luke 10,16; cf. Matt 10,40), for in their mission he wanted to pass on to them the mission he had received from his Father: "As the Father has sent me, so I send you" (John 20,21; cf. 17,18). This mission includes therefore also the anointing with the Holy Spirit, because Jesus himself was the Messiah, the Christ, the one anointed with the Holy Spirit. And this "Spirit of truth" (John 14,16–17.21.26; 15,26) will always remain with the Church; he "will teach you all things and bring to your remembrance all that I have said to you" (John 14,26). At Pentecost this Spirit descended once and for all upon the apostles and the Church (Acts 2,2–4.17–21.32–33). From this day on, the apostles and disciples of Christ carried the message of Christ for the salvation of all into the world as the "good news" (*euangelion* Isa 61,1; Mark 1,14f.; Rom 1,1.9; 1 Cor 4,15) as the word of God, not a mere human word (1 Thess 2,13; 2 Cor 4,3–6), accompanied by many signs and wonders (Acts 4,29f.; 6,8; 14,3) and at the risk of their lives (2 Cor 6,3–12). In the name of Christ (in the place of Christ and on behalf of Christ, *hyper Christou*, 2 Cor 5,20) they demand faith and obedience for "their gospel," which cannot be replaced by any "other gospel," not even if it were proclaimed by angels (Gal 1,6–9).

Apart from the apostles as a group, Christ promised to *Peter alone* the power to bind and to loose (Matt 16,19); to him alone he entrusted his whole flock (John 21,15–17); to him alone he gave the assurance of his special prayer, "that your faith may not fail," in order that he might strengthen his brothers (Luke 22,32).

Finally, "the household of God," which is the "Church of the living God," in which bishops and deacons act as stewards, is the "pillar and bulwark of the truth" (1 Tim 3,15; cf. 3,1–15) against "deceitful spirits and doctrines of demons" (1 Tim 4,1). Thus John can say, "Whoever knows God listens to us, and he who is not of God does not listen to us. By this we know the Spirit of truth and the spirit of error" (1 John 4,6). "If you put these instructions before the brethren, you will be a good minister of Christ Jesus, nourished on the words of the faith and of the good doctrine which you have followed" (1 Tim 4,6).

b) In the tradition of the fathers this apostolic spirit continued to be effective. Like his great master, the apostle John, Polycarp, bishop of Smyrna (d. 154) fought against heresies (he calls Marcion the firstborn of Satan) by appealing to the unalterable doctrine of the Church's tradition: "Let us therefore leave aside the empty talk of the masses and false doctrines and turn to the doctrine that has been passed on to us from the beginning" (*Ad Phil* c 7). In his fight against Gnosticism Polycarp's student Irenaeus of Lyons (d. 202) developed the principle of "tradition," which is supported by the principle of "succession." The rule and norm of faith (*regula veritatis*) is the tradition of the apostles that continues to live in the Church through their successors, the bishops. Thus he writes, "It is within the power of all, therefore, in every Church, who may wish to see the truth, to contemplate clearly the tradition of the apostles manifested throughout the whole world; and we are in a position to reckon up those who were by the apostles instituted bishops in the Churches and [to demonstrate] the succession of these men to our own times" (*Adv. Haer.* III,3,1). And he explicitly reckons up the list of Roman bishops (*Adv. Haer.* III,3,3). "Since therefore we have such proofs, it is not necessary to seek the truth among others which it is easy to obtain from the Church; since the apostles, like a rich man [depositing his money] in a bank, lodged in their hands most copiously all things pertaining to the truth: so that every man, whosoever will, can draw from her the water of life. . . . Suppose there arise a dispute relative to some important question among us, should we not have recourse to the most ancient churches with which the apostles held constant intercourse, and learn from them what is certain and clear in regard to the present question?" (*Adv. Haer.* III,4,1). "[M]ost vain is the affirmation of these sophists who affirm that the apostles did with hypocrisy frame their doctrine according to the capacity of their hearers, and gave answers after the opinions of their questioners . . . and not according to the truth" (*Adv. Haer.* III,5,1).

In his orthodox period Tertullian of Carthage (d. after 220) stressed even more that tradition is binding in the Church as lived faith, even when no scriptural proof is possible. "We must not introduce anything according to our whim . . . we have as our guarantee the apostles of the Lord who themselves did not choose anything according to their whim to introduce it. Rather they faithfully passed on to the nations the doctrines they received from Christ" (*De cor.* 3f.). A little later (397) Augustine even says, "I would not believe the Gospel, if the Church's authority would not urge me to" (*Contr. ep. Man.* 5,6). Augustine's words on Luke 22,32 should always be remembered as a permanently valid response to Calvin's misunderstandings (*Inst.* IV 7,27): "How do you wish to oppose the words of him who said, Peter, I have prayed for you . . . (Luke 22,32). Do you dare to assert, Despite Christ's prayer that Peter's faith would not fail, his faith did become weak, when he wanted it to fail . . . ? As if Peter could have wanted anything different than what Christ prayed for on his behalf. . . . Because 'the will is prepared by the Lord' (Prov 8,35), Christ's prayer for him could not be in vain. Why then did he ask in his prayer that his faith may not fail unless he wanted him to have a completely free, completely confident, completely invincible and tenacious will? See how the freedom of the will can be defended in harmony with grace, but not in opposition to it. For it is not through freedom that the human will attains grace, but rather through grace freedom and a joyful permanence and invincible strength to endure" (*De corrept. et grat.* 8,18). When the conciliar principle had already come into use for the securing of truth in the Church, Vincent of Lerin (d. before 450), in his struggle against Augustine's doctrine of grace, expressed the principle of tradition in his first *Commonitorium* in the well-known form, "Our concern is to preserve what has been believed everywhere, always, and by all; for this is what is in the true and authentic sense Catholic" (III,5). Nevertheless, in the same work, Vincent also points to the necessary progress in the understanding of faith, *"crescat . . . vehementerque proficiat . . . intelligentia, scientia, sapientia* (that [faith] might grow and progress mightily through understanding, science and wisdom)" (ibid. 23,4).

When the Church was freed under Emperor Constantine, the securing of truth and the guarantee for inerrancy in the Church was sought above all in the synods of elders and leaders. Already in 257 bishop Firmillian demanded that "they should gather every year, in order to order everything entrusted to their care" (*Ep. ad. Cypr.* 75,4). The Council of Nicaea even wanted to make it a rule to hold a synod twice a year (can. 5). In 359 Athanasius wrote concerning this first council of the Church (Nicaea 325), "What the fathers passed down in writing is not their innovation, but it is what the apostles have already taught" (*Ep. de syn.* 5). "The word of the Lord remains, uttered by the ecumenical Council of Nicaea, in eternity" (*Ep. ad Afr.* 2). The creed of Nicaea remained binding for the declarations of the following councils. Ambrose stressed this point when he wrote to the emperor Valentinus, "I follow the declaration [*tractatum*] of the Council of Nicaea and neither death nor the sword can separate me from it" (Ep. 21,14). Cyril of Alexandria in his struggle against Nestorius (Ep. 3) and Pope Leo I in his letter to the fathers at Chalcedon (DS 2185f.) appeal to this council. Augustine once wrote to Januarius, "That which is not found in Scripture, but is still preserved by tradition, must be understood and kept as binding tradition, either as coming from the apostles, or from the great councils [*plenariis conciliis*] which carry authority in the Church in questions of salvation" (*Ep.* 54,1,1). Pope Julius I (337–352) had already stressed the importance of Nicaea in his letter to the Eusebians in 341. Gregory the Great (d. 604) spoke the famous words that the first four councils are to be esteemed as the four Gospels, "he who thinks otherwise, let him be anathema" (*Ep.* 25 *ad Joan. Const.*, PL 77,478).

The special importance of the Roman See for the preservation of truth was already stressed by Irenaeus: "Due to the pre-eminence of the Roman church, every Church and believers everywhere must agree with it" (*Adv. Haer.* II,2) because of the "charism of truth" (*Adv. Haer.* IV,26,2). Many fathers, esp. Cyril of Alexandria (PG 72,915) and Ambrose (*De fide* IV 5,56) appeal to Luke 22,32 in support of this view. According to Cyprian, to be in communion with Cornelius, the bishop of Rome, is to be in communion with the Catholic Church (*Ep.* 55,1 *ad Anton.*). Tertullian explicitly interprets Peter's actions in Antioch criticized by Paul (Gal 2,11–18) as an error in behavior, not as an error in doctrine (*conversationis, non praedicationis*). In 419 Peter Chrysologus (d. 450) wrote to Eutyches, "St. Peter, who sits on his see and presides, offers to those who seek it the truth of faith" (2). Especially the popes, understandably, pointed to their authority, at least after the fifth century. Many texts from the early period quoted in the Middle Ages and especially after Melchior Cano and Bellarmine are part of the inauthentic collection of the "Pseudoisidoran Decretals." Innocent I seems to have been the first pope who explicitly stressed the pre-eminence of the Roman bishop in matters of the truth of faith. In 417 he wrote to the Synod of Carthage,

In your pursuit of the things of God, . . . following the examples of ancient tradition . . . you have made manifest by your proper course of action the vitality of our religion . . . when you agreed to have recourse to our judgment, knowing what is due to the apostolic See, since all of us placed in this position wish to follow the apostle [Peter], from whom have come this episcopate and all the authority belonging to this dignity. . . . Moreover, in safeguarding the ordinances of the Fathers with your priestly zeal, you certainly believe that they must not be trodden underfoot.

They decreed, not with human but with divine judgment, that no decision (even though it concerned the most remote provinces) was to be considered final unless this See might confirm whatever just decision was reached. From this See the other Churches receive the confirmation of what they ought to ordain. . . . (DS 217)

In a similar manner he wrote to the fathers of the Synod of Mileve (417) and added, "If an object of faith is at stake, I consider that all our brothers and fellow bishops may report only to Peter, i.e., to the origin of their name and rank, just as your love has now reported a matter which can be of use to the whole world." Canon 28 of the Canones of the African Church (419, controversy about the African Church's appeal to Rome) mirrors this norm proposed by Innocent I (cf. Hefele, CG II, 127–134). In the condemnation of the African Pelagians and Donatists, this Roman decision was exemplified particularly clearly. At the conclusion of the second session of the Council of Ephesus, the papal legate, the presbyter Philip, thanked the fathers, "that the holy members joined themselves to the holy head, knowing well that Peter is the head of the entire faith of all apostles." He also asked for the texts of all synodal decrees so that the legates could confirm (*bebaiōsomen*) them according to the instructions given by Celestine I (Hefele, CG II 200).

Rome's consciousness of its responsibility became especially clear in the activity of Leo I, in his rejection of the "robber synod" at Ephesus (449), in his confirmation of the decrees of Chalcedon and his rejection of canon 28 of this council. In 453 Leo wrote to Theodoret of Cyrus, "Our help is in the name of the Lord, who . . . confirmed through the irrevocable assent of the whole brotherhood what he had decided earlier through our office (cf. Leo's letter to Flavian, *Ep.* 28). In this way he showed that he was truly the origin of this decision which was first made by the first of all sees [*sedes*] and then received by the judgment of the whole Christian world, in order that in this matter too the members might agree with their head" (*Ep.*

120,1). In a sermon on the feast of Peter and Paul (*Sermo* 83,2) Leo comments as follows on the promise of the keys given to Peter, "It was not without reason that the power in which all share [Matt 18,18] was entrusted to one [Matt 16,18]. Peter's authority is conferred upon him especially, because the person of Peter stands above all leaders of the Church. Peter's pre-eminence holds also for his successors as often as they, filled with his power of judgment, pronounce a certain judgment." In the same sermon (83,3) he also comments on Christ's prayer for Peter (Luke 22,31f.): "All apostles are subject to the same danger of succumbing to fear. . . . Nevertheless, the Lord is especially concerned for Peter and prays for Peter's faith in particular, because the attitude of the others is more constant when the courage of the head remains unconquered. In Peter the strength of all is confirmed and the assistance of divine grace is regulated in such a way that the strength bestowed by Christ upon Peter passes through Peter to the other apostles."

Pope Hormisdas (414–523), who struggled for the unity between Rome and Constantinople, wrote in his famous *libellus fidei*,

The first demand for salvation is to keep the right rule of faith and never to depart from the decrees of the fathers. We cannot leave aside the words [*sententia*] of Christ to Peter, "You are Peter. . . ." [Matt 16,18] These words are confirmed by the course of events, because the Catholic religion has been preserved unstained [*immaculata*] by the Apostolic See (in Rome). In our striving never to separate ourselves from this faith and this hope, and following the constitutions of the fathers, we condemn all heresies . . . Novatian . . . Eutyches . . . Acacius . . . we accept all of Leo's writings on this subject and confirm them. . . . The names of those who do not agree with the Apostolic See are not to be mentioned in the memorial of the Holy Mass [the diptychs]. (DS 363ff.)

In the middle of the ninth century the Pseudoisidoran Decretals were composed as a four-part collection of various pseudepigraphical and inauthentic documents intended to defend the rights of suffragan bishops vis-à-vis the metropolitan bishops, provincial synods, and secular powers. Significantly, although the decretals were not composed by Roman officials, part of their strategy in this defense was to stress the power of the Roman bishops and their exclusive right of confirming councils. Rome began to use the decretals only in the eleventh century and in the investiture controversy. It was from these decretals that Thomas Aquinas drew the many unverifiable patristic quotes contained in his treatise *Contra errores Graecorum* which was commissioned by Pope Urban IV in about 1263. This defect also affects chapter 36 about the pope's inerrancy, where Thomas writes, "It must also be shown that it is proper to the Pontiff to decide what belongs to faith . . . and that it is necessary for salvation [*de necessitate salutis*] to subordinate oneself to the Roman Pontiff." This treatise was used and confirmed at the Second Council of Lyons (1274) which dealt with union with the Greeks after the schism of 1054. "The holy Roman Church possesses the supreme and full primacy and authority [*principatum*] over the universal Catholic Church . . . (Matt 16,18). And, as it is bound above all to defend the truth of faith, so too, if any questions should arise regarding the faith, they must be decided by its judgment" (DS 861; *Decr. Gratiani* II 9,3,12; quoted in Vatican I, DS 3067).

What is one to do with the difficulty that arises when a dogmatic decision of the Church is supported by inauthentic or falsified texts of the fathers, as happened in the case of Thomas Aquinas and the Second Council of Lyons? For a mere theological position taken by a theologian, the reasoning based on Scripture, tradition, and reason is decisive. Such a position can claim validity only as far as its premises can do so. However, the Church's definitions, especially those promulgated by a council, are decisively "confessional" in character, i.e., they express a conviction of faith that is prior to any possible theological reasoning.

Faith is not the result of logical reasoning based on proven premises. Faith is not only an intellectual act; it is also a personal act comparable, for example, to a human act of love, which is not created by, and cannot be canceled by, rational proof. In addition, the act of faith springs forth not only from the freedom of the human heart but even more from the grace of God, which is gratuitous and prevenient.

The decrees of the Second Council of Lyons (1274) were repeated and confirmed by the Council of Florence (1439) under Pope Eugene IV (DS 1328; 1307).

An "Enlightenment" that no longer understands "simple faith" (*philē pistis*, Origen) before God and the Church, but bases its faith only on its own understanding of the word of Scripture and upon the more narrow "understanding of history" developed by Humanism, gave up these truths of faith together with their theological arguments as soon as it discovered the above mentioned falsifications. This is what happened in the time of the Reformation, especially in the *Ecclesiastica Historia* composed by the so-called Magdeburg Centuriators.[109] Errors and moral defects in the private lives of popes were collected and used as arguments against faith in the infallibility of the Church and the pope. Robert Bellarmine (d. 1621) discusses such arguments in detail in his polemical writings.[110] After stating and explaining the Catholic position, "that the pope, when he acts as the teacher of the universal Church, can in no case err in matters of faith, morals, and all things necessary for salvation" (c 1–6), he turns to the arguments presented by the Magdeburg Centuriators (more than thirty cases drawn from the history of the Church, c 7–14) and continues with a more particular defense of the pope's power of jurisdiction (c 15–21). According to Bellarmine, the historical arguments brought against the Church deal with cases in which the conditions required for infallibility were not present and which, therefore, contain no binding papal teaching.

The articles of the clergy of Gaul (1682), which require

the confirming consent of the Church (the clergy) for an infallible decree by the pope, were explicitly condemned by Pope Alexander VIII in 1690 (DS 2284).

The Church's faith in the infallibility of the pope found its final formulation in the First Vatican Council. Vatican II confirmed these formulations. Vatican I states:

It is a divinely revealed dogma that the Roman Pontiff, when he speaks *ex cathedra*, that is, when, acting in the office of shepherd and teacher of the universal Church, he defines, by virtue of his supreme apostolic authority, a doctrine concerning faith or morals to be held by the universal Church, possesses through the divine assistance promised to him in the person of Blessed Peter, the infallibility with which the divine Redeemer willed His Church to be endowed in defining the doctrine concerning faith or morals; and that such definitions of the Roman Pontiff are therefore irreformable of themselves, not because of the consent of the Church [*ex sese, non autem ex consensu ecclesiae*]. (DS 3074)

Vatican II adopted this dogmatic definition of Vatican I. It widened it by the perspective of the episcopal college and deepened it by recourse to the teaching of the Vatican I peritus Father Vincent Gasser (d. 1879).

This infallibility, however, with which the divine Redeemer wished to endow his Church in defining doctrine pertaining to faith and morals, is co-extensive with the deposit of revelation, which must be religiously guarded and loyally and courageously expounded. The Roman Pontiff, head of the college of bishops, enjoys this infallibility in virtue of his office, when, as supreme pastor and teacher of all the faithful—who confirms his brethren in the faith (cf. Luke 22,32)—he proclaims in an absolute decision a doctrine pertaining to faith or morals. For that reason his definitions are rightly said to be irreformable by their very nature and not by reason of the assent of the Church, inasmuch as they were made with the assistance of the Holy Spirit promised to him in the person of Blessed Peter himself; and as a consequence they are in no way in need of the approval of others, and do not admit of appeal to any other tribunal. For in such a case the Roman Pontiff does not utter a pronouncement as a private person, but rather does he expound and defend the teaching of the Catholic faith as the supreme teacher of the universal Church, in whom the Church's charism of infallibility is present in a singular way. The infallibility promised to the Church is also present in the body of bishops when, together with Peter's successor, they exercise the supreme teaching office. Now, the assent of the Church can never be lacking to such definitions on account of the same Holy Spirit's influence, through which Christ's flock is maintained in the unity of faith and makes progress in it. Furthermore, when the Roman Pontiff, or the body of bishops together with him, define a doctrine, they make the definition in conformity with revelation itself, to which all are bound to adhere and to which they are obliged to submit; and this revelation is transmitted integrally either in written form or in oral tradition through the legitimate succession of bishops and above all through the watchful concern of the Roman Pontiff himself; and through the light of the Spirit of truth it is scrupulously preserved in the Church and unerringly explained. The Roman Pontiff and the bishops, by reason of their office and the seriousness of the matter, apply themselves with zeal to the work of enquiring by every suitable means into this revelation and of giving apt expression to its contents; they do not, however, admit any new public revelation as pertaining to the divine deposit of faith. (LG 25)

Just as the rejection of the Vatican I doctrine of infallibility by the circle around Döllinger was nurtured in the Old Catholic Church, a new struggle against this doctrine arose after the Vatican II declaration on infallibility, brought on by H. Küng's book *Unfehlbar? Eine Anfrage* (1970). Reactions to the book were carefully reviewed in a collection, also edited by Küng, *Bilanz: Fehlbar* (1973). In order to understand this controversy it may be useful to look at a prefatory remark in the paperback edition of Küng's *Wahrhaftigkeit* (Freiburg 1971), "Thus the two books about *Wahrhaftigkeit* [veracity, honesty] and *Unfehlbarkeit* [infallibility] function as two interpretive wings to the big picture which was drawn in the major work *Die Kirche* (Freiburg 1967)." Perhaps one should also point to Küngs's *Strukturen der Kirche*, which appeared in

1962. The source of these new difficulties is Küng's and others' rejection of the hierarchical understanding of the Church, as well as their rejection of the meaning of truth and language in the classical traditional (metaphysical) understanding of the Church. The Church is seen in more synodal and conciliar terms. Language and truth are seen in more pragmatic, functional and situational (historical) terms, not in their correspondence to being, their anchoring in metaphysical reality or the mystery of the Church. Thus Küng, together with Walter Kasper, arrives at the following understanding of the concept "infallible":[111]

Rightly understood, it (i.e., the reality signified by "infallibility") is the confidence of faith that the Church is basically preserved by the Spirit of Christ, despite various specific errors. "Infallible" should accordingly be understood dynamically, not statically. In and through the Church there occurs at all times the conflict with the powers of untruth, of error and of lying; according to the conviction of faith, the truth will always have the upper hand, it will never be lost. Thus it is precisely in the conflict about the authentic recognition of truth that the Church, on the basis of its faith [which Küng seems to conceive more in terms of hope], can be a sign of hope for human society. Through its own example the Church can be a witness that it is never meaningless, but always necessary, to continue the search and to walk on in the conviction that truth will prove itself.[112]

These assertions do not do justice to the Catholic understanding of the Church and of the Church's infallibility. Indeed, the Church's history clearly shows that they are erroneous. For, on the path of faith and knowledge plotted by Küng one cannot explain the numerous heresies, which often led to the founding of new churches. This vision of "the truth which proves itself" (it is Hegel's teaching about "the idea in the element of the community" *Phil. of Rel.* III, part III) is incorrect even in the sphere of the natural sciences, much more so in the science of faith (theology). Natural knowledge can be endangered or prevented by inaccurate observation, defects of logic in experiments and insufficient ability in assembling an objective synthesis. Likewise the knowledge of faith can be endangered or prevented by various moral weaknesses and personal defects. Revelation is purely the gift of God, not a human achievement. In the same way, the understanding of faith, which, according to the teaching of the Council, is nothing but the further unfolding of revelation through the grace of the Spirit of God in the reflection of believers, must be a gift of God, i.e., it must be secured in this world through a concrete institution or authority given by God. This authority is not the Church, understood in synodal (or democratic) terms, the "people" of the Church as such. Christ himself did not hand over his word and sacrament to the "crowd," so that it would trade with it, in the conviction that these realities "would prove themselves and would prove themselves in the truth." Rather, Christ expressly chose from the core group of his disciples the still smaller circle of the apostles and Peter, and he gave to them the responsibility of carrying his word and his work into the world (cf. Matt 28,19f.). In the same way the hierarchical principle must secure the truth and the work of Christ in the Church of Christ through all time. The following reflections may show in greater detail what this means.

The Subject of Infallibility in the Church

The true place of infallibility is the Church as a whole, as the *sacramentum universale salutis*. And the true cause of infallibility is the presence of Christ and his Spirit in it. As pointed out above, this Church has at least three areas of life: the area of the word of revelation, the area of the sacraments, and the area of the hierarchical ministerial office (pope, bishop and priest, deacon, and lay minister). These areas are themselves personal in character and are rooted in the three tasks of Christ as teaching office, priestly office, and pastoral office. Vatican II has for the first time clearly stressed that all members of the Church, according to their special ministry, share in Christ's three offices in the whole of the Church and that they, therefore, share also in the special character of the magisterial office, namely, infallibility.

a) Thus the Council teaches:

The holy People of God shares also in Christ's prophetic office: it spreads abroad a living witness to him, especially by a life of faith and love and by offering to God a sacrifice of praise, the fruit of lips praising his name (cf. Heb 13,15). The whole body of the faithful [*universitas fidelium*] who have an anointing that comes from the holy one (cf. 1 John 2,20.27) cannot err in matters of belief. This characteristic is shown in the supernatural appreciation of the faith of the whole people [*supernaturali sensu fidei totius populi*], when, "from the bishops to the last of the faithful" they manifest a universal consent in matters of faith and morals. By this appreciation of the faith [*sensus fidei*, not *sensus fidelium*, i.e., opinion of the faithful], aroused and sustained by the Spirit of truth, the People of God, guided by the sacred teaching authority [*sub ductu sacri magisterii*], and obeying it, receives not the mere word of men, but truly the word of God (cf. 1 Thess 2,13), the faith once for all delivered to the saints (cf. Jude 3). The People unfailingly [*indefectibiliter*] adheres to this faith, penetrates it more deeply with right judgment, and applies it more fully in daily life. (LG 12)

The Council continues by pointing to charismatic gifts (1 Cor 12–14) through which individual believers receive from the Holy Spirit the capacity for special works and ministries in the Church. However, the Council adds, "Extraordinary gifts are not to be rashly desired, nor is it from them that the fruits of apostolic labors are to be presumptuously expected. Those who have charge over the Church should judge the genuineness and proper use of these gifts, through their office not indeed to extinguish the Spirit, but to test all things and hold fast to what is good (cf. 1 Thess 5,12.19–21)" (LG 12). In these texts the whole people of God is quite clearly described as the addressee and the bearer of the word of truth in this world, always, of course, in the life-space of the hierarchically organized Church. The infallibility of the believed and lived truth of revelation is anchored in this whole people of God, as life must be anchored and guaranteed in an organism as a whole. However, individual persons can recognize and fulfill their task as "proclaimers of the truth" only in dependence upon this whole and as a service benefitting this whole.

b) The point just made in the perspective of the Church as a whole finds its particular application to those organs in the Church that are in a special way called to proclaim and to lead, namely, in the first place, the bishops. Thus the Council says,

Although the bishops, taken individually, do not enjoy the privilege of infallibility, they do, however, proclaim infallibly the doctrine of Christ on the following conditions: namely, when, even though dispersed throughout the world but preserving for all that amongst themselves and with Peter's successor the bond of communion, in their authoritative teaching concerning matters of faith and morals, they are in agreement that a particular teaching is to be held definitively and absolutely (cf. DS 2879; 3011). This is still more clearly the case when, assembled in an *ecumenical council*, they are, for the universal Church, teachers of and judges in matters of faith and morals, whose decisions must be adhered to with the loyal and obedient assent of faith (CIC c 1322–1323). (LG 25)

Again, the Council stresses the inner unity and communion of the bishops (*communio* or *corpus episcoporum*) among each other and with their head, the pope. This unity is present not only in a council but also in the daily proclamation of bishops in their dioceses and of their diocesan clergy. The two recently defined dogmas about Mary (the Immaculate Conception, 1854; and the assumption, 1950) were not prepared by a council, but by questionnaires and by asking for the *petitio* (the petition that the Church dogmatize a particular doctrine). On the basis of these steps, the doctrines were then proclaimed by the pope as "doctrines of the Church" (cf. Pope Paul VI, "On the Evangelization of Today's World," Dec. 8, 1975). The final decision about the infallibility of proclaimed truth cannot, of course, rest with individuals or subordinate authorities (national or provincial synods, etc.). This decision is tied to the Church as a whole and has its final guarantee in the pope, in his explicit proclamation or his tacit approbation.

c) The first or final and supreme subject or bearer of this infallibility is thus the head of the college of apostles, the Church's supreme shepherd, the vicar of Christ on earth in the Church's external guidance, namely, the bishop of Rome as the successor of St. Peter. He is this subject or bearer "in virtue of his office, when, as supreme pastor and teacher of all the faithful—who confirms his brethren in the faith (cf. Luke 22,32)—he proclaims in an absolute decision [*definitivo actu:* cf. LG 25; *ex cathedra:* DS 3074] a doctrine pertaining to faith or morals." The meaning and limits of this declaration will become clearer by discussing the question of the object of infallibility.

The Object of Infallibility

a) The true object of proclamation, and thus of the Church's infallibility, is the *depositum fidei,* i.e., the truths of faith, the orders and norms of Christian moral life and the revealed facts necessary for salvation. What is contained in Scripture and tradition must be "transmitted integrally . . . ; and through the light of the Spirit of truth it is scrupulously preserved in the Church and unerringly explained." The Church expects no "new public revelation as pertaining to the divine deposit of faith" (LG 25).

b) Of course, inasmuch as faith does not merely consist in the adherence to the word of Scripture, but demands an understanding of revelation as well as action on its basis, all philosophical systems in which the human understanding of the world and humanity attempts to find critical expression, as well as the various assertions of the sciences dealing with the human person and with nature by which our various philosophical systems are called forth and supported, must be submitted to the judgment of faith and thus to the judgment of the Church (cf. Vatican I on faith and reason, DS 3042–3043). This situation raises problems that differ from those connected with the pure truths (mysteries) of faith. For, the progress of the natural sciences as well as of theology enlarges the sphere covered by each, so that the points of intersection between them must be clarified anew each time. This demands on both sides respect for both the scientific as well as the creedal-moral conscience. The openness of the theological conscience of faith and the hypothetical nature of the ever-growing conclusions of natural science demand on both sides critical self-limitation as well as readiness to humbly serve truth and reality as a whole. Classical theology developed the distinctions (discussed by the introduction to dogmatic theology) between *fides divina* and *fides ecclesiastica*, between primary truths of revelation and secondary conclusions and dogmatic facts. These distinctions can be helpful only if they are seen and used in the light of the unity and wholeness of truth and reality.

c) Especially the growth of critical historiography, of the experimental human sciences (psychology, sociology) and the growth of the natural sciences spurred by new developments in mathematics, experimental methods and technology have made the common and mutual understanding of realities and truths more difficult. This difficulty already appeared in the condemnation of the Jansenist propositions by Pope Innocent X (1653; DS 2001–2007). In our time it has appeared even more clearly in the questions of historical (not merely theologically postulated) monogenism (cf. the encyclical *Humani Generis*, DS 3896–3897). Various factors must always be kept in mind when facing these difficulties: respect for the freedom of research; the possibility of a narrow worldview underlying particular scientific developments (materialism, evolutionism, idealism); the hypothetical or statistical character of many scientific claims; a sensitivity to possible consequences for the moral self-understanding of the human person, which may uncover errors in the approach of a particular line of research.

d) Finally, it is important to insist that despite the clear distinction between faith and knowledge, not only with regard to their method, but also with regard to their object (*non solum principio sed etiam obiecto,* DS 3015), despite the recognition of the supernatural character of faith, "there can never be a real discrepancy between faith and reason, *nulla tamen umquam inter fidem et rationem vera dissensio esse potest"* (DS 3017; cf. the whole Vatican I discussion of faith and reason DS 3015–3020). The nineteenth century materialist worldview has been overcome by the new atomic physics and electronics and this has made it possible for the Church to have a new and positive relation to the secular sciences. In Vatican II this improved relationship led to a new openness to human autonomy and freedom as well as for the autonomy of earthly affairs.

If by the autonomy of earthly affairs is meant the gradual discovery, exploitation, and ordering of the laws and values of matter and society, then the demand for autonomy is perfectly in order: it is at once the claim of modern man and the desire of the creator. By the very nature of creation, material being is endowed with its own stability, truth and excellence, its own order and laws. These man must respect as he recognizes the methods proper to every science and technique. Consequently, methodical research in all branches of knowledge, provided it is carried out in a truly scientific manner and does not override moral laws, can never conflict with the faith, because the things of the world and the things of faith derive from the same God. [There follows a passage in which the Church distances itself from the former treatment of Galileo.] However, if by the term "the autonomy of earthly affairs" is meant that material being does not depend on God and that man can use it as if it had no relationship to its creator, then the falsity of such a claim will be obvious to anyone who believes in God. (GS 36)

For these statements to be universally valid, certain conditions must be met. In conclusion we turn now to these conditions.

The Conditions for Infallible Statements in the Church

a) The object and the subject of infallibility as discussed above are part of these conditions. As for the form of infallible statements, the only condition is that the Church (the pope) consciously and expressly intends to propose a given statement as definitively binding for the whole Church. Although a special solemn form, as was used for the Immaculate Conception (1854) and the Assumption of Mary (1950), is not necessary, the will to declare a truth infallibly must still be clearly expressed by formulations such as "we define and declare that it is altogether necessary for salvation to believe . . . , *definimus et declaramus omnino esse de necessitate salutis credere.* . . ."

b) Conciliar decrees take on their binding character in the specific form of recognition by the pope. This binding character is present not only in conciliar *canones,* but also in the chapters themselves, insofar as they have the character of definitions. The arguments given in these chapters are not infallible. Infallibility applies only to the statements expressing the faith.

c) The history of dogma and of the papacy shows that historical circumstances, too, must be taken into account for the correct understanding of the binding character of infallible statements. It is only in this way that one can understand why the intention of Pope Boniface VIII to define "that the two swords, the ecclesiastical and the secular power, are subject only to the Church and the Pope" (bull *Unam Sanctam*, DS 783) or the condemnation of Galileo's heliocentric teachings under Pope Urban VIII (1633) by reference to Josh 10,12f. cannot be called infallible, because they refer to matters that are not the object of the infallibility of saving doctrine and because the historical circumstances made this insight difficult at the time. In addition, the pope must enjoy complete moral freedom, a freedom that may under certain circumstances be limited or absent due to personal or political conditions (such as imprisonment).

The decisive point remains that all sides should understand the charism of infallibility as a gift to the world, as a service for truth and for humanity, not as a means for power.

After these discussions of infallibility, the remaining question to be clarified about the office of the pope is the question of the relation between the office of the pope and the tasks of the worldwide episcopate.

7. THE OFFICE OF PETER AND THE APOSTOLIC OFFICE: THE POPE AND THE WORLD-WIDE EPISCOPATE

As a conclusion to the discussion about the episcopal office and the college of bishops as well as the discussion of the papacy and its primacy we must turn to the question, raised by the two Vatican Councils (1870 and 1962–1965) about the inner unity of the Church's pastoral offices. In the eighteenth century (and up to about 1848) this question was discussed extensively.[113] Vatican I placed such decisive emphasis on the primacy of the Roman bishop, without pointing to the college of apostles, that, almost up to Vatican II in 1962, the question of the unity of the Church's pastoral office was seen only in terms of the papacy. (A possible exception is the well-known controversy about Bismarck's circular, 1872, the collective response by the German bishops, and Rome's response to it:

cf. DS 3112–3117). By returning to the great tradition, especially that of the first millennium, the question of the sacrament of orders as well as that of the pastoral office in the Church was seen and answered in a new way.

a) Above, when discussing the primacy of jurisdiction we introduced the two texts from *Lumen Gentium* 22b in which supreme pastoral power in the Church is attributed to the pope as well as to the bishops. The coordinating of these two assertions called forth significant theological efforts during the Council itself, and the clarification of questions connected with them remains the task of further theological reflection.

During the Council itself an initial clarification was made by the *nota praevia*, the "Preliminary Explanatory Note" read on November 16, 1964, by the Council's general secretary, Cardinal Pericles Felici "at the behest of higher authority" in connection with the *Notae* on chapter 3 of *Lumen Gentium*.[114] The *nota* discusses (1) the concept of the episcopal college; (2) the way in which one becomes a member of this college; and (3–4) the relationship between the pope and the college of bishops. The following passage is particularly important,

[The distinction between the Pope and the college of bishops] is not a distinction between the Roman Pontiff and the bishops taken together but between the Roman Pontiff by himself and the Roman Pontiff along with the bishops. The Pope alone, in fact, being *head* of the college, is qualified to perform certain actions in which the bishops have no competence whatsoever, for example, the convocation and direction of the college, approval of the norms of its activity, and so on (cf. modus 18). It is for the Pope, to whom the care of the whole flock of Christ has been entrusted, to decide the best manner of implementing this care, either personal or collegiate, in order to meet the changing needs of the Church in the course of time. The Roman Pontiff undertakes the regulation, encouragement, and approval of the exercise of collegiality as he sees fit [*secundum propriam discretionem*]. The Pope, as supreme pastor of the Church, may exercise his power at any time, as he sees fit [*suam potestatem omni tempore ad placitum exercere potest*], by reason of the demands of his office [*munere*]. . . . Clearly it is the *connection* of bishops *with their head* that is in question throughout and not the activity of bishops *independently* of the Pope. (*Nota praevia*, Preliminary Explanatory Note, 3–4, 425–426)

This text clarifies that what is at issue in this hierarchical system is always the single top, whether one sees it more as the college of bishops with the pope as head, or as the pope alone as single head. It rejects both a monarchy in a human sense and the view that the pope and the college of bishops are in a juridical sense two independent functions of leadership next to each other.

The recognition of the episcopate of the Eastern Church, which is not "in fact" ordered to the leadership of Rome, but whose activity is fully acknowledged by Rome (cf. OE 27; UR 15,3) led to an addendum to the *nota praevia*. "The ontologico-sacramental function, which must be distinguished from the juridico-canonical aspect [*munus sacramentale ontologicum, quod distinguendum est ab aspectu canonico-iuridico*], cannot be discharged without hierarchical communion" (ibid. p. 426). Concerning sacramental theology and the sacraments of the Eastern Church, this statement raises the question discussed since Augustine of the distinction between licit and valid dispensing of the sacraments. The answer to this question is explicitly left open for further theological discussion. At any rate, the validity of the sacraments of the Eastern Church, in cases in which questions of form do not pose an obstacle, is implied in the recognition of ordinations performed in the Eastern Church.

By the emphasis it places on the unity of the Church's leadership in its head, the *nota praevia* does most justice, not only to the biblical foundation and the development of the hierarchy in the course of the Church's history, but also to contemporary historical developments through which the world and humanity have increasingly become a single visible unity.

b) The *nota* does well to mention the clear distinction between a juridical and a dogmatic perspective. This distinction is of great value for many other theological questions. Quite apart from this distinction, the *nota* allows one to pinpoint some opinions on the relation between the two aspects (the pope and the episcopal college) in the one function of leadership that cannot be reconciled with the text and intention of *Lumen Gentium* chapter 3. Some examples: (1) The pope and the college of bishops are two equal bearers of the one supreme pastoral power in the Church. (2) The person of the pope is the only bearer of the supreme pastoral authority and he merely authorizes the college of bishops as his subject so that it can engage in collegiate action, an action it cannot perform out of itself, but only due to papal authorization. (3) The only bearer of the supreme pastoral office is the college of bishops, which the pope must represent as a member of this college, chosen and appointed to represent it in such a way that he remains tied to the will of that college. (4) There is probably a fourth unacceptable position, namely, that the collegiate form of exercising the pastoral office, e.g., in an ecumenical council, is the "ordinary manner" of exercising this office, while independent action by the pope constitutes an "extraordinary manner." This opinion, which would allow the exercise of the papal office only in extraordinary cases, does justice neither to the Church's actual history nor to the text of the *nota praevia*.

c) Following the *nota praevia*, the new "Outline of a Post-Conciliar Canon Law" (Regensburg 1979, p. 197) distinguishes a "canonical interpretation" of the unity of the pastoral office, exercised by the college of bishops (with the pope as head) and by the pope alone (as head of the universal Church), for which it "assumes two not completely distinct bearers of the supreme pastoral authority in the Church," from "the declaration made by dogmatic theologians, according to which the two modes of the exercise of supreme authority in the Church constitute a merely functional duality, which does not impair a fundamental unity of the subject of this authority." "The only bearer of supreme pastoral power in the Church is the college of bishops with the pope as head. The college can act in two ways, either in a strictly collegiate way which must be initiated and confirmed by the pope (e.g., a Council), or through its head (alone). Even in the latter case, the college of bishops is at work through its representative, the pope."

The final sentence needs to be clarified. The *nota praevia* says, "The pope, as supreme pastor of the Church, may exercise his power at any time, as he sees fit. . . . But as the Church's tradition attests, the college, although it is always in existence, is not for that reason continually engaged in *strictly* collegiate activity. In other words it is not always in full activity (*in actu pleno*) . . ." (*nota praevia*, 4, p. 426). For example, individual bishops act in the ordinary leadership of the "churches" (2 Cor 8,23) as the successors of the apostles, not through a participation in the pope's pastoral authority over the whole Church, though still in agreement with their head.

The Church cannot be understood philosophically in the abstract, nor can it be understood in the concrete in terms of earthly power, as the state is understood.[115] Its "reality" must be understood through signs in terms of the sacramental mystery. Thus the Constitution on the Church says,

This college [of bishops], in so far as it is composed of many members, is the expression of the multifariousness and universality of the People of God; and of the unity of the flock of Christ, in so far as it is assembled under one head. In it the bishops, whilst loyally respecting the primacy and pre-eminence of their head, exercise their own proper authority for the good of their faithful, indeed even for the good of the whole Church, the organic structure and harmony of which are strengthened by the continued influence of the Holy Spirit. (LG 22)

Collegiate unity is also apparent in the mutual relations of each bishop to individual dioceses and with the universal Church. The Roman Pontiff, as the successor of Peter, is the perpetual and visible source and foundation of the unity both of the bishops and of the whole company of the faithful. The individual bishops are the visible source and foundation of unity in their own particular churches, which are constituted after the model of the universal Church; it is in these and formed out of them that the one and unique Catholic Church exists. And for that reason precisely each bishop represents his own church, whereas all, together with the pope, represent the whole Church in a bond of peace, love and unity. (LG 23)

The outward sign that distinguishes the pope from the other bishops, with whom he shares the one episcopal consecration, is the "Roman See" which he alone occupies. (As the only outward secular sign he wears a white robe, the only bishop of the Western Church to do so. Pope Paul VI began to wear a simple episcopal mitre instead of the "tiara," which had been an outward sign of the papacy since Innocent III).

d) The letter to all bishops of the Catholic Church (Feb. 22, 1967) in which Paul VI announced the "Year of Faith" as the nineteen hundredth anniversary of the martyrdom of the two princes of the apostles, Peter and Paul, states in its introduction, "Peter and Paul are the apostles whom the faithful people rightly calls the pillars of the Roman See and of the Church spread over the whole world." Beyond its local significance for the city of Rome, this statement can stimulate valuable reflections about the question of the unity of the pastoral office in the Church. Peter, one of Christ's first disciples (cf. John 1,40–42), who appears in Scripture as the spokesman of the twelve apostles and whom Christ appointed expressly as the "shepherd of the whole flock," as the foundation of his Church and the special keeper of the keys, and as the guarantor of the confession of truth, is here called "a pillar of the Roman see" together with a man who was not part of the original college of Twelve (Mark 3,16–19), who was not even cho-

sen by the other apostles as a replacement for Judas Iscariot (Acts 1,21–25), but who was called in an extraordinary
manner by the transfigured Lord (Acts 9). Paul is given this
joint title with Peter, because, as "a chosen instrument"
(Acts 9,15) he opened up the great world mission of which
the first history of the Church, the Book of Acts, tells us.
Since among the many bishops of the worldwide Church
only very few bishops (mainly of the Eastern Church) can
point to the "See of one of the twelve apostles" as the
origin of their office, one should reflect whether succession, in addition to more or less specific "personal" derivation from one of the twelve apostles, should not rather be
seen again as founded on the commission and activity
that flow from the apostolic missionary command (Matt
18,19). This approach might show more clearly the inner
equilibrium between the Petrine pastoral commission and
the apostolic missionary commission to go into the whole
world. In this way it might help to mitigate historical tensions (cf. Gal 2,11–14) that were still felt to be at work
when this question was discussed in Vatican II.

After these reflections on the episcopal and papal office,
our remaining task is to discuss, at least in outline, the
office of the priest, the office of the deacon, and, if one
wishes to recognize such an office, the world-office of the
laity.

The Presbyterate; The Priesthood

With our previous discussion of the sacrament of orders
serving as background, let us discuss some supplementary
points on the priesthood as a state of life and on the relationship between bishop and priests.

I. HISTORICAL ASPECTS

We have already spoken about the multiplicity and organization of offices in the Church (X). The office or state of

the presbyterate derives in its original concept from the Israelite-Jewish constitution,[116] where "presbyter" referred to the head of a synagogue, and also to the members of the Sanhedrin in the Jerusalem Temple. These two meanings were probably the origin of the Christian "presbyters," who made their first appearance in Jewish Christian communities, as in Jerusalem around James (Acts 11,30; 21,18; Jas 5,14). In gentile Christian communities, presbyters are mentioned as leaders of the communities during the first missionary journey of Paul and Barnabas, who appointed presbyters in the newly founded communities of Asia Minor and recommended them to the Lord with prayer and the imposing of hands (Acts 14,23). At first, these presbyters are mentioned together with the apostles (Acts 15,2.4.6.22f.) and they appear to be of a rank equal to that of the *episkopoi* (Acts 20,17.28).

In the pastoral epistles "the presbyters" always appear in the plural (college of elders: Tit 1,5; 1 Tim 4,14; 5,17) while the *"episkopos"* is always mentioned in the singular (Tit 1,7; 1 Tim 3,2). (The term used for the 24 elders, *presbyteroi*, in Revelation and the presbyter in 2 John 1 and 3 John 1 is not the title of an office). In *1 Clement* and the *Shepherd of Hermas* the leadership of the community is in the hands of the presbyter. A quite different and clearly hierarchical order of the community appears in the letters of Ignatius of Antioch (d. 116): the *episkopos* stands at the head, while the presbyters (the presbytery) and the servants (*diakonoi*) of both are clearly subordinated to the *episkopos*. The *episkopos* presides in the place of God, and the presbyters in the place of the apostles (*Magn.* 6,1). Obedience to the *episkopos* is determined by God, obedience to the presbyters by the law of Christ (*Magn.* 2). This Antiochean church order appears to have been at first a special case. In the following period there are even cases in which the offices of leadership and of teaching are separated (Clement of Alexandria).

It was only in the ecclesiastical order of Hipploytus of Rome (d. 235), which soon prevailed also in the Orient, that the order of the letters of Ignatius, interpreted in more juridical terms, became binding. In the respective rites of ordination, the *spiritus principalis* was called down upon the bishop as successor of the apostles (accordingly, only the bishop has the power to ordain). By contrast, the *spiritus gratiae* was called down upon the presbyters, who were compared to the presbyters (elders) who acted as Moses' helpers.[117] The following explicit norm was laid down: "The presbyters shall not do anything without the decision of the bishop; for it is to him that the people of God is entrusted, and it is from him that an account about the souls is demanded."[118] Thus Pope Innocent I writes in his letter to Bishop Decentius (416), "Presbyters, as priests of second order, do not possess the full height of the spiritual office; *presbyteri, licet secundi sint sacerdotes, pontificatus tamen apicem non habent*" (DS 215). Although, beginning in the Middle Ages, the sacrament of orders was seen primarily in priestly ordination, rather than episcopal ordination, the pre-eminence of the bishop was still maintained. Thus the Council of Trent taught in 1563 that, "besides the other ecclesiastical grades, the bishops, who have succeeded the apostles, principally belong to this hierarchical Order . . . they are superior to priests, confer the sacraments of confirmation, ordain ministers to the Church . . ." (DS 1768; cf. also DS 1777).

2. THE TEACHING OF VATICAN II

The early Christian understanding of the relation between episcopate and presbyterate was validated in a new way by Vatican II which expressly taught again that the true sacrament of orders is episcopal ordination. "The bishop, invested with the fullness of the sacrament of Orders, is 'the steward of the grace of the supreme priesthood'" (LG 26).

Christ . . . has, through his apostles, made their successors, the bishops namely, sharers in his consecration and mission; and these, in their turn, duly entrusted in varying degrees various members of the Church with the office of their ministry. Thus the divinely instituted ecclesiastical ministry is exercised in different degrees by those who even from ancient times have been called bishops, priests and deacons. Whilst not having the supreme degree of the pontifical office, and notwithstanding the fact that they depend on the bishops in the exercise of their own proper power, the priests are for all that associated with them by reason of their sacerdotal dignity; and in virtue of the sacrament of Orders, after the image of Christ, the supreme and eternal priest, they are consecrated in order to preach the Gospel and shepherd the faithful as well as to celebrate divine worship as true priests of the New Testament. On the level of their own ministry they share [*participes*] in the unique office of Christ. . . . The priests, prudent cooperators of the episcopal college and its support and mouthpiece [*ordinis episcopalis providi cooperatores eiusque adiutorium et organum*], called to the service of the People of God, constitute, together with their bishop, a unique sacerdotal college [*presbyterium*] dedicated to a variety of duties. In each local assembly of the faithful they represent in a certain sense the bishop, with whom they are associated in all trust and generosity; in part they take upon themselves his duties and solicitude and in their daily toils discharge them . . . they should be eager to lend their efforts to the pastoral work of the whole diocese, nay rather of the whole Church. (LG 28)

From these statements the Council draws the necessary practical conclusions for the relation of the bishops to their priests, of the priests to their bishops, and of the priests among each other, as well as for the activity and the life of priests in this world for the kingdom of God. These conclusions are contained, above all, in the Decree on the Ministry and Life of Priests (*Presbyterorum Ordinis*). In the perspective of the ontic unity of the sacrament of orders, despite all hierarchical order of tasks and ministerial functions, the relation between the bishop and the presbytery is introduced as follows: "All priests share with the bishops the one identical priesthood and ministry of Christ. Consequently the very unity of their consecration and mission requires their hierarchical union with the order of bishops" (PO 7). In the pastoral spirit of the whole Council, the subsequent sections (PO 8–9) unfold the relation between bishop and priests as a relation of trust and love, of care and obedience. They also portray the inner cohesion of the whole presbyterate as a witness for the world and for the building of the kingdom of God in the Church of Christ.

3. THE ONE PRIESTHOOD AND THE TASKS CONDITIONED BY THE WORLD

Independently of this ontic and functional hierarchical order, a variety of "offices" in the Church arose in the course of time, conditioned by secular honors and secular tasks, e.g., the order of "arch-priests" (since the fourth century) as representatives of the bishop, still in use today in the principal Roman basilicas, St. Peter and S. Maria Maggiore. "Arch-priests" were also introduced when associations of parishes were formed in the Carolingian period. After the Middle Ages, "deans," commissioned by the bishops in the interest of the diocese, were put in charge of larger groups of parishes (deaneries) in order to fulfill and coordinate the more comprehensive pastoral tasks, even those regarding the clergy.[119]

Dominated as it is by the division of labor, the modern age stimulated the formation of many "offices" in the Church which are conditioned by various tasks in the service of the schools and of education (professors, religion teachers), of law and administration (tribunals and chanceries), of cultural and social needs of various kinds (youth work, work with the elderly, charities, etc.) and even of comprehensive pastoral needs in counseling and the liturgy, etc.

The fundamental and decisive norm is this: in all "offices," whatever their particular tasks may be in this world, priests must live and fulfill their apostolate in the power of consecration and mission and in the power of following Christ in a total self-giving for his cause, the kingdom of his Father in this world.[120]

The Diaconate

Why should we discuss the diaconate in the Church at this point, namely in the perspective of hierarchical offices, after discussing the apostolic or episcopal office and the priesthood? We do so, not only because the diaconate is confirmed as a "ministerial" office by the Church's explicit doctrine (Council of Florence, DS 1326; Council of Trent, DS 1765) and by a long tradition going back to the very beginning, but, in addition, because we wish to show the ontological difference between the priesthood and the diaconate and the specific form of the diaconate within the unity of the one sacrament of orders. This approach will, at the same time, prepare the way for a "postscript" on the possibility and necessity of a distinct world-office of the laity.

I. HISTORICAL ASPECTS

a) It is probably right to assume that the Semitic messenger law, which early Judaism had developed into the juridical institution of the *Shaliach*, was given a special, personal and comprehensive form by Jesus, who "sent" the twelve apostles (and their numerous successors). This new form is evident in the manner in which the apostles (and their successors) carried out their office, namely, as "world-missionaries" who were sent for the whole and one community (Church) of Christ. It was only later that the Church's geographical extension made a geographical division of this whole necessary.

On the other hand, the institution of the presbyter introduced by the apostles and their successors, which grew out of the Israelite tribal and urban aristocracy, was, in the

Church just as in its original setting, a collegiate office which came into use for smaller, mainly urban communities.

The term "deacon" was first applied to all "servants" in Christ's kingdom, to the apostles as well as to their collaborators and assistants, and it always expresses the idea of service in a personal rather than an impersonal order. Thus Paul writes, "Having gifts [*charismata*] that differ according to the grace given to us, let us use them: . . . if service [*diakonia*], in our serving; . . . he who is a leader, with zeal; he who does acts of mercy, withy cheerfulness. Let love be genuine; . . . love one another with brotherly affection; outdo one another in showing honor. Never flag in zeal, be aglow with the Spirit, serve the Lord [*solicitudine non pigri, Spiritu ferventes, Domino servientes*]" (Rom 12,6–11). It is in this sense that one should probably understand the following exhortation addressed only to deacons in the list of the virtues necessary for the diaconate given in 1 Tim 3,8–13. "They must hold the mystery of the faith (of the pure faith) with a clear conscience (in inner personal obedience to the Spirit of the truth of faith)" (1 Tim 3,8). For this reason the consecration rites of some Churches (e.g., the Western Syrian and the Maronite Churches) compare the service of deacons with that of angels, and most other rites refer to the example of the inspired martyr Stephen. (At least after Irenaeus, the seven "*diakonoi*" of Acts 6,1–6 were understood as "deacons." Contemporary exegetes (e.g., Gächter) prefer to interpret them as presbyters for the hellenistic communities.) Many rites of consecration also quote 1 Tim 3,13: "those who serve well as deacons gain a good standing for themselves and also great confidence in the faith which is in Christ Jesus." This quote is historically confirmed by the ease with which good deacons gained access to the higher offices, the presbyterate and even the episcopate, a development that led to the eventual abolition of the independent diaconate.[121]

b) The history of the diaconate, especially in the Eastern Churches, shows that the tasks of deacons differed in different places and different periods.[122] Three tasks are generally mentioned. The first is charity, not merely private charity, but the first ecclesiastical social institution (it was probably originally connected with the episcopate, cf. Phil 1,1, and worked between various communities in the service of the whole Church, cf. 2 Cor 8 and 9; Acts 2,44f.). Deacons soon became administrators of ecclesiastical property, especially property in the hands of the bishop (cf. *Ign. Trall.* 2,3; *Herm. Sim.* 9,26; Basil founded a separate "hospital"). In the second and third centuries (Hippolytus) deacons increasingly acted as servants of the bishops and priests in the liturgy. They were responsible for keeping order in the church building (Justin, *Apol.* I,65 and 67), they helped with the instruction of catechumens, with baptisms (of men), and with distributing communion (esp. communion brought to the sick, *Ordines Rom.* I–IV).

c) The early Church had a distinct institution of deaconesses (Rom 16,1), which was probably often identical with the order of widows (cf. 1 Tim 5,9–16, Titus 2,3–5). The ministry of deaconesses, apart from service at the altar, which was reserved for deacons, was the same as that of deacons, especially in the ministry toward women. The deaconesses were also ordained by the bishop through the imposition of hands (which was expressly called *cheirotonia* in the East). However, various canons decreed that the consecration of deaconesses is not a sacrament (Nicaea, can. 19; Laodicea, can. 11; Hippolytus, *Trad. Ap.* 37 and 47). With the rise of monastic orders, deaconesses disappeared, in the West by the fifth century, in the East by the seventh.[123]

d) The diaconate was preserved as a distinct state in the Eastern Church; in the Western Church it became a mere step on the way to the priesthood. Work for the poor was taken over by ecclesiastical groups of lay brothers, until charismatic figures (e.g., Giovanni di Dio and Vincent de

Paul) founded separate orders, also orders of women, for this purpose. In the Reformation Calvin called again for the office of the deacon to take care of the poor (*Inst.* IV,3,9). Luther, on the other hand, called upon secular authorities to fulfill this task. After the Enlightenment, civic philanthropic associations took on charitable work. In the Catholic sphere a number of congregations for men and women were formed for this purpose in the nineteenth century. Following the pattern of the "sisters of Clement" in Münster, Protestant churches set up the institution of "deaconesses" (J. H. Wichern in Hamburg) and, after 1948, the *"Innere Mission."* However, these institutions cannot be equated with the diaconate of the early Church.

In the Catholic Church only the so-called *"archdiaconate"* maintained itself until recently. It was developed in the fourth century. Beginning in the Carolingian period, it asserted itself more and more as a "factor of power" beside the priesthood and even the episcopate. In its inner nature it can no longer be understood in terms of the hierarchical order of offices.[124]

2. THE EARLY CHRISTIAN DIACONATE AS RENEWED BY VATICAN II

a) In the Eastern Churches the early Christian diaconate has been maintained as an independent *ordo* for the liturgy. In the Western Church there have been repeated efforts to bring the early Christian diaconate to life again as a separate order. This happened for the first time at Trent and especially after World War II, due to the shortage of priests. The movement originated in Germany (Cologne and Freiburg), spread in France, and was advocated especially by the missionary orders. Vatican II picked up these efforts and offered initial guidelines in the Constitution on the Liturgy (SC 35), in the Decree on the Catholic Eastern Churches (OE 17), in the Decree on the Church's Missionary Activity (AG 15f.), and, above all, in the Constitution on the Church (LG 29). The *Motu Proprio "Sacrum di-aconatus ordinem"* of June 18, 1967, left it up to the individual conferences of bishops to ask Rome for permission to introduce the independent diaconate. It already set down some norms about the age, training, tasks, and celibacy requirements of independent deacons and gave a formula for the consecration of deacons, which follows the mainstream of tradition.

Generally speaking the tasks of the independent diaconate are primarily in liturgical, catechetical, and pastoral areas, rather than in the area of charitable work, because ecclesiastical institutions for charity were already in place. On August 15, 1972, Pope Paul VI published two Apostolic letters, *Ministeria Quaedam*, on the non-sacramental offices of lector and acolyte (cf. *Vatican Council II*, pp. 427–32), and *Ad Pascendum* for the sacramental diaconate (ibid., pp. 433–40). The arduous struggle for the reintroduction of the early Christian diaconate was thus brought to a blessed conclusion.

b) The doctrine of Vatican II on the tasks of the independent deacon was expressed as follows in the *Motu Proprio* and in the later rite of ordination:

They will draw new strength from the gift of the Holy Spirit. They will help the bishop and his body of priests as ministers of the word, of the altar, and of charity. They will make themselves servants of all. As ministers of the altar they will proclaim the Gospel, prepare the sacrifice, and give the Lord's body and blood to the community of believers. It will also be their duty, at the bishop's discretion, to bring God's word to believer and unbeliever alike, to preside over public prayer, to baptize, to assist at marriages and bless them, to give viaticum to the dying, and to lead the rites of burial. Once they are consecrated by the laying on of hands that comes to us from the apostles and are bound more closely to the altar, they will perform works of charity in the name of the bishop or the pastor. From the way they go about these duties, may you recognize them as disciples of Jesus, who came to serve, not to be served. (Pontifical, pp. 159–60)

c) What we said above about the episcopate and the priesthood raises the question, How can the diaconate be integrated as a third rank into the unity of the sacrament of orders? We must show its specific relation to Christ and his offices and thus to the whole Church and to what is innermost in it.[125] The Vatican II Constitution on the Church expressly declares, "Thus the divinely instituted ecclesiastical ministry is exercised in different degrees by those who even from ancient times have been called bishops, priests and deacons" (LG 28). "The holy synod teaches, moreover, that the fullness of the sacrament of Orders is conferred [only] by episcopal consecration" (LG 21). The priests are second in rank and depend in the exercise of their power on the bishop (LG 28). "At a lower level of the hierarchy are to be found deacons, who receive the imposition of hands 'not unto the priesthood, but unto the ministry.' For, strengthened by sacramental grace they are dedicated to the People of God, in conjunction with the bishop and his body of priests, in the service of the liturgy, of the Gospel and of works of charity" (LG 29).

(1) There is only one sacrament of orders. Since episcopal consecration, priestly ordination, and ordination to the diaconate bring about three ranks or levels in the one ecclesiastical office that is shaped by the sacrament of orders, the office itself, which must be understood as related to three terms, Christ, his Church and the bearer of the office, must have a different rank or level in each of these three relations. For the deacon, these relations are as follows.

In the context of his task, the deacon is ordered to the people of the Church with the same complete personal dedication and responsibility as the other two ranks or levels, the priests and the bishops. In the Church as a hierarchically organized institution, his task is determined by the respective tasks of the two superior ranks, the priests and the bishops. However, he owes his dignity and the power of his office only to the bishop (not to the priests), because he receives his consecration and mission only from the bishop.

The bearer of an ecclesiastical office, as an "official person," is essentially qualified and determined through his service, a service that is always service for human beings, service for the Church as an institution, and finally and primarily service for Christ and his cause. Hence the deacon must serve Christ always and everywhere with his whole person, because it is in Christ alone that all consecration and mission is anchored. This service implies the continuous and complete gift of self, ever anew, to the Lord (totus tuus, the motto of Pope John Paul II). With all that can serve others on this earth he will serve each person entrusted to him and thus the Church as the People of God. This service implies self-sacrificing deeds of love and of concern for the salvation of others. The scope of this ministry, its special tasks in the Church, is determined by the commission conferred on him by the bishop and by priests, but it must also be seen and realized ever anew by the deacon. The character of this service is determined by trusting, respectful, and engaged obedience.

Finally, the deacon's gift of self to the Lord Jesus Christ, seen from the perspective of the deacon's office, must be related to the three offices of Christ: priest, teacher, and shepherd. The question thus arises how the deacon's rank should be defined in his relation to Christ. The answer is difficult, because Christ's offices cannot be seen as impersonal tasks, but must be seen in personal terms. Christ himself is the way (the pastoral office) the truth (the magisterial office) and the life (the priestly office) (cf. John 14,6).

With regard to the office of leadership, the difference in rank can be shown by the external distinction between various tasks. The bishop leads the diocese and is responsible for the whole Church, not only in a council, but always as a member of the order of bishops (apostles). The priest has a more particular sphere of responsibility (parish, religion teacher, etc.), but through the sacrifice of the Mass and the dispensing of the sacraments he is likewise intimately tied and connected to the whole Church as the *universale sacramentum salutis*. The deacon exercises his office of leadership more in the space that prepares this living mystery. Still, his personal charisma may have important things to contribute in this space for the whole Church as *mysterium salutis*.

It is more difficult to show differences of rank in the magisterial office, because truth, especially the truth of faith, is always concerned with the whole. Nevertheless, a clear difference in rank appears with respect to the "order or 'hierarchy' of truths" contained in the Christian faith (UR 11). It appears also in the commission to teach and, above all, in the "certain gift of truth [*charisma certum veritatis*]" (DV 8).

The most difficult thing is to explain the difference in rank between bishops, priests, and deacons with respect to the priesthood. Bishops and priests are of equal rank in the central mysteries of the priestly office, the offering of the sacrifice of salvation and the forgiveness of sins. Nevertheless, the fullness of the sacrament of orders belongs only to the bishop. Only the bishop can pass on the sacrament of orders. But how should the deacon's rank be characterized, because in the preparation of the sacrifice and in the distribution of communion he really does no more than what lay ministers do? However, this activity of lay ministers is really an ad hoc solution dictated by necessity. It belongs by right to the office of the deacon. The correctness of this answer can be seen more clearly if one does not conceive the priesthood only in terms of the priestly functions of the sacrifice of the mass and the forgiveness of sins, as the Middle Ages tended to do, but rather in terms of the inner participation in the activity of Christ. Given this perspective one can say that whatever the deacon does in fulfillment of his office, he does "in and with and through Christ." His activity represents in all things Christ's activity, even when he does the same things he did earlier as a layman. The priestly office is primarily a personal determination and marking of a man out of which, secondarily and in terms of function, his activity flows as a priestly activity.

(2) These remarks about the priesthood suggest that we return at this point to the offices of Christ in order to meditate on it anew. In the face of the question of the deacon's rank in the priesthood, a rank he has on the basis of the one ordination, the one sacrament of orders, the list of Christ's offices as "teacher, pastor, and priest," which was introduced by Calvin (*Inst.* II, 15) and adopted by Catholic theology in the seventeenth century, appears problematic in at least three ways.

First, in the medieval spirit, this list understands the priestly office completely in terms of the priest's functions, in terms of his power to celebrate the redeeming sacrifice of Christ and of distributing his redeeming grace in the forgiveness of sins, especially in the sacrament of reconciliation. Christ's true priesthood, however, is rooted in his person, not in his work. His work only receives its true significance from his person. Christ became priest in his incarnation. Here, only here in the person of Christ the God-man, lies the root of the mystery of the New Testament priesthood, which differs, therefore, completely in both form and essence from the Old Testament priesthood. This original Christian truth is missing in Calvin. Also the Middle Ages no longer saw it clearly enough with reference to Christ's priesthood. In the time of the great christological struggles of the fourth and the fifth centuries the original Christian truth was recognized by fathers like Athanasius, Gregory of Nazianzen, Augustine, and Leo the Great. They expressed it in such formulas as: "In Christ God has become man, in order to divinize us." "The incarnation of God was necessary for our salvation." Only the rediscovery of the great theology of the fathers in the nineteenth century led to the view of the "priest as another Christ, *sacerdos alter Christus.*"

Second, only if priesthood is thus understood in the New

Testament perspective in terms of the person of Christ can one understand the difference in rank between bishop and priest. The difference cannot be sufficiently grasped in terms of the capacity to offer the sacrifice of the mass and the sacramental power to forgive sins. Just as mature life is necessary for the passing on of natural life, the bishop's capacity to pass on the sacramental priesthood, as a sort of procreation, is a sign of the fullness of the sacrament in the bishop, a fullness lacking in the priest, although he can perform the priestly acts of the sacrifice of the mass and the forgiveness of sins like the bishop.

Third, if we rightly see the priesthood of Christ in the light of the person of the God-man, we realize (especially when thinking about the diaconate) that we have increasingly overlooked a feature in the priesthood of Christ, partly because of the misleading juxtaposition of the priesthood with the office of teacher and pastor as initiated by Calvin. It is a feature that is part of the biblical image of Christ as well as of the instructions for the New Testament priesthood, namely, the work of salvation performed for concrete persons. As the "Servant of the Lord" in Isaiah (Isa 61,1; 35,5f.; Matt 11,4f.) and the miracle worker of the Gospels (Mark 1–3; 5–8), Jesus again and again performed this work; he demanded it of his disciples when giving them their mission ("Heal the sick, raise the dead, cleanse lepers, cast out demons": Matt 10,8; cf. Luke 9,1–6) and he showed it in the account of the final judgment as the criterion of God's judgment (Matt 25,35f.; 42f.: hungry, thirsty, naked, sick, in prison). Due to certain cultural and social changes, the letter of these instructions may demand a new interpretation today. Still, the spirit of Jesus' demands, and example remains forever binding for the Christian priesthood. This may be the deeper intention of the present day charismatic movement when it appeals for its action to the early Christian charisms as witnessed to by Paul in Corinth (1 Cor 12,4–11).

If what we have just said corresponds to revelation, then

the more correct view of Christ's offices is this: Christ's true "calling," which determines his person as a whole, is his mission as savior. In a New Testament perspective, this is the calling we must see in the life and office of the priesthood. All salvation is founded and contained in Christ's person. This "calling" takes its effect in three offices: the first, namely the teaching office, is directed at the spiritual-intellectual dimension of the human person; the second, the office of shepherd and leader, aims at the human person under the aspect of will and praxis; following Christ's words, "The Son of man came not to be served but to serve" (Mark 10,45; Matt 20,28; Luke 22,26), the third office could be called "an office of service" aimed at the whole concrete person.

According to this perspective the three levels of consecration share in Christ's personal priesthood according to their rank. As for the three "offices" that flow from this priesthood, the bishop is characterized above all by the teaching office, the office of a "watchman"; the priest, in his pastoral task, is ordered rather to the office of shepherd; and the deacon, as the texts of his consecration indicate, is given the office of service (*diakonia*), in which he serves people in their specific situation in the world.

In this way the development of a renewed early Christian diaconate leads into the depth and breadth and can help the Church's overall understanding of offices to achieve what Vatican II intended when it used the term *ministerium* (serving office), rather than *potestas* (power) to refer to ecclesiastical offices. On this basis it could become a reality (at least a reality always desired and aimed at) that bishops, priests, and deacons, who stand under the one sacrament of orders, form that inner unity of activity and life that intends not only a collegiality on the basis of common tasks, but a *communio hierarchica* rooted in the one Lord and brother, the priest Jesus Christ. The *nota praevia* to *Lumen Gentium* says in this context, "Without *communio hierarchica* the sacramental function cannot be fulfilled in its inner nature [*munus sacramentale on-tologicum*] which must be distinguished from the juridical and canonical aspect" (*nota praevia*, p. 426; transl. altered).

In this light one must see and answer the question of celibacy, which is rooted in the persoanl relationship to Christ. In all the ancient Churches celibacy is obligatory for the episcopal office; in the Roman rite it is also binding for the priesthood. In the struggles for a renewed early Christian diaconate it became an important question.

3. LECTOR AND ACOLYTE

The episcopal office, the priesthood, and the diaconate (as a step to the priesthood and as a full or part-time office) constitute together the one hierarchical office in the Church. "Entrance into the clerical state and incardination into a diocese are brought about by ordination to the diaconate" (*Ad Pasc.*, Vatican Council II, p. 440). *Ad Pascendum* thus eliminated tonsure as the reception into the clerical state; it also elininated the so-called "lower orders": exorcist, porter, and subdeacon. The offices of lector and acolyte were given a new liturgical scope. They are interpreted as a nonsacramental installment into a ministry, to be carried out as a preparation for the subsequent ordination to the diaconate or the priesthood. Lay men can also be installed in them for special services in the Church (such as sacristan, lector, cantor, etc.). The Apostolic letter *Ministeria Quaedam* (August 15, 1972) unfolds these two nonsacramental ministries in detail.

The Question of the Secular Office of the Laity

The question of "offices" in the Church cannot be considered completely covered by a discussion of hierarchical offices, if the intentions and teachings of Vatican II are to be sufficiently appreciated in their future-oriented depth. It would be a relapse into the historically conditioned error of the Middle Ages if one followed the *Decretum Gratiani* (C 7 C XII; PL 187,884f.) and distinguished "two kinds of Christians," ecclesiastical and secular, perfect and imperfect. We therefore wish to present some ideas that proceed from the comprehensive view of the priesthood that B. Durst presented in his book about the threefold priesthood.[126] Durst distinguishes between a sacramental priesthood of the hierarchy, a separate baptismal priesthood of Christians, and, finally, a creational priesthood found in every person as a creature of God. The Council did not adopt these distinctions. Still, it repeatedly stressed the importance of the laity in a new Christian understanding. The Decree on the Church's Missionary Activity, for example, writes, "The Church is not truly established and does not fully live, nor is a perfect sign of Christ unless there is a genuine laity [*laicatus veri nominis*] existing and working alongside the hierarchy. For the Gospel cannot become deeply rooted in the mentality, life and work of a people without the active presence of lay people" (AG 21). After a lengthy discussion of the task of the laity, the text continues, "[B]oth pastors and laity each retain their own special functions and obligations" (AG 21). The purpose of our brief discussion cannot be that of unfolding a theology of the laity in the Church. We will focus only on those aspects of such a theology through which the idea of a lay office in the Church can become intelligible and justifiable.

1) The Council speaks of a lay state (*status laicorum*), of a laity, and of lay people (*laicatus, christifideles laici*). It attributes to lay people "a special and indispensable role in the mission of the Church. Indeed, the Church can never be without the lay apostolate; it is something that derives from the layman's very vocation as a Christian" (AA 1). The lay apostolate is thus not something to which lay

people are only called by the hierarchy, as it was assumed in *"Azione Cattolica* (Catholic Action)," the lay organization established by Pope Pius XI in 1925:

present circumstances, in fact demand from lay people an apostolate infinitely broader and more intense. For the constant increase in population, the progress in science and technology, the shrinking of the gaps that have kept people apart, have . . . given rise to new problems which require from the laity an intelligent attention and examination. All the more urgent has this apostolate become, now that autonomy—as is only right—has been reached in numerous sectors of human life. . . . Besides, in many regions where priests are very scarce . . . it is hard to see how the Church could make her presence and her action felt without the help of the laity. (AA 1)

The laity are made to share in the priestly, prophetical and kingly office of Christ [*muneris . . . participes*]; they have therefore, in the Church and in the world, their own assignment in the mission of the whole People of God. In the concrete, their apostolate is exercised when they work (in society) at the evangelization and sanctification of human beings; it is exercised too when they endeavor to have the Gospel spirit permeate and improve the temporal order [*rerum temporalium ordo*]. . . . The characteristic of the lay state [*status l.*] being a life led in the midst of the world and of secular affairs [*negotia saecularia*], lay people are called by God [not only by the hierarchy] to make of their apostolate, through the vigor of their Christian spirit, a leaven in the world. (AA 2)

2) Following the teaching of the Council, the mission of lay people in the world of today can be characterized as follows.

a) It is the task of the Church, and thus also of the laity, to bear witness to and communicate Christ's redeeming grace and his Spirit to the world and thus to return creation to its creator. The world is not an original reality, and so it does not have its goal within itself, contrary to what secularism always assumed and still assumes.[127] Once God the creator and the mystery of God's incarnation in Christ as well as the presence of the Spirit of God in the Church are taken seriously, not only in the knowledge of faith but as the basis of our activity in daily life, the cultural mission we received from God ("fill the earth and subdue it" Gen 1,28) can be fulfilled again in its original manner. The world as creation, the human and subhuman, the living and nonliving world, the whole material world with its possibilities and powers, all of this is the special sphere of lay activity. The Council developed a theocentric and anthropocentric perspective on this world (cf. e.g., the Council's great final document, the Pastoral Constitution on the Church in the Modern World), for, according to Christian doctrine, the world has been created for the sake of the human race, and the human race can and should continue God's work of creation in this world, in a limited way as befits a creature, but nevertheless in the power of spiritual freedom that is the image of God. Christ, the incarnate Son of God, as the world's Alpha and the Omega, is the measure of this continuation (Col 1,13–23).

b) It is the fundamental mystery of the human person that this mission into the world can only be fulfilled in "free freedom." This full freedom is not an automatic fact contained in human nature, but only a possibility of that nature and a religious and moral task. In the particular situation of this world, which is subject to original sin, it is also a gift of divine grace, for which we must ask in freedom. For this reason it can happen that human beings, although they are endowed with spiritual capacities, completely fail in this mission by forgetting, ignoring, rejecting, and denying God, contrary to their state as creatures made in God's image. They can declare that they, who are only creatures and parts of creation, are the center and the goal of their own world. In this hubris they lose themselves, contrary to their own will, to the subhuman world and become its slaves, while they should be its lords and stewards according to God's will. Forgetting God, self-glorification, and abandonment to the world: these are the three basic attitudes that classical theology expressed in the term "original sin" (Augustine also uses the term *concupiscentia*). They entail the loss of the inner freedom in which persons, as creatures of God, can experience and live their nature as images of God and by which they can attain their final goal in immortality as children of God.

c) As long as we live on earth we live in this need and danger. It is overcome only in Jesus Christ, in grace, in the Spirit of Christ. Christ understood himself and his whole life in terms of God, his Father, and he sought nothing else in his life and action than to fulfill the Father's will. In this free reception of himself and gift of himself to God, he showed to the world the archetype of the human person. Through his life and death as "sacrifice for the sin of the world" (John 1,36; Eph 5,2; Heb 10,12) he took our sin upon himself (including the constraints of original sin) and opened for us a way to salvation. He gave us the possibility and capacity "in him and through him and for him" (Col 1,16) "to lead the world back to God and thus to sanctify it" (AA 6).

d) Through ordination and mission, the servant of Christ in the hierarchical office (the bishop, priest, and deacon) is given the task and responsibility of God's way toward the world. The lay person, on the other hand, has been given responsibility for the world (the *temporalia* and *saecularia:* AA 2; 7; 29; LG 31; AG 15; 21) and stands thus in the midst of the world. This is the nature of the lay call or mission into the world, which is a good world as God's creature (Gen 1,10.12.18.21.25.31), but which is as such neither good nor bad (indifferent) for humanity. Through baptism (deepened by the other sacraments—confirmation, reconciliation, Eucharist, and matrimony) Christian lay persons "in their own way share the priestly, prophetic and kingly office of Christ" (LG 31; AA 2; 10; AG 15). The Constitution on the Church summarizes the task of Christian lay people as follows:

Their secular character is proper and peculiar to the laity. . . . By reason of their special vocation it belongs to the laity to seek the kingdom of God by engaging in temporal affairs and directing them according to God's will. They live in the world, that is, they are engaged in each and every work and business of the earth and in the ordinary circumstances of social and family life which, as it were, constitute their very existence. [LG 36 and AG 21 mention, in addition, the cultural tasks.] There they are called by God that, being led by the spirit to the Gospel, they may contribute to the sanctification of the world, as from within like leaven, by fulfilling their own particular duties. Thus, especially by the witness of their life, resplendent in faith, hope and charity they must manifest Christ to others. It pertains to them in a special way so to illuminate and order all temporal things with which they are so closely associated that these may be effected and grow according to Christ and may be to the glory of the Creator and Redeemer. (LG 31)

The other decrees mentioned above contain similar statements.

3) With these preliminary reflections as background, let us raise the question whether one can assume an ecclesial world-office of the laity in addition to the hierarchical ecclesiastical office. The documents of Vatican II do not speak about a "ministry [*ministerium*]" of lay people, but only of their "task [*munus*]." The situation is similar in the secular world, where the term "office" is used only in the political and social sphere, while the term "task" or "achievement" is used in the economic and cultural sphere. However, one should reflect more deeply on the center of the Christian world view, which is a personal reality. God, the creator of the universe, Christ, the redeemer and center of all things, and the human person, the goal and intended lord of creation, must all be understood in personal terms. Since everything that is Christian finds its fulfillment only "in Christ," the Christian understanding of the world may require a different terminology than the secular, non-Christian understanding, so that one can

speak of "office" even in the economic and cultural sphere. In addition, every Christian is consecrated by baptism and shares in the offices of Christ and, on the basis of the world's character as a creature, the call to a secular task can be understood as a mission given by God. Every Christian is part of "a chosen race, a royal priesthood, a holy nation, God's own people, that you may declare the wonderful deeds of him who called you out of darkness into his marvelous light" (1 Pet 2,9). Every Christian is addressed by the exhortation, "Like living stones be yourselves built into a spiritual house, to be a holy priesthood, to offer spiritual sacrifices acceptable to God through Jesus Christ" (1 Pet 2,5).

To summarize, the idea of an "ecclesial world-office of the laity," developed out of the spirit of the Council, could help to clarify the place of lay people in the Church and their consecration and mission for their secular tasks, overcoming thereby the Lutheran denial of a distinct sacramental priesthood (WA 6,407) as well as an anti-ecclesiastical laicalism. This could be a way, over against modern secularism, of recalling to our age the fact that the world is God's creature, and over against materialism, that the ground of all reality is divine and spiritual.

With these signposts for the future, let us conclude this long discussion about offices in the Church.

XII

The Marks or Essential Attributes
of the Apostolic Church

The Church's Essential Attributes or
Proper Marks

Our intention in concluding this chapter on manifestations of the Church's being, life and activity with a discussion of its marks or essential characteristics is dogmatic,
not apologetic. Just as God is brought close to us human
beings in the Scriptures through the human concepts of his
"attributes," the mystery of the Church, as the Church
itself has spoken about it, is clarified and deepened by
speaking of certain marks. Our goal in this section is not to
prove that our Church is the true Church, but to reach a
deeper understanding of the Church itself. At the same
time, as we will soon see, reflection on the marks of the
Church will help us to see the inner connection between
the topics discussed in Part Three and those to be discussed in Part Four, i.e., between the Church's nature and
its task, between its historical obligation and its eschatological task and possibility. As we discuss these
marks, we will notice that the Church has been understood better by the immediate confession of its faith than
by its theology and its rational endeavors.

I. HISTORICAL ASPECTS

How did the idea of the marks of the Church arise and

grow? The Church has always confessed and presented itself in its confessions of faith. From the very beginning (already in the *Epistola Apostolorum*) it has used the attribute "holy" in this confession and it has never been missing to this very day.

The profession of faith or creed, which had its first fixed place in the baptismal liturgy from which it was taken over into the central liturgy of the eucharist, probably had originally three parts like the baptismal formula (Father, Son, and Holy Spirit). As a parallel to the five loaves mentioned in the multiplication of loaves (Mark 6,39), two elements were added: the confession of the "holy Church" and the "forgiveness of sins" (in Egypt the second element was the "resurrection of the body"). After Rufinus called the Roman creed "the Apostles' Creed," controversies arose about this title on several occasions. After the sixteenth century and the struggles with the churches of the Reformation, it was shown that this creed is not a genuine work of the apostles but grew in the course of time as the Church's understanding of itself and of the world. The "Apostles' Creed" is the expression of a new understanding, depending on certain historical conditions, of the ancient and always identical faith.[128] After the controversies with the followers of Huss in the fifteenth century, and above all after the Reformation, the dogmatic meaning of the Church's attributes was given an increasingly apologetic emphasis. The primary concern was to show that these attributes were found only in the "one holy Roman Catholic and apostolic Church" (cf. *Decretum Gelasianum* [A.D. 350], DS 354; against the Waldensians, DS 684; the decree for union with the Greeks, DS 1351; against the Reformation churches, DS 1862 and 1868; Vatican I, DS 3001). Vatican II did not simply identify the Roman Church with "the Church." It stated, rather, "This Church, constituted and organized as a society in this world, subsists in the Catholic Church [N.B., the Council does not say "Roman" Catholic Church], which is gov-

erned by the successor of Peter and by the bishops in communion with him" (LG 8). The statement that the Church
"subsists in" the Catholic Church implies that the true
Church can be found in the Catholic Church, which is not
to deny that it can be found in other churches, especially
the ancient Eastern Churches.

What are the attributes this Church attributed to itself
in the course of time, reflectedly or unreflectedly? The
oldest formulas (*Epistola Apostolorum*, around A.D. 170,
and Hippolytus, around 217) refer to the Church as "the
holy Church." The liturgical Der-Balizeh Papyrus calls it
"the holy catholic Church" (DS 2). This formula was most
widely accepted and is found even in later times. Around
348 Cyril of Jerusalem speaks about "the one holy and
catholic Church" (DS 41). The Symbol of Epiphanius of
Salamis (A.D. 374) is the first text in which we find the
formula, "one holy, catholic and apostolic Church" (DS
42). The formula recurs in the so-called *Constitutiones
Apostolorum* (ca. 380). It became binding, at least for the
West, through the Creed of the First Council of Constantinople (381) as determined by the Council of Chalcedon
(451) (cf. DS 150), and through the use of that creed in the
celebration of the eucharist. Following Ambrose (*Ep.* 42,5;
PL 16,1125) and Pope Leo the Great (*Sermo* 23,6; PL
54,207) the West called its own baptismal creed *symbolum apostolicum* (or *Apostolorum*), although the attribute "apostolic" was originally not part of it. "Apostolic"
was introduced in the "Apostles' Creed" only after Trent
by the catechism of Petrus Canisius, taken over from the
creed used in the mass. In the popular consciousness of the
Western Church, which had been nourished by the Apostles' Creed, the attribute "apostolic" was not present.
It was used (especially in the last two centuries) as the
background of hierarchical thinking for everything connected to Rome, e.g., "Apostolic See," "Apostolic nun-
cio," "Apostolic Letter."

2. THE INNER UNITY OF THE FOUR MARKS

The Church found these four attributes, neither by accident nor by theological deduction, but in the attempt to understand itself and the world for which it has been founded by Christ and for which it is filled with life by Christ's Spirit. It found them at the exact time at which it worked out its trinitarian understanding of God and thus its own "Christian" understanding of the world and of itself. The four attributes possess an inner unity in which each includes the other three.

The Church's *unity* refers to the inner fullness of life of the "holy catholic apostolic Church." It expresses the essence of this universal sacrament of salvation in the world. The Church's *catholicity* corresponds to the outer sign of that sacrament; its *holiness* to inner grace; and its historical *apostolicity* to the institution by Christ.

The Church's confession of its holiness was historically the first attribute to be used. This fact expresses the experience of the unique meaning and purpose of this new community initiated and held in existence by the triune God, a community that must transform all of humanity into the people of God, and all human beings into children of God. While the Church's unity is sacramental, its holiness is eschatological.

The Church's catholicity is also an eschatological attribute. It points to the Church's universality as a community intended for the whole of humanity. This universality must be realized in time through God's grace and free human decision.

Apostolicity, on the other hand, refers primarily to the unique historicity of this Church as the mystical body of Christ in this world. It speaks, not of the end times, but of the historical beginning. Of course, this historical beginning points, in turn, to its trans-historical origin in the mystery of the triune God, who transcends time.

Our human reflection about the Church and its attributes finds thus no natural limit and no justifiable end. We are left only with the saying of Paul as he stood before the mystery of the triune God and his plan for the world, "O the depth of the riches and wisdom and knowledge of God! How insearchable are his judgments and how inscrutable his ways! For who has known the mind of the Lord, or who has been his counselor? Or who has given a gift to him that he might be repaid? For from him and through him and to him are all things. To him be glory (*doxa*) for ever. Amen" (Rom 11,33–36).

3. NOTES ON THE INDIVIDUAL MARKS

When confronted with a whole, human thinking must break it up again and again, not in order to transform it into a unity composed from multiplicity, which would miss the whole (the whole is always more than the sum of its parts), but in order to grasp the whole anew and more deeply in each part and to draw closer to it in an intellectual and affective meditation. Thus, this discussion of the individual attributes of the Church must always keep the basic perspective that underlies the attempt made in this whole volume on the Church, the perspective, namely, of raising from various angles the question of the Church's inner mystery. Part One laid out the biblical foundations and the way in which they were unfolded historically; Part Two showed those structural features of the Church that are accessible to natural reason; Part Three attempted to present and explain the inner life of this Church as it manifests itself in various functions of its being and life, especially in what are called offices. It is thus particularly important for the question of the Church's attributes; it clarifies the meaning of the Church's apostolicity: all offices of the Church derive in some way from the apostles of the Lord. As a conclusion to Part Three, let us therefore get a clearer grasp of this apostolicity.

The Church's Apostolicity

The Church's apostolicity opens up a perspective from the Church's origins to the Church as a whole and to its inner dimension as the community of God, the family of Christ, and the temple of the Holy Spirit, i.e., as the universal sacrament of salvation. Paul's words apply to humanity as a whole: "For we are his workmanship, created in Christ Jesus for good works, which God prepared beforehand, that we should walk in them" (Eph 2,10). "You are fellow citizens with the saints and members of the household of God, built upon the foundation of the apostles and prophets, Christ Jesus himself being the cornerstone, in whom the whole structure [oikodomē] is joined together and grows into a holy temple [naos] in the Lord; in whom you also are built into it for a dwelling place [katoiketērion] of God in the Spirit" (Eph 2,19–22). Let us unfold the depth of these words in a few theological propositions.

1. The Church as a living social body, as the community of God, the family of Christ, and the temple of the Holy Spirit, is maintained in this world by three factors: the human person as free, as endowed with a mission, and as filled with the Holy Spirit. Mission and being filled with the Spirit belong together; the visible and the invisible, the external and the internal, the historical and the transhistorical, freedom and its power to choose, all of them are called for and made possible by mission and the Spirit.

2. The beginning is God's inner triune life. In our human theology we express this life by speaking about the Father as *ungenerated* origin, about the *generation* of the Son from the Father, and the *spiration*, the breathing, of the Spirit by the Father and the Son in the timeless eternity of the divine nature. This life within God is the reason why the timeless and eternal, the nonextended and all-present God created a world in time and space. More specifically, it is the reason why there can be, and are, free beings (human beings and angels) in this creation.

God's mystery breaks "bodily" (Col 2,9) into the world through the incarnation of the Son of God (John 1,14; Phil 2,6f.), Jesus of Nazareth. In him the dynamism of God's inner life arrives in this world in the form of mission." The Johannine Jesus presents himself to his contemporaries, especially to the apostles, as "the one sent by the Father" (John 3,17.34; 5,36; 6,57; 10,36; 11,42; 17,3.8.18.21.23.25). He can say about himself, "Whoever receives me, receives not me but him who sent me" (Mark 9,37; cf. Luke 4,18; 9,48; 10,16; Isa 61,1). For this reason the author of the Letter to the Hebrews can call Jesus "the apostle and high priest of our confession" (Heb 3,1). Jesus himself conferred his "being an apostle," his mission, on the twelve whom he called "apostles" (Luke 6,13). "As the Father has sent me, so I send you" (John 17,18; 20,21).

3. Yet those who have been called must again and again "freely follow" this call (Luke 4,19f.21f.; John 1,43; 6,66–69). And they must receive the Spirit before they begin to work for God's reign on earth on the basis of their mission (John 16,7–15; Acts 1,4–8), just as Christ began his public ministry, his mission into the world, after his anointing as the Messiah was manifested through the descent of the Holy Spirit "in bodily form" like a dove during his baptism (Mark 1,9–11; Mark 3,16f.; Luke 3,21f.; John 1,32ff.). The sending of the Holy Spirit upon the apostles was expressly promised by Christ (John 14,26; 15,26) and it was fulfilled at Pentecost (Acts 2,1–4). It is in the power of the Holy Spirit that the apostles acquire the confidence (parrēsia Acts 2,29; 4,13.29.31; Eph 6,18f.; Phil 1,20; Heb 3,6; 10,35) which flows from strong faith in the grace of Christ (Heb 4,16; 10,19).

4. The term "apostolic" was for the first time theo-logically narrowed in the second century (in the struggle against Gnosticism). Around A.D. 135 Justin Martyr called the Gospels "memoirs [apomnēmoneumata] of the apos-tles" (Dial. with Trypho, cap. 99–103, 13 times). Around 185, Irenaeus of Lyons spoke extensively about apostolic tradition (ab apostolis traditio, paradosis), which he sees

in two things, the doctrinal tradition and succession in the episcopal office. "It is in the power of all, therefore, in every church, who may wish to see the truth, to contemplate clearly the tradition of the apostles manifested throughout the whole world; and we are in a position to reckon up those who were by the apostles instituted bishops in the churches and [to demonstrate] the succession of these men to our times" (*Adv. Haer.* III,3,1). Irenaeus gives this demonstration for the Roman episcopal see. Succession is so normative for him that he does not need to appeal to the doctrinal tradition as documented all the way to the apostles. "How should it be if the apostles themselves had not left us writings? Would it not be necessary to follow the course of the tradition which they handed down to those to whom they did commit the churches? To which course many nations of those barbarians who believe in Christ do assent, having salvation written in their hearts by the Spirit, without paper or ink, and, carefully preserving the ancient tradition" (*Adv. Haer.* III,4,1–2).

Tertullian went a step further when he wrote (ca. A.D. 204) about "apostolic communities" (*Praescr.* 20), not only about the connection between the truth and teaching and the bishops with the apostles. "There are, then, many and numerous churches, and yet they are only one Church, that first Church from the apostles [*ab apostolis prima ecclesia*] from which they all stem. They are all in this way original and apostolic by being all together one. As proof of unity we have: the mutual giving of peace [*communicatio pacis*], the greeting of brotherhood [*appellatio fraternitatis*], and the assurance of hospitality [*contesseratio hospitalitatis*], three rights which exist for no other reason than because of one tradition of the same teaching of faith [*unius sacramenti una traditio*]" (*Praescr.* 21). "It is thus certain that the doctrine which agrees with those apostolic churches, the mother churches and original churches of the faith [*ecclesiis apostolicis, matricibus et originalibus fidei*], must be considered true, because without doubt it has that which the churches received from the apostles, the apostles from Christ and Christ from God." Tertullian summarized this truth in his Rule of Faith (*regula fidei*, cap. 13) in which "the Church" is, however, not yet mentioned as an object of faith. Also in Augustine (d. 431; *Sermo* 215) and still later in Rufinus (d. 532) the Church is less object of faith than mediatrix of eternal salvation (*vitam aeternam per sanctam ecclesiam catholicam*, DS 21 and 22).

5. Corresponding to Tertullian's terms "mother churches and original churches," it became customary, at least after the developments of the patriarchates in the fourth century (Nicaea, can. 6, applied the title "patriarchate" to Rome, Alexandria, and Antioch), to reserve the attribute "apostolic" for those churches that could give historical proof of having been founded by a well-known apostle. However, human ways of thinking were all too quick to transform a grace given to humanity into rights and power. Thus Constantinople, the *Roma junior*, demanded the "primacy of honor, *primatus honoris*" next to Rome; and in his *Dictatus Papae*, Pope Gregory VII (d. 1085) demanded that Rome alone be called "Apostolic See, *sedes apostolica*" on the grounds that Rome possessed the graves of Peter and Paul. In addition, primacy was to belong to the pope also in the political sphere, and he alone was to be called "pope," a name that was still used for all bishops. The political side of these ancient Roman honors declined in the "Babylonian" exile of the popes in Avignon and in the papal schism of the fourteenth and fifteenth centuries. It disappeared with the disappearance of the ecclesiastical state (1870). A new theological meaning was given to these titles in the new geopolitical situation of the twentieth century. Important factors in this process were the Lateran Concordat of Feb 11, 1929, and especially Vatican II in its clarification of the relationship between the pope and the bishops. At the end of the Council, Pope Paul

laid aside the tiara, the *insignium* of the medieval eccle-siastical state. Since then the popes wear only the mitre (the medieval episcopal hat). Vatican II gave to the title "apostolic" more of the sound and the meaning it had in the third and the fourth centuries.

6. Since the third century, "apostolic" has been under-stood as a normative characterization of the "rule of faith" (i.e., of the Church's faith which grows from the *traditio apostolica*). Until the sixth century "rule of faith" referred to more than the creed. The creed is merely a concise formula or version of the rule of faith and it can, therefore, be refomulated at various times by various theologians (cf. the Creed of Paul VI). Of course, it must not be overlooked that even a concise formula must preserve the essentials of the doctrine of faith in the understanding of the "apostolic tradition" and cannot be determined by the "questions and demands of the present."

7. "Apostolic" is especially a mark of the Church's of-fices, inasmuch as all orders must be understood in terms of the apostles. In this way the mark "apostolic" expresses what is historically essential in the community of God and the family of Christ. We will discuss the three other marks, unity, catholicity, and holiness, in the context of the discussion of the Church's tasks and paths.

Part Four

The Church's Tasks and Its Ways
to Self-Realization in the World

*As indicated above, the list of the Church's "marks" is not an accidental juxtaposition of attributes. It is, rather, a means for understanding the inner nature of the Church by looking at it from various angles, which is generally the manner of human seeing and thinking. These perspectives arose very early in the Church's consciousness itself, rather than being introduced from the outside; and they have brought to light essential features (*notae, inner marks*).*

We will turn first to the mystery of the Church's unity and unicity. *After a brief systematic theological discussion of this mark, XIII will unfold it by discussing the Church's missionary nature, and XIV by discussing ecumenism, which is one of the Church's essential tasks in this world, because its unity has over and over again been endangered and actually damaged.*

While unity is primarily an existential demand placed upon the Church, catholicity is an "eschatological mystery," a special task given to the Church until the end of time. After a brief systematic reflection, XV will discuss the Church's relationship to humanity, its role in the salvation of humanity as a whole ("no salvation outside the Church"). XVI will continue the subject of the Church's catholicity by discussing its relationship to the world and its tasks in the world, its relationship to the state, society, the economy, politics, culture and science.

Chapters XVII and XVIII will take up the eschatological mystery of the Church's holiness. XVII will clarify this mark by discussing the Church's relationship to the communion of saints, XVIII by discussing its relationship to the kingdom of God in the light of Mary, who stands at the Church's heart. As mentioned above, these three marks of the Church share an important feature: they are not primarily given as parts of the Church's nature, as is the case with the Church's apostolicity, but they are given to it as a task; with the grace of God they must find their fulfillment in space and time and in freedom.

XIII

The Church's Unity and Unicity;
Its Missionary Nature

"Go therefore and make disciples of all nations, baptizing them . . . , teaching them to observe all that I have
commanded you; and lo, I am with you always, to the
close of the age" (Matt 28,19–20). Whatever the exact
wording may have been, this final command given by Jesus
to the apostles before his ascension is not only the command to carry the kingdom of Christ and of God into the
whole world; it also draws the world with all its fullness
and manifoldness of peoples and cultures (and religions)
into this new Church of Christ. Already at the very beginning it raises the question of the external and even more of
the internal unity of the Church in the world, a unity for
which all people of all times and of all places are called to
pray, "thy kingdom come." Before pursuing these ideas,
we must see the question of the Church's unity and unicity as a theological problem and attempt to answer it in
this perspective.

The Church's Unity and Unicity

I. THE BIBLICAL FOUNDATION

It is difficult for systematic theology today to lay out the
biblical data for a particular doctrine in such a way that

357

revealed truth remains visible as a whole. On the one hand systematic theology must preserve the Catholic understanding of faith according to which tradition has not obscured or disfigured revealed truth as a whole, but has achieved an ever deeper and more comprehensive grasp of it, even if at times by going through certain detours. On the other hand systematic theology must not ignore the valuable differentiations between various New Testament statements that modern exegesis has brought to light with its historical critical method. Historical critical thinking often posits a radical distinction, to the point of separation, between the pre-Easter and the post-Easter Jesus, between the intentions of Jesus and the mystery of Christ, and thus between the Jesus of the Synoptics and the Christ of Paul as well as the Lord of the Gospel of John. The historical critical approach can, therefore, not provide the guiding thread for finding the "whole" that alone can be the basis of our life, the life we must live on the basis of the Catholic understanding of God, the world, and humanity. The history of dogma shows, however, that this whole is often in danger of being turned into something merely human. Human beings are always tempted to claim that their thoughts are those of God, instead of making God's thoughts their own. As a corrective of this defect, the historical critical approach of modern exegesis can be very important.

With these preliminary reflections in mind, let us now approach the question of the biblical foundation of the doctrine of the Church's unity and unicity. On the whole, the pre-Easter Jesus of the Synoptics did not say much in the abstract about this topic. His task was to purify the Old Testament revelation in the understanding of his time and to direct people anew to God, the Father, and to his reign in this world. His point of departure is the message of the ancient prophets, but he went decisively beyond this message. Already in the Synoptics, however, Jesus has a more central concern than such instruction. He wants to

gain people for his "person," in order to lead them as the
Son of God to his Father. This concern becomes especially
clear in his relation to the disciples. Before the Synoptic
Gospels were composed in their present form, Paul developed his apparently quite novel view of the importance of
the mystery of Christ for understanding the intentions of
Jesus. By doing so he does not, however, stand in opposition to the eyewitnesses of the life of Jesus, although as "a
chosen instrument of mine to carry my name before the
Gentiles and kings and the sons of Israel" (Acts 9, 15), he
sees more of the depth and interiority of revelation. Even
today, second-generation witnesses can often know more
and see more deeply than many contemporaries and eyewitnesses. What is required for grasping a great matter is
not so much space and time but greatness of spirit. In
religious matters, what is decisive is inner depth and the
wealth of grace and of the divine Spirit. The same thing
applies to John, the beloved disciple. One cannot overlook
what Paul himself says, [The gospel which was preached
by me is not man's gospel. For I did not receive it from
man, nor was I taught it, but it came through a revelation
of Jesus Christ (Gal 1,11–12).]

What are, then, the biblical foundations for understanding the Church's unity and unicity? It has been the
Church's faith from the very beginning that Jesus Christ
founded "his Church," as the Gospels say (Matt 16,18;
John 21,15–17). He did so by choosing and sending out
"apostles" whom he instructed about his intentions (probably there was more instruction than the Gospels report),
by entrusting to them his message and his holy signs, especially the sacrament of baptism, the holy Eucharist and the
forgiveness of sins. He himself, aided by the power of the
Spirit given from above, became the ground of the unity
and unicity of his Church, because he is "the way, the
truth and the life" (John 14,6). Being a Christian means
first of all following Christ (19 times in Mark) or, as Paul
says, "imitating Christ" (1 Thess 1,6; 2,14; 1 Cor 11,2).

Already in his first letter to the Corinthians (ca. A.D. 55) Paul unfolded the idea that the Church of Christ must by its very nature possess inner unity. Against the divisions in the Corinthian church he says, "I appeal to you . . . that all of you agree and that there be no dissensions among you, but that you be united in the same mind and the same judgment. . . . Is Christ divided?" (1 Cor 1,10.13). The power that is the root of this unity is found in the gospel and in baptism (1 Cor 1,12–17). Jesus Christ himself, upon whom the Church is founded, is this power, and so is God's Spirit and his inspiration which overcomes all divisions (cf. 1 Cor 3). "Now there are varieties of gifts, but the same Spirit; and there are varieties of service, but the same Lord; and there are varieties of working, but it is the same God who inspires them all in every one" (1 Cor 12,4–6). The Church's unity is a living unity, "For by one Spirit we were all baptized into one body—Jews or Greeks, slaves or free [male or female, Gal 3,28]—and all were made to drink of one Spirit" (1 Cor 12,13). The multitude of members forms a single body, and each member needs the others. The same unity must exist also among various communities, which is why the rich communities collect money for the poor and the poor pray for the rich (1 Cor 16,1–3). The most important thing is love (1 Cor 13).

This idea of the Church's unity as the body of Christ dominates especially the letters to the Colossians and Ephesians written during Paul's imprisonment in Rome (61–63). Christ is "our peace" (Eph 2,14). The Christian is a "new person" who must be "eager to maintain the unity of the Spirit in the bond of peace. There is one body and one Spirit, just as you were called to the one hope that belongs to your call, one Lord, one faith, one baptism, one God and Father of us all, who is above all and through all and in all" (Eph 4,2–6). The source of this unity is even deeper: Christ is the beginning of creation, the redeemer of his body, the Church, "he is before all things, and in him all things hold together. He is the head of the body, the Church; he is the beginning, the first-born from the dead, that in everything he might be pre-eminent. For in him all the fullness of God was pleased to dwell, and through him to reconcile to himself all things, whether on earth or in heaven . . ." (Col 1,13–23). "For in him the whole fullness of deity dwells bodily, and you have come to fullness of life in him, who is the head . . ." (Col 2,9–10). Baptism expresses the same unity, "For you have died, and your life is hid with Christ in God. When Christ who is our life appears, then you also will appear with him in glory" (Col 3,3–4). It is impossible to surpass this description of the unity and unicity of Christ's Church in scope or depth.

In the Acts of the Apostles, Luke, Paul's companion, draws an ideal image of the communitarian life of the first Christians. "And they devoted themselves to the apostles' teaching and fellowship, to the breaking of bread and the prayers (*proseuchais* = liturgical community prayer: "and sing psalms and hymns and spiritual songs with thankfulness from your hearts to God" (Col 3,16; Eph 5,19). "And all who believed were together and had all things in common; and they sold their possessions and goods and distributed them to all, as any had need" (Acts 2,42.44–45).

The biblical teaching on the Church's unity and unicity took on a new form in the Gospel of John around the turn of the century, because the Church's external unity had evidently been endangered by heresies (Matt 7,15; Col 2,16; Acts 20,29; 1 Tim 1,3–11; 2 Tim 2,14–3,9; Tit 1,10–16) and by the tepid life of many Christians (Phil 3,18f.; 2 John 7; 1 John 2,18: antichrists). The Church's unity is a gift of God, and a good in this world which must again and again be acquired and for which one must pray to God. John has Jesus himself pray for this unity in his farewell discourses.

Holy Father, keep them in thy name, which thou hast given me, that they may be one, even as we are one. . . . I do not pray for these only, but also for those who believe in me through their word, that they may all be one; even as thou, Father, art in me, and I in thee, that they also may be in us, so that the world may believe that thou hast sent me. The glory which thou hast given me I have given to them, that they may be one even as we are one, I in them and thou in me, that they may become perfectly one [*teteleiōmenoi eis hen*], so that the world may know that thou hast sent me and hast loved them even as thou hast loved me. . . . O righteous Father, the world has not known thee, but I have known thee; and these know that thou hast sent me. I made known to them thy name, and I will make it known, that the love with which thou hast loved me may be in them, and I in them. (John 17,11.20–23.25–26).

This text states quite clearly that the Church's unity is guaranteed by all that Jesus brought from the Father and entrusted to the apostles so that they would pass it on in his name: his word and his sacrament, his glory and his love, his spirit and his "name," in which all who are Christians" on this earth are baptized (Matt 28,20; Acts 2,38; 8,16; 10,48; 19,5).

2. HISTORICAL ASPECTS

In Clement's letter to the Corinthians (ca. A.D. 98) the episcopal office already plays an important role in preserving the unity of the Church. The situation is similar in the Pastoral Epistles (1 Tim 3,1–7; 2 Tim 1,13f.; 2,1–26). Disobedience or resistance against the bishops or presbyters is the cause of divisions in the Church. Like Paul, Clement demands obedience to the bishop, fraternal love, and justice, for the preservation of the unity which flows from the one God, the one Christ, and the one call and love of Christ (1 *Clem.* 42–69). In his letters Ignatius of Antioch struggles in a similar way for the unity of faith (*Eph.* 2–9; *Magn.* 6–8; *Trall.* 2–11). The struggle against the first great heresy in the Church, Gnosticism, emphasized these means for preserving unity: keeping the faith, obeying the leadership, and living an ordered life (cf. Irenaeus, *Adv. Haer.* V,20.)

Tertullian writes that enmity against the bishop is the mother of all division (*On Baptism*, 17).

In this way the apostles founded communities in city after city. The later communities took a shoot of faith and seeds of doctrine from these, and still do so today, in order to become ecclesial communities. For this reason even these later communities can be considered apostolic, because they derive from apostolic Churches. Every species must be classified according to its origin. Thus there are many and numerous Churches, and yet they are only one, that apostolic original Church from which they all stem. All of them are original and apostolic in this world by being all together one [Church].

As proof of unity we have: "the mutual giving of peace, the greeting of brotherhood, and the assurance of hospitality, three rights which exist for no other reason than the one tradition of the same faith" (Tertullian, *Praescr.* 21).

Around A.D. 250 Cyprian of Carthage wrote the first treatise "On the Unity of the Catholic Church" against schismatics and heretics in which he warns against inner divisions in this time of external persecutions. Here one finds his famous sayings, "The one who does not have the Church as a mother cannot have God as a Father" and "No salvation outside the Church (as outside Noah's ark)" (c. 6; *Ep.* 73,21; *Ep.* 74,7). Even martyrdom outside the Church cannot lead to salvation. Cyprian wrote to Pope Cornelius in Rome, "There is only one Catholic Church which can be neither split nor divided" (*Ep.* 51,2). With thirty other Numidian bishops he erroneously rejected the baptism of heretics for the sake of unity. Still, "There is only one baptism, only one Spirit and only one Church, which Christ our Lord founded in the unity of its origin and constitution on Peter" (Ep. 70,3). It is significant that in the fourth century, when membership in the Church became easier because of the political freedom granted to the Church, the ideal image of the Church's unity as drawn by Acts 2,45, the Letter to Diognetus (*Diogn.* 5,1–6) or Aristides (*Apol.* 15) and Justin (*Apol.* I,14) disappeared. The imperfect and sinners found room in the Church and still its unity was not threatened.

Ambrose and especially Augustine portrayed the Church's relation to its Christ, not so much in the Pauline image of body and head, but above all as a "bridal relation" as between Adam and Eve, or between the bride and the bridegroom in the Song of Songs (*De civ. Dei* XVII 20; *Doct. cgr* II 6). Augustine often stresses that the Church on earth, the earthly city of God, includes people who will be lost at the end (*De civ. Dei* I 35). "How many evil persons are in the Church! One womb carries them, until they are separated off at the end. And the good complain about the bad and the bad in turn about the good, and they quarrel in the womb of the one mother" (*In Jo* XI 10; cf. *Ep.* 25,8.21–24; *Ep.* 41 to Emeritus). In addition to the image of the "one mother," Augustine uses the image of the "one sheepfold" for the "one Church" (*In Jo* 45,5: Christ's sheepfold is the Catholic Church, but heretics do not enter through the door, cf. ibid. 47,4).

Especially after the great Councils, heretics were excluded from the Church and thus various "heretical churches" sprang up alongside the old Church. The Church's unity was thus visible only in "one's own Church." Heresy and schism obscured the image of the universal one Church," although Christians never lacked the sense that Christ and his Church are undivided, that they must be one body and one head.

How can belief in "one Church" and the actual multiplicity of churches be reconciled in an understanding of the Church illumined by faith? In the course of history, especially since the Middle Ages, three attempts at answering this question have been developed.

a) The first attempt consists in the summary of the relevant biblical and patristic teaching, without any consideration of the historical reality of divided "Christian churches." It found its clear expression in the bull *Unam*

Sanctam of Boniface VIII (November 18, 1302). This was the prevalent approach of the Catholic Church, and in some way also of the Orthodox Churches, until it was clarified and given a new form in our time through the problem of ecumenism. The point of departure in this approach is the knowledge that there is *one* Church, outside of which there is no forgiveness of sins and no salvation.

It represents one mystical body; the head of this body is Christ, but the head of Christ is God. In her there is "one Lord, one faith, one baptism" (Eph 4,5). There was also one ark at the time of the flood, which is an image of the Church. It had one helmsman, Noah; and outside of it everything on earth perished, as we read. This Church we revere as the one and only [*unicam*] Church, as the Lord says in the prophet, "Save my life [*animam*] from the sword and my one and only [*unicam*] from the power of the dog" (Psalm 21,21). He prayed for his life, i.e., for himself, head and body. He calls his body the "one and only" Church, because of the unity of the bridegroom, of faith, of the sacraments, and of the Church's love. She is the Lord's "seamless garment" (John 19,23) which was not divided but given away by lot. This one and unique Church, therefore, has not two heads like a monster, but one body and one head, namely Christ and his vicar, Peter's successor, for the Lord said to Peter personally, "Feed my sheep" (John 21,17). "My" he said in general, not individually, meaning these or those; whereby it is understood that he confided all his sheep to him. If therefore Greeks or others say that they were not confided to Peter and his successors, they must necessarily confess that they are not among Christ's sheep, for the Lord said in John, "there shall be one fold and one shepherd." (John 10,16) (*Unam Sanctam*, DS 870–872)

The Church is thus a visible community, organized by Christ and the apostles with their successors. The word, sacrament, and apostolic office are the foundations of this visible community. The problem of these medieval statements lies in the perspective of power that gives a historically conditioned meaning to the Scripture quotes used. This distortion is especially clear in the statements made by the same bull on the relation between spiritual and secular power.

b) The second attempt to deal with the above-mentioned tension was developed by Luther. In his sermon on Matt 16,13–19 (June 29, 1522) Luther claims that the "one rock" means "the Christian Gospel truth which proclaims Christ to me; for through this truth I base my conscience upon Christ." He declares that the early Church's interpretation in terms of Peter (and his faith: Augustine) is false. "The whole papal rule is built upon sheer marshland, upon lies and blasphemies against God, and the pope is the greatest blasphemer by applying these words to himself, although they are only meant to apply to Christ." Quite logically Luther says about the promise of the keys, "Thus it is no one in particular to whom the keys are given, but only the Church, i.e., those who place themselves upon this rock (i.e., Christ). Only the Christian Church has the keys. Nobody else does. Of course, the pope and the bishops can use them as the officials to whom the keys are entrusted by the community. A pastor administers the office of the keys . . . not out of himself, but out of the community. Even if he is a wicked man, he is a servant of the whole community, to which the keys are given." Luther then interprets the power to bind and to loose in terms of pastoral exhortation, not in the light of John 20,22f., in terms of the forgiveness of sins in the name of Jesus (WA 10,3, p. 208ff.). In his interpretation of John 17, 10–12 he defends Christ's real presence in the Eucharist, probably against the enthusiasts, but immediately interprets Christ's "being in us" as our "being in Christ's word" (WA 28, p. 140f.). In the Great Catechism he speaks about the Church as "a holy community on earth, consisting all of saints under one head, Christ, called together by the Holy Spirit, in one faith, one attitude and one manner of thinking, with various gifts, yet unanimous in love, without divisions and splits" (article 3). The Smalcaldic Articles present the Church as "the holy believers and the sheep who hear the voice of their shepherd"; the Church's holiness consists in "the word of God and orthodox faith." Calvin looks at the Church principally in terms of the idea of predestination. He sees its offices not in terms of apostles but in terms of the community. They are anchored in the community (*Inst.* IV, c. 1–12).

The problem with these views is that the Church remains basically invisible and that faith is understood primarily in terms of conscience, while the historical element of "apostolic mission" with succession and tradition, which has been of fundamental importance in the Church from the very beginning, disappears.[1] Therefore, in his writings on this subject, Robert Bellarmine stressed especially the Church's visibility and its historicity in office and tradition.[2]

c) Perhaps since 1870, and especially since World War I, there has been a third attempt to reconcile the reality of faith and historical reality: the realization that Christ's Church is one and unique and that history has given rise to many "Christian churches." The question of ecclesiastical office turned out to be especially important in this attempt. The Catholic Church reached a peak in its teaching about office in the Vatican I definitions on the office of the pope (1870). From this peak the apostolic office, and thus the whole question of offices, was addressed anew in the Second Vatican Council. The apostolic office, which even in the Catholic Church since the Middle Ages had not been seen sufficiently in the spirit of the first millennium (as the question of the sacrament of orders shows), was emphasized in its central form. The Council thus displayed more clearly the Church's historical foundation in this world in its original meaning and in the spirit of the great tradition of the first millennium. At the same time, at least since the beginning of the twentieth century, one can observe a new departure in the churches of the Reformation, especially in the Lutheran Church. Through renewed reflection on the doctrine of justification and the

Eucharist these Churches are seeking communion with the ancient Churches of the East and the West, without giving up the basic intentions of the Reformation, which have in large part become part of the contemporary worldview. There are as yet no signs, however, of a return to the apostolic office. What hinders the way to communion in this respect is the old accusation that the Catholic Church's view on apostolic succession falls into "legalism." During Vatican II the Catholic Church, together with the Eastern Churches, overcame the barriers of excommunication. Following the wish of Pope John XXIII it "opened the windows to the world" in the documents on religious liberty, ecumenism, and the Church's missionary activity, as well as in the Pastoral Constitution on the Church in the Modern World and its new self-portrait in the Dogmatic Constitution on the Church. In this way it prepared the ground for preserving faith in the Church's unity and unicity in the spirit of the early Churches of the first millennium, and for respecting in a theologically responsible way the historical reality of the "multiplicity" of Christian churches. This multiplicity is conditioned in part by the multiplicity of peoples, cultures, and religions, and in part by the related multiplicity of human understandings of the one Christian heritage.

In section 2. of this chapter XIII we will discuss the question of the Church's unity from the perspective of the first difficulty: What is the Church's unity in the face of the multiplicity of peoples, cultures, and religions? We will seek an answer to this question by reflecting about the Church's missionary nature. In XIV we will then discuss the same question from the perspective of the various human understandings of the one Christian heritage by focusing on the new development of ecumenism. First, however, let us give a systematic overview of the points made so far.

3. SYSTEMATIC OVERVIEW

As the point of departure we will take again the basic idea of the Church as "the universal sacrament of salvation." Let us take the three aspects contained in each sacrament as our guiding thread.

a) A sacrament is an "outward sign." Four forms of unity exist in this external sphere of the outward sign in the Church. (1) The fundamental aspect is the human and social unity among Christians of which Scripture and tradition speak. For the sake of brevity, let us summarize the various features of the Church's ideal image by quoting a famous Pauline text on love. "Love is patient and kind; love is not jealous or boastful; it is not arrogant or rude. Love does not insist on its own way; it is not irritable or resentful; it does not rejoice at wrong, but rejoices in the right. Love bears all things, believes all things, hopes all things, endures all things. Love never ends" (1 Cor 13,4–8). In all of his letters Paul speaks about this fundamental social attitude among Christians. Tertullian summarizes it as "peace, brotherhood, hospitality and communion (*pax, fraternitas, hospitalitas, communio*). The cause of this attitude is life "in Christ," nourished by his meal, his spirit, his sonship before the Father in heaven. These are gifts of grace and at the same time existential demands placed upon every individual and every community in relation to others, because the Church is Christ's body," Christ is the "head," and every individual and community is a "member" of this living unity.

(2) In order to live personal communion, human beings also need common ground in ideas and ideals by which the human heart and spirit lives, by which it is nourished, propelled and drawn, and from which it derives its enthusiasm (*voluntatum, studiorum, sententiarum summa consensio*, Cicero, *Laelius* 4,15; *omnium divinarum humanarumque rerum cum benevolentia et caritate consensio*, ibid. 6,20). In this way the Church's unity is rooted in a

special way in the unity of faith, in hope and in love, understood not only in a subjective way, but even more so in their objective meaning. This objectivity is extremely important here because we are dealing with supernatural revealed truths, which are given by God and cannot be found by unaided human reason. Still, once revealed, they can be accepted and loved as "the good news" and the foundation for a new life. At this point one can see how important the Church's doctrine and its magisterium are for its unity. Every truth, whenever it is grasped deeply, is affected among us human beings by the limitations of the human spirit and thus by the multiplicity of personalities and societies. Nevertheless, there is a certain communality in linguistic expression, and this communality is necessary for the external aspect of community, even though the one truth itself can and must grow in the Church's faith in scope and depth. This is the authentic place of living tradition.

(3) The truth of faith demands also religious action as something that flows from this truth. Only the one "who does what is true comes to the light" (John 3,21; John 1,6; 2,4). In this way not only moral-religious behavior based on faith but especially worship and the sacraments take on great importance for the Church's inner unity. Already in Paul's time the Church had to struggle for this communality in the sacrament, particularly in questions of baptism and the Eucharist (cf. 1 Cor 1,12–16; 10,17; 11,18–30). Here is the place of the important early Christian word that is being re-discovered today in our search for ecumenism, the word *koinōnia* (communion) (Acts 2,42; 2 Cor 9,13; 1 John 1,3.7) which means "communion with Christ" (1 Cor 1,9), "with his blood and his body" (1 Cor 10,16), "with his cross and suffering" (Phil 3,10), "with his gospel" (Phil 1,5; Gal 1,11f.).[3]

(4) The sacraments, the liturgy, the gospel, and faith necessarily point to the apostolic office, which is a pre-eminent source and manifestation of visible unity.

Without unity in this office, unity in the believing people is not possible or guaranteed. The shepherds have at all times been ministers of the Church's unity or, conversely, the causes of division and quarrels. In the past this was often the case with "apostolic" shepherds (i.e., bishops); in more recent times it has often been the case with "believers" who have become the shepherds of the communities founded by them. For, the hierarchical element is not merely founded in Christ; it is also an original human order, which cannot be eliminated even in a democratic constitution.

b) The element of the apostolic office expresses at the same time the second aspect of a sacrament, namely, its institution by Christ and the necessarily connected elements of succession and tradition.

c) The third constitutive element of the Church as the universal sacrament of salvation is the inner effect of grace. The Church's unity and unicity in this dimension is guaranteed by the living triune God himself, in whose name the sacraments are dispensed and who is the source of all grace in this world, his creation, which fell into sin. This ground of unity is the deepest and strongest; yet it is not visible for our eyes in our visible world. This invisibility was felt especially strongly by the churches of the Reformation. Although they appealed to this dimension of unity as the communion of saints, they were in fact from the very beginning a plurality of churches. The later development of a multitude of sects confirmed this point. The invisibility of this aspect of unity, however, allows us also to preserve the truth which Christ expressed in the parables of the net with good and bad fish (Matt 13,47–50) and of the wise and foolish virgins (Matt 25,1–13), namely, that the visible Church on earth includes good and evil people, saints and sinners. They can freely decide to convert or to fall away as long as they live on earth. They must decide with God's grace (cf. below, XVII).

After these general reflections on the Church's unity

and unicity, let us turn to that feature in the Church's nature in which unity and unicity must prove themselves especially and in which the Church shows its face as a living unity.

The Church's Missionary Nature

I. PRELIMINARY REMARKS

"The Second Vatican Council has helped us to realize that 'mission' is the Church's true name and in some way its definition. The Church becomes itself when it fulfills its mission" (Pope John Paul II, Epiphany 1979). Nowhere can the Church's true reality be felt more clearly than in its missionary work. Dogmatic theology, due to its limitations as a particular academic discipline, can only give an outline of the whole and deal with the questions that fall within its competence. We will discuss these questions by taking a brief look at the "Church as mission" and by clarifying the teaching of Vatican II on mission.

First, then, a few remarks on the basic problems of modern missiology without which theological statements about the Church could not be complete.

a) To begin with, let us take a look at some statistical data on the world religions. Although numbers are not a measure of the inner value and external importance of a spiritual reality, they are nevertheless a challenge for the bearers of such values to examine their consciences about their own commitment, which is a measure of their own subjective evaluation of the objective good. It is a fact that today, almost two thousand years after Christ's birth, less than a third of humanity is Christian (a fifth is Catholic). More than two-thirds belong to other religions. In addition, between 1900 and 1965 the Christian population of the earth decreased from thirty-five percent to twenty-eight percent. This is mainly due to the decrease of popula-

TABLE 1

Unbaptized		Baptized	
Muslim	440	Anglican	40
Confucian	420	Calvinist	42
Hindu	370	Lutheran	72
Buddhist	300	Prot. Sects	110
Native	250	Orthodox	170
Atheist	120	Catholic	570
Shintoist	100		
Jews	12		

From the year 1964: collected by the Pontifical
Missionary Institute in Bavaria; assumes a total
world population of 3.1 billion; numbers in
millions.

TABLE 2

Unbaptized		Baptized	
Islam	546	Christian (total)	1139
Sunnite	350	Catholics	709
Shiite	86	Lutheran	70
Confucian	310	Anglican	55
Buddhist	300	Orthodox	87
Hindu	519	Other	205
Shinto	61		
Taoist	29		
Sikh	10		
Dshaina and Parsi	2.7		
Jews	14.5		

The *Calendario Atlante de Agostino* of 1980 assumes a total
world population of 4.5 billion; it gives no numbers for atheism
and nature religions; numbers in millions.

tion in the industrialized countries and to the "population explosion" in the Third World. Seventy percent of all Christians live in Third World countries and only thirty percent in industrialized countries. Of course, the numbers of these statistics are largely estimates (approximate values). They often shift quite quickly, e.g., because of the rapid decline of the old nature religions (although many of the basic ideas and values of these religions continue to exert their influence after conversion) and because of the losses (difficult to estimate) which atheistic world communism inflicted on traditional religions, including Christianity (see the statistics in the accompanying tables).

b) Missiology, which developed only at the beginning of this century, has as its goal the scientific investigation of missionary activity as a whole. It uses all relevant disciplines of knowledge: geography, ethnology, cultural history, linguistics, and so forth. This leads to new insights into the various missionary processes which will, one hopes, provide answers to the kinds of problems that appeared in the controversies surrounding the Chinese missions. "Western Christianity" is joined by other forms of Christianity, an "African," and "Indonesian," a "Chinese" Christianity, each with its own attempt to formulate a Christian theology. The encounter with non-Christian religions is being thought through anew. The achievement of early Christianity which flowed from the enthusiasm of the faith of the beginnings (the "first love," Rev 2,4) was not always a positive achievement (see the history of heresies). This achievement must now be made intelligible. Of course, such an effort at understanding cannot replace the power of following Christ and the inner enthusiasm of love. In this respect Vatican II gave new directions of which we must speak below.

c) The whole world, which science and technology have made more transparent and more subject to our overview, is engaged in a spiritual struggle between materialism and secularism on the one side and the original human search and religious beginning on the other. On the part of Christ's messengers, this struggle requires moral strength, religious depth, and constancy in faith. We can observe these virtues in Paul's unique missionary letters and in many writings of the Fathers and the theological tradition in every century, but we must struggle for them and pray for them again and again. Christ himself said, "From the days of John the Baptist until now the kingdom of heaven has suffered violence [*biazetai*, against itself in giving itself to God], and those who use violence take it by force" (Matt 11,12). "Strive [*agōnizesthe*] to enter by the narrow door; for many, I tell you, will seek to enter and will not be able" (Luke 13,24; cf. 16,16f.; Col 2,1; 4,12). Similarly the First Letter to Timothy says, "For this end we toil and strive, because we have our hope set on the living God, who is the Savior of all men, especially of those who believe" (1 Tim 4,10). Likewise the Letter to the Hebrews says, "Therefore, since we are surrounded by so great a cloud of witnesses [i.e., martyrs, cf. Heb 11], let us also lay aside every weight [*onkon* or *oknon*, fear and laziness] and sin which clings so closely [original sin, cf. Rom 5,15: forgetfulness of God, self-glorification, abandonment to the world], and let us run with perseverance the race [*agōn*] that is set before us, looking to Jesus the pioneer and perfecter of our faith, who for the joy that was set before him endured the cross (cf. Phil 2,5–11), despising the shame, and is seated at the right hand of throne of God" (Heb 12,1–2).[4] After these preliminary remarks, let us turn to the two aspects of the missionary Church.

2. THE MISSIONARY CHURCH IN ITS HISTORY

The Church is "mission," because it lives from the mission that the Father gave to the Son and that the Son passed on to his apostles. This mission lives in the Church through the Holy Spirit whom the Father and the Son sent at Pentecost, thus calling the Church into life, and it lives in her through the exalted Lord ("I will be with you always," Matt 28,20), until at the end of time God himself in his final judgment will justify the missions which proceeded from him. The Church's missionary life through the ages shows the inner unity and cooperation between outward mission, human achievement and failure, and God's inner grace (as strength and mercy).

a) In the first century the Church's missionary work was carried out by the apostles and their companions, presbyters and deacons, pastors, teachers and prophets and the first believers in general. Important missionary means, besides the word of proclamation, were charismatic deeds (miracles), the new convincing communion of life, and the formation of the community out of the Eucharist. A major achievement was the transition of the new message from the Jewish sphere to the Greco-Roman sphere. God himself initiated this transition and blessed it with success in his instructions to Peter (Acts 10, Cornelius) and in the call of Saul-Paul (Acts 9). In the world of antiquity this transition was prepared for by the Jewish diaspora (e.g., proselytes), by philosophy with its explicitly religious dimension, by the political and cultural unity of the Greek and the Roman world (*pax Augusti romana*) and by the advance of the Oriental mystery religions (Mithras) next to the ossified official religion of the state. The main task was to give a permanent written form to Jesus' oral message (the New Testament writings) and thus to find and create the necessary means of expression for the new Christian truth in the international language of that time (koiné Greek).

b) Even in the apostolic period the young Church of Jews and Greeks began its struggle with the spiritual and political powers of antiquity. The first well-educated Christians, the Apologists, defended the new Christian doctrines and Christian life against the suspicions and accusations of the powerful. In the persecutions that flared up in almost every generation, numerous believers of all social classes gave witness to their faith by heroically dying for Christ. The new Christian understanding of God, the world and the Church found its summary expression around 220 in the canon of Scripture. A difficult theological struggle overcame the first heresies, the one-sided or destructive subjective selections (*hairesis* = taking a part = heresy) of aspects taken from the whole of the Christian message and world view. For 350 years the Church struggled to grasp the mystery of Christ and thus to clarify the new understanding of God, trinitarian monotheism, which has no Jewish or pagan parallels. It was the first and true struggle for the very existence of Christianity. The new doctrine took hold on all levels of the population, rich and poor, educated and uneducated. When Christianity, which was experienced as something altogether new, was first officially tolerated and then supported by Constantine, about one-eighth of the population of the Roman empire around the Mediterranean was already Christian. In certain areas, such as the cities of Asia Minor and Egypt, they were as much as half of the population.

c) The promulgation of the Edict of Milan (A.D. 313) by Constantine and Licinus inaugurated a new era for the missionary Church, apart from a few setbacks under Julian the Apostate and others. The official recognition of the Church had both good and bad effects. In addition to private donations, the Church began to receive large public subsidies. In the cities, Christian churches were built in the style of the large public buildings (basilicas). The bishops became officials of the state. The Christian message penetrated into the countryside (*pagani* = pagans) and into the areas at the borders of the empire (in the apostolic period individual missionaries had already taken up the challenge of India and Africa). Christians had come to *Germania* and *Brittania* as members of the Roman army. The geographical and social expansion of Christianity confronted the Church with new tasks in doctrine, life, and organization.

d) A new situation arose with the fall of the world of

antiquity, brought about, in part, by the fight of the Christian emperors against the ancient state religions and hastened by the catastrophe of the migration of peoples (after the fifth century), which brought the Church into great difficulties but also opened up new possibilities and tasks for it. Christianity had to be brought into the context of the young Germanic and Slavic peoples who in turn received certain essential elements of the culture of antiquity along with Christianity. In Spain (Visigoths: Ulfilas) and Northern Africa (Ostrogoths and Vandals), in Italy (Langobards) and Southern France (Burgundians and Franks under Clodwig in 496) the Aryan peoples that had passed through the Byzantine empire entered the Roman Church between the fifth and seventh centuries. Ireland (Patrick), Scotland (Columba) and England (Augustine of Canterbury with his thirty-nine companions in 596) were Christianized and soon sent their missionaries to Germany. Two great events shaped this period of the missionary Church. The first event was the rise of monasticism, which had begun in Palestine and Egypt in the fourth century and which became the main missionary force in Germany after Benedict founded the Benedictine order. The second event was the rise and the successful military campaigns of the new Arab religion founded by Mohammed (570-632) which almost completely destroyed the Church in Palestine, Egypt and Spain.

e) While this great Church of the Fathers and monks in the South was destroyed, the Germanic peoples of the North, who had at first received the education of antiquity as a curiosity, were newly missionized by Irishmen (Fridolin, Columba, Kilian) and Franks (Rupertus, Emmeram, Corbinian). In Rome's name, the Anglo-Saxon Boniface (672-754) created a new ecclesiastical heirarchy in this area. The order of St. Benedict (480-574) was mainly responsible for the German missions, until Charlemagne (768-814), the first German emperor, crowned by the pope, laid the foundation of the "Holy Roman Empire of German

Nation." From the seventh to the eleventh centuries the Church carried its faith to the Germanic peoples in the North and to the Slavic peoples in the East through monks and missionary bishops. The path of conversion was for the most part not the individual, as it had been in antiquity. The conversion of local rulers or kings led, rather, to the conversion of individual tribes and peoples. Political and military powers were part of the process. What had thus been gained externally had to be purified and deepened by the highly spiritual activity of the monasteries. Soon knights and monks were to become the most important missionary workers. New continuity with antiquity was sought (Carolingian Renaissance). Ecclesiastical Latin (which spread after the third century) had been the main means of communication. Now translations were made into the Germanic languages.

f) The situation of the missionary Church from the eleventh to the fifteenth centuries was quite different. The great ancient churches of the Greek East (Russia had been missionized from Byzantium beginning in the tenth century) were engaged in a bitter spiritual and military struggle against the advances of Islam. Through the fateful separation between East and West in 1054 and the tragic misunderstandings and events during the Crusades, the Eastern Churches suffered a heavy blow, losing much land and many members. Precisely for this reason, however, they maintained the heritage of early Christianity and of Greek antiquity. New cities with a new bourgeoisie arose in the West, in the new realm of the German emperors. In connection with the Crusades the old Germanic tribal nobility was transformed into the new institution of the knighthood, first as a Christian power, then also as a political force. Of great importance for the missionary Church were the new pastoral orders in the cities, the Franciscans (Francis of Assisi, 1181–1226) and the Dominicans (Dominic from Caleruega in Castile, 1170–1221) which carried the faith into the newly opened territories, especially to

Mongolia, Persia, and China. After losing the Near East, the orders of knights shifted their missionary work to Eastern Germany and Spain. Particular attention was paid to the upper classes of society, and the local cultures were treated with greater circumspection than in the Benedictine missions of the early Middle Ages.

At the end of the Middle Ages the Christian Church experienced internal and external difficulties, similar to those experienced by the ancient religions at the end of antiquity. There had been a brief flowering of theology, stimulated by the reception of Aristotle's work, and a similarly brief flowering of the papacy in its struggle for power against the German emperors and the Italian nobility. However, a decline began in 1300 and tiredness as well as superstition spread among the people.

g) The spirit of the Crusades and of the Conquista, which had freed Spain from Islam, brought a new beginning, a new missionary age, in the fifteenth century. Since Islam blocked the way into the East, one sought new ways to the West by which one hoped to encircle Islam. The new flowering of the mathematics and geography of antiquity provided navigators with new possibilities. By sailing to the West from Spain they attempted to reach India. (At least after Peter d'Ailly, d. 1420, the earth was generally thought to be a sphere.) Columbus discovered America in 1492. At the same time (1497–1498) Vasco da Gama found a way to India by sailing around Africa. P. A. Cabral discovered South America (around 1500) and the way through Brazil to China. From the very outset these discoveries went hand in hand with a missionary spirit, although political and economic questions soon pushed themselves into the foreground. The popes supported the voyages sponsored by Spain and Portugal and in 1494 they published three bulls which entrusted the world to the west of the Atlantic (America) to Spain, and the East (India, China) to Portugal. It was not only a question of rights of trade, but quite explicitly one of missionary work. Yet the new missionary spring was soon trampled down by struggles for power.

h) The Reformation led to a deep division of Western Christianity, which soon took its toll in the populating of America. At the beginning the Churches of the Reformation were little interested in mission. When they began to send their missionaries to Africa and Asia in the nineteenth century, the problems of the Reformation schism were brought also to these missionary territories. On the other hand, the Counter-Reformation gave to the old Church new confidence and trust. The new order of the Counter-Reformation, the Jesuits, wanted to gain not only the old world, but the great new world, especially Asia, for Christ. The papacy, which had been reformed at the Council of Trent, set up the *Congregatio de propaganda fide* (Gregory XV; January 6, 1622). This has been the central institution for the Catholic missions since then. It had been suggested in the sixteenth century by Francis Borgia and the foundation of a new missionary congregation by the Carmelites. Under Pope Urban VIII, the *Collegium de propaganda fide* was joined to the congregation. At the same time a multilingual publishing house (the Vatican *Polyglotta*) was formed, so that a well-furnished missionary center existed in the papal curia.

This new institution was soon plagued by grave difficulties which had a very negative effect in the eighteenth century. Before that time, however, great missionary works were carried out. The need for more and better-educated missionaries led to the founding (in 1659 under Alexander VII) of the *Missions Etrangères de Paris* under the guidance of the Jesuit order. In 1663 it was officially recognized by Louis XIV. The Lazarists, Spiritans and similar congregations were founded in the same century, so that France became the leading force in Catholic missionary work.

i) Yet the eighteenth century dissolved much that had bloomed so promisingly. Nowhere is the simultaneous action of good and evil powers, of human weakness and human virtue, more evident than in the Church's missionary activity. There was first the "Conflict of Jurisdiction" between the Jesuits, who had been working in Asia since the beginning of the seventeenth century under the Roman *Congregatio de propaganda fide,* and the Franciscan and Dominican missionaries who had come to the same area at the end of the seventeenth century. The only way to solve this conflict was to introduce hindering exemptions and privileges. In addition, the still more difficult controversy about rites arose within the Jesuit mission and spread to the whole Chinese mission. The translation controversy was a related problem. To what extent should pagan rites be integrated into the Christian liturgy and thus be christianized? Which Chinese phrases can be considered appropriate expressions of Christian truths, especially truths about God? The tolerant approach to these questions favored by the Jesuits directed by Rome (Ricci) was opposed by the Franciscans and Dominicans under the protectorate of the Portugese crown. From 1645 to 1700 the struggle went back and forth and Rome itself gave conflicting responses, depending on the form of the questions. In 1700, after the Sorbonne of Paris intervened with an opinion of its own, Pope Innocent XII gave in to the wish of the Dominicans and curtailed the theological (not the political) freedom of Jesuits in their missionary work. When the emperor of China heard of these controversies, he allowed only those missionaries who followed the freer line of the Jesuits to work in China. After the death of the emperor Kang Hi, the first persecutions of Christians took place in China. In response, Pope Benedict XIV (1742) rescinded the freedoms granted to the Jesuits, which brought the thriving missions in the Far East to a halt.

Five other events in Europe did great damage to the missionary spring in the East. In the Jansenist controversy the rigorists prevailed over the moderates, at least at first. The new philosophy of the Enlightenment weakened the impact of religious thought to a great extent. The doctrine of unlimited state power, which stems from the Enlightenment, led to the disaster of colonialist thinking and nationalism, which took hold also of the new peoples. The freedom of the person, which is a foundation of the Christian understanding of the world, had no room in these ideas. In addition Pope Clement XIV suppressed the Jesuits (1773), who had at that time twelve hundred missionaries in various missionary territories. The French Revolution (1789) destroyed the very basis of the French missionary orders and so the great initiative of 1622 was halted.

k) It was only in the nineteenth century, after the Napoleonic wars, that the Church began a new missionary initiative. There were three reasons for this new beginning. The horrors of the French Revolution had shown the value of Christianity in comparison with Enlightenment thought, and the Revolution had given to the "people" a new sense of mission. A second reason was the movement of Romanticism, which developed a new historical consciousness and thus a new sensitivity for tradition and religious values (especially in the Middle Ages). A third reason was the German *Kulturkampf* in the 1870s, which strengthened Catholic self-confidence in the measure in which it wanted to suppress it in Germany. These experiences gave new impetus to the missionary idea and the missionary spirit, and this strength expressed itself in the founding of new missionary societies and associations in France and especially in Germany. For a while Germany took a leading role in the missions. There were some additional factors: the technological conquest of the world; the development of trade, especially with China and Japan; colonialism, which despite its dark sides often had a benevolent attitude toward the missions; and the abolition of slavery to which the Church made a great contribution. Let us mention only some of the missionary works that were formed in this period. The "Work of Spreading the

Faith" was founded 1822 in Lyons. It soon spread to all European countries and was recognized by the Pope. "The Work of the Holy Childhood of Jesus" was founded 1843 in Nancy. It also spread over all of Europe and contributed to the awakening of the idea of mission among children. In 1889 women founded the "Liebeswerk des HL. Apostel Petrus," which propagated the idea of training local clergy in the missionary countries and contributed much to this training. There were also numerous local missionary societies and associations of men, women, and young people. Pope Gregory XVI (1831–1846) was the great missionary pope of the century and in his missionary encyclical *Sancta Dei Civitas* (Dec. 3, 1888) Pope Leo XIII proclaimed the missionary duty of every individual Christian and of the whole Christian people. A large number of missionary journals disseminated the idea of mission among the people.

l) In the twentieth century diocesan clergy entered missionary work, which had been done mainly by men and women religious (Priester-Missions-Bund).

The decisive thing, however, happened in the missionary countries themselves. The number of Catholics grew rapidly in Africa (13 million in 1935; 35 million in 1958; 48.5 million in 1978) and in Indonesia. A local Church with its own clergy and many missionary assistants (catechists and brothers) is being formed in missionary countries. Foreign missionaries are often indispensable, but the local hierarchy is of the greatest importance in the various political conditions. There is a growing school system including universities (Japan) and an extensive social network. In addition to these bright lights there are, however, also shadows: the split between the Christian churches engaged in mission; the growing political power of Islam; the Communist danger in the missionary countries themselves; secularism and anti-Christian currents in the liberal economic world of Europe. These shadows are aggravated by the crisis in the global economy, which aggravates the great tensions between rich and poor in the missionary countries, between the rich industrial nations of the North and the poor agrarian developing nations in the South. Important discussions about the great missionary problems went on during Vatican II, to which we now turn.

3. SYSTEMATIC ASPECTS: VATICAN II

a) The teaching outlined briefly and clearly in the Constitution on the Church (LG 17) was developed in a theological and pastoral perspective in the Decree on the Church's Missionary Activity (AG). To understand the teaching of this decree correctly one must take a look at the Declaration on the Relationship of the Church to Non-Christian Religions (NA) and the Declaration on Religious Freedom (DH), because these documents clarify how the struggle for the truth of faith and of the various religions is ordered to the respect for the dignity of the person as to its principle. These documents understand and see the person with equal insistence in terms of the freedom of human conscience and in terms of the duty of orienting and forming this conscience by growing insight into the truth of faith and of all reality. Each person is unique *and* linked to social and cultural, political and economic forms of communion, which shows that the various communities can make the claims on the free persons that are necessary for such communities. This respect for human dignity leads to a deeper understanding of the positive values found in non-Christian religions and cultures, which are often older as shapers and guides of humanity than the Christian faith. "The Catholic Church rejects nothing of what is true and holy in these religions . . . (which) often reflect a ray of that truth which enlightens all men" (NA 2). In this context the decree expressly mentions Hinduism with its mysticism, Buddhism with its ethos, and Islam with its image of God and trust in God. Special attention is given to the Jewish religion, with which Christianity is most intimately united, not only through Jesus and the apostles, but also through the basic mystery of the whole history of salvation with its religious truths and values. In the Church's name the Council fathers accuse themselves that the Church in its long history has often forgotten these truths and Christian love which is related to them ("He who does not love does not know God" 1 John 4,8). These "new insights" and basic attitudes have become more conscious today, certainly not without the spiritual transition of the eighteenth and nineteenth centuries. The Council explains and clarifies them in the light of the word and spirit of Christian revelation itself. It is in terms of this new spirit that the Decree on the Church's Missionary Activity can be rightly understood. Let us look at five basic themes developed by the Council.

b) "The Church on earth is by her very nature missionary" (AG 2). The basis of this teaching is the new understanding of the Church as the "pilgrim people of God" which must bear and realize God's history of salvation in the history of humanity. Mission is thus not understood as one enterprise of the institutional Church among others (e.g., pastoral care in Christian countries). It is, rather, a function, indeed the first function, of the Church's life. "In the present state of things which gives rise to a new situation for humankind" through science and technology, the Church as "the universal sacrament of salvation" must "save and renew every creature" (AG 1). The Church as mission, like its very existence, is understood in terms of the inner divine love between Father, Son, and Spirit, and thus in trinitarian terms as the continuation of the divine missions (John 20,21; 15,26f.). The Code of Canon Law of 1917 still said, "All care [cura] for Catholic missions in the world is reserved only to the apostolic See" (CIC can. 1350 §2). After the Council one can perhaps say with greater precision: For the sake of unity, the organization of the world Church and thus also of the missions remains the exclusive task of the apostolic see. But the *care* for the missions as an actualization of the Church must be the care of the whole people of the Church, of every believer, every diocese and every parish (AG 18; 35). "The theology of communion and the relationships among particular churches, which have theological reasons (LG 23; AG 9; CD 6), demand a practice of communion, a juridically (pastorally) grounded cooperation which benefits above all the younger churches."[5] Following the Decree on the Church's Missionary Activity, the motu proprio *Ecclesiae Sanctae* (Aug. 6, 1966) further specifies that the coordination of all missionary activities (of the various missionary orders and associations of diocesan priests) is the responsibility of the *Congregatio de propaganda fide* and that "national and regional" mission councils should be formed (parallel to episcopal conferences and dioceses).

c) The Constitution on the Sacred Liturgy (SC) established certain norms for the central area of the Church's life, the liturgy, which are designed to allow missionary activity in the "spirit of openness" for everything that is true and good in this world. (1) Of greatest importance is the permission to use the vernacular in the Church's liturgy (SC 36). This permission soon led many to forget another norm laid down in the same section, "The use of the Latin language, with due respect to particular law, is to be preserved in the Latin rites." At any rate, the use of the vernacular in the liturgy is necessary for a true inculturation of the Christian faith. One should not forget that the preservation of ecclesiastical Latin in the Germanic missions was a great enrichment for the culture of these peoples, because it allowed them to absorb the culture of antiquity. It is difficult to say to what extent the preservation of Latin was a religious impoverishment for these peoples. The Germanic religions, like many primitive religions today, were inferior and corrupt, in contrast to the major world-religions of Hinduism, Shintoism, Buddhism, Islam.

(2) "Even in the liturgy, the Church has no wish to impose a rigid uniformity [*rigidam unius tenoris formam*] in matters which do not involve the faith or the good of the whole community" (SC 37). This significant opening of the Church to the values and goods of various cultures does not eliminate the duty of carefully investigating in the spirit of each cultural sphere the differences in the value of various forms and rites (e.g., in music, dance, and traditional customs) before adopting them in the Christian liturgy.

(3) "Provided that the substantial unity of the Roman rite is preserved, provision shall be made, when revising the liturgical books, for legitimate variations and adaptations to different groups, regions and peoples, especially in mission countries" (SC 38).

(4) The competent ecclesiastical authority (usually the episcopal conference of various countries) should "specify adaptations, especially as regards the administration of the sacraments, sacramentals, processions, liturgical language, sacred music and the arts, according, however, to the fundamental norms laid down in this Constitution" (SC 39).

(5) The next passage is particularly important.

In some places and circumstances, however, an even more radical adaptation of the liturgy is needed and entails greater difficulties. Therefore: (1) The competent territorial ecclesiastical authority . . . must, in this matter, carefully and prudently consider which elements from the traditions and genius of individual peoples might appropriately be admitted into divine worship. . . . (2) To ensure that adaptations are made with all necessary circumspection, the Apostolic See will grant power to this same territorial ecclesiastical authority to permit and to direct, as the case requires, the necessary preliminary experiments over a determined period of time among certain groups suitable for the purpose. (3) Because liturgical laws often involve special difficulties with respect to adaptation, particularly in mission lands, experts in these matters in question [i.e., local and lay persons as mem-

bers of an ecclesiastical commission] must be employed to formulate them. (SC 40)

All of this demands an extraordinary measure of knowledge about the liturgy and its history, of empathy and critical judgment about the Church's ancient liturgy and the
secular and religious rites and forms. This demand applies
especially to missionaries, who must often make the preliminary decisions.

d) This openness of the Church to the religions and cultures of mission lands raises again the question of the
unity and unicity of the Church as an internal spiritual
communion of life, as the mystical body of the one Christ.
A fundamental condition is that one see the Church with
the eyes of faith and that one assent within this vision to
the Church's leadership in the one college of bishops (represented by the episcopal council of the whole Church at
the Holy See) under the guidance of the pope. On this
foundation the genuine problems which result from the
Church's new openness for the true human values in the
whole world will always be seen and resolved in the depth
of lived faith, in obedience and love, in patience and thus
in the tolerance necessary for all human relationships. But
further, the people of God on earth, which is now larger,
will see a way from the multiplicity of "theologies," "liturgies," and "ways of life," which are the first result of
such openness, to a new and higher unity in Christ and his
Spirit. If the Church's external unity in its leadership is
rightly understood and lived, its inner unity, which is always a task and a gift of development and of the conscious
growth of individuals and communities, will be honestly
sought, seen, and realized, even in all the multiplicity of
human opinions and needs. This point is of special importance for the "theologies" of the third world. The Ecumenical Association of Third World Theologians (EAT-
WOT) was founded at Dar es Salaam (1976) to discuss the
liberation theology of South America and the new theo-

logical experiments in Africa and Asia (India, Indonesia, the Philippines, China, Japan). The first conference took place in Accra (Ghana) 1977; the second in Sri Lanka 1979.[6]

e) After this discussion of the new understanding of mission, let us raise the question of the meaning and goal and the inner reason of the Church's missionary activity. It cannot be denied that the Church's missionary work in the past not only gained large peoples for Christ, but christianized them in an authentic sense. It also cannot be denied that great goods and values contained in the cultures of ancient peoples, indeed ancient peoples themselves together with their cultures (e.g., in America Indians such as the Incas), suffered great damage from human weakness in carrying out this missionary work. Liberal spirits, especially since the Enlightenment, have often disapproved of missionary work and have demanded that each person should be left to become happy in his own way (Frederick I of Prussia). The history, psychology, and sociology of religion have raised the critical question of the "absolute character of Christianity."[7] From the perspective of liberalism and indifferentism this question must be answered in the negative.

For the Catholic Christian, Christianity is not just in a history of religions perspective the "highest development among the various religions of the world," but it is the unique gift of the self-revelation of the one triune God through Jesus Christ in the history of humanity. On the basis of this self-understanding the Council proposed various reasons for the Church's missionary activity. Let us present at least four of them. Seen in their inner unity they can clarify the inner meaning of missionary activity from both a divine and a human perspective.

(1) The Constitution on the Church (LG 17) bases the Church's missionary activity on Christ's missionary command (Matt 28,18ff.; cf. Mark 16,15–18). The Church received this command from the apostles. And it must fulfill

it to the ends of the earth (Acts 1,8) until Christ himself "will also be subjected to him who put all things under him, that God may be all in all" (1 Cor 15,28). One could call this the *incarnational* reason of the Church's missionary activity, because it is based on the historical event in which God's trans-historical reality entered this historical world, and because the mission of the apostles and their successors as well as the whole Church and each individual Christian remains forever tied to the mission that the Son received from the Father (John 20,21; 17,18).

(2) The Decree on the Church's Missionary Activity (AG 2–9) takes up the idea of mission as just explained and builds upon it to see the deeper reasons for mission in the history of salvation, in christology and in soteriology. God's "fountain-like love" is the eternal ground, and the union of humanity and divinity in Christ is the temporal ground of the mission and work of Jesus Christ for the salvation of the human race and for the recapitulation and renewal of the whole world in earthly history (Eph 1,2–23; 2,10; Col 1,13–20). "God our Savior . . . desires all men to be saved and to come to the knowledge of the truth. For there is one God, and there is one mediator between God and men, the man Christ Jesus, who gave himself as a ransom for all" (1 Tim 2,3–6). "And there is salvation in no one else" (Acts 4,12).

(3) Seen from the time of our world, the Church's missionary activity must be seen in historical-eschatological terms. "The period between the first [incarnation] and second coming of the Lord [his parousia as judge of the world, Matt 25,31–46; Rev 20,11–22,5] is the time of missionary activity [of the Church's missionary nature]" (AG 9). The missionary command in Mark 16,15f. is related to this comprehensive view, "Go into all the world and preach the gospel to the whole creation. He who believes and is baptized will be saved; but he who does not believe will be condemned."

(4) A fourth reason for the Church's missionary activity

is necessarily linked with the three mentioned so far and can be gathered from the more practical instructions of the Decree on the Church's Missionary Activity. It is an ecclesiological-existential reason and rests on the fact that the action of God's eternal love in Christ and his Spirit for the salvation of every person demands from every person the response of love which urges one to lead all things and all people back to God. This basic attitude is expressed in the words of Paul, "Woe to me if I do not preach the gospel" (1 Cor 9,16; cf. Luke 17,10). "The love of Christ urges us on, because we are convinced that one has died for all; therefore all have died. And he died for all, that those who live might live no longer for themselves but for him who for their sake died and was raised" (2 Cor 5,14–15).

This should really be the first and the deepest reason. In our human poverty, however, Christ's historical missionary command will probably always occupy the first place and our love of Christ will determine in each case in what spirit and power of self-abandonment we will understand and fulfill this command. For the love of Christ has not even been able to make us completely one as brothers and sisters of Christ in one Church. Let us, therefore, turn to the question of ecumenism, which Vatican II proposes as a preparatory issue for successful Christian missionary work.

f) One final question, however, remains: namely, the question of the basic structure of missionary activity. Quite different answers have been given to this question, depending on the spirit of the various missionary periods: at times baptism stood in the foreground (the Germanic missions, St. Francis Xavier), at times instruction did, at times the liturgy. The only valid answer to this question can be taken from the missionary command. Mark formulates it as follows, "Preach the gospel to the whole creation" (Mark 16,15); in Matthew the command has four parts, as discussed above. For Mark "the gospel" is not a doctrine, but the person, the event, and the work of Jesus

Christ (Mark 1,1; cf. 1 Cor 15,1–5). This perspective leads to several conclusions about mission. (1) The basic act of missionary activity is to "make disciples" (*mathēteusate;* Matt 28,19; 13,52; cf. Acts 14,21). "Make disciples" means "Lead people to Jesus so that they can hear his personal call and follow him." Thus Luke calls the apostles "disciples of Jesus" until the scene at Gethsemane after which they no longer followed the Lord (Luke 22,45). After this point they are only called "the Eleven" or "those with him." The title "disciple" is only taken up again in Acts 6,1 where it is applied to the first Christians.[8] "Disciple (as a title) always implies the presence of a personal bond which forms the whole life of the disciple and which, in its specific character, excludes any doubt as to who has the forming power."[9]

(2) Since the power that forms the disciples is the person of the "master" (*rabbi, disdaskalos*), the missionary command in Matthew continues, "and baptize them in the name of the Father and of the Son and of the Holy Spirit" (Matt 28,19). For the living triune God himself generates and forms the "Christian" as a brother or sister of Christ in the sacraments and in grace.

(3) Since the forming element is not a neutral truth but a personal wisdom of life, the missionary command continues, "and teach [*didaskontes*] them to observe [*tērein*] all that I have commanded you" (Matt 28,20). Communicate and pass on (tradition) my instructions to them, not the "law" of tradition, but my lived instructions for following Christ.

(4) This is why the final sentence of the missionary command is, "and lo [*idou*, which means: Pay attention! The most important thing is coming now!], I am with you always, to the close of the age" (Matt 28,20). This means that the missionary can and should lead people to Christ only in order that Christ may bring them to the Father (John 14,1–14). The missionary is thus only the "unworthy servant" (Luke 17,10). The giver of all gifts is the Spirit, the

bearer of each office is the Lord, and the one who acts in all is God (1 Cor 12,4–7).

Everything through which missionaries can gain people for Christ and lead them to Christ as his disciples is a useful and necessary part of their missionary activity. And they must accept everything with gratitude which makes them aware that the one who acts in everything is God, not they themselves (this includes suffering and failure). Their prayer for their "children" (1 Cor 4,14–16) must have the same ultimate form as Paul's words: I do not cease to give thanks for you, remembering you in my prayers, that the God of our Lord Jesus Christ, the Father of glory, may give you a spirit of wisdom and of revelation in the knowledge of him (Jesus), having the eyes of your hearts enlightened, that you may know what is the hope to which he has called you, what are the riches of his glorious inheritance in the saints, and what is the immeasurable greatness of his power in us who believe, according to the working of his great might which he accomplished in Christ when he raised him from the dead and made him sit at his right hand in the heavenly places (Eph 1,16–20; cf. 1 Cor 1,4; Rom 1,8; 2 Cor 1,3–11; 1 Thess 1,2; 2 Thess 1,3; Phil 1,3–11; Col 1,3–12).

XIV

Ecumenism as an Essential Task of the Church in the World

Our reflections on the Church's missionary nature have shown us how the Church's unity and unicity must prove themselves as it spreads over the whole world and to all peoples with their different religions and cultures and how, at the same time, it must find an ever new face in its own growth and maturation as a being in this world. The following reflections about "ecumenism as an essential task of the Church in this world" will show us some of the reasons of the dividedness of Christ's one Church in this world and some of the paths which can lead to the single Church, to the unity of the Church. The World Council of Churches in Geneva, of which the Catholic Church is not a member, is composed of almost three hundred churches, but it does not constitute a unity in the sense of the "one holy catholic and apostolic Church." This situation raises many questions. We must at least outline these questions to approach a correct understanding of the problem of the Church's unity and unicity from this perspective. We will address the questions in a "systematic" part after a brief historical sketch has shown us how this situation came about. First, however, let us prepare the ground with four preliminary points.

I. PRELIMINARY REMARKS

a) The word *ecumenical* (*coikoumenē* means the space

in which people live) referred first of all to "the inhabited and cultivated world." (According to the author of the treatise "On the World," which is found among Aristotle's works, this *oikoumenē* includes Europe, Asia, and Africa; it is 40,000 stadias wide and 70,000 long; 393 b 18–22). This is why the great councils of the Church, at least after Ephesus in 431, were called "ecumenical Councils." The word acquired a new meaning in the nineteenth century when the various Christian churches that had been formed in the course of history began to seek unity among themselves, especially for the sake of cooperating in the missions. Of course, this unity was understood in very different terms. "Ecumenical" now refers to a process of re-unification, which is to bring about this much-desired unity.

b) In order to understand this process, one must understand the reasons for the divisions that led to the multiplicity of Christian churches today. The forms of separation from the one Church are usually characterized today by the terms "schism" and "heresy." The reasons for these two forms of division in the Church's unity are quite various.[10]

The meaning of the term "heresy" shifted in the course of history. Originally, and especially in Hellenistic usage, "heresy (*hairesis*)" referred simply to a philosophical or religious school (cf. Diogenes Laertius, I, Proem XIII, 19; Acts 5,17; 18,5). In Christian usage the term referred from the very beginning to a form of life and doctrine that deviates from the general norm, because the life and doctrine of Christ's one Church is incompatible with any deviation. For this reason Paul immediately connects the term "heresy" with "schism": "For, in the first place, when you assemble as a church [*ekklēsia*], I hear that there are divisions [*schismata*] among you; and I partly believe it, for there must be factions [*haireseis*] among you in order that those who are genuine among you may be recognized" (1 Cor 11,18f.).[11] Already in 2 Peter the word "heresy" has the

special meaning of "deviation from doctrine" or "false separate doctrine": "But false prophets also arose among the
people, just as there will be false teachers [*pseu-
dodidaskaloi*] among you, who will secretly bring in destructive heresies [*haireseis*], even denying the Master
who bought them, bringing upon themselves swift destruction. And many will follow their licentiousness, and
because of them the way of truth [*hodos tēs alētheias*] will
be reviled" (2 Pet 2,1–2; cf. Tit 13,10). This meaning of
"heresy" soon prevailed in the Church. It was only in the
controversy about the validity of sacraments, especially in
the Donatist controversy, that a more precise distinction
was made between schism as separation from the Church
and heresy as false doctrine. Thus Augustine says, "Heresy
means a sect of people who follow another doctrine;
schism, on the other hand, is the separation of people who
follow this doctrine from the Church. *Haeresis est diversa
sequentium secta; schisma vero eadem sequentium sep-
aratio*" (*Contr. Cresco.* II 3,4; PL 43,469). The schismatic
is not defined by another doctrine but by the rupture of the
bond of communion. Christ again and again warns against
false prophets and wicked shepherds (Matt 7,15; Luke
21,8; Mark 13,5f.); so does Paul (Rom 16,7f.; Gal 1,6ff.; 1
Cor 11,2ff.); and the Pastoral Epistles give special attention to this theme (1 Tim 1,3–11; 2 Tim 2,14–26; 4,1–6; cf.
1 John 4,1–6) and demand "sound doctrine" (1 Tim 1,10;
6,3).

c) Theology has often dealt with these two forms of
"gangrene" (2 Tim 2,17) which harm the Church's unity.

(1) Let us first look at *schism*. In the early Church
schisms appeared for the most part as divisions in local
churches (cf. the histories of heresy by Hippolytus, The-
odoretus of Cyrus, Epiphanius, etc.) and they soon disappeared. It was only in the third century that more permanent schisms were formed (Marcion, the Nestorians,
Monophysites). The fundamental aspect of unity was seen
in the liturgy (the eucharistic liturgy of the bishop with his

presbytery and his people; cf. Ignatius, *Magn.* 7,2; *Apostol. Const.* VIII 47,31 Funk 673). Schism is thus the breaking of ecclesial communion. The apostolic *Canones* mention above all "lust for power" as a reason for this break. Since the Gregorian reform in the Middle Ages, schism has been seen primarily as a separation from the Church's hierarchy (the pope and the bishops) which implies, at the same time, a separation from the Church's communion of love. Thus Thomas Aquinas writes that the sin of schism is a special sin, because it consists in the intention of separating oneself from the communion of love, which exists not only between individual persons, but unites the whole Church in the unity of the Spirit. This unity consists both in the communion (*communicatio*) of members among each other and their subordination under a common head (cf. Col 2,18f.). This head is Christ and his vicar on earth, the pope (cf. *Summa Theol.* II–II, q. 39). Thomas Aquinas, as later J. A. Möhler,[12] combines in his vision the Church's inner unity which stems from the divine Spirit of love and its external unity through the hierarchical institution. This comprehensive view of the Church's unity explains the multiplicity of reasons for schisms: personal, spiritual, and temperamental dispositions; political, economic, and social power struggles; questions of doctrine and liturgical practice; questions of discipline; and differences in conceiving the ecclesial ideal of communion. Since nationalism combines many of these factors, it has often become the source of schisms. The decisive thing is that the insistence on one's own will leads not only to separation from the "old" Church, but to the formation of one's own "Church," which is then proclaimed to be the "universal Church" and opposed to the old Church. Of course, the behavior of the old Church was often also responsible for the behavior of the "new Church."

(2) According to Thomas Aquinas, the sin of heresy is more serious than the sin of schism. Schism often preserves the great realities of faith (teachings, sacraments

and offices: cf. the schism between the Eastern and the Western Church). Heresy, on the other hand, is unbelief; it thus destroys these inner bonds of unity and turns directly against God, who is Truth itself (cf. *Summa Theol.* II–II, q. 39, a. 2). Yet, is heresy simply unbelief? The concept of heresy was variously understood in the history of the Church. In antiquity it was defined in more ecclesiological terms and even the Middle Ages often draw no clear distinction between heresy and schism. Every conciliar anathema was interpreted as pointing out heresy. If heresy is understood as a sin, it cannot be described only in objective terms as a deviation from revealed truth. There must be personal wrongdoing, an attitude Augustine called *pertinacia* (*Ep.* 43,1; PL 33,16) or *contumacia* (*De Gen. ad litt.* VI 9,13; PL 35,160). In addition this pertinacious denial or doubt must be externally and publicly proclaimed and defended so that it disturbs the Church's external unity (cf. CIC of 1917, can. 1325, §2).

In our time of Enlightenment and individualism, the true problem lies probably more in the "inner emigration" of "believers" from the Church which is rooted in eclecticism and a liberal indifferentism. True reality is always greater than our human knowledge of it, and it can be grasped by numerous methods and on often quite different paths. "Enlightenment" is the basic attitude in which one attempts to grasp and to define reality definitively and exclusively with the rational mind, even if one concedes that this grasp is always an ongoing process. Enlightenment dissolves tradition and authority in a manner quite foreign to real being. We will return to this issue in the context of the correct understanding of ecumenism. *Sapere aude* (Horace, *Ep.* I 2,40) does not mean "Dare to use your mind," as Kant misinterpreted it. In Horace it means, "Make a new beginning, immediately, in order to find the true life [*recte vivendi*] which lets you become wise [*sapere-sapientia:* not only to know reality in order to govern it, but to taste it]"[13]

d) In conclusion, let us point to the objective space in which the ecumenical endeavor must unfold itself today. Among the baptized, in the "Christian space," four different groups must be mentioned: In the first place the orthodox churches, which were one with the Catholic Church during the first millennium and which still hold the same essential doctrines of faith (the Trinity, faith in Christ, sacraments, apostolic office, priesthood, and basic liturgical forms). In addition to the "Old Catholic" Church of Utrecht, one must mention the Anglican Church, in which patristic tradition plays an important role, although in other respects the Anglican Church resembles the Churches of the Reformation. Among the Churches of the Reformation (Lutherans, Calvinists, and sects), the Lutheran Church found a closer ecumenical contact with the Catholic Church, due to its special understanding of the Eucharist. Still, the question of ecclesiastical office presents many difficulties, just as it does in the other Churches of the Reformation.

The Catholic Church is bound to ecumenical dialogue especially with these Christian churches. At least in these preliminary remarks we must, however, mention the dialogue with the Old Testament people of God, with the Jewish community of faith. The religion of Israel cannot be viewed as the other non-Christian religions, because Israel's religion and its whole history are in a unique way ordered to the Christian religion. Thus Paul says, "So you see that it is men of faith who are sons of Abraham. And the Scripture, foreseeing that God would justify the Gentiles by faith, preached the gospel beforehand to Abraham, saying, In you shall all the nations be blessed . . . that in Christ Jesus the blessing of Abraham might come upon the Gentiles, that we might receive the promise of the Spirit through faith. . . . Why then the law? It was added because of transgressions. . . . But the Scripture consigned all things to sin, that what was promised to faith in Jesus Christ might be given to those who believe . . . in Christ

Jesus you are all sons of God through faith. . . . And if you are Christ's, then you are Abraham's offspring, heirs according to promise" (Gal 3,7–29). In the Letter to the Romans, Paul deals extensively with the mystery of Israel and the Church in the history of salvation, and he offers the following image: "If the root is holy, so are the branches. But if some of the branches [Jews] were broken off [from the noble olive tree which is Israel], and you, a wild olive shoot [a Gentile], were grafted in their place to share the richness of the olive tree, do not boast over the branches. If you do boast, remember it is not you that support the root, but the root that supports you. . . . For if you have been cut from what is by nature a wild olive tree [the Gentiles], and grafted, contrary to nature, into a cultivated olive tree [the promise to Abraham], how much more will these natural branches be grafted back into their own olive tree. . . . As regards the gospel they are [now] enemies of God, for your sake; but as regards election they are beloved for the sake of their forefathers. For the gifts and the call of God are irrevocable" (Rom 11,16–29).

The Jewish history of salvation, the basis of the religion of Israel as we find it in the Old Testament,[14] is the historical foundation of the Christian history of salvation and revelation. This connection remains intact although according to our faith something completely new, the new covenant (Jer 31,31–34; Luke 22,20; 1 Cor 11,25; Heb 7,1–10,18), God's definitive revelation in this world, was realized in Jesus of Nazareth, the Messiah and true Son of God ("For in him the whole fullness of deity dwells bodily" Col 2,9). No "new" revelation will come beyond Christ, although in all this "newness" of the New Covenant, "the creation waits with eager longing for the revealing of the sons of God" (Rom 8,19; cf. 8,1–30) at the resurrection of the dead in the final judgment (1 Cor 15,22–28) so that God may be revealed as being "all in all" (1 Cor 15,28). On the basis of these Scriptural teachings contemporary exegetes assume that "according to Rom 11,26–32 Israel will reach

salvation through the *parousia,* not through a mass conversion preceding the *parousia* (F. W. Maier), but only
through an initiative of the all-merciful God which is completely independent from the behavior of Israel and the
rest of humanity, an initiative which consists concretely
in the *parousia* of Jesus."[15] Of course, for human thinking
this divine initiative seems to compromise the freedom of
Israel's conversion. Yet God can "guide" us without com-
promising our freedom. Grace brings about true freedom!
"In Christ we are free" (Gal 2,4; 5,1.13).

2. HISTORICAL ASPECTS OF ECUMENISM

In this brief historical sketch we will concentrate on
those processes that point to basic principles needed for a
correct understanding of ecumenical attitudes from the
perspective of the Catholic Church.

a) The Catholic Church, which understands itself as a
unity founded externally by Christ and supported inter-
nally by him and his Spirit, was for a considerable period
divided by an extraordinary schism, the Great Western
Schism from 1378 to 1418. There were two to five "popes"
side by side. Despite these confusing political circumstances, a line of authentic popes (as opposed to anti-popes)
can be traced. When the Council of Constance demanded
the abdicaton of Pope Gregory XII, it did not intend to
declare him illegitimate, but merely to open the possibility of new elections as a solution to the schism between
the three popes (new elections were held on November 11,
1417, after Gregory's death). Despite the idea of conciliarism, which had become dominant after 1379, there never
was a doubt that the Church of Christ can as a matter of
principle have only one legitimate head, i.e., that its structure is hierarchical in the traditional sense.

b) From the very beginning there have been various
"theological schools" in questions of faith. However,
when the issue was the Church's faith, these schools

found a common basis in a single linguistic formulation (the conciliar documents) in terms of which divergent views had to be judged and condemned as heresy. This fact is attested by the eventful history of heresies, especially in the early Church, when the questions of God, of Christ, of the sacraments, and of grace were decided by the ecumenical councils. No compromises were made in true questions of faith. When compromises were attempted (in "formulas of union"), which usually happened for political reasons, they never served true unity and were for the most part short-lived.

c) Despite the great spiritual tensions between the two cultures, the struggle about the Church's unity in the clashes between the Greek East and the Latin West was due only to political conditions, beginning with the First Council of Constantinople (the second Rome!) in A.D. 381, intensified at Chalcedon in A.D. 451 and under Photius in A.D. 879 until the tragic separation in 1054 under Michael Cerularius in the East and Pope Leo IX with his Secretary of State Humbertus of Silva Candida in the West. This separation was sealed by the Crusades, especially the Fourth Crusade during the reign of the emperor Alexius IV in Constantinople and Pope Innocent III. Constantinople was sacked in 1204. Human weakness as well as unfortunate political circumstances thus deepened the schism. The various attempts at union (Lyons 1274 under Gregory X; and Florence under Eugene IV) could not heal the schism. It became evident that the spiritual and religious reality of the Church's unity could be smashed by political factors, but could not be re-established by them. A series of letters initiated in 1958 was exchanged between Pope John XXIII and Ecumenical Patriarch Athenagoras (1886–1972) who was imbued with the spirit of Christian love and a sense of worldwide responsibility. These exchanges culminated in the memorable meeting between Ecumenical Patriarch Athenagoras and Pope Paul VI (January 5, 1964) on the Mount of Olives in Jerusalem. The relic of the head of the apostle Andrew which had been stolen during the Crusades, was returned to Constantinople. The mutual anathemas imposed by Rome and Constantinople in 1054 were lifted by mutual agreement on December 7, 1965. The dialogue between these two churches can now build upon this basis. The churches seek union in the visible communion of the Eucharist, that *koinonia* for which Christians pray in obedience to the Spirit of unity.

The Decree on Ecumenism writes on this point, "Although these [Eastern] churches are separated from us, yet they possess true sacraments, above all—by apostolic succession—the priesthood and the Eucharist, whereby they are still joined to us in a very close relationship. Therefore, some worship in common [*communicatio in sacris*], given suitable circumstances and the approval of Church authority, is not merely possible but is recommended" (UR 15). And the Decree on the Catholic Eastern Churches says, "Eastern Christians who are separated in good faith from the Catholic Church, if they are rightly disposed and make such request of their own accord, may be given the sacraments of penance, the Eucharist and the anointing of the sick. Furthermore, Catholics may ask for these same sacraments from those non-Catholic ministers [of the Eastern Church] whose churches possess valid sacraments, as often as necessity or a genuine spiritual benefit recommends such a course of action, and when access to a Catholic priest is physically or morally impossible" (OE 27). Of course the agreement of the local authorities of the various churches is presupposed (UR 27).[16]

d) The questions of ecumenism are different and more complex in the case of the Catholic Church and the Churches of the Reformation. Soon after the end of the Thirty Years' War (1618–1648), attempts were made to reunite Christians. Letters about the possibility of a reunification of confessions were exchanged between Bishop J.-B. Bossuet (1677–1704) and the scientist and philosopher G. W. Leibniz (1646–1716) as well as Cardinal de Noailles

(1651–1729) and the Pietist Count N. L. Zinzendorf (1700–1760). In the nineteenth century, important Catholic theologians attempted to prepare the ground for a possible reunification in the face of the strongly negative voice of the Spanish Jesuit J. L. Balmes (1810–1848) against the Protestant Francois Guigot (1787–1874), and the resistance of Pope Pius XI against a participation of Catholics in the "Association for the Promotion of Unity among Christians" (APUC) in England 1864. Especially J. A. Möhler (1796–1838) showed in his brilliant *Symbolik* (an account of the doctrinal differences between Catholics and Protestants; published in 1832) that many differences between the confessions were originally differences between schools of thought. As soon as the bond of ecclesial communion was broken, these differences turned into insuperable oppositions. Also the collection of dogmatic definitions, the *Enchiridion Symbolorum et Definitionum* compiled by the Würzburg theologian H. J. Denzinger (1819–1883) was intended to serve the dialogue between the confessions by clarifying the traditional Catholic doctrine. It was written in response to the lectures of the Protestant theologian H. W. G. Thiersch "On Catholicism and Protestantism" (Würzburg, 1947/48). Indeed, faithfulness to the innermost conviction of faith is the presupposition for finding the true unity of the one Church in the face of the word of Scripture and tradition. Even the strictly Lutheran orientation of the Erlangen School founded by A. Harlefs (1806–1879) must be seen in this context.

è) Re-unification with the Churches of the Reformation calls for the search for new paths, since the reasons for the break between these Churches and the old Church were not national and spiritual, but true differences of faith. In addition, the Churches of the Reformation were from the outset divided among themselves by divergent faiths. Ecumenism had to take root in their own mutual relations if it was to be effectively implemented in relation to the ancient churches. Two Protestant movements were in the forefront of furthering these efforts. In addition to the pietism of the seventeenth and eighteenth centuries[17] one must mention the critique of the Enlightenment formulated by leading Lutherans in the nineteenth century. K. Harms (1778–1855) composed his 95 theses against the Enlightenment, and the Danish theologian N. Grundtwig (1783–1872) attempted to understand the different churches as different "theological schools" in order to prepare the ground for "brotherly communion" among them. Also S. Kierkegaard's critique of pietism in terms of the paradox of a living understanding of God must be mentioned in the context of the critique of the Enlightenment.

In addition, Anglican theology with its appreciation of tradition and its pietism (as reflected in the Book of Common Prayer) took on a special importance for the ecumenical movement in the Churches of the Reformation. Especially effective was the Oxford Movement founded by J. Keth (1792–1866), E. Pusey (1800–1882) and John Henry Newman (1801–1890). Since 1867 the archbishop of Canterbury has been convening the Lambeth Conference, which takes place about every ten years and includes the Anglican bishops of the whole world. In 1888 the Conference passed the "Lambeth Quadrilateral," which laid down four conditions for Christian unity: (1) the recognition of the entire Scriptures; (2) the assent to the Nicaean Creed and the Apostles' Creed; (3) the practice of the sacraments of baptism and the Eucharist as instituted by Christ; (4) the acknowledgment of an ecclesiastical office instituted by Christ. In his Tract Ninety, J. H. Newman interpreted the 39 articles of Anglicanism (1563) in a Catholic key. This interpretation remained the norm of "Anglo-Catholicism" even when Newman personally ignored the goal of the Oxford Movement, which was the corporate re-unification of churches, by converting to the Catholic Church (1845). The Oxford Movement developed what is known as the "branch theory," which completely leaves out Protestantism and seeks a new triune unity of the Church between the Orthodox Church, the Catholic Church, and Anglo-Catholicism. In a similar way, V. S. Soloviev (1853–1900) sought his home in a Russian (Orthodox) Church united with the Roman Church under Peter. More recent Orthodox theologians proposed a reunification along the lines of a branch theory between the Orthodox (Johannine) Church, the Protestant (Pauline) Church, and the Roman (Petrine) Church.

Two religious realities were brought to new light in the Oxford Movement and in Russian theology of the nineteenth century: the figure of the "living Christ" as the unique Lord of the Church, and the idea of the "kingdom of Christ" as Augustine unfolds it in his *City of God.* This kingdom had been somewhat misunderstood in the Middle Ages, which made the distinction between a secular state and a monastic Christianity on the basis of a mistaken interpretation of Matt 22,21 ("Render to Caesar the things that are Caesar's, and to God the things that are God's"). In contrast, Newman and Soloviev realized the inner unity of the "city of God" in a Christianized world to which the Church belongs. They reached this insight just after the destruction of the ecclesiastical state (1870) and the new image of the Church in this world made necessary by this destruction. A shift in Roman terminology occurred also at this time. Pope Leo XIII no longer referred to the other Churches simply as heretics and schismatics, but began to use the names which they give themselves. In 1895 Leo XIII dedicated the novena of Pentecost to prayer for the unity of Christians and in 1897 he returned to this prayer in the encyclical *Divinum Illud.* Still, in the encyclical *Satis Cognitum* he saw the realization and guarantee of the Church's unity only in the hierarchical Church founded by Christ with the pope as head.

f) The ecumenism of the twentieth century began with the great movement of Protestant Christians which found its first expression in the World Missionary Conference of Edinburgh in 1910. American Episcopalians played a leading role at this conference. The Orthodox Church and the Catholic Church did not participate. John Mott (1865–1955), the founder of the World's Student Christian Foundation (WSCF), was its president. The main components of this new movement were thus the idea of mission, the student movement, and American Anglicanism (as shaped by the Episcopalian Church). In the same year the Episcopalian Church called for an ecumenical conference with the theme "Faith and Order," but it was prevented by World War I (1914–18). It took place for the first time in 1927 (Lausanne). The themes of the seven task forces of this conference have remained at the center of attention to this day: (1) the call to unity; (2) the gospel for the world; (3) the nature of the Church; (4) the common confession of faith; (5) the spiritual office of the Church; (6) the sacraments: baptism and the Lord's supper; (7) the unity of the Christian world and the Church. The movement organized international conferences with various emphases: Edinburgh (1937); Lund (1952); Montreal (1963); Louvain (1971). The International Missionary Council (IMC) was founded in 1921 in Lake Mohonk, New York. It organized conferences in Jerusalem (1928), in Tambaram, India (1938), in Whitby, Canada (1947), in Willingen, West Germany (1952), in Achimota, Ghana (1958), and in Mexico (1963). In 1961 (New Delhi) it joined the World Council of Churches. The Norwegian bishop Nathan Söderblom (1866–1931) founded the movement *Life and Work* (World Conference of Churches in Stockholm, 1925). The movement's second conference took place in 1937 in Oxford. It sought a more practical solution of the problem of reunification. In 1938 (Tambaram) the decision was made to merge *Faith and Order* and *Life and Work*. The merger was completed only in 1948 (Amsterdam) after World War II (1939–45). It was called the World Council of Churches and included 147 churches from 44 countries. Its headquarters are located in Geneva and the World Assemblies (technical name) of the World Council of Churches met in

Amsterdam (1948), Evanston, Illinois (1954), New Delhi (1961), Upsala (1968), Nairobi (1975), Vancouver (1983), and Canberra (1991). Today it includes almost 300 Christian churches, including the Orthodox Church. The Catholic Church has observer status. The following creedal formula was worked out in 1960 as condition of membership in the World Council of Churches: "The World Council of Churches is a community of churches which confess the Lord Jesus Christ according to Scripture as God and Savior and which therefore attempt to fulfill their common calling to the glory of God the Father, the Son and the Holy Spirit." The trinitarian conclusion was a contribution of the Orthodox Church. This great worldwide ecumenical movement is the space in which Catholic lay movements (since World War I) and official representatives of the Catholic Church (since World War II) entered into ecumenical dialogue with the Churches of the Reformation. All these events emphasized the essential task of the Church of Christ, which must bring salvation to the whole world however this task may be understood by individual Churches.

g) After the Lambeth Conference's call for dialogue among the various confessions (1920), the first Catholic attempts at such a dialogue were made with the permission of Rome. One of the first was the dialogue between Catholics and Anglicans organized in Mecheln under Cardinal Mercier (1921–26). The Barmen Theological Declaration (1934) of the German Evangelical Church paved the way for the German Confessing Church. All churches in Germany suffered under the regime of Adolf Hitler (1889–1945). In this situation the Catholic priest M. J. Metzger (1887–1944; executed in a concentration camp) founded the Christkönigsgesellschaft vom Weissen Kreuz which was the parent movement of Una Sancta. Already in 1939 Metzger proposed an ecumenical council for the re-unification of Christians. In 1944 he wrote to Pope Pius XII from the concentration camp, "Only a great and daring courage of faith, humility and love can bring a solution to this tragic Christian problem." In 1950 Thomas Sartory, O.S.B., started the journal *Una Sancta* and Robert Grosche founded the journal *Catholica* in Cologne. In his reports on the conferences of Stockholm and Lausanne, the Munich Jesuit Max Pribilla had in 1925 and 1927 already pointed to Catholic studies of Protestant theology as a path to fruitful dialogue. In 1957 Cardinal Lorenz Jäger founded the Adam Möhler Institute in Paderborn, which is dedicated to dialogue with Protestant theology.

h) A new ecumenical spring came in the pontificate of John XXIII (1958–1963), after the death of Pope Pius XII (1939–1958), who was rather reserved about ecumenism. It was a resurgence of ecumenism not only for the Catholic Church, but for all Christian churches. John XXIII's announcement of the Second Vatican Council on January 25, 1959, invited "the separated communities to the search for unity." For January 1960 he proposed the following prayer, "May all who seek the true Church recognize more deeply the desire of the heart of Jesus for the unity of his people and may they all be brought to unity by it." On Pentecost 1960, when he set up the various commissions for the Council, he also set up a special "Secretariat for Unity among Christians" under the direction of Cardinal Augustin Bea (1881–1968). The leaders of the most important ecclesial communities separated from Rome were able to participate in the Council through Cardinal Bea's mediation. In the Council's first three years, they acted as observers and influenced in important ways the Council's work on the three great texts promulgated in 1964: the Constitution on the Church, the Decree on Ecumenism, and the Decree on the Catholic Eastern Churches.

Pope Paul VI (1963–1978) adopted the ecumenical decisions of his predecessor as a binding heritage. In this way the spirit of John XXIII has continued to be effective to this day. Cardinal Bea formulated the basic idea of this work of unity as follows: "What is needed in the struggle for unity is not uniformity. The urgent requirements are prudent cooperation, mutual help, counsel and leadership. It is necessary to receive information, to give it, to further the mutual exchange of experience and to increase contacts. Perhaps the most important task is to awaken among Catholics the attitude of a truly ecumenical apostolate and to carry this attitude into every diocese, every parish, every social and professional group and every Christian life, however humble its level."[18] The main task of ecumenism is to make Christians aware of the fundamental Christian attitude of *communio*, of communion and communality. Among human beings, whether Christian or not, this attitude is never a matter of course, but always a task and a gift to be asked for in prayer from God.[19] The Vatican II Decree on Ecumenism, which deals separately with the situation of the Eastern Churches and with the Western Churches of the Reformation (Chapter Three), makes the following suggestions as paths toward realizing the ecumenical spirit: (1) avoid expressions, judgments and actions that do not represent the situation of separated Christians with truth and fairness and make relations with them more difficult; (2) promote dialogue between experts of the various churches; (3) common prayer; (4) cooperation in many areas (of culture and charity); (5) deepened obedience to Christ's will, expressed in renewal of the Church. The goal (6) is perfect ecclesiastical communion expressed in common celebration of the Eucharist (UR 4,2–3). Against the dangers of relativism, indifferentism, and irenicism, which are opposed to truth and depth, the Council demands "that the doctrine be presented in its entirety" without "obscuring its genuine and certain meaning." This must be done in humility and love for separated Christians and with due respect for the "hierarchy of truths" (UR 11). At the same time the Council points to the difference between the natural unity of humanity and the unity of Christians in faith (cf. the encyclicals by Pope John XXIII *Mater et Magistra*, May 15, 1961, and *Pacem in Terris*, April 11, 1963).

After the Council and its declarations on ecumenism, numerous ecumenical dialogues were begun. The churches themselves appointed official groups for dialogue. Separate chairs and institutes of ecumenical theology were formed in the universities. The collaboration of these institutes has already resulted in numerous documents of different value.[20]

3. SYSTEMATIC ASPECTS

Let us look at some of the principles of ecumenical dialogue and action.

a) At the very outset it must be stated that Christ's one Church, the one body of the one head, Christ, has not perished in this world, although this unity of the Church is difficult to recognize because of the disunity of Christians. This is why the Decree on Ecumenism begins with the call to "the restoration of unity among all Christians [*unitatis redintegratio inter universos Christianos promovenda*]" so that all may be "one in Christ [*unus in Christo*]" (Gal 3,27f.). "Those who believe in Christ and have been properly baptized are brought into a certain, though imperfect, communion with the Catholic Church [*in quadam cum ecclesia catholica communione, etsi non perfecta*]" (UR 3). "[I]t is through Christ's Catholic Church alone, which is the all-embracing means of salvation [*generale auxilium salutis*], that the fullness of the means of salvation can be obtained. It was to the apostolic college alone, of which Peter is the head, that we believe that Our Lord entrusted all the blessings of the New Covenant, in order to establish on earth the one Body of Christ into which all those should be fully incorporated who belong in any way to the People of God" (UR 3). Concerning the unity given by Christ to his Church, the Council says, "This unity, we believe, subsists in the Catholic Church [*in ecclesia catholica subsistere credimus*] as something it can never lose, and we hope that it will continue to increase until the end of time" (UR 4). The Constitution on the Church expresses a similar point, [T]he unique Church of Christ which in the Creed we avow as one, holy, catholic and apostolic. . . . This Church, constituted and organized in the world as a society, subsists [*subsistit*] in the Catholic Church, which is governed by the successor of Peter and by the bishops in communion with that successor, although many elements of sanctification and of truth are found outside its visible structure. These elements, however, as gifts properly belonging to the Church of Christ, possess an inner dynamism towards Catholic unity" (LG 8).

b) The true Church of Christ can only be grasped in faith. It is a mystery of faith, a mystery, however, which is a full historical reality in this world, just as the historical Jesus Christ, its Lord and its head, was a historical man. If we look only at the historical and sociological aspects of this earthly reality, we do not do justice to the reality we believe in. "But the society furnished with hierarchical agencies and the Mystical Body of Christ, the visible society and the spiritual community, the earthly [historical] Church and the [trans-historical] Church endowed with heavenly riches, are not to be thought of as two realities. On the contrary, they form one complex reality [*unam realitatem complexam*] which comes together from a human and a divine element" (LG 8).

c) Although Christ's one Church exists only in a concrete historical condition, it would be erroneous to hold that it exists only in the local churches and not rather equally and even primarily as the one comprehensive reality present in the single local churches. This comprehensive reality can be compared to the family, which also exists not only in the individual family members and their sense of family. It is a reality that encompasses all family members, even when they do not wish to acknowledge their membership anymore or are simply no longer conscious of it. The family is a community of descent and blood, humanly experienced through a history in which its members somehow share and through the values and goods rooted in this history. In a similar way the Church is the community of those who have been baptized in Jesus' name into the triune God, of those who live from his word and table, even if they appear differently according to country, history, and culture in the local churches of this world in which the one Church appears anew. "Between those Churches there is such a wonderful bond of union that this variety in the Universal Church, so far from diminishing its unity, rather serves to emphasize it" (OE 2).

d) The fundamental concern of Lutheran theology is the subject's concern for salvation (How may I find a gracious God?). From the Catholic perspective one must say: The question of the Church is not only a question of its salvific function for the individual. It is, rather, a question of its true saving reality for the whole world. This is why the Council mentions various degrees of membership in the Church: "to her there belong or are ordered in various ways . . . [ad eam variis modis pertinent vel ordinantur . . .]" (LG 13; UR 3; 13). The individual members of the various ecclesial communities, who usually belong to these communities by birth without a prior independent decision, can reach their full salvation through their own Church, even if they do not possess the fullness of the gifts of grace found in the one Church of Christ.

e) Regarding the present attempts of common action among various churches and the models of union presented so far one can, therefore, say: In almost all areas of cultural and social action in Christ's spirit, common action for the good of humanity is desirable, at least among the various larger churches, whenever this is possible without blurring the confessional differences. The same thing holds for liturgies of the word and benedictions apart from the celebration of the Eucharist.

f) The Anglican branch theory and some circles of the World Council of Churches propose the idea of a community of worship composed of different confessions which live in full recognition of each other. This idea is not com-

patible with the Catholic understanding of the Church.
The same point applies to the merely "federal unity" that
has been attempted in the South-Indian Church since
1947,[21] and to the "conciliar" unity of the Church proposed
by the fifth congress of the World Council of Churches in
Nairobi (1975).[22]

g) Mixed marriages cannot be seen as paths that further
the re-unification of Christians in the one Church of
Christ, although in ideal cases they can contribute to improved knowledge about the other's Church and to a deepened understanding of one's own. Even less can "intercommunion" be seen as a path to the Church's unity.
Participation in Christ's one sacrificial meal is the expression for an already existing unity in faith and in Christ, a
unity grasped by faith. This is why the Council expressly
promulgated certain norms for the Catholic Church about
mixed marriage and common communion with the Eastern Churches. When these norms are recognized by an
Orthodox Church (as in the case of Moscow), mixed marriage and communion can be a sign of unity between these
two ancient Churches (cf. OE 14–18; 26f.).

h) Very important is the question of "corporative
union," which was proposed by Newman in his second
period and which is being pursued by many circles of the
Anglican Church. In the relation between the Catholic
Church and the ancient Eastern Churches, the corporative
way is probably the correct way to be pursued, because the
differences in life and doctrine, when correctly interpreted, hardly touch any essential points. Union between
the Catholic Church and the Churches of the Reformation
is a more difficult question. As long as no unity is found by
the churches themselves, individual conversion in obedience to one's own conscience remains a possible path
toward the desired unity of the Church.

i) Some final remarks on the path toward the unity for
which Christ prayed, but which he did not demand. (1) The
first thing demanded of all churches that seek the unity of

Christ's one Church in this real world with seriousness of conscience and action is the demand of honest self-reflection, linked with the readiness to confess one's own guilt in the spirit of penance, humility, and love. Every Church lives in its people as a whole. And so no Church can claim to live what it believes while having to admit that it is a witness of "catholicity," that is, of inner wholeness and thus of conformity to the Church founded by Christ, only in what it believes, not in its life of faith.

(2) The Catholic Church's special task is to realize that its comprehensive possession of realities and truths of faith is not its own work, but a gift of God. It must also recognize with humility and gratitude that elements and realities of the Church remained and were further developed in other ecclesial communities after their separation, and it must strive to realize these elements also in itself.

(3) "Further, this Council declares that it realizes that this holy objective—the reconciliation of all Christians in the unity of the one and only Church of Christ—transcends human powers and gifts" (UR 24). For this reason our union with Christ's high priestly prayer (John 17) is the most important path toward this unity. Christ did not "command" this unity, but he prayed for it. We human beings can also not "make" it, but must ask for it.

(4) "This sacred Council urges the faithful to abstain from any frivolous or imprudent zeal, for these can cause harm to true progress toward unity. Their ecumenical activity cannot be other than fully and sincerely Catholic, that is, loyal to the truth we have received from the Apostles and the Fathers, and in harmony with the faith which the Catholic Church has always professed, and at the same time tending toward that fullness in which our Lord wants his Body to grow in the course of time" (UR 24). Thus the dialogue between the Churches and their theologians must have the patience of aiming not only at a "theologically grasped" reality, but at a reality which is to be sought in faith and lived in grace. This dialogue can there-

fore not be defined exclusively by the rules of natural her-
meneutics.[23] Also the "collision theory" (P. Lengsfeld)
must not ignore this point when it attempts to do particular justice to the complexity of ecumenical events and
activities. Dialogue among the Churches is especially important here. As a living conversation (not an artificial
literary form) it presupposes that the partners have cleared
themselves of prejudices and resentment and are attempt-
ing to find a common basis of discussion. They must assent to this basis, learn from each other, come to know and
appreciate themselves and each other better in their dialogue. Their purpose is not to "convert" each other, but to
arrive at common action for Christ.

As a means for promoting dialogue, various agencies
were called into existence: "The Secretariat for the Unity
of Christians" in 1960 with Cardinal A. Bea as president;
"The Secretariat for Non-Christians" in 1964 with Cardi-
nal P. Marella as president; "The Secretariat for Non-
Believers" in 1964 with Cardinal F. König as president;
"The International Mixed Catholic-Anglican Dialogue
Commission" in 1969; and "The International Mixed
Catholic-Orthodox Dialogue Commission" in June, 1980.

The Orthodox theologian J. Panagopoulos (Athens) is
quite correct in pointing to "eucharistic existence" as the
foundation of unity in the Church. "The primary thing is
not unity as such, but unity in Christ and directed toward
Christ. . . . One easily falls into absolutizing unity and
into understanding it as an end in itself. Caught in this
misunderstanding one develops a static understanding of
the Church, as if it were only an earthly organism, an
institution, whose unity one must restore as one strives
toward a goal. . . . But this unity is not a program, not a
limited goal, not a working hypothesis. It is also not a
demanded and proclaimed unity. The Church's unity,
given to it by Christ, is rather the definitive overcoming of
any demanded, proclaimed or sought after unity and, beyond this, the radical negation and judgment of any such

unity."[24] This Orthodox judgment is certainly justified as a corrective for our Western ecumenical endeavors.

In conclusion: Nowhere does the mystery of the Church's unity and unicity become clearer than in its missionary nature and in its ecumenical endeavor and prayer.

Let us look at the question of ecumenism again from the perspective of our understanding of the Church as the universal sacrament of salvation. In terms of the institution of the sacraments by Christ, all Churches are given the task of seeking earnestly the unity that Christ alone gives and for which he expressly prayed to his Father. However, since the sacraments are not abandoned to the whim of the Churches but have their own inner shape (sign and word; matter and form), sacraments can remain the true and exclusively effective sacraments of Jesus Christ, even in Churches not in full communion (*koinonia*) with the one Catholic and apostolic Church. In Vatican II, the Catholic Church explicitly acknowledged this point in the case of the ancient Churches of the East. Provided these Churches consent, there can be a mutual reception of the sacraments in specific cases even though external and internal unity with these Churches must still be sought.

The positing of an external sign in the dispensation of a sacrament (except for baptism in emergencies) requires a legitimately ordained and commissioned minister who stands under the law of living succession through his ordination and in whom the gift of living tradition is present. Vatican II acknowledged that this requirement is fulfilled in the Eastern Churches, as we showed above.

Regarding the sacrament's inner effect of grace, the Council declared itself in favor of a certain "*communicatio in sacris*" with the ancient Churches of the East in situations of external or internal need, although full communion with these Churches is not yet realized but must still be sought. The reason for this position lies in the salvific importance of the sacraments.

In no way do we wish to imply that the sacraments of the Churches of the Reformation or of the Church of the 1870 schism are fruitless. Still, the Catholic understanding of faith cannot accept them as fully valid sacraments, because there are no validly ordained ministers.

XV

The Church's Catholicity and Its Necessity for the Salvation of Humankind

We have seen how the Church's unity becomes an issue in its missionary task and in ecumenism in the face of confessional and organizational divisions in today's Christianity. In discussing the Church's catholicity we will, therefore, have to pay particular attention both to the objective nature of this attribute as well as to how it is understood by the various Churches. Catholicity is claimed today not only by the (Roman) Catholic Church, but, as a matter of course, by the Orthodox Churches (due to their tradition) and by the Churches of the Reformation (in their worldwide missionary activity). After clarifying the original meaning of *katholon* we will give a brief historical survey. In a systematic way, we will then discuss the question of the inner connection between the Church's catholicity and its necessity for the salvation of humanity. The following chapter (XVI) will deal with the connection between the Church's catholicity and its task in the world.

The Meaning of the Word *Catholic*

I. THE CONCEPT OF ''CATHOLICITY''

a) Analysis of the word: The word "Catholic" is not

found in the New Testament, although the reality it expresses is clearly present in these founding documents of Christ's Church. It is contained in the command to missionize the whole inhabited world (Matt 24,14) and the whole cosmos (Matt 26,13), in Christ's demand that we give ourselves completely to God (Matt 22,37; Deut 16,5; cf. John 9,14) and in Christ's conferring the office of shepherd over the whole flock to Peter (John 21,15–17). Ignatius of Antioch (d. 110) was the first to apply this word to the Church: "Wherever the bishop appears let the congregation be present [*plēthos estō*]; just as wherever Jesus Christ is, there is the Catholic Church [*katholikē ekklēsia*]" (*Smyrn.* 8,2).

"*Katholikos*" is a composite word derived from the prepositional phrase "*kath' holon.*" The basic meaning of the preposition "*kata*" is "from, down from" (with the genitive) and "across, toward" (with the accusative). The first use is often connected with the idea of "cause" and the second with the idea of "purpose." Occasionally the two uses are combined in the meaning "across the whole." The second part of the compound, "*holon,*" refers to a whole as opposed to a part (*totum-pars*) or a whole in a quantitative or qualitative sense. Metaphysics, which has brought out important aspects of being in its reflection on the relation between whole and part, distinguishes the "essential whole" (matter, form, and the act of being), the "universal whole" (a species in relation to its individuals, a genus in relation to its species), and the "integral whole" (brought into unity through time or movement in space); it distinguishes between the "natural (organic) whole" and the "artificial (technical: machine) whole" and speaks of entities that include both, such as human communities (e.g., the people or the state; cf. the mixed metaphor in which Paul calls the Church both "God's field" and "God's building," 1 Cor 3,9).[25]

A decisive aspect of the form of each whole is that the whole is entitatively more than the sum of its parts. For this reason the whole is not only linked with the idea of "unity" but also with the ideas of "truth," "authenticity," and "perfection." Aristotle says on this point:

A "whole [holon]" means (1) that from which are absent none of the parts of which it is said to be naturally a whole, and (2) that which so contains the things it contains that they form a unity; and this in two senses—either as being each severally one single thing, or as making up the unity between them. For what is said of the whole [toward the whole, katholou] and wholly [holos], as if it were [in itself] a whole [holon] is so universal [katholou] because it contains many, inasmuch as it is predicated of each and all together are one, as each [is one] [hen hapanta einai hōs hekaston]. . . . Wholeness is in fact a kind of oneness. Again (3), of quanta that have a beginning and a middle and an end [archē-meson-eschaton], those to which the position [thesis] does not make a difference are called totals [pan], and those to which it does wholes [holon]. (Met 5,26; 1023 b 26–1024 a 3)

In the context of logic, "katholon" refers to the universal (which is predicated of several things: cf. Aristotle, Peri Hermeneias 7, 17 a 39) as opposed to the particular (hekaston). In his theological Elements Proclus extensively unfolds the question of the relation of a whole to its parts (Stoich. Prop. 66–74) and he stresses that every whole is always an existing thing either prior to its parts, or through its parts, or in its parts (Prop. 67; cf. Dodds, n. 63–71). So much for the analysis of the word. Although words undergo many transformations in any living language, certain basic elements of meaning nevertheless remain important for understanding them.

b) The application of the word to the Church: The tension between a more quantitative and a more qualitative meaning, which we brought out in the analysis of the word "katholon," is preserved in the application of this term to the Church. At different times this tension led to different emphases. Ignatius's phrase "Catholic Church" has already been interpreted either as "the worldwide Church as a whole" or as "the Church of comprehensive truth." At

the beginning of the *Martyrdom of Polycarp* (A.D. 166)
the word is understood in a quantitative sense: "all communities [*paroikiai*] in all places of the Catholic Church."
In 16,2, however, Polycarp is called "apostolic and prophetic teacher of the bishops of the Catholic Church,"
while the Latin translation speaks of "Jesus Christ, the
shepherd of the whole Catholic Church [*catholicae totius
ecclesiae*]." "Catholic" is thus understood in a qualitative
sense.

2. HISTORICAL SURVEY

The encompassing meaning of "Catholic" was preserved from the creed of the First Council of Constantinople (A.D. 381) to the end of the Middle Ages. It refers to the
true Church of Christ, which was instituted by him,
which spread over the whole world in accordance with his
missionary command, and which is present in each legitimate local church whose bishop lives in the communion
of faith (*koinonia, communio*) with the other bishops of
the universal (Catholic) Church. The Egyptian Constitutions (Funk II, 110) and the baptismal symbol of Epiphanius (DS 42 and 44), as well as, by derivation, the creed of
Constantinople (DS 150), contain this sense of "Catholic."
In his struggle against the Donatists (388–430) Augustine
simply uses the term *"catholica"* (240 times) for the
Church of Rome, usually as an echo of the Psalm verse,
"The Lord said to me, You are my son . . . I will make
the nations your heritage and the ends of the earth your
possession" (Psalm 2,7–8; cf. 21,28; *Ep.* 49,2; 53,2 with a
list of popes up to the present; 76; 151; 185; *De unitate
ecclesiae* I: MS 4,1 p. 481 note 14). Cyril of Jerusalem once
explained the meaning of "Catholic" as follows:

The Church is called Catholic because it has spread over the
whole world, from one end to the other; because it proclaims
comprehensively and without defect all the doctrines of faith
which we must know, about the visible and the invisible, about

heavenly and earthly things; because it brings the whole human race, princes and subjects, the educated and the uneducated, to the right worship of God; and finally, quite in general, because like a doctor it heals all sins which have been committed either with the soul or the body; it also possesses every kind of virtue, whatever it may be called, in action and words and every kind of spiritual gift. (*Cat.* 18,23; PG 33,1044; *Ep.* 838)

This text gives a clear and comprehensive description of "Catholic," both in its quantitative aspect, the entire world and the whole of humanity, and in its qualitative aspect in doctrine and liturgy, saving efficacy and virtue as well as spiritual gifts. This comprehensive sense was preserved in the whole Middle Ages, beginning with Boethius (*De Trinitate*, c. 1), the great theologians of the High Middle Ages and into the fifteenth century.[26] It is above all the understanding of the Church as body of Christ which provides the foundation of this comprehensive interpretation of catholicity. In the work of Wycliffe and Ockham, and especially in the apologetic perspective on the Church in the struggle against the Reformation theologians, catholicity was understood almost exclusively in quantitative terms in space and time. R. Bellarmine, for example, writes, "Only the Roman Church has spread over the whole world and through all times; heretical communities spread only at certain times and in certain countries" (*Controv. Epithome Li* 4 *De notis ecclesiae*). The qualitative aspect of catholicity has only recently been brought out again and seen in a new way by theologians who have made the Church a subject of dogmatic theology (M. Schmaus, Y. Congar).

3. SYSTEMATIC ASPECTS OF THE CONCEPT "CATHOLIC CHURCH"

The great theology of the Fathers assembled many paradigms and ideas to clarify the meaning of catholicity. Let us list only the most important of these. For the quantitative aspect, the parallel between Adam and Christ (Rom 5,12–21; 1 Cor 15,22) turned out to be especially fruitful, because early Judaism interpreted Adam as the progenitor of the human race and as its permanent head (like Christ) and because the four letters of "Adam" were taken to refer to the four directions of the compass: "Who does not know that the whole race stems from him and that the four letters of his name refer to the Greek names of the four directions, namely East, West, North, South [in Greek: *anatolē*, *dysis*, *arktos*, *mesēmbria*]" (Augustine, *In Jo* 2 *tr.* 9,14). In the same sermon (on the wedding at Cana) Augustine introduces Adam and Eve and the wedding between Christ and the Church (according to Eph 5,31f.), as well as the image of Noah's ark, the ark that contained all animals and human beings who were saved from the flood, and Abraham, who received the promise that all peoples would be blessed in him. These images were used again and again to interpret the Church's catholicity. The most important image, however, is the Pauline image of the body of Christ, which expresses the quantitative aspect of catholicity, and even more so its qualitative aspect. The term "Catholic" expresses the Church's unity and wholeness, its authenticity and truth, its importance for salvation as well as its living growth through all times and spaces of this world. The foundation of this attribute lies in the Lord's missionary command (Mark 16,15f.; Matt 28,19f.; Matt 24,14; 26,13).

The Catholic Church and Its Necessity for Human Salvation

I. HISTORICAL ASPECTS

The deeper meaning of the qualitative understanding of catholicity comes to light when one reflects on the fact that the Catholic Church is necessary for the salvation of

humanity. The oldest image for the Church's necessity
and efficacy for salvation is the image of Noah's ark (Gen
7,23; 7,1–9,17) which is already used in 1 Pet 3,20ff. to
express the efficacy of baptism. Around A.D. 160 Ignatius
of Antioch stressed that only those are saved who are in
Jesus Christ or who return to the unity of the Catholic
Church (*Phil.* 3,2). Around A.D. 195 Clement of Alexandria
characterized baptism, through which entrance is gained
into the Church, as follows, "Through baptism we are illumined, as illumined we are accepted as children of God, as
children of God we attain perfection and reach immortality" (*Paed.* I 6,26,1). Around A.D. 250, Origen formulated the principle, "Outside the Church no one is saved
[*extra ecclesiam nemo salvatur*]" (*In Jesu Nave hom.* 3,5).
Around A.D. 251, Cyprian wrote in his work "On the Unity
of the Church," "No one who leaves the Church can attain
the reward of Christ. He is a stranger, a man of this world,
an enemy of Christ. The one who does not have the
Church as mother cannot have God as Father" (c. 6). Cyprian erroneously concludes that baptism by heretics is
invalid and that martyrdom outside the Church is fruitless. When meditating on Noah's ark, Augustine repeatedly dwells on the saving importance of the Church: "One
and the same water, but a different water, saved those who
were in the ark and destroyed those who were not in it.
Similarly, one baptism saves good Catholics [*catholici*]
and destroys bad Catholics and heretics" (*De bapt., Contr.
Don.* V 28/39; *Contr. Faust.* XII c. 14–22; *De civ. Dei* XV c.
26). Augustine, like all theologians of the Middle Ages
after him, understands the axiom of the Church's necessity for salvation in an exclusive sense. In his last work,
"On the Perseverance of the Saints" he writes that even
those who are baptized in the true Church perish if they do
not live according to their baptism, in other words, if they
did not have "the gift of perseverance" (*De persev.* VI 10).
The exclusive interpretation of the axiom is especially
clear in the bull *Unam Sanctam* (Boniface VIII, 1302; DS

870) and in the Decree for the Jacobites of the Council of Florence in A.D. 1442 which "firmly believes, professes and preaches that no one remaining outside the Catholic Church, not only pagans but also Jews, heretics or schismatics, can become partakers of eternal life" (DS 1351).

The awareness of God's universal saving will and of heretics who live without personal fault in heresy prevailed only slowly. It was only in A.D. 1713, in the struggles against the Jansenist Quesnel, that the following proposition was explicitly condemned: "No grace is granted outside the Catholic Church" (DS 2429). In his allocution "Singulari Quaedam" of the year 1854, Pius IX discussed this axiom in the form "no one can be saved outside the apostolic Roman Church [extra Apostolicam, Romanam Ecclesiam salvum fieri neminem posse]" which expressly limits it to the Roman Church (not even called "Catholic"). He expressly excepted all those, however, who do not know the true religion and he stressed that no one can define the limits of this ignorance (D 1647; not reproduced in DS). In the year 1863, in his encyclical against indifferentism, he condemns as a "grave error" the position that those who live in error and outside the Catholic unity can attain eternal life. Still, he concedes the possibility of grace outside the Church in cases of "invincible ignorance" (DS 2865–67).

In quite a new way the axiom has been understood inclusively, not exclusively, since Vatican II. The Decree on Ecumenism says:

[S]erious dissensions appeared and large communities separated from full communion with the Catholic Church, for which, often enough, men of both sides were to blame. However, one cannot charge with the sin of the separation those who at present are born into these communities and in them are brought up in the faith of Christ, and the Catholic Church accepts them with respect and affection as brothers. For those who believe in Christ and have been properly baptized are put in some, though imperfect, communion with the Catholic Church. . . . Moreover, some, even very many, of the most significant elements and endowments which together go to build up and give life to the Church itself, can exist outside the visible boundaries of the Catholic Church: the written Word of God; the life of grace; faith, hope and charity, with the other interior gifts of the Holy Spirit, as well as visible elements. All of these, which come from Christ and lead back to him, belong by right to the one Church of Christ [*haec omnia, quae a Christo proveniunt et ad ipsum conducunt, ad unicam Christi Ecclesiam iure pertinent*]. (UR 3)

The Declaration on the Relationship of the Church to Non-Christian Religions goes one step further. In this age of scientific and technological progress, the Church is "aware of its duty to foster unity and charity among individuals, and even among nations." The Counci goes on to make the following statement about non-Christian religions:

Men look to their different religions for an answer to the unsolved riddles of human existence. The problems that weigh heavily on the hearts of men are the same today as in the ages past. What is man? What is the meaning and purpose of life? What is upright behavior, and what is sinful? Where does suffering originate, and what end does it serve? How can genuine happiness be found? What happens at death? What is judgment? What reward follows death? And finally, what is the ultimate mystery, beyond human explanation, which embraces our entire existence, from which we take our origin and towards which we tend? (NA 1)

"Therefore the Church reproves, as foreign to the mind of Christ, any discrimination against people or any harassment of them on the basis of their race, color, condition in life or religion" on the basis of the scriptural teaching that "he who does not love, does not know God" (1 John 4,8). These points are further unfolded in the Declaration on Religious Liberty.

The Vatican Council declares that the human person has a right to religious freedom. Freedom of this kind means that all men should be immune from coercion on the part of individuals, social groups and every human power so that, within due limits, nobody is forced to act against his convictions nor is anyone to be restrained from acting in accordance with his convictions in religious matters in private or in public, alone or in associations with others. The Council further declares that the right to religious freedom is based on the very dignity of the human person as known through the revealed word of God and by reason itself. (DH 2)

As the same decree states, conscience is not merely a subjective organ of the person. It is ordered to objective final values. It is not only a gift but a task. The issue of the truth of various religions can thus not be considered settled together with the issue of religious liberty.

On the background of these teachings of the Church, what is the enduring meaning of the axiom "no salvation outside the Church [*extra ecclesiam nulla salus*]"?

2. SYSTEMATIC ASPECTS

a) The first point to be laid down is that the axiom has always been a dogmatic statement, not a geographical, sociological, or psychological statement. It states that salvation is always and essentially a gift of God's grace and that this grace has a salvation history revealed to us in Scripture, a history of creation, redemption, and sanctification which proceeds from the one triune God. Thus Paul says, "He [God] is the source of your life in Christ Jesus, whom God made our wisdom, our righteousness and sanctification and redemption [*sophia–dikaiosunē–hagiasmos–apolutrōsis*]; therefore, as it is written, Let him who boasts, boast of the Lord" (1 Cor 1,30–31). On this basis Paul says, "What have you that you did not receive? If then you received it, why do you boast as if it were not a gift?" (1 Cor 4,7). Augustine again and again quotes this sentence against the Pelagians and applies it above all to faith itself. "The sentence, 'What have you that you did not receive,' applies to faith itself, which has its seat in the will, not because faith and lack of faith are not a matter of the free human will, but because in the elect 'the will is prepared by God' (Prov 8,35 LXX)" (*De Praed.* V, 9f.).

b) Since faith and grace as objective realities are located in the history of salvation, the axiom of the Church's necessity for salvation has an objective historical meaning. It means that all graces, even those given outside the historical Church of Christ in general and outside the Catholic Church, flow from the one Catholic Church and dwell in it, because there is only one Church of the one Christ, his mystical body in this world. The objective sense of faith, which does not, of course, exist without the subjective act of faith in this historical world, is implied in the new prayer for the feast of St. Peter's Chair (February 22), which speaks about the "rock of Peter's apostolic confession [*apostolicae confessionis petra*]," not about Peter himself, as the rock on which Christ built his Church according to Matt 16,18.

c) The Council maintains that everything that proceeds from Christ and leads back to him belongs by right to the single historical Church of Christ (UR 3). In the same way the Fathers understood the wisdom of the ancients, the effects of which can already be observed in the holy Scriptures of the Old Testament and the New Testament, as revelations of the same one God and they used this wisdom for their theological work.[27]

d) The axiom "no salvation outside the Church" is rooted in two statements of Scripture: Unless one is born of water and the Spirit one cannot enter the kingdom of God (John 3,5.17f.), and God wants all to be saved and to come to the knowledge of the truth (1 Tim 2,4). Karl Rahner in this connection invented the expression "anonymous Christian."[28] The meaningfulness and justification of this concept depends on whether one can and may equate being a Christian on the basis of belonging to the historical Church of Christ with being a pious God-fearing person on the basis of assent to the values and good

proposed by the message of Christ. Although the fulfillment of Christian ethical norms is a genuine and legitimate way to salvation, even when one encounters these
norms outside of historical Christianity, it is questionable
whether one should use the expression "anonymous
Christian." It is questionable even though all salvation,
even the salvation possible outside the historical Church
of Christ, is rooted in and founded upon the person and
work of Christ in this world. As shown by the first use of
the term "Christian" in Antioch (Acts 11,26), the authentic foundation of this name is the personal relation of its
bearer to the historical person of Jesus Christ. For the sake
of the historical reality of Christ's Church, it should not be
used differently.

e) A nuanced understanding of the Church's catholicity
can be achieved in terms of the understanding of the
Church as the universal sacrament of salvation, as indi-
cated above in our presentation of conciliar texts. From the
perspective of its external sign, the Catholic Church of
Christ (in its pilgrimage, not its fulfillment) exists in the
Church of Rome and in all other (especially Eastern)
Churches inasmuch as these agree with it in the revealed
truths of faith, the sacraments, and ecclesiastical offices.
Regarding its inner grace, one must say that all grace in all
Christian Churches, and also all grace outside these
Churches in the other religions of the world, are somehow
rooted in Christ and his redemptive work, due to the unity
of God's history of salvation. They are rooted in Christ not
only "anonymously" with respect to their value-content,
but historically inasmuch as they approach and correspond to the truth and demand of Christ. This point raises
the final element, institution by Christ, which refers not
only to the fact of institution but to the measure and form
of what is instituted. The Eastern Churches speak rather
platonically about "participation (*methexis-participatio*)"
of the various particular churches in the one Church of
Christ. The Western Church prefers to speak (in a Jewish

way) of various degrees of the presence of the one Church of Christ in the various particular Churches, in order to express more clearly that the Church has the character of a grace and that it is Catholic.

Let us now turn to the second aspect of catholicity, the Church's task in this world.

XVI

The Church's Tasks in the World: Church and State, Society, Economy, Science, and Culture

I. THE CHURCH AND THE WORLD

The Catholic Church is not of this world, but it is within this world (John 17,11–21). Above all, it has been founded for this world, in order to realize God's eternal saving will in it and with it (John 3,17; 12,47: "I did not come to judge the world but to save the world"; Eph 1,102: "to unite all things in Christ, things in heaven and things on earth"). For, Christ is the head, not only of the Church, but of the whole cosmos "and in him all things hold together" (Col 1,17; cf. 1,13–20). The Church's understanding of and relationship to the world varied greatly in the course of history. Even in the Hellenistic period, Judaism preserved a rather positive and unbroken relation to the world that surrounds humanity. This relation dates back to the nomadic origins of Israel and stems from the Jewish awareness that God is the creator and lord of the world. Within early Christianity, on the other hand, a divided or broken relationship to the world soon made itself felt, perhaps due to Eastern and gnostic influence. In Paul and John one can already hear certain dualist notes: "so that we may not be condemned with the world" (1 Cor 11,32; Gal 6,14); "Do not love the world or the things of this world. . . .

For all that is in the world, the lust of the flesh and the lust of the eyes and the pride of life, is not of the Father" (1 John 2,15–16); "The whole world is in the power of the evil one" (1 John 5,19). These dualistic notes are rooted not in the proclamation of Jesus but in the decaying pagan culture of antiquity, against which the early Church had to struggle. If one reads side by side the history of Rome (e.g., that of Ammianus Marcellinus, A.D. 353–378) and Jesus' Sermon on the Mount, one can understand this broken relationship to the world quite well. It is in terms of high Jewish moral doctrine, and even more so of Jesus' doctrine, that one must read Paul's statements about "sin" (Rom 5,12.20f.; 7,17.20: "sin which dwells within me"), about the continuously effective original sin of forgetting God, of self-glorification and abandonment to the world (cf. Gen 3,1–7) which deeply affects the human person "in this world" (John 8,23; 12,31), which "is passing away" (1 Cor 7,31), the very person who is made in the image of God (Gen 1,26) and who is called to be a child of God (Luke 20,36; 1 John 3,1f.). The high spirit of Old Testament creation faith, as expressed in the creation Psalms, and Jesus' parables about the lilies of the field and the birds of heaven, which go back to these Psalms, as well as the high world-affirming message of love found in the New Testament, never permitted the victory of the dualistic spirit in the true Church of Christ. Rather, they gave to this spirit its legitimate place as a warning against an un-Christian indiscriminate assent to the world, subordinate to the Christian understanding of the world as a creation "in Christ" (Col 1,16; John 1,10). This understanding is clear in the relationship of the great Church Fathers to the literary culture of antiquity and also in the monastic rules of the period immediately following the persecutions, which were hard in their asceticism but never dualistic. In all periods of history one can observe this tension between the world and God, between sin and grace, between asceticism and grateful joy in the world, between human cultural achievement in all its problematic nature and faith in divine creation with its mysterious greatness and terror.

Vatican II expressed new acknowledgment and esteem for humanity and its cultural work. (This attitude can be understood, at least in part, as an expression of the spirit of reconstruction after the terrors of World War II). Soon, however, the Council also had to warn against an indiscriminate assent to the world, which stemmed from a secularized view of the world. Today, twenty years after the Council, doubts have been raised even outside the Church about the faith in progress characteristic of that time. In this world we are not assured a permanent balance between sacrifice and enjoyment, between self-preservation and self-donation. Whenever the *via media* is found for a while, it is always a task and a gift of grace. All of this, however, cannot change the fact that the world that surrounds us is a gift and a task belonging to our being, our development, and our maturation. Despising or neglecting it can only lead to an impoverishment of humanity and is, therefore, un-Christian.

2. KATHOLON AND THE WORLD

In this perspective one can see the deeper meaning of *katholon* that we expressed in the phrases "from the whole and toward the whole, according to the whole." For in Jewish and Christian thought, "world" does not refer to the ordered cosmos, as it does in antiquity, but to the world in time and to humanity in its history, to the *"aiōn"* in which we live.[29] As God's creation, the world had a beginning (Luke 11,50; Matt 25,34), it hurries toward its end (Matt 13,40; 1 John 2,17; 1 Cor 7,31) and God himself will give "a new heaven and a new earth" (Isa 65,17; 66,22; 2 Pet 3,13). In the New Testament message this concept of "world" is understood not only in terms of God, the creator, but in terms of Christ, the savior, and in terms of the ultimate end of all things. "In Christ" the world of sin, the world of enmity to God, has already been vanquished. The new world (the history of salvation) has already begun. In this way Christ can say to the Jews, "You are from below, I am from above; you are of this world, I am not of this world" (John 8,23). Christians are now "in Christ" ("It is no longer I who live, but Christ who lives in me" Gal 2,20). Through the Eucharist (cf. John 6,49–58) they have been "delivered from the dominion of darkness and transferred into the kingdom of his beloved Son" (Col 1,13). In Christ there already begins the "new creation" (Gal 6,15; 2 Cor 5,17), which comes into this world through Christians and which is destined for the whole world ("For creation waits with eager longing for the revealing of the sons of God" Rom 6,19). Like Christ, Christians are sent into the world to save the world (John 4,42; 1 John 4,14), but the world does not know them, just as it did not know Christ (John 1,9–14; 1 John 3,1). But they have the grace to know that he who is in them "is greater than he who is in the world" (1 John 4,4; 5,19). Even if they are hated by the world (1 John 3,13–18) they can experience that their faith in Christ "is the victory over the world" (1 John 5,4). This is the Catholic "worldview," this theological, christological-soteriological, and eschatological vision, which explains and preserves both the reality of grace and the Christian task in this world.

3. THE CHURCH AND THE MODERN WORLD

The decisive and new element of the Pastoral Constitution on the Church in the Modern World, an element that could not be gathered immediately from Pauline or Johannine theology, is that it stresses the natural human and earthly values and goods in their importance for the task of the Christian and of the Church in this world. This point applies already to Chapter One (The Dignity of the Human Person), in which the greatness and dignity of the human spirit are stressed. "By diligent use of his talents through the ages man has indeed made progress in the empirical sciences, in technology, and in the liberal arts. In our time his attempts to search out the secrets of the material universe and to bring it under his control have been extremely successful" (GS 15,1). Of course the Council also points to the necessity for deeper wisdom. "Indeed, the future of the world is in danger unless provision is made for men of greater wisdom" (GS 15,3) who are to grow from the depth of their "conscience" and the "dignity of their freedom." The Church wants to enter into a living "dialogue" with the modern world, to serve this world and so also to learn from it. "Whatever truth, goodness, and justice is to be found in past or present human institutions is held in high esteem by the Council. In addition, the Council declares that the Church is anxious to help and foster these institutions as far as is possible and compatible with its mission" (GS 42,5). The Council expressly rejects any rejection of the world in which we "shirk our earthly responsibilities" (GS 43,1). But the Council likewise rejects an indiscriminate immersion in "earthly activities" (GS 43,1). The Church

profits from the experience of past ages, from the progress of the sciences, and from the riches hidden in various cultures, through which greater light is thrown on the nature of man and new avenues of truth are opened up. . . . In this way it is possible to create in every country the possibility of expressing the message of Christ in suitable terms and to foster vital contact and exchange between the Church and different cultures. Nowadays when things change so rapidly and thought patterns differ so widely [pluralism], the Church needs to step up this exchange by calling upon the help of people who are living in the world [lay people], who are expert in its organizations and its forms of training, and who understand its mentality, in the case of believers and nonbelievers alike. (GS 44)

The Council does not fail to stress, of course, that all things are centered upon Christ: "The Lord is the goal of human history, the focal point of the desires of history and civilization, the center of mankind, the joy of all hearts, and the fulfillment of all aspirations" (GS 45,2; cf. Eph 1,10).

4. DETAILS OF THE CHURCH'S TASKS IN THE WORLD

The most important points of a Christian view of the world have already been mentioned in Volume Three, *The World—God's Creation* (esp. Section V, Chapter 5). At this point let us focus only on those elements especially helpful in clarifying the relation between the Church and the world. After a brief explanation of basic principles and a few historical notes we will systematically treat the most important individual questions.

a) *Principles*

The incomprehensible infinity of the creator and the finitude of all created being and thinking, which must be experienced again and again, necessarily leads to tensions between a purely human perspective on reality and the perspective of faith. This tension demands a dialectical intellectual search, moral affective patience in the face of intellectual tensions and the preservation of personal identity in the deepest believing self. For this reason the following principles must be understood in their inner coordination and unity.

(1) Whatever our faith can recognize as God's creation in this world demands our grateful assent and our praise of the creator in his creation, our praise of the source of all human creativity in understanding and shaping a humane world.

(2) Whatever our natural reason can recognize as true, good, beautiful, noble, authentic, and sacred in our world calls for the response of recognition and joy, admiration

and wonder, reverence and commitment. In the same way falsehood calls for rejection, evil for existential mourning, ugliness for compassion, and inauthenticity for resistance.

(3) The unity of the world must be seen both in terms of God, the creator, and in terms of the human person, of each person's self. It is a unity that can be found only in the Person and work of Jesus Christ.

(4) Although the human person is part of the world, it is at the same time its center and its goal, both as a member of humanity and as an individual person and creator of a humane world.

(5) The world is God's gift to humanity as well as a task set for human life. Human work serves the continuation of God's plan of creation and human self-realization in the service of God.

(6) Temptation and failings (sin) can serve us in the struggle of finding, knowing, preserving, and proving ourselves, of conversion and self-realization by maturing in grace, whenever we overcome them in the footsteps of Christ through sacrifice and patience in the spirit of Christ.

(7) The signs of the sacred are traces of God in this world. They are a call to the healing and sanctification of the world and of humanity in Christ and his work of redemption, in his word and his sacrament.

(8) The ambivalence of earthly goods demands a religious suppleness that Ignatius of Loyola called "indifference" (to use the world as if one did not use it, 1 Cor 7,29–31, a foundation of the Ignatian Spiritual Exercises). And the tension between freedom and grace demands a paradoxical fundamental attitude: "Work out your salvation in fear and trembling, *for* God is at work in you, both to will and to work for his own good pleasure" (Phil 2,12–13).

(9) The transience of this world points beyond itself to a world to come (Mark 10,30), for which we may hope as

God's gift through Christ's death and resurrection as present and effective in his sacraments.

(10) Suffering and the cross as consequences of sin are God's gracious gifts in the cross of Christ and thus helps through which we can mature until we become children of God in Christ, the only Son of God (1 John 3,1–10).

(11) Human knowledge must always open up into faith if it is to serve human existence ("If you do not believe, you shall not know" or "you will not stand firm," Isa 7,9). Human wisdom must always be on the way to divine wisdom (1 Cor 2,1–16) which comes from the power of God's Spirit and the mind of Christ.

(12) Whatever we understand as "opposites" in this world must be understood by natural reason as unity in tension (as polarity) and as a dialectical way to wholeness and unity (Aristotle, "On the World" c. 5, 396 a 33–397 b 8). God the creator, the threefold and triune God, is the exemplar and ground of this world. He can never be comprehended, but faith must and can seek him from afar in the mystery of being and creation, of sin and redemption, of grace and perfection, in the Father, the Son and the Holy Spirit "and these three are one" (1 John 5,7).

b) Historical Aspects

The Church with its contrasts and changes is a historical being in this world. It is understandable that in the course of its history it was shaped by weakness or power, wealth or poverty, struggles or suffering, holy heroism or human failure. Yet at no time were the opposite elements completely absent, and at every time they showed their ambivalence. At different times all of them brought good as well as evil, rise as well as decline in the struggle of God's kingdom in this world, because all human action or suffering can turn into its opposite through human reflection and attitudes. Authentic piety of the heart can be devalued in vain spiritual self-mirroring. Profound human failure can lead to true humility and gratitude through interior conversion. External poverty can give rise to inner wealth and external wealth to inner poverty.

The persecutions of the third century gave to the Church a whole army of holy martyrs. In the same period the idealistic search for a deepened understanding of faith often led to uncharitable intellectual battles that left embittered heretics as enemies of the Church and even of Jesus. The religious renewal of monasticism in the fourth century produced Christians of great heroism and great leadership qualities in the Church, especially among the bishops, for whom official state recognition had become an acute danger. At the same time monasticism became in many respects an occasion for a loss of the world, which made the conversion of antiquity more difficult and contributed to its downfall. The Christianizing of the young Germanic peoples and the coronation of Charlemagne by the pope prepared the growth of high Western culture and of the Holy Roman Empire of the German nation. At the same time it led to the tearing of the Church into East and West. The power struggles between the pope and the emperor led to the Great Western Schism and the decline of the Eastern Church after the destruction of Constantinople. The East-West split was, in turn, one of the roots of the deep split in the Western Church brought about by the Reformation. The Judeo-Christian faith de-divinized the world of antiquity. It led to a new understanding of human greatness in the freedom given by Christ and thus brought about a new conquest of the world. Under the influence of the neo-pagan spirit of the Renaissance, however, it also led to the secularism that has destroyed even the pre-Christian natural piety of large segments of the peoples of Europe.

One could show the effects of the ambivalence of human virtue and weakness throughout the history of the Church. This should not lead one to indifferentism. It shows how complex the qualitative meaning of "catholic" really is. History must be perceived in its true dynamism rather than be pressed into a static intellectualist schema. Besides the high and the great, as exclusive agents of history, one must see also the critical function of the evil and the weak. Goodness and holiness in this world are not assured for ever. In a true Christian understanding they are always subject to the law of cross and resurrection, until God himself creates and gives a new heaven and a new earth and Christ lays everything at the feet of his father in the final judgment in order "that God may be all in all" (1 Cor 15,20–28; Rom 8,18–30). In Christian terms, the Church's history as well as the world's history, human history as well as cosmic history, can be understood only as an eschatological history, as a history that began in Christ, the one through whom all things were created and redeemed, as a history that has the center of its meaning in Christ's death and resurrection and will be fulfilled in the Lord's return as judge and bringer of final happiness.

c) Systematic Aspects

On the basis of these general remarks let us say something on the particular relations of the Church to the world, ordered according to areas. The great history of concepts and ideas in each of these areas must be left to more detailed treatment. Let us present only the most important problems and answers for our age, grouped according to the political, economic, cultural and social spheres.

(1) FOUNDATION IN NATURAL LAW Before entering into these areas, however, let us mention the concept of natural law—the idea of a law prior to all human positive law—which arose in early Christian thought through the adaptation of Stoic ideas and was further developed by Scholasticism. In recent times this concept has increasingly become the foundation of Catholic political, economic, and social doctrine. Quite apart from the question

of the sources, the criteria and the foundations of natural law (divine revelation, human reason, natural ordination, and desires of the individual or society), Catholic theology maintains that there exists an order that God the creator himself placed into creation and that is prior and normative in relation to all positive legal decisions. Today the foundation and unfolding of this natural law is seen in different ways, even within Catholic thinking: either more statically or more dynamically. Faith, conscience, and reason (understood in terms of metaphysical psychology, not merely experimental psychology) are the means for understanding this natural law.

(2) THE POLITICAL SPHERE In the context of the Church's tasks in this world, the political realm should be mentioned first, because it brings to light the Church's relationship to the world in the most comprehensive way. At least in the countries and peoples whose histories have been shaped by Europe (e.g., America), membership in the Church and in the state overlap to a great extent, so that the manifold tensions between the Church and the world appear in all spheres of the world. The Council lays down the following general principle: "It is clear that the political community and public authority are based on human nature, and therefore that they need to belong to an order established by God; nevertheless, the choice of the political regime and the appointment of rulers are left to the free decision of the citizens. It follows that political authority . . . must be exercised within the limits of the moral order and directed toward the common good . . . according to the juridical order legitimately established or due to be established" (GS 74,2–3). In their origin, goal, and nature, the Church and state differ fundamentally. They are "autonomous and independent of each other in their own fields" (GS 76,1–3).

In the High Middle Ages, the Church wanted to subject the state to itself in the light of the theologically misunderstood "two swords doctrine" (Luke 22,35–38).[30] As the modern states developed, the Church was forced, conversely, to struggle for its independence from the state and for its freedom. Leo XIII (1878–1903) criticized the idea of state omnipotence, which grew out of the spirit of the Enlightenment (cf. the encyclicals *Immortale Dei* Nov. 1, 1885 and *Diuturnum Illud* June 29, 1881). He argued for the Church's internal and external autonomy by pointing to its essence as *societas perfecta*, which implies autonomous legislative, judiciary, administrative, and executive power. While the Church requires full freedom in its own sphere, it is aware that its members are also members of the state, and it therefore seeks harmonious cooperation with the state, wherever this is possible and desirable for the common good. The Council extensively discussed this issue above all in the Declaration on Religious Liberty (*Dignitatis Humanae*). The right to the free exercise of religion is based, the Declaration says, "on the very dignity of the human person" (DH 2). This dignity is also the source of the right to come together in various ecclesial communities (DH 4). This freedom of religion must be anchored, above all, in the laws governing marriage, the family and education. "The civil authority therefore must undertake to safeguard the religious freedom of all the citizens in an effective manner by just legislation and other appropriate means. It must help to create conditions favorable to the fostering of religious life so that the citizens will be really in a position to exercise their religious rights and fulfill their religious duties and so that society itself may enjoy the benefits of justice and peace, which result from man's faithfulness to God and his holy will" (DH 6,2). "The freedom of the Church is the fundamental principle governing relations between the Church and public authorities and the whole civil order" (DH 13,1). The Council explicitly points to the recognition of religious freedom in the constitutions of various states and in international documents (cf. article 18 of the General Declaration on Human Rights of Dec. 10, 1948; DH 15) and to the importance of this demand for the preservation of world peace especially in our time in which all peoples with their different religions are increasingly growing into a global family due to international politics in this technological age.

The Church is not tied to any form of the state, although it cannot be overlooked that the absolutist one-party state after the French Revolution of 1789 can hardly do justice to the freedom of the person and to the various social forms of the modern age. Despite its weakness, liberal democracy corresponds better to these demands, if it does not lead to a "separation between Church and state" that is detrimental to the common good when it is conceived as a separation which expresses opposition to the Church. Due to the continuous transformation of the thinking of individuals, communities, and states, the relation between Church and state must always be cultivated, purified, sought anew, and expressed in law. In many countries, concordats between the Holy See and the state contribute to this goal, for the good of persons, states, and the Church, and to the honor of God.[31]

An important contribution within the Church's political task in this world is the striving for world peace, as expressed in the Pastoral Constitution on the Church in the Modern World (GS 77–90) and in numerous recent documents of the magisterium.

(3) THE FIELD OF ECONOMICS Economic conditions and forces, in addition to political forces and institutions, play a great role in the establishment and preservation of peace and of an order that guarantees human personal freedom. Let us look at four areas in which the dignity and freedom of the person, and thus the Church's task in this world, are expressed with particular clarity: (a) property; (b) labor and wages; (c) rich and poor nations; (d) ecology and a humane world.

(a) *Property* The human person is part of this created world, destined by God to subject the earth, to administer the world God entrusted to us, and to form it in insight and freedom. At least in part this world is subject to the divisions of public and private property. Whatever the particular legal framework of property may be, property as such is rooted in human needs (both material and spiritual-personal needs); it contributes to the self-expression and unfolding of the person. It helps us to fulfill our tasks in the family and toward neighbors, society, the people, the economy, and human culture in general. Just as human society develops into ever-more-differentiated forms on the basis of the primal form of the family, so forms of property and legal property rights become more and more complex as human civilization progresses. Property is not merely material possession; it is also present in the form of legal claims on the basis of work and services rendered to various forms of society. Private property and common property should not come into conflict with each other, but must complete and support each other according to the principle of subsidiarity. Both private and public property are not only rights: they imply certain duties. The balance between the two must be regulated, not by the power of the private or public owner, but by the needs of both, as well as by the capacity and readiness for service present in each. "In the sphere of economics and social life, too, the dignity and entire vocation of the human person as well as the welfare of society as a whole have to be respected and fostered; for man is the source, the focus and the end of all economic and social life" (GS 63,1). All economic enterprises must therefore serve the human person, the unfolding of the freedom and dignity of the person. Whenever the state must nationalize private property for the sake of the common good, it must make sure that just compensation is given to the former owner. Nationalization of private or common property without just compensation is robbery and cannot be excused.

(b) Work, Wages and Leisure "Human work exercised in the production and exchange of goods or in the provision of economic services surpasses all other elements of economic life, for the latter are only means to an end. Human work, whether exercised independently or in subordination to another, proceeds from the human person, who as it were impresses his seal on the things of nature and reduces them to his will. By his work a man ordinarily provides for himself and his family, associates with others as his brothers, and renders them service; he can exercise genuine charity and be a partner in the work of bringing divine creation to perfection" (GS 67,1–2). Through work man unfolds himself and creates his own human world. It must be the Church's concern to work, through its preaching, for just wages, according to the economic conditions of various civilizations, peoples, and countries, and for humane working conditions in which human persons are not transformed into slaves of labor and in which they do not enslave themselves to work through ambition and greed, thus neglecting the rest and leisure necessary for the person's spiritual dimension (recreation, celebration of the Lord's day). Inasmuch as the labor market is determined by society and the economy, the individual right to work must be respected and supported. Of course, this right does not relieve the individual of the task of maintaining a job through sufficient training and a Christian moral attitude toward work or of acquiring and securing the right to a new job. Unemployment of larger groups challenges the Church and its Christian economic and social teaching to investigate the roots of this evil and to seek temporary or permanent solutions. As conditions become more and more complex through the rapid development of production and monetary systems and of the corresponding standard of living, a deeper understanding of economic life as a whole in a Christian perspective becomes more and more urgent, and the Church must engage itself more and more for the weaker side.

(c) Rich and Poor Nations: The North-South Differential
An economic and social, political and cultural North-South differential has been developing between the industrial nations of the northern hemisphere and the so-called developing nations (in Asia, Africa, and South America). The reasons for this differential lie in the industrial revolution in the middle of the nineteenth century; in the consequences of the collapse of the liberal global economy in World War I; in the repayment of war damages in Europe and the American depression, intensified since World War II through the liberation of the former colonies and the population explosion in these nations. For the Church and for its Christian message to humanity, the North-South differential presents a hard challenge. Since 1975 the "North-South Dialogue" sponsored by the Conference for International Economic Cooperation has attempted to overcome the differential. The "General Agreement on Tariffs and Trade," (GATT), located in Geneva, was set up in 1947 for international customs and trade agreements. Its purpose was to free international trade from the bonds of protectionism by reducing the customs duties and price controls of the numerous national economic units that had been formed after 1918. Its resolutions are binding for members. The first session of the United Nations Conference on Trade and Development (UNCTAD) took place in 1964 in Geneva, in accordance with a resolution of the United Nations plenary assembly. Its purpose was also the reduction of tensions between rich and poor nations. Its resolutions are nonbinding recommendations.

The Church, the oldest institution on this earth, must contribute, through cooperation in these international organizations, toward a shift in perspective—from the attention the liberal global economy pays to the *object* of economic activity to attention to the *subject* of economic activity, the human person. "To fulfill the requirements of justice and equity, every effort must be made to put an end as soon as possible to the immense economic inequalities which exist in the world and increase from day to day, linked with individual and social discrimination, provided, of course, that the rights of individuals and the character of each people are not disturbed" (GS 66,1). The fight against world hunger must be intensified in agriculture, especially in developing nations, through customs and price regulations as well as through specific development aid. In industrial nations, the main tasks are dictated by the problem of unemployment, the regulation of "progress," and the problem of foreign workers who contributed to the reconstruction of Europe after World War II. The governing principles in both areas must be the laws of Christian social and economic teaching. The Church must act through its numerous charitable institutions and it must urge its Christian principles in the international political, economic and social institutions in order to humanize the human condition.

(d) *Environmental Protection and Ecology* It is the task of lay people in the Church to introduce Christian principles into the new studies of ecology, in which economic and biology overlap. Ecology must serve not only the dignity of the person but the nobility and beauty of God's creation. Only the threat posed by environmental destruction to the human habitat has clarified the importance of ecology. Nevertheless, one does not see the full purpose of this new field of scientific and technological development if one does not see nature and everything on earth (as well as the cosmos) as God's creation for the good of humanity and the glory of the creator. If all endeavors in this field were motivated exclusively by concern for human survival, materialistic and egotistic motives would obscure the full scope of ecology and would miss its final goal.

Following ancient tradition, the Church proclaims its faith in creation in its prayers and songs, but this faith has been increasingly left aside in theology since the Renaissance and even more so since the Enlightenment. Ecology makes clear how important it is for the Church in our time to propose creation in a new and living way in its doctrine and celebrations. The analogy of being, the analogy of faith, and the natural law, all of which are built on the doctrine of creation, are indispensable for understanding the world and acting in it according to Christian principles. They must become basic ways of experiencing reality. For we live not only out of reality itself, but out of the image we ourselves make of it according to our knowledge. And an essential element of the Christian knowledge of reality is provided only by living faith made conscious through reflection.

(4) ART AND SCIENCE IN THE MODERN CHURCH'S CULTURAL TASK The Church's task and responsibility in the world are particularly visible and fruitful in the cultural sphere, in science and art. This is why Vatican II paid special attention to this subject. In the 114th plenary session on November 4, 1964, Bishop A. L. Elchinger of Strasbourg said, "Public opinion largely holds that the Church's attitude toward culture is fearful and defensive. The Church's fight against Modernism is still an open wound today and induces suspicion against the Church's magisterium in many people. The Church should, therefore, openly ask itself the following questions: Does it merely unwillingly tolerate the necessary autonomy of culture? Is it engaged in a dogmatic imperialism in which it judges all scientific progress superficially and hastily, as if claiming that the competence of faith extends to everything? Is its perspective on culture too limited to retrospect and is it suspicious of a new humanism? Does it merely apply the theological theses of a certain historical period to life, as if theological work were only the repetition of acquired knowledge? Does it neglect the pastoral care of the intellect? Does it have a neurotic fear of rationalism and critical thought, as if nothing valuable could be found in them?" After demanding that the Church reverse

its injustice against Galileo, Bishop Elchinger pointed to three tasks of the modern Church: It must encounter contemporary culture with openness, benevolence, and trust; it must recognize the freedom of scientific inquiry, even in the study of religion; it must encourage prudent and courageous action among Christians. Without falling into paternalism, it must make a strong contribution to cultural progress; it must protect culture against anthropocentrism as well as materialistic and technocratic utilitarianism and preserve its openness to the transcendent. In addition, the Church must increasingly integrate culture into its proclamation and found new scientific institutions.

The fruits of this speech can be seen above all in Chapter Two of the Pastoral Constitution on the Church in the Modern World (GS 53–62), which deals with the correct promotion of cultural progress. It contains an extensive discussion of the historical and social aspects of culture and its special situation in our time of rapid scientific and technological progress. In order to strengthen the Church's work and esteem in this world, the Council demands understanding for and cooperation with the spiritual search and research of the modern age as it tends toward a worldwide culture—a culture, however, that must respect the legitimate specific character of the culture of particular peoples, especially in the sciences. The Council calls upon individual Christians and the Church's institutions to do more for the promotion of culture according to the demands of the time and to open up and facilitate access to the achievements of the mind and of technology for all people without discrimination. Theologians should be more open to the secular sciences, and lay people should not ignore the problems and insights of philosophy and theology:

The faithful ought to work in close conjunction with their contemporaries and try to get to know their ways of thinking and feeling, as they find them expressed in current culture. Let the faithful incorporate the findings of new sciences and teachings and the understanding of the most recent discoveries with Christian morality and thought, so that their practice of religion and their moral behavior may keep abreast of their acquaintance with science and of the relentless progress of technology: in this way they will succeed in evaluating and interpreting everything with an authentically Christian sense. (GS 62,4)

The trusting openness of faith for the great achievements of human culture and the christianizing of this culture through lived faith—this is the task of the Christian and of the Church in our age. In this way, the Church's missionary spirit is again visible and active in the cultural life of our time and our world, in all areas of human culture and thus also in daily life, in science and technology, in natural science and the humanities, in literature and music, in architecture, sculpture and painting, in theater, dance and film, and in the culture of daily life, housing, eating, and entertainment. Historically relative and trans-historical ideas and forms should work together in order to reach the best result for our time, out of Christian spirit and modern culture, for the good of individual persons and peoples and, in the end, of the whole family of nations.

In the pursuit of this goal the Council called for the cooperation of Christians and of the Church in the various national and international associations and enterprises that serve this purpose and it called upon the Church itself to establish such institutions. Accordingly, Pope Paul VI set up the "Pontifical Council for the Laity" (*Motu Proprio "Catholicam Christi Ecclesiam"* of January 6, 1967) and the "Pontifical Commission for Justice and Peace" (*Justitia et Pax*). They were given their final statutes in the *Motu Proprio "Apostolatus Peragendi."* On April 30, 1969, Pope Paul VI founded the International Theological Commission, and on July 22, 1971, the Council for the Coordination of Charitable Activity in the Church. On June 3, 1971, the Pontifical Council for the Instruments of Social

Communications was founded (cf. the Pastoral Instruction *Communio et Progressio*, Vatican Council II, pp. 293–349) and on November 1, 1973, a separate "Committee for the Family." The Pontifical Academy of Sciences, founded in 1603 under the great Pope Clement VIII (Aldobrandini, 1592–1605), was given in 1936 an international and inter-denominational character under Pope Pius XI (*Accademia dei Lincei*). Finally, one should mention cooperation in numerous committees of UNESCO.

All of these things express the catholicity of the Church and the fulfillment of its task in the world. It is the duty of each individual Catholic to support this activity of the Church in his or her place in the modern world and thus to contribute to an awakening of the Church in people's hearts. Certainly, the Church's catholicity does not depend upon the number of people who are committed to it, nor upon the true christianizing of the world, which is an effect of the Holy Spirit in its members. The Church is not a question of mass and of cultural Christianity. God will give "a new heaven and a new earth" at the end of time (2 Pet 3,13). In his judgment which he handed over to his Son (John 5,22)—in the cross of Christ, which is a witness of both sin and grace—the Church's catholicity will become manifest as a reality that encompasses the whole world. In order to understand this point correctly, we must raise and address the question of the Church's holiness.

XVII

The Church's Holiness and Its Definition as the Communion of Saints

I. HISTORICAL ASPECTS

The most ancient attribute applied to the Church by the Fathers is the attribute "holy." Ignatius of Antioch (d. ca. 110) wrote "to the holy Church which is at Tralles in Asia" (*Trall.* 1,1). Circa 150, the Letter of the Church at Smyrna about the martyrdom of Polycarp greets "all holy and Catholic Churches" everywhere, and at about the same time, the Shepherd of Hermas mentions three times "the holy Church." Circa 220, Hippolytus of Rome introduced the following question into the baptismal vow: "Do you believe in the holy Church" (DS 10); the most ancient form of the baptismal creed in the Epistola Apostolorum confesses, "We believe in the holy (Catholic) Church" (DS 1–5). Since the Baptismal Creed of Jerusalem (Cyril of Jerusalem, DS 41) and the Symbol of Epiphanius (DS 42), this formulation has been part of all baptismal creeds.

In the controversy on second repentance (third century, after the persecution under Decius), the Church's holiness required particular explanation vis-à-vis various heretics who were so struck by the sinfulness of Christians (apostasy under persecution) that they either counted only true saints as members of the Church—for example, Novatian (ca. 250; *Trin.* 29,167.172) and Tertullian (ca. 220; *de Pud.* 21)—or limited the attribute of "holiness" to the spiritual Church. The second alternative became very important in the Middle Ages, for example, in the views of the Fraticelli (DS 911), of Wycliffe (d. 1377; DS 1121f.; 1187), of John Huss (d. 1415; DS 1221: the community of the predestined), and probably also of Martin Luther (d. 1546), who in his Greater Catechism sets up the phrase "the holy community of the Spirit" over against the phrase "communion of saints" and explains it as "a community in which there are only saints." Calvin's view is probably different (*Inst.* IV,1). Calvin interprets success in the world as a sign for the holiness of Christians. It was probably in the controversy on second repentance that the expression "*communio (coetus) sanctorum*" was first used, initially only in theology. "*Sancti*" refers to the perfect Christians. Thus Novatian writes that God "makes the Church in every place and every respect perfect (*perfectam et consummatam*)" (*Trin.* 29,167). Basing himself on Ephesians 5,27 ("that he might present the church to himself in splendor, without spot or wrinkle or any such thing, that it might be holy and without blemish"), he goes even further and teaches that God preserves it "incorrupt and unharmed, perfect in the holiness of virginity and truth [*incorruptam et inviolatam perfectam virginitatis et veritatis sanctitate*]."[32] According to Tertullian, the spiritual persons (pneumatics), not the bishops, are where the Church exists (*de Pud.* 21). In sharp contrast, Origen (*In Lev. Hom.* 7,2) and especially Augustine understood the Church on earth as a space for both the good and the bad, following Christ's parables about the kingdom (Matt 13,30.47).

How and when did "*communio sanctorum*" enter the creed and what is its meaning? Nicetas of Remesiana (d. after 414) appears to have received this formula at the end of the fourth century from Paulinus of Nola in southern Gaul, who used it to combat Vigilantius and his attacks on the veneration of saints and relics (cf. Jerome, *Contra Vig-*

ilantium). Nicetas then introduced the formula into the Roman baptismal creed (DS 19). In 394, the Synod of Nîmes decreed that the phrase should not be received into the creed of the Mass.[33] The Pseudo-Augustinian sermons 240–242, which were perhaps written by Alcuin (d. 804), introduced the formula in Rome as part of the Carolingean tradition. The original meaning of the phrase seems to have been personal: the one, holy Catholic and apostolic Church is the personal successor of the prophets and apostles and finally of the martyrs of the early Church (*"sanctorum"* derived from *"sancti"*). Perhaps under the influence of the controversy on second repentance and baptism in the third century—or of the Eastern usage, in which *"hagia"* refers above all to the eucharistic species (cf. *Apost. Const.* VIII,13, the cry at communion)—*communio sanctorum* was understood in a neutral sense (*"sanctorum"* derived from *"sancta,"* holy things). Thus Thomas Aquinas (d. 1274) understands the phrase in terms of the sacraments (*In Symb. Apost. exp.*, 10,987). In his bull *Unam Sanctam,* Boniface VIII writes that the Psalmist calls the Church Christ's only body (Psalm 21,21) "because of the unity of the bridegroom, of faith, of the sacraments, and of the love [of Christians] in the Church" (DS 871). Bellarmine (d. 1621) defines the Church as the "gathering of persons [*coetus hominum*] who confess the same Christian faith, who are united by the same sacraments under the government of the legitimate shepherds, especially the vicar of Christ, the Roman Pontiff" (*De eccl. mil.* c. II). For this reason he explicitly defends the presence of sinners in the Church. The Roman catechism of the Council of Trent (Peter Canisius) explains *"communio sanctorum"* in terms of the sacraments and the merits of the whole Church (article 9, n. 24f.). The reformers understand *"sanctorum"* above all as "faith and God's word" (Calvin, *Inst.* IV,1; Luther, *Great Cat.*, art. 3).[34]

2. SYSTEMATIC ASPECTS

After this historical introduction we must (a) explain the concept "holy" and (b) its use for the Church and (c) reflect on the reality and impact of sin and sinners in the Church.

a) What is Meant by "Holy"?

The meaning and transformation of the concept "holy" were explained in the volume on God (KKD 2, §45). Only God is "holy" in the true sense of the word. Everything other than God which is also called holy receives the right to this title through its relation to the holy, all-holy, thrice-holy (Isa 6,3) God. "Holy" is thus a term expressing not a certain value but God's *being*. In Hebrew (*qados*) and in Latin (*sanctus*) the word has a primarily cultic meaning and refers to the realm of the divinity reserved within the un-holy (profane) world. The Greek term (*hagios*) is taken from the human reaction to the divine (*hazomai*, to shudder), and the English "holy" is related to "whole" and "hale (healthy)" as is the German "heilig" (from "Heil," health, salvation, or from "Heila," magic, luck).[35]

In the Old Testament "holy" is applied to God's name, which stands for his being (Lev 20,2; 22,2) and alone deserves adoration (Psalm 33,1; 103,1). In this context one could speak of an *ontic* concept of *"holy."* In addition, the people Israel, which Yahweh chose as his own, is called *"holy"*: "a royal priesthood, a holy nation" (Exod 19,6; 1 Pet 2,9; cf. the holiness code, Lev 17–26). The covenant God made with his people is a "holy covenant" (Exod 24,4–8). This cultic meaning of the word is quite clear here and cultic "purity" is closely connected with holiness.[36] The prophets introduce a more ethical meaning of "holy." Isaiah connects God's external glory with his inner holiness (Isa 6,3), and Hosea sees God's holiness in his fatherly love of his people (Hos 11). In Jeremiah, Yahweh appears as "the holy one of Israel" (Jer 12,6; 17,7), and in Deuteronomy the holy God is not only judge, but even more so creator (Deut 41,20) and redeemer (Deut 41,16; 43,3; 47,4). In the later period of the Old Covenant the various meanings of the word appear side by side, as they do in the Revelation of John.

The word *holy* took on a new personal and ethical meaning in the New Testament in its application to Christ, son of David and Son of God (Rom 1,3f.; Luke 1,35). In the first exorcism reported by Mark, the demon calls him "the holy one of God" (Mark 1,24), and in early Christian preaching on the servant of God he is called "the holy one" (Acts 3,14; 4,27–30). The servant of Yahweh perspective brings out in a new way the cultic meaning of "holy," inasmuch as Christ is both priest and sacrifice (Heb 9–11). In the Johannine farewell discourses he says, "Holy Father . . . I make myself holy [i.e., I make myself a sacrifice to you] for them so that they too may be holy [a sacrifice]" (John 17,11.19).

A new concept of "holy," which should probably be called *charismatic-eschatological*, appears in the concept of the Holy Spirit, especially in Luke: "Holy Spirit will come upon you and the power of the most high will overshadow you; therefore the child to be born will be called holy, the Son of God" (Luke 1,35). The holiness of this Spirit is so unique that the sin against the Holy Spirit remains an "eternal sin" which is not forgiven either in this life or the next (Mark 3,29; Matt 12,32; Luke 12,10).

The concept is again different in Paul when he integrates his statements on Christ and the Spirit into his teaching on Christian life. One could speak of a personal-mystical and sacramental understanding of the word, which gives to the cultic element a new and transfigured form. "By taking up the images of the temple (1 Cor 3,16; 6,19; Eph 2,20) of sacrifice (Gal 5,2) and of the liturgical minister (Rom 15,16) Paul points to the cultic character of 'holy' and spiritualizes it."[37] The place for this new cultic vision is the Church as the "mystical body of Christ" (1 Cor 12,12–31), which brings us to the next question.

b) What Does the Attribution of "Holiness" to the Church Mean, Both with Respect to the Church and with Respect to Holiness?

The fundamental text for this new vision of the holy, of the Christian reality in general, is Eph 2,19–22, where Paul writes, "So then you are no longer strangers and so-journers, but you are fellow citizens with the saints and members of the household of God, built upon the foundation of the apostles and prophets, Christ Jesus himself being the cornerstone, in whom the whole structure is joined together and grows into a holy temple in the Lord; in whom you also are built into it for a dwelling place of God in the Spirit." Paul unfolds the meaning of this statement in the following words:

There is one body and one Spirit, just as you were called to the one hope that belongs to your call, one Lord, one faith, one baptism, one God and Father of us all, who is above all and through all and in all. But grace was given to each of us according to the measure of Christ's gift. . . . And his gifts were that some should be apostles, some prophets, some evangelists, some pastors and teachers, to equip the saints for the work of ministry, for building up the body of Christ, until we all attain to the unity of the faith and of the knowledge of the Son of God, to mature manhood, to the measure of the stature of the fullness of Christ; so that . . . speaking the truth in love we are to grow up in every way into him who is the head, into Christ, from whom the whole body, joined and knit together by every joint with which it is supplied, when each part is working properly, makes bodily growth and upbuilds itself in love. (Eph 4,4–7.11–13.15–16)

Heinrich Schlier comments on this text as follows: "In this growing up toward itself the dimension of holiness increasingly opens up."[38] This point, made in a chris-tological key in Ephesians, is unfolded in a more so-

teriological key in Colossians 1,13–23 and in a more pneumatological key in 1 Corinthians 12–14. Holiness, which
appeared in the Old Covenant temple cult primarily as an
external event between Yahweh, the God of the covenant,
and Israel, the people of the covenant, appears in the New
Covenant as a single inner event in Christ, in whom God
and man have become one person. In the Old Covenant,
holiness could be lost by the faithlessness of the Israel-
ites, but it has been imperishably assured once and for all
in the New Covenant through God's eternal faithfulness
in Christ. Although particular individuals may lose the
promise through their personal faithlessness, the promise
itself and, consequently, holiness in the New Covenant,
remains irrevocable, an eternal covenant (Heb 10,1–18).

The principles of a doctrine of the Church's holiness can
thus be unfolded as follows:

(1) Christ is "the holy one of God" as the "Son of God"
and "son of man," as the priest who is, at the same time,
the sacrifice (Heb 7–10). Christ is now the head of his
Church "which is his body, the fulness of him who fills all
in all" (Eph 1,23). This is why Paul prays for the Christian
community, "that according to the riches of his glory he
may grant you to be strengthened with might through his
Spirit in the inner man, and that Christ may dwell in your
hearts through faith; that you, being rooted and grounded
in love, may have power to comprehend with all the saints
what is the breadth and length and depth, and to know the
love of Christ which surpasses knowledge, that you may
be filled with all the fulness of God" (Eph 3,16–19).

(2) As Christians we are filled with God in Christ. Christians, who through baptism have become members of
Christ (Rom 6,3–14), are a new creation (2 Cor 5,17), which
lives no longer out of itself, but in which Christ lives (Gal
2,20). Through the eucharistic meal, Christians participate
in Christ himself: "The bread which we break, is it not a
participation in the body of Christ?" (1 Cor 10,16). For
Christ said, "The bread which I shall give for the life of the

world is my flesh. . . . He who eats my flesh and drinks
my blood abides in me and I in him. As the living Father
sent me, and I live because of the Father, so he who eats me
will live because of me" (John 6,51.56). "Christ loved the
Church and gave himself up for her, that he might make
her holy, having cleansed her by the washing of water with
the word, that he might present the Church to himself in
splendor, without spot or wrinkle or any such thing, that
she might be holy and without blemish" (Eph 5,25–27).
Christians are therefore "those made holy in Christ Jesus,
called as saints" (1 Cor 1,2). And since Christian sanctification flows out of Christ's sacrifice, Paul sees his missionary task as being "a minister of Christ Jesus to the
Gentiles in the priestly service of the Gospel of God, so
that the offering of the Gentiles [in which they offer themselves as a sacrifice] may be acceptable [before God], sanctified by the Holy Spirit" (Rom 15,16).

(3) In this light one can understand why Paul calls Christians simply, "the holy ones (saints)" (Rom 1,7; 15,25f.; 1
Cor 1,2; 16,1). This holiness is, of course, a gift of God, not
the unfolding of natural talents or the fruit of moral
achievement. The "inheritance (klēronomia)" (Acts 20,32)
is a "lot (klēros)" (Acts 26,18) given by God.

(4) The path toward this holiness is "sanctification."
Thus Paul says, "This is the will of God, your sanctification [hagiasmos]" (1 Thess 4,3). The human task is "to
continue in faith and love and holiness" (1 Tim 2,15). This
sanctification must manifest itself in three ways. The behavior of Christians must be "reverent and pure" (1 Pet
3,2). They must offer themselves as a sacrifice to God, as
Christ offered himself: "I appeal to you therefore, brethren, by the mercies of God, to present your bodies [i.e.,
yourselves] as a living sacrifice, holy and acceptable to
God, which is your spiritual worship" (Rom 12,1). "One
has died for all; therefore all have died. And he died for all,
that those who live might live no longer for themselves
but for him who for their sake died and was raised to life"

(1 Cor 5,14–15). Finally, holiness must prove itself in the love of neighbor. "Serve one another in love" (Gal 5,13). This love proves itself as a rich and varied gift of God's Spirit, as "love, joy, peace, patience, kindness, goodness, faithfulness, gentleness, self-control" (Gal 5,22).

(5) It is from such "service to the saints" (Rom 15,25; 1 Cor 16,15; 2 Cor 8,4) and "sharing in their needs" (2 Cor 9,13) that communion with them is born (the *communio sanctorum*). This communion is a fruit both of the holy sacraments and mutual love in the Church in the power of the sacraments. This is particularly important for Christian existence in the world which, according to 2 Peter and Hebrews, is an eschatological existence:

His divine power has granted to us all things that pertain to life and godliness, through the knowledge of him who called us to his own glory and excellence, by which he has granted to us his precious and very great promises, that through these we may escape from the corruption that is in the world because of passion, and become partakers of the divine nature [*theias koinōnoi physeōs*]. For this very reason make every effort to supplement your faith with virtue, virtue with knowledge, and knowledge with self-control, and self-control with steadfastness, and steadfastness with godliness, and godliness with brotherly affection, and brotherly affection with love. (2 Pet 1,3–7)

"Strive for peace with all, and for the holiness without which no one will see the Lord" (Heb 12,14). In the face of the approaching end, the final demand is "let the just still be just, and the holy still be holy" (Rev 22,11).

(6) The Church, however, is not only the holy people of God, the communion of saints. Theology, especially since the Middle Ages, sees in it the bride of the Song of Songs, the "bride of the lamb" (Rev 19,7; 21,9; 22,17). "Christ loved the Church and gave himself up for her, that he might make her holy" (Eph 5,25–26) and he "nourishes her" (Eph 5,29). Yet on earth the Church can only look for him with longing. In this intermediate time between

Christ's ascension and his return as judge, the following words apply to it and to every Christian: "If then you have been raised with Christ, seek the things that are above, where Christ is, seated at the right hand of God. Set your minds on things that are above, not on things that are on earth. For you have died, and your life is hidden with Christ in God. When Christ who is our life appears, then you also will appear with him in glory" (Col 3,1–3). The Second Vatican Council wanted to bring out especially this side of the Church, "the Church's true face" (Paul VI, Nov. 21, 1964), and to show "the mystery of the unity and faithful love between Christ and his Church (Eph 5,32)" from which comes "the family in which new citizens of human society are born and, by the grace of the Holy Spirit in baptism, those who are made children of God so that the People of God may be perpetuated throughout the centuries. In what might be regarded as the domestic Church, the parents, by word and example, are the first heralds of the faith with regard to their children. They must foster the vocation which is proper to each child, and this with special care if it be a religious vocation" (LG 11). The Council expressed the great fruitfulness of the union between Christ and the Church by describing the Church as the "universal sacrament of salvation" (cf. above VII). This description makes clear that the sanctification the Church brings to the world is not merely a moral and religious event and activity of human beings in the world. It is, rather, a holiness brought as a fruit of Christ's love, both human and divine, in the sacramental action of his bride, the Church, for the children who are the fruit of this love. (In this context it can be pointed out that in the Old Testament the Hitpael form of *kds*—hitkaddes—can be used not only reflexively, "sanctify oneself, purify oneself, and thus prepare oneself for sanctification by God," but in a permissive sense, "let oneself be sanctified": "Let yourselves be made holy and be holy; for I, the Lord, am your God. Keep my statutes and do them, I am the Lord who sanctifies you" (Lev 20,7–8; cf. Jos 3,5; Lev 11,44). "May the God of peace sanctify you wholly; and may your spirit and soul and body be kept sound and blameless at the coming of our Lord Jesus Christ" (1 Thess 5,23). This is the reason the Letter to the Hebrews gives for the incarnation: "For he who sanctifies and those who are sanctified have all one origin. That is why he is not ashamed to call them brothers . . ." (Heb 2,11; cf. 2,11–18).

(7) At its very end Scripture reveals an even more sublime image of the Church's holiness, so sublime that it can be expressed only in extraordinary images and metaphors. The Church in heaven is the transfigured reality of the "new Jerusalem, coming down out of heaven from God, prepared as a bride adorned for her husband" (Rev 21,2), everything within formed of purest glass and gold and radiant jewels. "Its temple is the Lord, the Almighty and the lamb . . . the glory of God is its light, and its lamp is the lamb . . . the kings of the earth shall bring their glory into it . . . the river of the water of life, bright as crystal . . . and on either side of the river, the tree of life with its twelve kinds of fruit . . . the throne of God and of the lamb will be in it . . . and they shall see his face and his name shall be on their foreheads . . . the Lord God will be their light and they shall reign for ever and ever" (Rev 21,22–22,5). Part of this transfigured Church are the "holy angels" (1 Thess 3,13)[39] and the saints of ancient times (Matt 27,52). The Church's final service, before God's face, is in hymns to God and the lamb, radiant joy in the Lord. "Now to him who by the power at work within us is able to do far more abundantly than all that we ask or think, to him be glory in the Church and in Christ Jesus to all generations, for ever and ever. Amen." (Eph 3,20). The "cultic" element is always present in the image and concept of "holiness." It serves the human person when the person glorifies God and it sanctifies the person who "hallows" (makes holy) God's name (Matt 6,9).

After these lofty aspects of the Church's holiness we

must turn to what is unholy, evil, and a failure in it. We must understand these aspects if our image of the Church is not to be idealist, surrealist, and thus unreal.

c) *The Meaning and Significance of the Unholy, of Evil, and of Human Failure in Christ's Church on Earth*

Even a superficial and highly benevolent survey of the Church's history inevitably turns up many things that cannot be reconciled from a Christian perspective with the Church's holiness in the sense discussed above. Without doubt, the first thing to be mentioned is the deep lack of love, expressed in various forms, in the fight against heretics and schismatics, in the Inquisition with all its inhuman brutality, in various wars of "religion," to leave aside the sins and crimes in the lives of individual Christians. One does not need to look for these evils, they are clearly visible. There are various forms of human failure, including the failures of the Church's leaders, beginning with Judas and Peter, in times of hardship (apostasy) as well as in times of wealth and abundance (forgetfulness of God; self-glorification; being lost to absorption in the world). Not only the message of the great penitential preachers, but the Church's very history (Bernard, Bernardino of Siena, Savonarola) is an eloquent witness to this fact. In comparison with these historical testimonies, the criticisms brought against the Church today are certainly quite minor.

The problem becomes clear when these testimonies of concrete history are confronted with the dogmatic image of the Church's holiness. The question, seen quite simply, is this: Where can one find the true Church? In the everyday experience of Christians? In theological reflection about scriptural revelation? In the Church's glory, which is a gift of grace, or in its human scandal? In pious *sentire cum ecclesia* (living with the Church) or in "holy" zeal for the house of the Lord which is being transformed into a den of thieves?

In order not to deny what is unholy and evil in the Church, more idealistic thinkers will think they owe it to their pious thinking about the Church to distinguish between "the Church" as the holy bride of the lamb and "Christians" in the Church as poor and wicked failures.[40] However, this would separate the mystical body of Christ from the new people of God, which leads to a Nestorian erroneous image of the Church and misses the reality of the Church, just as Nestorius destroyed the reality of the historical Christ. As Hans Urs von Balthasar has shown, Origen, perhaps as the first in the history of the Church, departed from the early Christian image of the "sinless Church" and used "Rahab, the whore" (Josh 2; 6,17–25) as an image of the Church (Rahab is part of Jesus' family tree, Matt 1,5).[41] Origin used this image to express the presence of sinners in the Church, "converted sinners" as he still thought. Augustine was the one who counted real sinners as members of the Church, e.g., in his interpretation of Jesus' parable of the field in which there are weeds among the wheat (In Matt. Sermo 83; cf. Sermo 213,7 in Symbolum). In addressing this question, the great theology of the Middle Ages used, in addition, the parable of the net with both good and bad fish (Matt 13,47ff.), and especially various women figures of the Old Testament.[42] Vatican II has a clear and terse statement on this point: "Christ, 'holy, innocent and undefiled' (Heb 7,26) knew nothing of sin (2 Cor 5,21), but came only to expiate the sins of the people (cf. Heb 2,17). The Church, however, clasping sinners to its bosom, at once holy and always in need of purification, follows constantly the path of penance and renewal" (LG 8,3).

Evil and failure belong to the Church on earth, as suffering and the cross belonged to Christ in this world. "Was it not necessary that the Christ should suffer these things and so enter into his glory?" (Luke 24,26). Would the

Church be Christ's Church if it were completely sinless and no longer needed the suffering and sacrifice of Jesus Christ? Christ has died once for all for our sins, he offered his sacrifice for us. Until the end of the world, the Church offers the daily and permanent eucharistic sacrifice at Christ's command. Is this sacrifice only symbolical play? Is it not rather the permanent presence of Christ's atoning sacrifice for his bride, the Church, who is in need of atonement because she is sinful? Are evil and failure not simply part of the Church in this world, of its pilgrimage, because human existence, as a pilgrim existence, is characterized not by secure possession but by permanent seeking in repentance, penitence, and conversion? Uncertainty and risk are the foundation of human faith in this world; similarly, conversion and yearning are the foundation of love in this world. Certainty, possession, and fulfilled blessedness are the prerogatives of our "home," not of our pilgrimage. Would the high negative virtues of poverty, humility, obedience, and virginity be thinkable in the Church in this world if there were no evil and failure? Even John the Evangelist, despite his seemingly gnostic-dualist image of the world (cf. 1 John 2,16; 3,9) says, "If we say we have no sin we deceive ourselves and the truth is not in us. If we confess our sins, he is faithful and just, and will forgive our sins and cleanse us from all injustice" (1 John 1,8–9). Were not the great saints of the Church particularly aware of their sinfulness and were they not the first to confess their sins? The unholy, evil, and failure throw into relief those holy goods in the Church that (besides holy people) constitute its holiness, namely, the holy sacraments, which are not the reward of a holy life but helps for a holy life and healing medicines against weakness and sin. Perhaps a "pious" Christian will ask Paul's question: "Are we to continue in sin that grace may abound?" (Rom 6,1). Paul's only answer is this: "By no means!" (Rom 6,2). Remaining in sin is different, however, from having to confess again and again, even after a good confession, because "the inte-

rior of the human heart is inclined to evil from its youth"
(Gen 8,21).

The humble acceptance of this weakness in the Church
brings to light the great gulf that separates the Church in
this world from the Church in the kingdom of God. This
gulf can be filled and will be filled only by God. In the
measure in which we understand ourselves as members of
the Church *in via* we must assent to the "Church of sinners." If we limited our image of the Church to that of the
spotless bride of the lamb, we would transform our own
Christian existence in this world into an idealistic day-
dream. Of course, also the assent to the "Church of sinners" can be a temptation to "excuse" our own sinfulness
instead of "resisting sin to the point of shedding blood"
(Heb 12,4). As often in the Christian understanding of the
world, we are brought to the paradoxical principle: live as
if you had to achieve of yourself what you are to be and
know that "God is at work in you, both to will and to work
for his good pleasure" (Phil 2,13; cf. Eph 2,10). Like everything in this world, the Church's holiness is a gift of the
triune God: of God the creator (the Father), without whom
nothing real exists; of God the redeemer (the Son) who
points to evil and deficiency in creation by his very existence; and of God the sanctifier, the perfector, without
whom nothing created and nothing redeemed can find its
fulfillment. And these three are—is—the one holy triune
God.

The final word remains thus that of the Church's holiness, because it is the Church of the triune God, although
for us human beings, who can think only in the categories
of this earth, this holiness will be fulfilled only beyond
this earth and this time. "Brother, thy high desire shall be
fulfilled in the last sphere, where all the rest have their
fulfillment, and mine too. There perfect, ripe, and whole is
each desire; in it alone is every part there where it ever
was" (St. Benedict to Dante in Dante's *Paradiso*, canto 22).
The three forms of the Church, the Church triumphant,

the suffering Church, and the Church militant are thus *holy* only by participation in the holy God. For Christians in the Church militant, of course, there is the mystery of freedom, the mystery of grace and of predestination, which leaves open two paths: one to fulfillment and the other to eternal lack of fulfillment. The mystery of iniquity remains, and because we are existentially so entangled in this mystery, it truly does remain a special "mystery" for our faith and thinking on earth, even though we know that it has been overcome by Christ the redeemer in the holy triune God.

Let us look at the Church's holiness in the light of the understanding of the Church as the universal sacrament of salvation. In terms of institution by Christ, the Church is the only and definitive space of all the sacraments of Christ and their saving efficacy for humanity, for all peoples (Matt 16,18; 28,19f.). In terms of the outward sign, the Church of Christ is the visible offer of salvation to "all the world and the whole creation. He who believes and is baptized will be saved; but he who does not believe will be condemned" (Mark 16,15–16). In terms of inner grace, the Church is the space of all graces, from conversion to sanctification and final glory, of grace in this world (Rom 3,29), and of eternal life (Rom 5,21), redemption, sanctification, and righteousness (1 Cor 1,30).

The mystery of the Church's holiness will thus become clearer to us when we reflect briefly on the Church's relationship to what Jesus called "the kingdom of God."

XVIII

The Church and the Kingdom of God; The Fundamental Marian Mystery of the Church

We must still insert the keystone in the cupola of the "one, holy, catholic, and apostolic Church." What is the physical-metaphysical reality of the Church? Although this keystone exceeds the scope of this little work and the power of its author, it should not be left out. A few outlines should show at least what really needs to be done if our theological discussion of the Church is to reach our contemporary faith in the Church in its entirety and in its true core. The two themes addressed in this chapter touch upon this ultimate and innermost element in our contemporary understanding of the Church. In their inner unity they point to the following fundamental question: Where can we see today, after Kant and Hegel and Heidegger and Wittgenstein, the "reality" (Newman) of the Church as "universal sacrament of salvation"? How can we describe this reality without succumbing to the influence of the criticist doctrine of knowledge, of idealism, of materialism and existentialism, of structuralism and personalism?[43]

The problem can be expressed quite simply in the following questions: 1. How can one reconcile Jesus' two statements, "The kingdom of God is in the midst of you" (Luke 17,21) and "My kingdom is not of this world" (John 18,36)? Where is the reality of this kingdom of God? What physical-metaphysical structure does this "sacrament"

Church have? 2. Within the Church as a political-social entity, how can one reconcile the creative element of sending and mission ("Go into all the world and preach the gospel to the whole creation" Mark 16,15), the element of violent struggle ("the kingdom of heaven suffers violence" Matt 11,12), and the receptivity that is the hallmark of all creaturely and of all Christian action ("What have you that you did not receive?" 1 Cor 4,7)? What is the inner reality of this Church which encompasses the Church militant, the suffering Church, and the Church triumphant? Is Mary, the Mother of Christ, the head of the Church, part of the Church's structure as the "handmaid of the Lord"? Let me attempt to say briefly the most important things on this topic, as far as I understand it.

The Church and the Kingdom of God

I. THE KINGDOM OF GOD IN THE NEW TESTAMENT

According to the Synoptic Gospels, the message of the *basileia,* of God's rule or kingdom in this world, is the center and innermost core of Jesus' message.[44] The phrase is used sixty-three times by Jesus. What is its meaning? Jesus' contemporaries were convinced that the old prophetic spirit had died out in Israel. To many, Christ appeared as the new bearer of the Spirit. In his own speeches, however, he stresses that he does not continue the spirit of the prophets, but is their fulfillment as God's definitive revelation to his people and to all of humanity (Matt 5,17; 13,17). The new beginning of God's rule in Christ, as experienced in his miracles (Mark 1,21–34), is the overcoming of the rule of Satan. This is how Peter describes Christ in the house of Cornelius: "God anointed Jesus of Nazareth with the Holy Spirit and with power; he went about doing good and healing all that were oppressed by the devil, for

God was with him" (Acts 10,38). Jesus' contemporaries see him as the one who overcomes Satan (Luke 11,20; Matt 1,24) and thus as the beginning of God's rule. According to Deutero-Isaiah, this rule is an eschatological reality (Isa 29,18; 35,5f.; 61,1f.), but in Christ it appears as a present power (Luke 17,20ff.). Of course, this presence of the kingdom of God points beyond itself to a future fulfillment of the world. Like the fig tree, God's rule, which began in Christ, announces a new spring (Matt 13,28f.), it is new wine which must be put into new skins (Mark 2,22f.). The bread of life he gives (Matt 7,24–30), the festive garment he requires (Luke 15,22; Matt 22,11), and the beginning of God's peace (Matt 10,12–15)—all of these point to a future kingdom. The new good news is proclaimed to the poor and to sinners (Mark 2,15f.; Matt 11,19; Luke 15,1; 19,7; 7,37.39) and its content is healing and the forgiveness of sins (Luke 15,7.10; 7,36–50). God's graciousness is present in Christ, but it still points to a future time of salvation, as shown by the eschatological discourses in Matthew (24,1–25,46) and Mark (13,1–37). The destruction of the temple and thus of the Old Testament cult are signs of a future final judgment. When people ask him whether only a few will be saved at the end, Christ answers only by speaking about the hard path and the narrow door which lead into the kingdom (Luke 13,23f.; Matt 7,13f.22–24). Thus God's rule began in Christ, but it is not present in its final openness (Mark 13,28f.). Jesus tells his disciples to continue the proclamation that the kingdom of God has approached (Matt 10,7; Luke 10,9.11) and he teaches them to pray "Thy kingdom come" (Luke 11,2). In Jesus' preaching, the kingdom of God is thus portrayed as an intermediary time which tends toward something definitive. As an intermediary time, however, it demands a quick and definitive decision for Christ and the kingdom which has arrived in him. The one who is called by Christ must follow quickly and without hesitation (Luke 9,59–62) and his messengers (apostles) are to lose no time with the customary greeting

on the road (Luke 10,4). The call to repentance which introduces the message of the kingdom (Mark 1,15) is made
particularly dramatic by threats (Luke 13,1–9), and the
parables of the ten virgins (Matt 25,1–12) and the great
banquet (Matt 22,1–10) point to this urgency of the end-
times. Those who do not want to hear this preaching of
repentance and grace are part of "this generation" (Mark
8,38; 9,19; 12,38–40), which will suffer quick and hard
judgment. The woes (Luke 17,28–30) and the hint that
"there are some standing here who will not taste death
before they see the kingdom of God" (Luke 9,27) express
the pressing urgency of this final time of God's rule with
particular clarity. At the same time, conversion must be
genuine and interior and immediate (Matt 5,25f.; Luke
16,1–13), otherwise one is a hypocrite (Matt 6,1–28) and
particularly threatened by punishment. One must reflect
on all of these elements to understand the time of God's
rule brought about by Christ.

2. HISTORICAL ASPECTS

Before raising the question of the relation between the
Church and the kingdom of God on the background of this
clear scriptural image of the kingdom, we must indicate
the basic transformations of Christ's clear message in the
Church's self-understanding and its actions in this world.
For Christ did not only proclaim a new message of the
kingdom of God in his time. For the intermediary time in
which this kingdom is to be proclaimed and established he
initiated a specific social order, namely, the Church, of
whose founding, foundation, and coming to be we spoke
above (Chapter VIII). In this way there is an intimate link
between the message of the kingdom of God and the
Church, the bearer of this message in the world. Our question cannot be fully answered without taking this link into
account. Otherwise the kingdom of God remains a mere
ideology, and the Church a mere secular reality.

First, Scripture itself contains statements that can be misunderstood, e.g., the statements about "the new heavens and the new earth" (Isa 65,17; 66,22; 2 Pet 3,13) and the image of a millennium of Christ's reign on earth together with his martyrs (chiliasm, Rev 20,1–6). In addition, the kingdom of God can be understood not only in terms of Christ, but also in terms of the Holy Spirit (Joachim of Fiore; the Franciscan *spirituales*). Further, the kingdom of God in this world is borne by faith, hope, and love. When speaking of the kingdom, individual persons and groups within the Church can at different times be shaped, therefore, more by faith, which demands a present reality, or by hope, which expects realization only in the future, or by love, which seeks and bears the ideal as something above experience. Given these tendencies, it can easily happen that the kingdom of God is seen as a spiritual and other-worldly reality, somewhat dualistically opposed to all earthly reality (the Montanists), or that earthly reality is idealized and the kingdom is viewed as something that must be developed and maintained by earthly power (apocalyptic theology, federal theology). The understanding of the kingdom of God thus plays a particularly important role in the Church's relation to the political powers of this world. Ideological misinterpretations of Scripture texts are usually brought in to support these erroneous views and attitudes, e.g., the misinterpretation of Jesus' words about the two swords (Luke 22,38) in High Scholasticism (Innocent IV, Boniface VIII) or John's statements about the anti-Christ (1 John 2,18.22; 4,3), which Luther used to support his doctrine of the two kingdoms. The Enlightenment, finally, simply transformed Christianity into a mere human ethics (Fichte) or it transferred the tasks of the kingdom of God from the Church to the absolute state in the light of an idealist understanding of the state (Hegel). Chiliastic and apocalyptic features are particularly pronounced among modern sects (Seventh Day Adventists, Jehovah's Witnesses, Mormons). Jewish thinking is concerned with the question of the messiah as bringer of salvation for the whole world. The messiah has either arrived already and been rejected as an impostor after his failure (Bar Kochba, etc.) or he is still to be expected. Secularized messianism is at work in the Marxist and Communist understanding of the state and the party, linking an old religious ideal with human power after Marxism turned into a major power after World War I.

The Christian biblical understanding of the kingdom of God and of the relationship between the kingdom and the Church holds onto the indissoluble tension between two simultaneous and seemingly paradoxical elements: the arrival of God, which has begun with power, and the parousia of God's rule, which must be awaited in lack of earthly power; the kingdom of God as pure grace, and the call of realizing the kingdom of God with all human effort (in grace); the supernatural reality and its realization in this created world.

3. THE KINGDOM OF GOD AND THE CHURCH

After these preparatory reflections, let us turn to the question of the relationship between the kingdom of God and the Church. In contemporary theological language the phrase "kingdom of God" expresses all that can be known of God, his being and his knowledge, his will and activity; of the goal, end, and meaning of his actions; of his power, which is his self-abandoning love. The world's creation, conservation, and government, the redemption of the fallen world in the history of salvation through Jesus Christ, the incarnate Son of God, the fulfillment and sanctification of the world in the Church through the Holy Spirit, who is sent by the Father and the Son, and the final fulfillment of all creation at the end of time through and in and with God—all of these elements are summarized in the phrase "kingdom of God." The importance of the

Church for this reality of the kingdom of God is most simply and clearly expressed in the Vatican II description of the Church as the "universal sacrament of salvation" (cf. above Chapter VII) in this world. This description has the following implications for the relationship between the Church and the kingdom of God.

a) The kingdom of God has begun in the Church of Christ in this world, and the Church is the only and the authentic instrument of God's kingdom in this world. The Church, however, is not identical with this kingdom, which is greater than this world in space and time. The well-known Modernist theologian A. Loisy (d. 1940) coined the saying: Christ announced the kingdom of God, but the Church came instead. Loisy misunderstands both realities and thus also their relationship to each other.

b) The more the Church is seen not only as the Church militant but as the suffering Church and the Church triumphant, the more one must say that in it the kingdom of God is already present and effective. Still, not even the Church triumphant is the entire kingdom of God, because the definitive separation between good and evil in the final judgment and the comprehensive revelation of the kingdom of God as the all-embracing rule of his love are still to come.

c) In the Church militant on earth one sees that the kingdom of God is a grace and especially that this grace implies an obligation for us to commit and exert ourselves. The suffering Church shows this grace in its aspect of patient suffering. In the Church triumphant the pure gratuitousness of the grace of God's kingdom is present in the participation in the glory of God's love. Our earthly theologizing will hardly be able to understand and express what the fulfillment at the end of time will add to this third form of the Church.

d) As it is certain that in God's universal plan of salvation the kingdom of God is at present still to come for the Church militant and the suffering Church, so it is certain that this kingdom is not developing in a worldly sense. It remains always and completely a freely given gift of the loving omnipotence of the triune God.

e) According to the history of salvation presented in Scripture, the definitive realization of the kingdom of God will come only after the final judgment in a new heaven and a new earth. Expressed in contemporary terms it will thus be a "cosmic," not merely a "transcendental," reality. Even our transcendental theological statements in this world fall short of the event of the "end of the world." All we can say is that God will be "all in all" (1 Cor 15,28). Also Christ, who became man in this our world, will subject himself to his Father at the end of the world. All our theological statements, which are formulated from the perspective of the time of this world, must, therefore, be adjusted to apply to eternal reality.

f) In the end, however, all earthly and human realities will be "themselves" in a new and final way, according to the law: the closer a creature is to the creator, the more it can become and be what it itself can be and is. "The new heavens and the new earth" can thus not be understood in terms of our earthly world-view, but only in terms of God, the creator. We cannot yet grasp concretely what they will be.

g) The decisive thing for our Christian existence in the world is: *sentire cum (in) ecclesia!* We must always be on the way to reach an ever-new understanding of ourselves in our Church, of our Church in Christ, and of Christ in God, by giving ourselves away and spending ourselves in serving this Church. The kingdom of heaven suffers violence, not in the sense of moral achievement, but in the sense of personal self-giving until God is all in all, the one, three-personal God in whom everything is person and in whom there is nothing a-personal. Only when we see God will we understand what "person" is and that this personhood is the foundation of the image of God in us (Gen 1,26). The importance of this personal element is already made clear by the fact that one becomes a Christian by simply, unconditionally, and definitively following Christ.

The Fundamental Marian Mystery of the Church

The mystery of the personal in Christianity and the Church which we just mentioned comes to light again in the fundamental Marian mystery of the Church. Vatican II specifically decided to include the new things it wanted to say about Mary in the final chapter (Chapter Eight) of the Dogmatic Constitution on the Church under the title, "On the Blessed Virgin Mary, Mother of God, in the Mystery of Christ and the Church." Much has since been written on this topic. Again let us sketch only a few basic ideas that are important for our contemporary understanding of the Church.

I. HISTORICAL ASPECTS

"God's Son, born of a woman" (Gal 4,4), the redeemer of the world and head of his Church, inevitably raised the question of this "woman" in his Church.

a) Already in the middle of the second century, the importance of Mary for the Church of Christ was expressed in the parallel between Eve and Mary which follows the parallel between Adam and Christ in Paul (Rom 5,12–19; 1 Cor 15,22). Justin mentioned this parallel (*Dial.* 100,5) and one generation later Irenaeus unfolded it in detail (*Adv. Haer.* III,22,4; V,19,1: she unloosened the bonds). Almost all other Fathers return to this theme (Epiphanius, *Pan. haer.* 78,18; Jacob of Batnae, etc.). Just as Eve is the mother of the whole sinful human race, so Mary, the mother of the redeemer Jesus Christ, is the mother of the whole redeemed human race. Bodily and spiritual motherhood are clearly brought together in this view.

b) Ambrose (*In Lk* X 24–25; II 7) and Augustine (*De s. Virginitate* 6) stressed the deep relatedness of this special motherhood to God by speaking about the "virginal motherhood" of Mary and of the Church. Mary is "mother of God" because she gave bodily life to the Son of God; the Church, in turn, gives birth to "children of God" through baptism. This truth is distinguished quite clearly from the pagan ideas on mothers of the gods.

c) A new image is unfolded by the Church's oldest prayer to Mary (*Sub tuum praesidium confugimus*) from the end of the third century, and by the legend of the Madonna with the protective mantle from the fifth century. Mary appears as the help of Christians, just as the Church is called the "mother" of Christians in Gal 4,26. In this use the term "mother" has a developed meaning which goes beyond mere natural motherhood.

d) Again a new image of Mary and the Church was developed by the commentaries on the Song of Songs in the early Middle Ages. The bridal relation between Mary and Christ or God's Spirit and between the Church and Christ was unfolded in a deep theological spirituality.

e) Two further images of the Church were unfolded by the medieval mysticism of suffering: the birth of the Church from the wounded side of Christ, like Eve from the side of Adam, and the image of the *Mater dolorosa* Mary under the Cross, when she was declared to be the mother of John (John 19,26f.) and through him of the Church.

f) A new form was given to the relationship between the Church and Mary in the theology of L. M. Grignion de Montfort (d. 1716) who came from the school of Berulle and interpreted all events surrounding Christ as exemplary for Christians. Thus he holds that "also in the human soul the birth of Christ happens through the cooperation of the Holy Spirit and the blessed Virgin Mary." Mary is "mother of Jesus," not only in an earthly and historical sense, but also in a mystical and existential sense in Christians.

g) These ideas played a considerable role in the discussions at Vatican II and at the end of the Council's third working period Paul VI addressed Mary with the title "mother of the Church" (in addition to the traditional titles "mother of God, mother of Christ, mother of Christians"). A fourth of the Council Fathers had asked for this title to be introduced. (In September of 1981 the German bishops decided to introduce the title "mother of the Church" into the Litany of Loretto between the titles "mother of Christ" and "mother of divine grace"). The Chapter on Mary in the Constitution on the Church proceeds from an understanding of the Church as the sacrament of salvation (Ch. 1,9,48,59). This approach leads us back from our historical sketch to a systematic discussion of Mary as the fundamental mystery of the Church.

2. SYSTEMATIC ASPECTS

Two preliminary remarks: (1) What is at issue is primarily "typological theology." Mary appears above all as the archetype of the Church and the Church as her antitype. The importance of Mary for the incarnation of Christ is seen with respect to the Church as the body of Christ, the body which is, in turn, the universal sacrament of salvation and thus the source and giving of new life. (2) In this perspective Catholic theology understands the Church as a comprehensive social reality prior to the people of God, not simply as the people of God itself which is seen (especially in Protestant theology) as the sum of individual Christians. Against this background let us attempt to understand Mary as the fundamental mystery of the Church.

a) The fundamental mystery which links Mary and the Church is the "mystery of grace." What the angel told Mary about being filled by God's grace, being filled with the Holy Spirit, and being the mother of the Son of God (Luke 1,30–37) is of ultimate importance also for the Church founded by Christ, filled by the Spirit and mother of all since its birth at Pentecost. The basic principles of Christian anthropology in Paul hold for Mary as well as the Church: "foreknown, predestined, called, justified, glorified" (Rom 8,29–30).

b) Mary as well as the Church responds to this grace as "handmaid of the Lord." And in this humble response of gratitude and obedience, the handmaid is transformed by the Lord himself into the "bride." All human service becomes bridal service in the grace of God. All toil is borne by the power and the wings of love.

c) In Mary as well as the Church, the meeting of divine grace and human self-donation is not merely a unique historical event. It becomes fruitful in a permanent "motherhood" in relation to all who belong to Christ and to God. Through their action "life" is passed on, although Christ remains the only mediator between God and human beings (1 Tim 2,5f.).

d) Christ offered his sacrifice for the salvation of the world only once, but he presents this sacrifice to His heavenly Father through all time until the end of the world (Heb 8–10). In the same way Mary's service in the saving work of Jesus is the unique bodily service of motherhood, but this motherhood continues as a spiritual motherhood (beginning in the communion of prayer in the cenacle before Pentecost, Acts 1,14) in care for Christians to the end of time. In the same way the Church's motherhood in relation to Christians, in which she gives birth to them once in the water of baptism, continues as spiritual motherly care even beyond the grave all the way to God's judgment. In this way Mary is the image of the Church in faith, love and perfect union with Christ (LG 63–64).

e) While Christ is the center and foundation of the office of the priesthood in the Church, Mary is the archetype and exemplar of the universal creational and baptismal priesthood of the Christian people. In this way she is the exemplar of all Christian virtues. Through her unique position in God's plan of salvation she introduces the meditation of Christians ever deeper into the living mysteries of God's kingdom of which the Church must be a witness in its teaching and its life. In this way an authentic veneration of

Mary leads to a deeper worship of Christ and a more interior adoration of God, just as all authentic veneration of
saints is a sure path and effective help for following Christ
personally.

f) As handmaid (daughter) of God, mother of Christ, and
bride of the Holy Spirit, Mary is the archetype and exemplar of the Church. The Church conforms to this archetype
when it lives its life effectively and fruitfully for the world
and for people of all times as handmaid in grateful service
within the order of creation, as mother in the self-sacrificing service of the order of grace, and as blessed bride in
the unconditional obedience of faith toward the Holy
Spirit in the order of action.

g) In his Constitution *Munificentissimus Deus* (Nov. 1,
1950), which proclaimed the bodily assumption of Mary
into heaven, Pope Pius XII said, "The great value of this
definition is that it points the human race toward the glory
of the most holy Trinity." This is indeed the mystery of all
veneration of the saints and in particular of the veneration
of Mary, that it preserves Christians (and the Church) from
the most dangerous temptation which besets Christian
life, or helps them to overcome it, namely, the temptation
toward "spiritual worldliness," as Dom Vonier once called
it, which puts worldly human "perfection" in the place of
Christian holiness. Christian holiness knows (as a holiness that depends upon this knowledge) that everything
that is truly great, every true human perfection, is God's
gift ("treasure in earthen vessels" 2 Cor 4,7) and not the
fruit of natural maturity or the achievement of human
effort. This is why Mary's *Magnificat* is the Church's song
of praise through all ages. Upon it depends the Church's
final task in our time, the apostolate of the laity, i.e., of all
Christians. The source of this apostolate lies in Marian
faith, in the faith which overcomes the world (1 John 5,4).
Its strength lies in the power which flows from Marian
"joy in the Lord" (Neh 8,10). It is rooted in the "love which
is strong as death" (Cant 8,6–7; cf. AA 4).

Epilogue

In the preceding pages, we have attempted to describe the Church as it shows itself in revelation and as it is understood by the Roman Church (and to a large extent also by the Eastern Churches), by discussing its marks as listed in the Creed of Constantinople. It is apostolic (in its offices), one (in its missionary and ecumenical nature), Catholic (in its mission into the whole world and to the whole human race) and holy (in its gifts and members). We concluded this discussion with the question of the specific form of reality of this Church, as far as we were able to answer it within the limits of our present possibilities. In my opinion, an answer to this question is possible only if we look at the Church from nine perspectives at once and see the unity of these perspectives.

1. The primal divine ground of the Church: This ground appears throughout the whole history of salvation, from the creation of the world and the human race to the fall, the incarnation of God, the redemption worked by Christ to the final judgment and the new transfigured world in which God will be all in all. The center is Christ, the primal sacrament, and the Church, the universal sacrament, head and body, the Christ of the hymn in Colossians (Col 1,13–24).

2. The Church as a social space of humanity, as the family of God: as the living communion of all who can be characterized by the central statements of Paul's anthropology with its salvation history perspective: foreknown, predestined, called, justified, glorified (Rom 8,28–30). They bear the Church and the Church bears them.

3. The Church under the mission of Christ (John 20,21)

as an apostolic, hierarchical institution for the life and the order of the (new) people of God: built on the rock foundation of Peter and the apostles, with Christ as the cornerstone. Without this aspect there is no Church.

4. The Church as the communion of saints, alive in living historical persons who live on earth in purgatory or in heaven in the knowledge of their faith, who fulfill God's will in his grace and who thus form the innermost realm of God's rule (*basileia*), following Christ in the power of the Spirit to the glory of the Father.

5. The Church as a part of the mystery of God's creation in which—since Adam—the reality of sin, opposed to God, is present. For the Church militant this presence implies struggle, repentance, and conversion, for the suffering Church blessed physical suffering and grateful yearning of the spirit for secure glory, and for the Church triumphant with the wounds of its sin (of forgetting God, glorifying the self, being absorbed and lost in the world: the original sin, Gen 3, 1–6; John 1, 29) adoration of the thrice-holy creator and exulting gratitude for his healing, creating and sanctifying grace. The center of this mystery of creation, however, is not sin, but the one sinless human being, Mary, and Christ in whom everything has been created, in whom everything that lets itself be redeemed is redeemed, and in whom everything that is sanctified is sanctified.

6. The Church as the universal sacrament of salvation, its life flowing from the primal sacrament, Christ, in the celebration of the seven individual sacraments and the sacramentals in the hierarchical Church for the salvation of individual members of the body of Christ and the historical cosmos whose center is Christ with his cross.

7. The Church as the community which worships God, in which the institutional, social and existential order cooperate, and in which three dimensions grow together to communion from God: the Church militant, which lives from revelation and faith, law and grace, charism and sacrament; the suffering Church with its blessed penitential

suffering; and the Church of the blessed with their all-encompassing praise of God. God himself in his omnipotence, wisdom and love builds up this Church.

8. The Church in the eschatological prospective of our earthly time: All earthly realities in it will be lifted by God into a new mode of being and existence, all its natural actions will be performed in a new, supernatural way as God's gift, completely and exclusively to the honor of the triune God who will fill all in all and who will thus give the eternal fulfillment of blessedness in his divine glory. At this point the divine ground of the Church's whole reality in this world will become visible for all behind the world's passing nature. In this Church of the blessed, the angels and saints with Mary, the queen of angels and saints at their head, will lead the liturgical dance.

9. The Church in its definitive transfigured being after the judgment: Revelation tells us three things about this Church: God will give a new heaven and a new earth (2 Pet 3,23); we human beings will be with Christ, our transfigured Lord and brother, with transfigured bodies (John 5,25.28f.); finally, "the Son himself will also subject himself to him who put all things under him, that God may be all in all" (1 Cor 15,28).

It seems that these three statements of revelation address and illumine three mysteries of our world in general: (1) The *mystery of creation* as a reality which appears to have been created by God, who fills all in all, in such a way that it is outside him, facing non-being and nothing. Now this world will be freed from facing nothing and placed into imperishable life, into participation in God's eternal life. (2) The *mystery of human beings* who are created in the image of God and called to be children of God (Gen 1,26; 1 John 3,1f.) but who, as revelation says, have become prey to death through sin (Rom 5,12), death in which the mortal body that weighs down the soul (Wis 9,15) returns to the dust of the earth from which it is taken while the soul returns to God (into immortality) who gave it (Qoh

12,7). The death of the body is overcome only by the transfiguration of the body, through participation in the transfigured Lord; and sin is overcome in the forgiving judgment of the Lord, through participation in the "joy of the
Lord" (Matt 25,21), the great and eternal joy which is given
as the reward of faithfulness in small things of earthly life.
God's superabundance,[1] in which the human person does
not suffocate but finds full freedom as God's image and full
identity and peace, removes all defects of annihilating sin,
and gives fulfillment to the created image of God. As the
queen of angels and saints, Mary, the mirror image of the
Church, will lead this dance of the blessed. The mystery of
the eternal deprivation of fulfillment in hell is hidden for
our earthly thinking in God's justice and holiness, but also
in God's love. Our light on earth does not penetrate into
these mysteries but we can abandon ourselves to them and
adore them. (3) The *mystery of the Christ*, the Son of God
made man, will reach the "solution" in which the first two
mysteries we mentioned are lifted above themselves and
brought home. The Son will subject himself to his Father
that God may be all in all.

Expressed in the perspective of our earthly thinking:
When creation and its time come to an end or, rather,
when it is transformed into the new, second creation, we
will meet the triune God as he—humanly speaking—has
been from eternity, before the foundation of the world
with its time and before the incarnation of the Son and the
sending of the Holy Spirit in time, as he is in eternity, one
and the same, the unchangeable one in himself as the
agent and Lord of the great history of salvation in the history of destruction initiated by his free creatures. Him we
will see, and in jubilant cries of Alleluia, we will experience his nature, which is love (Rev 21,1–22,5). What will
become of us Christians, who, as members of Christ, belong to the body of Christ and who, still, are only creatures, who cannot become one in being with God, the
creator, and who cannot enter "all in all" into God like the

Son, our brother? The incarnation of God is irreversible. Even as the Son who has subjected himself to the Father, Christ remains in eternity our brother; even as God, he remains our brother. Commenting on Christ's submission to the Father, Augustine writes:

For we shall contemplate God the Father, the Son, and the Holy Spirit when the man Christ Jesus, the mediator between God and men, shall have delivered the kingdom to God and the Father, so that our mediator and priest, the Son of God and the Son of man, will no longer plead for us, but he himself, inasmuch as he is a priest by the form of a slave that he assumed for our sake, will be subjected to him, who has subjected all things to him, and to whom he has subjected all things; inasmuch as he is God, he together with him will keep us in subjection; inasmuch as he is a priest, he together with us will be subjected to him. (*De Trin.* I, 10,20)

"In this vision God will be all in all, because nothing is sought (by us) beside him, but it is enough to be illumined by him and to enjoy him [*illustrari perfruique*] . . . Our Lord Jesus Christ will thus deliver the kingdom to "God and the Father" (cf. 1 Cor 3,1; Eph 1,3.17; 1 Pet 1,3; John 20,17) not by separating himself from believers, nor by a separation of the Holy Spirit from believers, when he leads them to the vision of God, when the end of all good works comes and eternal peace and eternal joy which shall never be taken from us." While the mystery of the incarnation is that the Son becomes our brother and still remains with the Father, the mystery of this eschatological submission of the Son under the Father is that he still remains with us as our brother.

In both cases, "remaining" belongs to the nature of this Christ. In this light we can understand Paul's word, "And we all who mirror with unveiled face the glory of the Lord, are being transformed into the same image from glory to glory as it proceeds from the Spirit of the Lord" (2 Cor 3,18). We can now grasp in a new way the innermost mystery of the Church as the universal sacrament of salvation, although it remains a mystery and even increasingly becomes one the more we attempt to enter into the mystery of God himself with our earthly thinking and meditating and the more God's grace makes us able to enter. Paul provides thus the conclusion: "Now to him who by the power at work within us is able to do far more abundantly than all that we ask or think, to him be glory in the Church and in Christ Jesus to all generations, for ever and ever. Amen" (Eph 3,20).

Notes

PREFACE TO THIS VOLUME

1. Cf. W. Pinder, *Das Problem der Generationen in der Kunstgeschichte Europas* (Munich, 1961).

2. Cf. R. W. Meyer, ed., *Das Problem des Fortschrittes—heute* (Darmstadt, 1969); R. Dubos, *Der entfesselte Fortschritt* (Bergisch Gladbach, 1970).

3. Cf. the report of the World Council of Churches: *Die Kirche als Faktor einer kommenden Weltgemeinschaft* (Stuttgart, 1966).

4. H. Küng, *Die Kirche* (Freiburg im Breisgau, 1967); ET: *The Church* (New York, 1968).

5. M. Schmaus, *Der Glaube der Kirche* 2 (Munich, 1970); ET: *Dogma* 4: *The Church* (Kansas City, 1972).

6. MS IV/1 (1972).

AN INTRODUCTION TO THE WORK OF JOHANN AUER

1. H. Rossmann and J. Ratzinger, eds., *Mysterium der Gnade. Festschrift für Johann Auer zum 65. Geburtstag* (Regensburg, 1975), p. 7.

2. For a brief biographical outline, see ibid. pp. 7–8.

3. *Die menschliche Willensfreiheit im Lehrsystem des Thomas von Aquin und Johannes Duns Scotus* (Munich, 1938).

4. Ibid. pp. 300–303.

5. *Die Entwicklung der Gnadenlehre in der Hochscholastik mit besonderer Berücksichtigung des Kardinals Matteo d'Acquasparta* (Freiburg im Breisgau, 1942; 1951).

6. Ibid. pp. 24–29.

7. Ibid. pp. 250–55.

8. Ibid. pp. 1–2.

9. H. Rossmann, "Das Schriftum von Professor DDr. Johann Auer," in *Mysterium der Gnade*, pp. 442–50.

PART ONE: PATHWAYS TOWARDS THE PROPER
UNDERSTANDING OF THE CHURCH

1. V. Rüfner, Psychologie (Paderborn, 1969), chap. 12.
2. LThK 5, cols. 84–92, with bibliography.
3. Epistolae X. 24.
4. E. Przywara, Gesammelte Schriften, Vol. III (Einsiedeln,
1962); W. Struve, Philosophie und Transzendenz (Freiburg im
Breisgau, 1969); J. Salaquarda, ed., Philosophische Theologie im
Schatten des Nihilismus (Berlin, 1971); E. Topitsch, Vom
Ursprung und Ende der Metaphysik (Vienna, 1958; Munich,
1972); J. Möller, Von Bewusstsein zu Sein (Mainz, 1962); K. Saur,
Transzendenz als Wirklichkeit, 2 vols. (Hamburg, 1965/1973).
5. Cf. D. von Hildebrand, Metaphysik der Gemeinschaft (Augsburg, 1930). K. Mannheim speaks in this connection of founding,
planning, and administering. Cf. K. Mannheim, Mensch und Gesellschaft im Zeitalter des Umbaus (Darmstadt, 1958). A. Weber
speaks of the spheres of society, civilization, and culture. Cf. A.
Weber, Einführung in die Soziologie (Munich, 1955).
6. Cf. M. Scheler, The Nature and Forms of Sympathy (London,
1954).
7. Cf. M. Buber, Ich und Du [Werke, Vol. I (Munich, 1962), pp.
77–170]; J. Lotz, Ich-Du-Wir (Frankfurt am Main, 1968); D. von
Hildebrand, Das Wesen der Liebe [Gesammelte Werke, Vol. III,
(Regensburg, 1971)].
8. D. von Hildebrand, Metaphysik der Gemeinschaft (Augsburg, 1930).
9. Cf. F.-X. Kaufmann, Kirche begreifen: Analysen und The-
men zur gesellschaftlichen Verfassung des Christentums (Freiburg im Breisgau, 1979); F. H. Tenbruck, Kritik der planenden
Vernunft (Freiburg im Breisgau, 1972).
10. O. Schreuder, Gestaltwandel der Kirche (Freiburg im
Breisgau, 1967); H. Hoefnagels, Kirche in der veränderten Welt
(Essen, 1964); K. Rahner, Strukturwandel der Kirche als Aufgabe
und Chance (Freiburg im Breisgau, 1972); ET: The Shape of the
Church to Come (London, 1974).
11. Cf. J. Lortz, Geschichte der Kirche in ideengeschichtlicher
Betrachtung, 2 vols., 21st ed. (Munich, 1962–1964).
12. Cf. K. Adam, Das Wesen des Katholizismus, 13th ed.
(Düsseldorf, 1957); A. Rademacher, Die Kirche als Gemeinschaft
und Gesellschaft (Augsburg, 1931); H. Petri, "Die Kirche als
Thema der Fundamentaltheologie," Theologie und Glaube 69
(1979), pp. 376–94.
13. Cf. M. Kaiser, Die Einheit der Kirchengewalt (Munich,
1956); J. Listl in GNKR.

14. DS 51.

15. Cf. H. de Lubac, *The Splendour of the Church* (London, 1956), pp. 13–25.

16. Cf. C. Eichenseer, *Das Symbolum Apostolicum beim hl. Augustinus* [*Kirchengeschichtliche Quellen und Studien* 4 (St. Ottilien, 1960)], pp. 357–77.

17. *De Baptismo* VI. 2, 11–14; cf. E. Benz, *Adam. Der Mythos vom Urmenschen* (Munich, 1955).

18. DS 60; *Apostolic Constitutions.*

19. DS 62–63; *Egyptian Church Order.*

20. Cf. Hippolytus and the liturgy of Aquileia until the fifth century.

21. Cf. Irenaeus, *Adversus Haereses* I. 2; ed. Harvey, I. 90ff.

22. *Baptismal Catecheses* 18, 26; PG 33, 1048–50.

23. Ibid. 18, 27.

24. Cf. *Sermo* 267, 3; 268, 2; PL 38, 1231ff.

25. DS 46: Athanasius.

26. Cf. *In Symbolum* 36; PL 21, 373A-B.

27. Cf. DS 150: *Missale Romanum;* Thomas Aquinas, *Summa Theol.* IIa. IIae., q. 1, a. 9, ad 5; *Catechismus Romanus* I. 10, 22.

28. LG 48.

29. R. Bultmann, in TWNT VI, p. 209.

30. DS 575.

31. DS 1351; D 714.

32. *Was ist Kirche?* (Freiburg im Breisgau, 1967), pp. 35ff.

33. Nos. 352–71.

34. See, G. Switek, S.J., "Discretio spirituum," *Theologie und Philosophie* 47 (1972), pp. 36–76; DSAM, Vol. III, cols. 1222–91; Peter Huizing and William Bassett, eds., *Experience of the Spirit* (New York, 1974, = *Concilium* 99).

35. Cf. *Bibel-Lexikon*, ed. H. Haag, 2d ed. (Einsiedeln, 1968), pp. 949–56; TWNT III, pp. 502–39.

36. Cf. Augustine, *Ep. ad Rom.* incoh. exp. I,2; PL 35, 2089, where he explains "*ecclesia ex vocatione, synagoga ex congregatione,*" and writes, "To be called together is more appropriate to human beings, to be gathered to sheep" ("*Convocari enim magis hominibus congruit, congregari autem magis pecoribus*"). Cf. TWNT III, pp. 533–35: *ekkalein* (*vocare*) means to "summon" and not to "call out."

37. Cf. Kluge-Mitzka, *Etymologisches Wörterbuch* (Berlin, 1967), p. 370.

38. Cf. F. van Teigt, *Die Geschichte der Patriarchen* (Mainz, 1963).

39. N. A. Dahl, *Das Volk Gottes*, 2d ed. (Darmstadt, 1963).

40. Cf. J. Scharbert, *Heilsmittler im Alten Testament und im alten Orient* (Freiburg im Breisgau, 1964).

41. Cf. M. Malmberg, *Ein Leib, ein Geist* (Freiburg im Breisgau, 1960), pp. 223–311.

42. Cf. J. Jeremias, *Die Gleichnisse Jesu*, 7th ed. (Göttingen, 1965).

43. Cf. E. Benz, *Adam. Der Mythos vom Urmenschen*, pp. 237–51.

44. Cf. H. U. von Balthasar, *Wer ist die Kirche?* (Freiburg im Breisgau, 1965), pp. 55–136; *Sponsa Christi* II (Einsiedeln, 1961).

45. Thomas Aquinas, *Summa Theol.* III, q. 62, a. 5, ad 1.

46. Cf. Pius XII, encyclical *Mystici Corporis*, June 29, 1943: AAS 35 (1943), p. 208.

47. Cf. Leo XIII, encyclical *Divinum Illud*, May 9, 1897: AAS 29 (1896–97), p. 650; Pius XII, encyclical *Mystici Corporis*, AAS 35 (1943), pp. 219–20; DS 3808; Augustine, *Serm.* 268.2: PL 38, 1232; John Chrysostom, *In Eph. Hom.*, 9,3: PG 62, 72; Didymus of Alexandria, *Trin.*, 2,1: PG 39, 449f.; and Thomas Aquinas, *In Col.*, 1,18, lect. 5 (Marietti ed., II, no. 46): "As one body is constituted by the unity of the soul, so the Church by the unity of the Spirit. . . ."

48. *Summa Theol.* III, q. 63, a. 1, ad 1.

49. *Glossa ord.:* PL 113, 844.

50. Cf. M. Luther, *Heidelberger Disputation*, theses 19–22; J. Ratzinger, *Das neue Volk Gottes. Entwürfe zur Ekklesiologie* (Düsseldorf, 1969), pp. 90–99.

51. M. D. Koster, *Ekklesiologie im Werden* (Paderborn, 1940).

52. Cf. Hugo Rahner, *Mysterium lunae* in *Symbole der Kirche. Die Ekklesiologie der Väter* (Salzburg, 1964).

53. Beginning with the reign of Boniface VIII. See, for example, *De potestate Papae* by Henry of Cremona and Angelus Nigri (ca. 1300); Herveus Natalia (1312); *De regimine principum* by Barthomolew of Lucca and Jacobus Capocci of Viterbo (1302); *De ecclesiastica potestate* by Aegidius of Rome (1302); Peter de Palude (1321); and Alexander of San Elpidio (1326).

54. See, for example, H. Riedlinger, *Die Makellosigkeit der Kirche in den lateinischen Hohenliedkommentaren des Mittelalters* (Münster, 1958); H. U. von Balthasar, "Die heilige Hure" in *Wer ist Kirche?* (Freiburg im Breisgau, 1965); W. Seiferth, *Synagoge und Kirche im Mittelalter* (München, 1964).

55. See, for example, M. Grabmann, *Die Lehre des heiligen Thomas von Aquin von der Kirche als Gottes Werk* (Regensburg, 1903); H. Beresheim, *Christus als das Haupt der Kirche nach dem heiligen Bonaventura* (Bonn, 1939); L. Ott, *Der Kirchenbegriff bei den Scholastikern, besonders bei Richard von Mediavilla, Fran-*

zisk. Studien 24 (1937), pp. 331–53; 26 (1939), pp. 38–64; 142–66; 296–312.

56. Cf. J. Betz, *Asz.* IV, 87–113.

57. Cf. the decree *Sacro sancta* of session V, April 6, 1415 and the decree *Frequens* of October 9, 1417. Cf. Basel, May 16, 1439: Mansi 29, 178f.

58. Cf. LG 25; R. Bäumer, *Die Entwicklung des Konziliarismus* (Darmstadt, 1976).

59. *De ecclesia militante*, chap. 2.

60. Cf. *Div. Com.* 32; cf. *Lexikon der Christlichen Ikonographie* (Freiburg im Breisgau, 1968) Vol. 1, pp. 562–78: Ecclesia und Synagoge; A. Mayer, *Das Bild der Kirche* (Regensburg, 1962).

61. *Symbolik* (1832).

62. Cf. M. D. Koster, *Ekklesiologie im Werden* (Paderborn, 1940).

PART TWO: PATHWAYS TOWARDS A THEOLOGICAL CONCEPT OF THE CHURCH

1. On the concept of structure, see H. Rombach, *Substanz, System, Struktur*, 2 vols. (Freiburg im Breisgau and Munich, 1965).

2. Cf. Jürgen Habermas, *Theorie und Praxis. Sozialphilosophische Studien* 4th ed. (Berlin, 1972); M. Riedel (ed.), *Rehabilitierung der praktischen Philosophie* (Freiburg im Breisgau, 1972).

3. Cf. "Laos," TWNT IV, pp. 32–57; Barnabas 13,2; cf. Mal 1,2.

4. Cf. Justin, *Dial.*, cap. 135ff., PG 6,788; Irenaeus, *Epideixis*, 93–95, TU 31,1 (1907) 48f.

5. Cf. Origen, PG 13,134; Athanasius, *Contr. Ar.* 4,29, PG 26,513; especially "ecclesia ab Abel" in Augustine, *In Ps. 118 Sermo* 29,9, PL 37,1589; cf. the article with the same title by Yves Congar in *Festschrift für Karl Adam* (Düsseldorf, 1952), p. 84ff.

6. Cf. Augustine, *In Ps.* 47,2, PL 36,533f.

7. Cf. Augustine, *Quattuor Evangelia* 1,2, cap. 40, PL 35,1355.

8. Cf. Thomas Aquinas, *Suppl.* III, q. 60, a. 1, ad 4.

9. Cf. H. E. Mayer, *Geschichte der Kreuzzüge* (Stuttgart, 1965); W. Eckert and E. L. Ehrlich, *Judenhass, Schuld der Christen?* (Essen, 1964).

10. Synod of Bern: H. Müller, *Bekenntnisschriften* (Leipzig, 1903), p. 46.

11. Cf. TWNT V, pp. 139–47.

12. Cf. "Mesitēs," TWNT IV, pp. 602–29.

13. Cf. J. Scharbert, *Heilsmittler im AT und im alten Orient* (Freiburg im Breisgau, 1964).

14. Augustine, *In Ps.* 127,1. Cf. the Encyclical *Mystici Corporis* of Pius XII, June 29, 1943; J. Bach, *Die Dogmengeschichte des Mittelalters vom christologischen Standpunkt . . . vom 8. bis 16. Jahrhundert*, 2 vols. (Vienna, 1847/1875); F. Malmberg, *Ein Leib—ein Geist, Das Mysterium der Kirche* (Freiburg im Breisgau, 1960); *Salmanticenses*, III, dist. 14, dub. 1, nr. 6–28; K. Binder, *Wesen und Eigenschaften der Kirche bei Kard. J. de Torquemada* (Innsbruck, 1955), pp. 151–95.

15. Second ed. (Athens, 1959), Book II, 5; pp. 316–22.

16. (Athens, 1956), pp. 259–92.

17. Cf. P. Plank, *Zur Entstehung und Entfaltung der eucharistischen Ekklesiologie Nikolaj Afanassieff* (Würzburg, 1980).

18. G. Gloege, *Reich Gottes und Kirche im NT* (Darmstadt, 1968), p. 260.

19. Cf. EC 11 (1953), pp. 660–62; NCE 8 (1962), pp. 188–95; H. Schlier, "Reich Gottes und Kirche nach dem NT," in *Das Ende der Zeit* (Freiburg im Breisgau, 1971), pp. 37–51.

20. Cf. Leonardo Boff, *Die Kirche als Sakrament im Horizont der Welterfahrung* (Paderborn, 1972), pp. 83–123; 206f., 237–330.

21. Cf. *Opera omnia*, ed. A. Houssaye, II (Paris, 1874), pp. 1180f.

22. Cf. N. Kabasilas, *Leben in Christus*, ed. V. Ivanka (Klosterneuburg, 1958), p. 19.

23. *Dogm. theol.*, vol. II (Paris, 1684), pp. 243, 250.

24. Goethe, *Dichtung und Wahrheit*, II, 7.

25. *Kath. Dogm.* III, p. 117.

26. *Von den Sakramenten*, vol. I, 5th ed. (Münster, 1844), pp. 12ff.

27. Cf. KKD VI, pp. 113–25.

28. O. Semmelroth, *Die Kirche als Ursakrament* (Frankfurt/Main, 1953); cf. the useful review by H. Zeller, *Zeitschrift für Katholische Theologie* 76 (1954), pp. 94–99.

29. De Lubac, *Betrachtungen*, 2nd ed. (Vienna, 1954), p. 145.

30. Cf. P. Teilhard de Chardin, *Der Mensch im Kosmos* IV, ch. 2, III: Omega as the center of all centers which is characterized by its own logic, by all-pervasive action, irreversibility, and transcendence.

31. Cf. KKD VI, pp. 37–45 and pp. 24–37.

32. MS IV/1 (1973), pp. 318ff.

33. Cf. AAS 35 (1943), p. 239.

34. H. Plessner, *Die Stufen des Organischen und der Mensch*, 2d ed. (Berlin, 1965); F. Hammer, *Die exzentrische Position des Menschen* (Bonn, 1957).

35. H. J. Schulz, "Eucharistie und Einheit der Kirche nach Basilius dem Grossen," in *Basilius, Heiliger der einen Kirche* (Munich, 1981); *Eucharistische Ekklesiologie: Regensburger ökumenisches Symposion* July 20–26, 1981 (Munich, 1982); P. Plank, *Zur Entstehung und Entfaltung der eucharistischen Ekklesiologie Nikolaj Afanassieff* (Würzburg, 1980).

36. E. Cassirer, *Wesen und Wirkung des Symbolbegriffs* (Darmstadt, 1969).

37. For the contrary position, cf. L. Boff, *Die Kirche als Sakrament,* pp. 147–81.

38. Cf. G. B. Winkler, "Kirchenkritik bei Bernhard von Clairvaux," *Theologische Praktische Quartalschrift* 126 (1978), pp. 326–35.

39. Cf. Luther, WA, VI, 277ff.; II, 85f.

40. Cf. J. Köstlin, *Luthers Theologie* (Darmstadt, 1968) I, pp. 396–400; II, pp. 256–90.

41. Cf. P. Wernle, *Der Glaube: Calvin* (Tübingen, 1919), pp. 49–67, 403ff.

42. Cf. P. Wernle, *Der Glaube: Zwingli* (Tübingen, 1919), pp. 193–201.

43. AAS 35 (1943), pp. 221ff.

44. AAS 42 (1950), p. 571.

45. According to Chrysostom, *Hom. 24 in Joh.,* catechumens still have nothing in common with the faithful.

46. *Sent.* IV, d.3, q.2, a.3, q.5, sol.

47. *De eccl. mil.,* cap. 2.

48. Cf. Mansi, 51,540f.

49. Cf. AAS 35 (1943), pp. 202f.

50. Cf. the commentary by Grillmeier in LThK Concil I, 194–200.

51. For this identification cf. the "creed" of Trent and Vatican I, DS 3001.

52. Cf. KKD VI, p. 56.

53. Cf. Ign. *Smyrn.* 8: unity of bishop and presbytery.

54. Cf. Chalcedon, can. 3 and 28; against this position, DS 306 and 351 (Decr. Gelasianum).

55. Cf. Marcus Eremita (d. 1430), *De his qui putant se ex operibus justificari* (On those who think they are justified through works), against the Messialians; PG 65, 929–65.

56. L. Hödl, *Zeitschrift für Katholische Theologie* 95 (1973), p. 7.

57. Cf. O. Casel, *"Mysteriengegenwart," Jahrbuch für Liturgiewissenschaft* 8 (1929), pp. 145–214; *Das Christliche Kultmysterium,* 4th ed. (Regensburg, 1960), pp. 196–236; cf. KKD VI (1970), pp. 61–70.

58. Funk, *Patres Apologetici* I, 200.
59. Cf. Hans Urs von Balthasar, *Geist und Feuer*, 2d ed. (1938), pp. 210f.
60. *Ancor.* 1; PG 42,834.
61. *In Ps. 90*, 2,1; PL 37,1159.
62. Cf. MS, IV/1, pp. 287–307 (W. Beinert).
63. Cf. RGG II, 2d ed. (1958), pp. 655–89.
64. R. Schnackenburg, LThK (1959), p. 1089.
65. G. Juenin, *Institutiones theologicae*, 3d ed. (Lugduni, 1704), pp. 473f.
66. Cf. de Lubac, *Betrachtung* (1954), pp. 47–58.
67. Gertrud von Le Fort, *Hymnen an die Kirche*, 5th ed. (Munich, 1948), p. 28.

PART THREE: MANIFESTATIONS OF THE CHURCH'S BEING, LIFE, AND ACTIVITY IN THE LIGHT OF ITS SACRAMENTAL STRUCTURE

1. Like Eve from the side of Adam: cf. Sebastian Tromp, *Gregorianum* 13 (1932), pp. 482–527.
2. A. Loisy, *L'évangile et l'église* (1902), p. 134.
3. A. Loisy, *Autour d'un petit livre*, p. 161.
4. Cf. A. Raffelt, *Wort und Wahrheit* (1972), pp. 193f.
5. Cf. A. Schweitzer, *Geschichte der Leben Jesu Forschung*, p. 254.
6. Cf. K. Weiss, *Exegetisches zur Irrtumslosigkeit und Eschatologie Jesu Christi* (Münster, 1916); W. Trilling, *Die Entstehung des Zwölferkreises*.
7. Irenaeus expressed this truth in the idea of the "recapitulation of the world's history"; cf. *Adv. haer.*, 3,21; E. Scharl, *Recapitulatio mundi* (Freiburg im Breisgau, 1941).
8. Cf. G. Feuerer, *Die Kirche im Kommen, Begegnung von Jetztzeit und Endzeit* (Freiburg im Breisgau, 1937).
9. *Zur Debatte* 3 (1972) No. 1/2.9f.; cf. J. Beumer, "Der Heilige Geist, 'Seele der Kirche,'" *Theologie und Glaube* 39 (1949), pp. 249–67; KKD V, pp. 108–15; H. Berkhof, *Theologie des Heiligen Geistes* (Neunkirchen, 1968).
10. Cf. TWNT I, pp. 403ff.
11. M. Philipon, "Die heiligste Dreifaltigkeit und die Kirche," in Baraúna, *Eccl.* I, pp. 252–75.
12. TWNT I, pp. 404.
13. Cf. C. J. Friedrich, *Die Philosophie des Rechts in historischer Perspektive* (Berlin, 1955).
14. First presented at the synod of bishops in Rome, Fall 1971.

15. Cf. *Kein Grundsatz der Kirche ohne Zustimmung der Christen* (Mainz, 1971).

16. Cf. *Herder Korrespondenz* (1978), pp. 623–32.

17. Cf. the Aristotelian distinction between *schēma, taxis,* and *thesis,* Bekker edition, 188a 23f.; 1278b 8ff.

18. Cf. *Strukturen der Kirche* (Freiburg im Breisgau, 1972), pp. 244–62; attenuated through a comparison with Vatican I, cf. p. 284.

19. Cf. H. Jedin, *Bischöfliches Konzil oder Kirchenparlament?* (Stuttgart, 1963), pp. 37f.

20. Cf. LThK 10 (1965), p. 462: M.-D. Chenu.

21. Cf. H. Jedin, LThK 6 (1961), pp. 532–34; R. Bäumer, ed., *Die Entwicklung des Konziliarismus* (Darmstadt, 1976).

22. Cf. E. V. Ivanka, LThK 9 (1964), pp. 841f.; J. Ratzinger, *Das neue Volk Gottes,* pp. 147–70.

23. Cf. LThK 6 (1961), pp. 476f.

24. Cf. Y. Congar, "Die Rezeption als ekklesiologische Realität," *Concilium* 8 (1972), pp. 500–14, with bibliography.

25. Directives for applying the decree are contained in the Motu proprio *"Ecclesiae sanctae"* of August 6, 1966.

26. Cf. J. Neumann, "Strukturprobleme der nachkonziliaren Kirche," *Stimmen der Zeit* 89 (1973), pp. 185–201.

27. Cf. W. Bayerlein, "Die Arbeit der Laienräte," *Internationale Katholische Zeitschrift* 8 (1979), pp. 129–41; cf. GNKR, pp. 333–37.

28. Cf. C. J. Hefele, J. Card. Hergenröther, *Conciliengeschichte,* 9 vols., 2d ed. (Freiburg im Breisgau, 1873–1890), vol. II, p. 748.

29. Cf. Richard of St. Victor, PL 196,340.

30. M. Kaiser, "Hierarchie nach dem Verständnis des CIC und des 2. Vatikanischen Konzils," in *Jus et Salus Animarum: Festschrift Panzram* (Freiburg im Breisgau, 1969), p. 119.

31. *Sent.* II, 9, praenot. 3; Ed. min., 235.

32. Ibid. a. un., q. 1, c; Ed. min., 241.

33. *Cat. had.* V (1962), pp. 715–21.

34. Cf. Kl. Mörsdorf, S. U., II, p. 6.

35. Cf. KKD VII, pp. 317–21.

36. Cf. KKD VII, pp. 56–61.

37. Cf. M. Kehl, *Die Kirche als Institution* (Frankfurt/Main, 1976).

38. Cf. *Politics,* III,7; IV,2; 1279ab.

39. Cf. W. Beinert, *Gottesherrshaft—Weltherrschaft* (Regensburg, 1980), pp. 53–66.

40. Cf. Y. Congar, "Die historische Entwicklung der Autorität

in der Kirche," in J. M. Todd, ed., *Probleme der Autorität* (Düsseldorf, 1967), pp. 145–85.

41. Cf. H. Peters in *Staatslexikon, Recht—Wirtschaft—Gesellschaft*, 6th ed., vol. II (Freiburg im Breisgau, 1958), pp. 560–94.

42. Cf. J. Ratzinger, "Fraternité," DSAM V (1964), cols. 1141–67.

43. Cf. "Reform in der Kirche," *Concilium* 8 (1972) fasc. 3; "Wahl, Consens und Rezeption in der Kirche," *Concilium* 8 (1972) fasc. 8/9.

44. Cf. J. Baumgartner, ed., *Wiederentdeckung der Volksreligiosität* (Regensburg, 1979); A. Exeler and N. Mette, *Theologie des Volkes* (1979).

45. Y. Congar, "Reception as an Ecclesiological Reality," in Giuseppe Alberigo and Anton Weiler, eds., *Election and Consensus in the Church* (New York, 1972, = *Concilium* 77), pp. 43–68.

46. Cf. Nell-Breuning, *Einzelmensch und Gesellschaft* (Heidelberg, 1950) and *Wie sozial ist die Kirche?* (Munich, 1972).

47. Cf. *Die Zukunft des Menschen* (Freiburg im Breisgau, 1973), pp. 313–20.

48. Cf. G. May, *Demokratisierung der Kirche* (Vienna, 1971).

49. Cf. *Um die Erklärung der Menschenrechte. Ein Symposium. Mit einer Einführung von Jacques Maritain.* Europa V (1951); A. Bogan Andrej, *La communità internazionale o la libertà religiosa. Il problema della discriminazione religiosa nei documenti delle nazione unite* (Rome, 1965); "Kirche und Menschenrechte," *Concilium* 15 (1979) fasc. 4.

50. Cf. Horst Hermann, *Ein unmoralisches Verhältnis. Bemerkungen eines Betroffenen zur Lage von Staat und Kirche in der BRD* (Düsseldorf, 1974); H. Hermann, *Die sieben Todsünden der Kirche* (Munich, 1976); K. Deschner, *Die Kirche des Unheils* (Münster, 1979).

51. Cf. K. Röttgers, "Autorität," HWPh I (1971), pp. 724–32.

52. Cf. K. Nusser, "Gehorsam," HWPh I (1971), pp. 146–54.

53. Cf. J. Daniélou and H. Vorgrimler, eds., *Sentire Ecclesiam* (Freiburg im Breisgau, 1969).

54. Cf. *Ubi arcano*, December 23, 1922.

55. On the universal priesthood of the laity, M. Keller, *Kath. Aktion* (Paderborn, 1935); J. Will, S.J., *Handbuch der Katholischen Aktion* (Freiburg im Breisgau, 1934).

56. Cf. K. Rahner, "Der Einzelne in der Kirche," *Stimmen der Zeit* 72 (1947), pp. 260–76.

57. A. Von Harnack, *Entstehung und Entwicklung der*

Kirchenverfassung des Kirchenrechts in den zwei ersten Jahrhun-
derten (Leipzig, 1910).

58. Cf. K. Kertelge, ed., *Das kirchliche Amt im Neuen Testa-*
ment (Darmstadt, 1977).

59. Cf. G. Backes, "Frühkatholizismus," *Osservatore Romano,*
German edition, 1979, 2, pp. 8ff., with bibliography.

60. Cf. TWNT II, pp. 81–88.

61. J. P. Michael, LThK 1, p. 455.

62. J. Brosch, LThK 1 (1957), p. 457.

63. Cf. LThK 6 (1961), pp. 74–77.

64. L. Hödl, *Wahrheit und Verkündigung* (Munich, 1967), pp.
1785–1806.

65. Cf. M.-D. Chenu, "Die Laien und die 'consecratio mundi',"
in: Baraúna, *Eccl.,* II, pp. 289–307.

66. Cf. W. Trilling, "Die Entstehung des Zwölferkreises," in
Die Kirche des Anfangs (Freiburg im Breisgau, 1978), pp. 201–22.

67. A. Javiere, in Hans Küng, ed., *Apostolic Succession* (New
York 1968, = *Concilium* 34), pp. 16–27.

68. Cf. W. Seibel, L. A. Dorn, *Tagebuch des Konzils,* 2. Sessio,
pp. 22–177.

69. Cf. S. Lyonnet in Baraúna, *Eccl.,* II, pp. 106–24.

70. Cf. J. Hajjar in Baraúna, *Eccl.,* II, pp. 125–47.

71. Cf. J. Ratzinger in Baraúna, *Eccl.,* II, pp. 61–68.

72. Cf. Kl. Mörsdorf, LThK 2 (1958), pp. 501–05.

73. Cf. R. Kottje, "The Selection of Church Officials: Some
Historical Facts and Experiences," in A. Müller, ed., *Democratiz-*
ation of the Church (New York 1971 = *Concilium* 63), pp. 117–
26; *Concilium* 7 (1971) fasc. 3; LThK 2 (1958), pp. 501–05.

74. Cf. A. Lang, *Fundamentaltheologie* II, 4th ed. (Munich,
1968), pp. 91–95.

75. O. Cullmann, TWNT VI (1959), pp. 94–112); *Pietro nella*
Scrittura (Florence, 1975).

76. Cf. R. E. Brown, K. P. Donfried, and J. Reumann, eds., *Der*
Petrus der Bibel. Eine ökumenische Untersuchung (Stuttgart,
1976).

77. Cf. A. Lang, *Fundamentaltheologie* II, 4th ed. (Munich,
1968), pp. 133–40.

78. Cullmann, p. 82.

79. Cf. E. Kirschbaum, *Die Gräber der Apostelfürsten*
(Frankfurt/Main, 1959).

80. Cf. M. Garducci, *Hier ist Petrus* (Regensburg, 1967).

81. Cf. O. Cullmann, pp. 177–263; K. H. Schelke, *Theologie des*
Neuen Testaments IV/2, pp. 96–103.

82. Cf. L. Baeck, *Aus drei Jahrtausenden* (Tübingen 1958), pp.

199–202; cf. Cullmann, pp. 209, 238–63; J. Jeremias, TWNT III, p. 749.

83. Cf. J. Jeremias, *Die Sprache des Lukasevangeliums* (Göttingen, 1980), p. 291.

84. Cf. J. Schmid, RNT 3 (1940), p. 237.

85. Cf. A. Lang, *Fundamentaltheologie* II (Munich, 1958), pp. 57–84 with bibliography.

86. Cf. *Conc. Oecum. Decreta* (Freiburg im Breisgau), 76.

87. Cf. Ph. Schmitz, *Geschichte des Benediktinerordens* III (Einsiedeln, 1955).

88. Cf. R. Bäumer, ed., *Die Entwicklung des Konziliarismus* (Darmstadt, 1976).

89. Cf. *Trid.* ses. XXV, c 21 de ref.; KlP 4 (1972), cols. 1046–48]; LThK 8 (1963), p. 613.

90. Cf. C. 2,4 X de transl. I,7 C 3 in VI de elect. I 6; cf. also M. Maccarone, *Vicarius Christi. Storia del titulo papale* (Rome, 1952); K. J. Kuschel, *Stellvertreter Christi? Der Papst in der zeitgenössischen Literatur* (Zürich, 1980).

91. Cf. LThK 9 (1964), pp. 695f.; H. Grisar, *Zeitschrift für Katholische Theologie* 4 (1880), pp. 468ff.

92. Cf. Lietzmann, *Geschichte der alten Kirche* III (1953), p. 335.

93. Cf. O. Betz, "Felsenmann und Felsengemeinde," *Zeitschrift für Neutestamentliche Wissenschaft* 18 (1957), pp. 49–77.

94. J. Schmid, *Das Evangelium nach Matthäus* (Regensburg, 1948), p. 177. Cf. Chrysostom, *In Matth Com.* 54,2; Ambrose, *In Luc* 9, 18–22, no. 93.

95. Cf. J. Specht, *Die Lehre der Kirche nach dem heiligen Augustinus* (Paderborn, 1892), pp. 129ff, 143ff; J. Lessel, "Christuspetra, Petrus-petra" *Verbum Domini* 24 (1944), pp. 15–24; 55–61; R. Graber, *Petrus der Fels* (Ettal, 1949); J. Betz, "Christus-Petra-Petrus," in *Kirche und Überlieferung* (Freiburg im Breisgau, 1960), pp. 1–21; A. Rimoldi, *L'apostolo San Pietro* (Rome, 1958).

96. Cf. K. Adam, "Zum ausserkanonischen und kanonischen Sprachgebrauch von Binden und Lösen," *Tübinger Theologische Quartalschrift* 96 (1914), pp. 49–64; 161–97; reprinted in *Gesammelte Aufsätze* (Augsburg, 1936), pp. 17–52.

97. Adam, *Gesammelte Aufsätze.*

98. Ibid. p. 49.

99. Ibid.

100. Ibid. p. 50.

101. Cf. I. *Der Primat des Petrus in der orthodoxen Kirche,* N. Afanassieff and N. Koulomzine (Paris); J. Meyendorff and J. Schmemann, New York (Zürich, 1961); II. *Papstum als*

ökumenische Frage, ed. Arbeitsgemeinschaft ökumenischer Universitätsinstitute (Munich and Mainz, 1979).

102. Cf. "Die kirchliche Disziplin," *Concilium* (1975) fasc. 8–9.

103. Cf. J. Listl, GNKR, par. 25, pp. 204–09.

104. Cf. Kl. Mörsdorf, "Heilige Gewalt," in *Sacramentum Mundi* II, pp. 582–697; M. Kaiser, "Aussagen des II. Vat. Konzils über die Kirchengewalt, in Audomar Scheuermann, ed., *Jus Sacrum: Klaus Mörsdorf zum 60. Geburtstag* (Munich, 1969), pp. 240–45.

105. Wetzer-Welte, *Kirchenlexikon* 12 (1901), pp. 240–45.

106. Cf. A. Lang, *Die Loci theologici des M. C. und die Methode des dogmatischen Beweises* (Munich, 1925).

107. Cf. the proposition of 1544; A. Lenz in *Gregorianum* 23 (1942), pp. 348–74.

108. M. Schmaus, J. R. Geiselmann, A. Grillmeier, and S. Scheffczyk, eds., *Handbuch der Dogmengeschichte* (Freiburg im Breisgau, 1955ff.), vol. III, 3d, p. 65.

109. Flacius Illyricus, Basel 1559–74, 8 vols.

110. Ingolstadt 1586–93: *Contr. III lib. IV de potestate spirituali Summi Pontificis.*

111. Similar formulations are found in the work of Walter Kasper, who likewise stresses the historicity of truth.

112. *Unfehlbar?*, pp. 162f.

113. Cf. J. Beumer, "Die Kollegiale Gewalt der Bischöfe für die Gesamtkirche nach der Theologie des 18. Jahrhunderts," *Gregorianum* 45 (1964), pp. 280–315.

114. *Vatican Council II*, ed. A. Flannery, pp. 424–26; for a commentary on this passage by J. Ratzinger cf. LThK II. Vat. Vol. I (1966), pp. 348–54.

115. Cf. W. Schätzel, *Der Staat* (Birsfeld-Basel, n. d.).

116. Cf. G. Bornkamm, TWNT (1959), pp. 651–83.

117. *Const. eccl. Aegypt.* I and II, Funk II,98 and 102ff.

118. Funk I,577.

119. Cf. J. Listl, GNKR, pp. 299–302.

120. Cf. F. Klostermann, *Das christliche Apostolat* (Vienna, 1962).

121. Cf. *Diaconia in Christo*, pp. 57–91.

122. Cf. *Diaconia in Christo*, pp. 31–56.

123. Cf. A. Kalsbach, *Die altkirchliche Einrichtung der Diakonissen* (Freiburg im Breisgau, 1926); LThK 3 (1959), pp. 327f.

124. Cf. LThK 1 (1957), pp. 824f.

125. Cf. H. J. Weber, "Zur theologischen Ortsbestimmung des Diakonats im einen Weihesakrament," in *Der Diakon* (1980), pp. 104–21.

126. B. Durst, *Dreifaches Priestertum* (Neresheim, 1946).
127. Cf. GS 36; F. Gogarten, *Verhängnis und Hoffnung der Neuzeit* (Munich, 1958); *Catholic* 12 (1958), pp. 67–75.
128. Cf. H. Lietzmann, *Symbolstudien I-XIV* (Darmstadt, 1966); J. N. D. Kelly, *Early Christian Creeds* (London, 1950); H. Riley, *Christian Initiation* (Washington, 1974).

PART FOUR: THE CHURCH'S TASKS AND ITS WAYS
TO SELF-REALIZATION IN THE WORLD

1. P. Wernle, *Der evangelische Glaube nach den Schriften der Reformatoren*, 3 vols. (Tübingen, 1918–1921).
2. *Controv.* II lib 3: *De ecclesia militante;* lib 4: *De notis ecclesiae*, where he lists 15 marks.
3. J. Hainz, *Koinonia. "Kirche" als Gemeinschaft bei Paulus* (Regensburg, 1982).
4. Cf. E. Stauffer, *"Agōn,"* TWNT I, pp. 134–41; G. Schrenk, *"Biazomai,"* TWNT I, pp. 608–13.
5. *Grundriss des nk. Kirchenrechtes* (Regensburg, 1980), pp. 433–35; *Gemeinsame Synode der BRD* (1976), pp. 807–46 with bibliography.
6. *Herder Korrespondenz* 33 (1979), pp. 416–21; *Theologie im Kontext: Zeitschriftenschau seit Januar 1980* (Missionswissenschaftliches Institut Missio, Aachen).
7. Cf. A. Lang, *Fundamentaltheologie* II (Munich, 1958), pp. 214–21 with bibliography; U. Mann, *Das Christentum als absolute Religion* (Darmstadt, 1970); W. Kasper, ed., *Absolutheit des Christentums* (Freiburg im Breisgau, 1977).
8. TWNT IV, pp. 445, 450, 465.
9. TWNT IV, p. 444; Mark 2,18ff.
10. Cf. MS 4/1 (1972), pp. 411–57.
11. H. Schlier, TWNT I, pp. 181f.
12. J. A. Möhler, *Die Einheit der Kirche oder das Prinzip des Katholizismus im Geiste der Kirchenväter der ersten drei Jahrhunderte* (Tübingen, 1925).
13. HWPh 1 (1971), pp. 620–35; N. Hinske, ed., *Was ist Aufklärung: Beiträge aus der Berlinischen Monatsschrift* (Darmstadt, 1973).
14. On the further development in Talmud and Midrash, cf. L. Strack, *Einleitung in Talmud und Midrasch*, 6th ed. (Munich, 1976); H. H. Ben Sasson, *Geschichte des jüdischen Volkes*, 3 vols. (Munich, 1978–1980).
15. F. Mussner, *Traktat über die Juden* (Munich, 1979), pp. 59f.
16. Cf. Ch. Konstantinidis and E. Ch. Suttner, *Fragen der*

Sakramentenpastoral in orthodox-katholisch gemischten Gemeinden. Eine Handreichung für die Seelsorge (Regensburg, 1979).

17. Cf. RGG 5 (1961), pp. 370–83.

18. Augustin Cardinal Bea, *Einheit in Freiheit* (Stuttgart, 1964), p. 207; ET: *Unity in Freedom* (New York, 1964).

19. Cf. O. Saier, *Communio in der Lehre des II. Vat. Konzils* (Munich, 1973); P. C. Bari, *Koinonia: L'idea della Communione nel ecclesiologia recente e nel NT* (Brescia, 1972); J. Hainz, *Koinonia: "Kirche" als Gemeinschaft bei Paulus* (Regensburg, 1982).

20. Cf. R. Frieling, *Ökumene in Deutschland* (Göttingen, 1970); H. Meyer, H. J. Urban, L. Fischer, eds., *Dokumente wachsender Zusammenarbeit* (Paderborn, 1982).

21. Cf. H. W. Gensichen, "Die Kirche von Südindien," *Weltmission heute: ein Studienheft* (Stuttgart, 1957).

22. Cf. P. W. Scheele, *Nairobi, Genf und Rom* (Paderborn, 1976).

23. Cf. M. Seckler, O. H. Pesch, J. Brosseder, and W. Pannenberg, eds., *Begegnung. Beiträge zu einer Hermeneutik des theologischen Gespräches* (Graz, 1972); W. Beinert, "Theologie und christliche Existenz," in *Catholica* 30 (1976), pp. 94–110; bibliography in note 3.

24. J. Panagopoulos, "Eucharistische Existenz in dem einem Leib des Herrn," in *Die Einheit der Kirche* (Wiesbaden, 1977), pp. 2–15; here p. 10.

25. Cf. HWPhil 3 (1979), pp. 3–12.

26. Cf. J. D. Labrunie, "Les principes de la catholicité d'après S. Thomas," *Revue des Sciences Philosophiques et Théologiques* 17 (1928), pp. 633–58; J. Lang, "Strukturen und Anliegen des Kirchenverständnisses bei S. Bonaventura," in *S. Bonaventura 1274–1974*, vol. 4 (Assisi, 1974), pp. 387–420.

27. Cf. J. Daniélou, *Platonisme et théologie mystique* (Paris, 1944); J. Daniélou, *Méssage évangelique et culture héllénique* (Paris, 1961); ET: *Gospel Message and Hellenistic Culture* (Philadelphia, 1973); M. Spanneut, *Le Stoicisme des Pères de l'Eglise* (Paris, 1957); R. Arnou, "Platonisme des Pères," DThC 12, cols. 2294–2392; "Salut des Infideles," DThC 7 (1922) cols. 1726–1930.

28. Cf. Bert van der Heijden, *Karl Rahner, Darstellung und Kritik seiner Grundpositionen* (Einsiedeln, 1973), pp. 252–96, esp. pp. 254–59; Fritz Rendtdorff, *Christentum ausserhalb der Kirche. Konkretionen der Aufklärung* (Hamburg, 1968); E. Klinger, ed., *Christentum innerhalb und ausserhalb der Kirche* (Freiburg im Breisgau, 1976) with 16 articles.

29. Cf. J. Sasse, "Aiōn," TWNT I, pp. 197–207; J. Sasse, "Kosmos," TWNT III, pp. 867, 879, 896.

30. Cf. LThK 10 (1965), pp. 1429f.

31. Cf. Kl. Mörsdorf, "Konkordat," LThK 6 (1961), pp. 454–59.

32. Cf. H. J. Vogt, *Coetus Sanctorum: Der Kirchenbegriff Novatians und die Geschichte seiner Kirche* (Bonn, 1966), p. 74.

33. Cf. C. J. Hefele and J. Card. Hergenröther, *Conciliengeschichte* Vol. II (Freiburg im Breisgau, 1875), p. 62.

34. Cf. J. N. C. Kelly, *Early Christian Creeds*, 2d ed. (London, 1952), pp. 388–97.

35. Cf. N. Wokart, HWPh 3 (1974), pp. 1034–37.

36. Cf. J. Hauck, "*Hagnos*," TWNT I, pp. 123f.

37. TWNT I (1948), p. 106.

38. H. Schlier, *Der Brief an die Epheser* (Düsseldorf, 1957), p. 145.

39. Cf. R. Michl, RAC, vol. 5 (1962), pp. 114f.

40. Cf. Ch. Journet, *Théologie de l'église* (Paris, 1958), p. 236.

41. Cf. Hans Urs von Balthasar, *Origenes: Geist und Feuer*, 2d ed. (Salzburg, 1938), pp. 221–39.

42. Cf. Hans Urs von Balthasar, *Wer ist die Kirche?* (Freiburg im Breisgau, 1965), pp. 55–136.

43. Cf. W. Härle and E. Herms, *Rechtfertigung: Das Wirklichkeitsverständnis des christlichen Glaubens* (Göttingen 1980); R. Grimm and J. Hermand, eds., *Realismustheorien in Literatur, Malerei, Musik und Politik* (Stuttgart, 1975).

44. Cf. M. Meinertz, TWNT I, pp. 27–146; J. Jeremias, *Neutestamentliche Theologie*, Vol. 1 (Gütersloh 1971), pp. 40–44; 51–123.

EPILOGUE

1. Cf. M. Theobald, *Die überströmende Gnade* (Würzburg, 1981).

Select Bibliography

Prepared for the English translation by Michael A. Fahey, S.J.

BIBLIOGRAPHICAL RESOURCES

Dulles, Avery, and Patrick Granfield. *The Church: A Bibliography*. Wilmington, DE, 1985.

REFERENCE WORKS

Carlen, Claudia, ed. *The Papal Encyclicals.* 5 vols. Wilmington, NC, 1981.
Solesmes, Monks of. *Papal Teachings: The Church.* Boston, 1962.
Tanner, Norman P., ed. *Decrees of the Ecumenical Church.* 2 vols. Washington and London, 1990.

GENERAL WORKS

Adam, Karl. *The Spirit of Catholicism.* New York, 1929.
Bouyer, Louis. *The Church of God: The Body of Christ and Temple of the Holy Spirit.* Especially 3–155. Chicago, 1982.
Butler, B. C. *The Idea of the Church.* Baltimore, 1962.
Döpfner, Julius Cardinal. *The Questioning Church.* Montreal, 1964.
Dulles, Avery. *A Church to Believe In.* New York, 1982.
Dulles, Avery. *Models of the Church.* New York, 1974.
Duquoc, Christian. *Provisional Churches: An Essay in Ecumenical Ecclesiology.* London, 1986.
Fiorenza, Francis Shüssler, and John Galvin, eds. *Dogmatic Theology: A Roman Catholic Perspective.* 2 vols. Especially chapter on Church by Michael A. Fahey. Minneapolis, 1991.
Gratsch, Edward J. *Where Peter Is: A Survey of Ecclesiology.* Staten Island, NY, 1975.
Jay, Eric G. *The Church: Its Changing Image through Twenty Centuries.* Atlanta, 1980.
Journet, Charles. *The Church of the Incarnate World.* New York, 1955.

Kasper, Walter. *Theology and Church.* New York, 1989.

König, Franz Cardinal. *Where is the Church Heading?* Interview with G. Licheri. Slough, UK, 1986.

Lubac, Henri de. *The Splendour of the Church.* New York, 1956.

Maritain, Jacques. *On the Church of Christ.* Notre Dame, 1973.

Moltmann, Jürgen. *The Church in the Power of the Spirit: A Contribution to Messianic Ecclesiology.* London, 1977.

Pannenberg, Wolfhart. *The Church.* Philadelphia, 1968.

Paul VI. *Ecclesiam Suam.* In *The Papal Encyclicals 1958–1981,* English translation, edited by Claudia Carlen, 135–60. Wilmington, NC, 1981.

Pius XII. *Mystici Corporis.* In *The Papal Encyclicals 1939–1958,* English translation, edited by Claudia Carlen, 35–63. Wilmington, NC, 1981.

Provost, James H., ed. *The Church as Communion.* Washington, 1976; 1984.

Ratzinger, Joseph, and Karl Lehmann. *Living with the Church.* Chicago, 1978.

Schmaus, Michael. *Dogma 4: The Church.* Kansas City, 1972; 1976.

Sullivan, Francis. *The Church We Believe In: One, Holy, Catholic and Apostolic.* New York, 1988.

VATICAN II AND ITS IMPACT

English Translations:

Abbott, Walter M., and Joseph Gallagher, eds. *The Documents of Vatican II.* New York, 1966.

Flannery, Austin, ed. *Vatican Council II: The Conciliar and Postconciliar Documents.* Northport, NY, 1982.

Flannery, Austin, ed. *Vatican Council II: More Postconciliar Documents.* Northport, NY, 1982.

Commentaries

Alberigo, Giuseppe, Jean-Pierre Jossua, and Joseph A. Komonchak, eds. *The Reception of Vatican II.* Washington, 1987.

Congar, Yves, Hans Küng, and Daniel O'Hanlon, eds. *Council Speeches of Vatican II.* London, 1968.

Hastings, Adrian, ed. *Modern Catholicism: Vatican II and After.* New York, and London, 1991.

Kloppenburg, Bonaventure. *The Ecclesiology of Vatican II.* Chicago, 1970.

Latourelle, René, ed. *Vatican II: Assessment and Perspectives,*

Twenty-Five Years After (*1962–1987*). 3 vols. New York, 1988–1989.

Miller, John H., ed. *Vatican II: An Interfaith Appraisal.* Notre Dame, 1966.

Ratzinger, Joseph. *Theological Highlights of Vatican II.* New York, 1966.

Ratzinger, Joseph. "The Ecclesiology of the Second Vatican Council." In his *Church, Ecumenism and Politics: New Essays in Ecclesiology,* 3–28. New York, and Middlegreen, UK, 1988.

Vorgrimler, Herbert, ed. *Commentary on the Documents of Vatican II.* 5 vols. Especially 1:105–305 on Lumen Gentium. New York, 1967.

PART ONE: PATHWAYS TOWARDS THE PROPER UNDERSTANDING OF THE CHURCH

I. Individual Approaches towards Understanding the Church

1. Challenges to the Church

Berger, Peter L. *The Heretical Imperative: Contemporary Possibilities of Religious Affirmation.* Garden City, NY, 1979.

Gannon, Thomas. *World Catholicism in Transition.* New York, 1988.

Küng, Hans. *Structures of the Church.* New York, 1964.

Küng, Hans. *The Church.* New York, 1968.

Küng, Hans. *On Being a Christian.* Garden City, NY, 1976.

Legaut, Marcel. *True Humanity.* New York, 1982.

Staniloe, Dumitru. *Theology and the Church.* Crestwood, NY, 1984.

2. Ecclesiology and Sociology

Baum, Gregory. "The Impact of Sociology on Catholic Theology." *Catholic Theological Society of America Proceedings* 30 (1975):1–29.

Baum, Gregory. "Sociology and Salvation: Do We Need a Catholic Sociology?" *Theological Studies* 50 (1989):718–43.

Berger, Peter L. *A Rumor of Angels.* Garden City, NY, 1970.

Berger, Peter L. *The Sacred Canopy: Elements of a Sociological Theory of Religion.* Garden City, NY, 1967.

Fichter, Joseph. *Organization Man in the Church.* Cambridge, MA, 1964.

Greeley, Andrew M. "Sociology and Church Structure." In *Struc-*

tures of the Christian Church, edited by Jimenez Teodoro Urresti. New York, 1970. (= *Concilium* 58:26–35.)

Komonchak, Joseph. "Ecclesiology and Social Theory: A Methodological Essay." *The Thomist* 45 (1981):262–83.

O'Day, Thomas G. *Sociology and the Study of Religion.* New York, 1970.

Troeltsch, Ernest. *The Social Teaching of the Christian Churches.* 2 vols. New York, 1930.

Weber, Max. *From Max Weber: Essays in Sociology,* ed. Hans H. Gerth and C. W. Mills. New York, 1946.

Winter, Gibson. *The Suburban Captivity of the Churches.* New York, 1961.

II. Foundations for Understanding the Church in the Revelation of the Old and New Testaments

Banks, Robert J. *Paul's Idea of Community.* Grand Rapids, 1980.

Brown, Raymond E. *The Churches the Apostles Left Behind.* New York, 1984.

Brown, Raymond E. *The Community of the Beloved Disciple.* New York, 1979.

Brown, Raymond E., and John P. Meier. *Antioch and Rome: New Testament Cradles of Catholic Christianity.* New York, 1983.

Cerfaux, Lucien. *The Church in the Theology of St. Paul.* New York, 1959.

Congar, Yves. *The Mystery of the Church.* Baltimore, 1960.

Cwiekowski, Frederick J. *The Beginnings of the Church.* New York, 1988.

Dunn, James D. G. *Unity and Diversity in the New Testament: An Inquiry into the Character of Earliest Christianity.* Philadelphia, 1977.

Fiorenza, Francis Schüssler. *Foundational Theology: Jesus and the Church.* Especially chapters 3–6. New York, 1984.

Gager, John G. *Kingdom and Community: The Social World of Early Christianity.* Englewood Cliffs, NJ, 1975.

Holmberg, Bengt. *Paul and Power: The Structure of Authority and Power in the Primitive Church as Reflected in the Pauline Epistles.* Philadelphia, 1980.

Malherbe, Abraham. *Social Aspects of Early Christianity.* Baton Rouge, 1977.

McKelvey, R. J. *The New Temple: The Church in the New Testament.* London, 1969.

Meeks, Wayne A. *The First Urban Christians.* New Haven, 1983.

Meeks, Wayne A. *The Moral World of the First Christians.* Philadelphia, 1986.

Minear, Paul S. *Images of the Church in the New Testament.*
    Philadelphia, 1960.
Schmidt, Karl L. *"kaleo/ekklesia* (to call, church)." In *Theological
    Dictionary of the New Testament* [TDNT], translated and
    edited by G. W. Bromily, 3:487–536. Grand Rapids, 1964–1974.
Schnackenburg, Rudolph. *The Church in the New Testament.*
    New York, 1965.
Theissen, Paul. *Social Setting of Pauline Christianity.* Phila-
    delphia, 1977.

1. The Church as Mother

Lubac, Henri de. *The Motherhood of the Church.* San Francisco,
    1982.
Lubac, Henri de. *Particular Churches in the Universal Church.*
    San Francisco, 1982.
Plumpe, Joseph C. *Mater Ecclesia: An Inquiry into the Concept of
    the Church as Mother in Early Christianity.* Washington, 1943.

2. The Church as the Body of Christ

Mersch, Emile. *The Theology of the Mystical Body.* St. Louis,
    1958.
Mersch, Emile. *The Whole Christ: The Historical Development
    of the Doctrine of the Mystical Body.* Milwaukee, 1938.
Mura, Ernest. *The Mystical Body of Christ.* St. Louis, 1963.
Pelton, Robert S., ed. *The Church as the Body of Christ.* Notre
    Dame, 1963.
Robinson, John A. T. *The Body: A Study in Pauline Theology.*
    London, 1952.
Schweizer, Eduard. *The Church as the Body of Christ.* Richmond,
    1964.

III. A Brief History of the Development in the Catholic Understanding of the Church

Aubert, Roger, et al., eds. *Church in a Secularized Society.* Chris-
    tian Centuries 5. New York, 1978.
Bowe, Ellen. *A Church in Crisis: Ecclesiology in Clement of
    Rome.* Minneapolis, 1988.
Congar, Yves. "The Idea of the Church in St. Thomas Aquinas."
    In *The Mystery of the Church.* Especially chap. 3. Baltimore,
    1960.
Dulles, Avery. "The Church According to Thomas Aquinas." In *A
    Church to Believe In,* chap. 10. New York, 1982.
Evans, Robert F. *One and Holy: The Church in Latin Patristic
    Thought.* London, 1972.

Grabowski, Stanislaus J. *The Church: An Introduction to the Theology of Saint Augustine.* St. Louis, 1957.

Hill, Edmund. "Church." In *The New Dictionary of Theology*, ed. Joseph Komonchak, 185–201. Wilmington, DE, 1988.

LeGuillou, M. J. "Church: I. History of Ecclesiology." In *Sacramentum Mundi* 1:313–17. New York, 1968.

McFarlane, K. B. *John Wycliffe and the Beginnings of English Nonconformity.* London, 1952.

Pascoe, Louis B. *Jean Gerson: Principles of Church Reform.* Leiden, 1973.

Ryan, John J. *The Nature, Structure and Function of the Church in William of Ockham.* Missoula, MT, 1979.

PART TWO: PATHWAYS TOWARDS A THEOLOGICAL CONCEPT OF THE CHURCH

IV. Structural Elements for a Theological Concept of the Church: The Biblical Images

1. People of God/Body of Christ

Congar, Yves. "The Church: The People of God." In *The Church and Mankind*, ed. Karl Rahner and Edward Schillebeeckx. New York, 1965. = *Concilium* 1:11–37.

Schnackenburg, Rudolph, and Jacques Dupont. "The Church as the People of God." In *The Church and Mankind*, ed. Karl Rahner and Edward Schillebeeckx. New York, 1965. = *Concilium* 1:117–29.

2. God's Building

Congar, Yves. *The Mystery of the Temple.* Westminister, MD, 1962.

Schnider, Franz, and Werner Stenger. "The Church as a Building and the Building of the Church." In *Office and Ministry in the Church*, ed. Bas van Iersel and Roland Murphy. New York, 1972. = *Concilium* 80:21–34.

3. The Kingdom of God

Schnackenburg, Rudolph. *God's Rule and Kingdom.* New York, 1963.

van Rad, Gerhard, Karl Georg Kuhn, and Karl L. Schmidt. "*basileus/basileia* [king/reign]." In *TDNT* 1:564–93.

V. The Church as a Sacramental Reality; The Use of Models; Ordering and Interpretation of the Structural Elements Drawn from Scripture

1. The Church as Sacrament

Dulles, Avery. "The Church: Sacrament and Ground of Faith." In *Problems and Perspectives of Fundamental Theology*, ed. René Latourelle and Gerald O'Collins, 259–73. New York, 1982.

Latourelle, René. *Christ and the Church: Signs of Salvation.* Staten Island, NY, 1972.

McNamara, Kevin. *Sacrament of Salvation: Christ and the Church.* Dublin, 1977.

Rahner, Karl. *The Church and the Sacraments.* New York, 1963.

Schillebeeckx, Edward. *Christ the Sacrament of the Encounter with God.* New York, 1963.

Semmelroth, Otto. *Church and Sacrament.* Notre Dame, 1965.

2. Models of the Church

Dulles, Avery. *Models of the Church.* Garden City, NY, 1974.

Ramsey, I. T. *Models and Mystery.* New York, 1964.

VI. The Christian, the Community, Particular Churches and the Church; The Sacramental Church in Space; Diversity in Unity

1. Community

Hamer, Jerome. *The Church is a Communion.* New York, 1964.

Hauck, Friedrich. *"koinos/koinonia* [common/communion]." In TDNT 3:789–804.

Hertling, Ludwig. *Communio: Church and Papacy.* Chicago, 1972.

The Jurist. "The Church as Communion." Vol. 36. No. 1–2. 1976.

2. Local/Particular Churches

Brown, Raymond. "The New Testament Background for the Emerging Doctrine of 'Local Church'." In *Biblical Exegesis and Church Doctrine*, 114–34. New York, 1985.

Komonchak, Joseph. "The Church Universal as the Communion of Local Churches." In *Where Does the Church Stand?* ed. Giuseppe Alberigo and Gustavo Gutiérrez. New York, 1981. = *Concilium* 146:30–35.

Komonchak, Joseph. "The Local Realization of the Church." In *The Reception of Vatican II*, 77–90. Washington, 1987.

Lubac, Henri de. *The Motherhood of the Church*. San Francisco, 1982.

Lubac, Henri de. *Particular Churches in the Universal Church*. San Francisco, 1982.

Zizioulas, John. "The Local Church in a Perspective of Communion." In *Being as Communion*, 247–60. Crestwood, NY, 1985.

Zizioulas, John. "The Local Church in a Eucharistic Perspective." In *In Each Place: Towards a Fellowship of Local Churches Truly United*, ed. World Council of Churches, Faith and Order, 50–61. Geneva, 1977.

3. *Membership in the Church*

Congar, Yves. "What Belonging to the Church Has Come to Mean." *Communio* 4 (1977):146–60.

Dulles, Avery. *Church Membership as a Catholic and Ecumenical Problem*. Milwaukee, 1974.

O'Neill, Colman. "St. Thomas on the Membership of the Church." In *Vatican II: The Theological Dimension*, Special issue of *The Thomist* 27 (1963):88–140.

Rahner, Karl. "Membership of the Church According to the Teaching of Pius XII's Encyclical 'Mystici Corporis'." *Theological Investigations* 2:1–88. New York, 1963.

Sauras, Emilio. "Church: Membership of the Church." In *Sacramentum Mundi* 1:332–37. New York, 1968.

Willems, Boniface. "Who Belongs to the Church?" In *The Church and Mankind*, ed. Karl Rahner and Edward Schillebeeckx. New York, 1965. = *Concilium* 1:131–51.

VII. The Church from the Foundation of the World, since Christ and until the End of Time; The Sacramental Church in Time

Bonsirven, Joseph. *Theology of the New Testament*. London, 1963.

Kasper, Walter. "Hope in the Final Coming of Jesus Christ in Glory." *Communio* 12 (1985):368–84.

Mussner, Franz. *Christ and the End of the World: A Biblical Study in Eschatology*. Notre Dame, 1965.

Rahner, Karl. "The Church and the Parousia of Christ." In *Theological Investigations* 6:295–312. Baltimore, 1969.

Ratzinger, Joseph. "Eschatology and Utopia." *Communio* 5 (1978):211–27.

Theisen, Jerome P. *The Ultimate Church and the Promise of Salvation*. Collegeville, MN, 1976.

PART THREE: MANIFESTATIONS OF THE
CHURCH'S BEING, LIFE, AND ACTIVITY IN
LIGHT OF ITS SACRAMENTAL STRUCTURE

VIII. The Founding, the Basis, the Genesis of the Church; The Beginning (arché) of the Sacramental Church

Balthasar, Hans Urs von. "Life and Institution in the Church."
    Communio 12 (1985):25–32.
Burghardt, Walter, and William G. Thompson, eds. *Why the
    Church?* New York, 1977.
Cody, Aelred. "The Foundation of the Church: Biblical Criticism
    for Ecumenical Discussion." *Theological Studies* 34 (1973):3–
    18.
Conzelmann, Hans. *A History of Primitive History.* Nashville,
    1973.
Filson, Floyd Vivian. *A New Testament History: The Story of the
    Emerging Church.* Philadelphia, 1964.
Küng, Hans. *The Church.* New York, 1968.
Warnach, Viktor. "Church." In *Sacramentum Verbi* 1:101–16.
    New York, 1970.

IX. The Structures of the Church's Being; Orders and Organization in the Church; The Constitution of the Sacramental Church

1. Fundamental Structure of the Church

Küng, Hans. *Structures of the Church.* New York, 1964.
Mörsdorf, K. "Hierarchy." In *Sacramentum Mundi* 3:27–29.
Rahner, Karl. *The Shape of the Church to Come.* New York and
    London, 1974.
Rahner, Karl. "Constitution of the Church." In *Sacramentum
    Mundi* 1:327–30.

2. Democracy and Obedience in the Church

Bassett, William, and Peter Huizing, eds. *Judgment in the Church.*
    New York, 1977. = *Concilium* 107.
Coriden, James A., ed. *Who Decides for the Church?* Hartford,
    1971.
Moltmann, Jürgen, and Hans Küng, eds. *Who Has the Say in the
    Church?* New York, 1981. = *Concilium* 148.

Müller, Alois, ed. *Democratization of the Church*. New York, 1971. = *Concilium* 63.

Ratzinger, Joseph. "Free Expression and Obedience in the Church." In *The Church: Readings in Theology*, ed. Hugo Rahner et al., 194–217. Compiled at the Canisianum, Innsbruck. New York, 1963.

3. Subsidiarity

Kossel, Clifford. "Global Community and Subsidiarity." *Communio* 8(1981):37–50.

4. Magisterium

Metz, Johann Baptist, and Edward Schillebeeckx. *The Teaching Authority of Believers*. New York, 1985. = *Concilium* 180.

Müller, Alois. *Obedience in the Church*. Westminister, MD, 1966.

O'Donovan, Leo, ed. *Cooperation between Theologians and the Ecclesiastical Magisterium*. Washington, 1982.

Orsy, Ladislas. *The Church Learning and Teaching*. Wilmington, NC, 1987.

Rahner, Karl. *Free Speech in the Church*. New York, 1959.

Ratzinger, Joseph. "Freedom and Constraint in the Church." In *Church, Ecumenism and Politics*, 183–203. New York, and Middlegreen, UK, 1988.

Sullivan, Francis A. *Magisterium: Teaching Authority in the Catholic Church*. New York, 1983.

X. Vocations or Charisms, Ministries, Offices or Commissionings in the Missionary Church as Universal Sacrament of Salvation

1. Offices and Charisms

Conzelmann, Hans, and Walter Zimmerli. *"chairo/charis/charisma* [to greet, gift, charism]." In TDNT 9:359–415.

Duquoc, Christian, and Casiano Floristan, eds. *Charisms in the Church*. New York, 1977. = *Concilium* 109.

Küng, Hans. "The Charismatic Structure of the Church." In *The Church and Ecumenism*, ed. Hans Küng. New York, 1965. = *Concilium* 4:41–61.

Mühlen, Heribert. *A Charismatic Theology: Initiation in the Spirit*. New York, 1978.

Rahner, Karl. *The Dynamic Element in the Church*. New York, 1964.

Ratzinger, Joseph. "Office and Unity in the Church." *Journal of*

Ecumenical Studies 1 (1964):42–57. Also in *Theology Digest* 14 (1966):95–100.

2. Christian Laity and the Church

Congar, Yves. *Lay People in the Church: A Study for a Theology of the Laity.* Westminster, MD, 1957; rev. ed. New York and London, 1985.

Congar, Yves. "My Pathfindings in the Theology of the Laity." *The Jurist* 32 (1972):169–88.

Vatican II. "Decree on the Apostolate of the Laity" *Apostolicam actuositatem.*

XI. The Hierarchical Offices of the Apostolic Church

1. The Apostolic Office as the Central Office of the New Covenant, Bishops as Successors to the Apostles

a. Apostles in the New Testament

Agner, F. H. *Apostolos in the New Testament: The Origin of the Concept and the Term. A Bibliographical Survey.* Denver, 1973.

Schmithals, Walter, *The Office of Apostle in the Early Church.* London, 1971.

Schütz, J. H. *Paul and the Anatomy of Apostolic Authority.* London, 1975.

b. The Twelve

Regensdorf, K. H. *"manthano/mathētēs* [to teach/disciple]." In TDNT 4:390–461.

Rigaux, Béda. "The Twelve Apostles." In *Apostolic Succession: Rethinking a Barrier to Unity,* ed. Hans Küng. New York, 1968. = *Concilium* 34:5–15.

c. Apostolic Succession

Küng, Hans, ed. *Apostolic Succession: Rethinking a Barrier to Unity.* Especially articles by Antonio Javierre, Hans Küng, Johannes Remmers, Avery Dulles, Arnold van Ruler, and Maurice Villain. New York, 1968. = *Concilium* 34.

Rahner, Karl, and Joseph Ratzinger. *The Episcopate and the Primacy.* Freiburg, 1962. = *Quaestiones disputatae* 4.

d. Bishops

Beyer, Hermann W. *"episkopē/episkopos* [oversight, overseer]." In TDNT 2:599–622.

Group of Les Dombes. "The Episcopal Ministry." *One in Christ* 14 (1978):267–88.

Mallett, James K., ed. *The Ministry of Governance.* Washington, 1986.

Swidler, Arlene, and Leonard Swidler, eds. *Bishops and People.* Philadelphia, 1970.

Vatican II. "Dogmatic Constitution on the Church" [Lumen Gentium] and "Decree on the Bishops' Pastoral Office in the Church" [Christus Dominus].

2. The Apostolic Office and the Office of Peter: The Papal Office

a. Peter in the New Testament

Brown, Raymond E., Karl P. Donfried, et al., eds. *Peter in the New Testament.* New York, 1973.

Cullmann, Oscar. *Peter: Disciple, Apostle, Martyr.* London, 1961.

Karrer, Otto. *Peter and the Church: An Examination of Cullmann's Thesis.* Freiburg, 1963. = *Quaestiones disputatae* 8.

Lutheran/Roman Catholic International Commission, 1981. "The Ministry in the Church." In *Growth in Agreement,* ed. Harding Meyer and Lukas Vischer. New York, 1984. = *Ecumenical Documents* II:248–75.

b. Papacy—Succession; Jurisdiction

Balthasar, Hans Urs von. *The Office of Peter and the Structure of the Church.* San Francisco, 1986.

De Satge, John. *Peter and the Single Church.* London, 1981.

Granfield, Patrick, *The Papacy in Transition.* New York, 1980.

Granfield, Patrick, *The Limits of the Papacy.* New York, 1987.

Hendrix, Scott H. *Luther and the Papacy: Stages in a Reformation Conflict.* Philadelphia, 1981.

Jean (Quidort) of Paris. *On Royal and Papal Power,* trans. Arthur P. Monahan. New York, 1974.

Küng, Hans, ed. *The Papal Ministry in the Church.* New York, 1971. = *Concilium* 64.

McAdoo, H. R., J. C. H. Aveling, and D. M. Loades. *Rome and the Anglicans: Historical and Doctrinal Aspects of Anglican–Roman Catholic Relations.* Berlin and New York, 1982.

McCord, Peter J., ed. *A Pope for All Christians?* New York, 1976.

Ohlig, Karl-Heinz. *Why We Need the Pope: The Necessity and Limitations of Papal Primacy.* St. Meinrad, 1975.

Ratzinger, Joseph. "The Papal Primacy and the Unity of the People of God." In *Church, Ecumenism and Politics,* 29–45. New York, and Middlegreen, UK, 1988.

Tillard, Jean Marie. *The Bishop of Rome*. London, 1983.

c. *The Power of the Keys*

Cunningham, Agnes. "The Power of the Keys: The Patristic Tradition." In *The Papacy and the Church*, ed. Bernard Cooke, 141–60. New York, 1989.

Jeremias, Joachim. *"kleis* [keys]." In TDNT 3:487–536.

d. *The Power of Binding and Loosing*

Büchsel, Friedrich. *"deo/luo* [to bind/to loose]." In TDNT 2:60–61.

Derrett, J. Duncan M. "Binding and Loosing." *Journal of Biblical Literature* 102 (1983):112–17.

Hiers, Richard H. "'Binding' and 'Loosing': The Matthean Authorization." *Journal of Biblical Literature* 104 (1985):233–50.

e. *The Image of the Shepherd*

Jeremias, Joachim. *"poimēn* [shepherd]." In TDNT 6:485–502.

Schnackenburg, Rudolph. *The Gospel According to St. John*. 3 vols. New York, 1968–1982.

f. *Infallibility (of the Church/Pope)*

Butler, Cuthbert. *The Vatican Council: The Story Told from Inside in Bishop Ullathorne's Letters*. 2 vols. London, 1930.

Chirico, Peter. *Infallibility: The Crossroads of Doctrine*. Wilmington, DE, 1983.

Küng, Hans. *Infallible? An Inquiry*. New York, 1971.

Hasler, August. *How the Pope Became Infallible: Pius IX and the Politics of Persuasion*. Garden City, NY, 1981.

Salmon, George. *The Infallibility of the Church*. London, 1888, 1923.

Tierney, Brian. *The Origins of Papal Infallibility (1150–1350)*. Leiden, 1973.

g. *Pope and Bishops*

Bertrams, Wilhelm. *The Papacy, the Episcopacy and Collegiality*. Westminister, MD, 1964.

Küng, Hans, and Jürgen Moltmann, eds. *Who Has the Say in the Church?* New York, 1981. = *Concilium* 148.

Legrand, Hervé, et al., eds. *The Nature and Future of Episcopal Conferences*. Washington, 1988.

Oakley, Francis. *Council Over Pope? Towards a Provisional Ecclesiology*. New York, 1969.

Ratzinger, Joseph. "The Doctrine of Collegiality of Bishops." *Concilium* 1. 1964.

Ratzinger, Joseph. "The Structure and Tasks of the Synod of

Bishops." In *Church, Ecumenism and Politics*, 46–62. New York, and Middlegreen, UK, 1988.

Reese, Thomas J., ed. *Episcopal Conferences: Historical, Canonical and Theological Studies*. Washington, 1988.

Tierney, Brian. *Foundations of Conciliar Theory*. Cambridge, 1955.

Vooght, Paul de. "The Results of Recent Historical Research on Conciliarism." In *The Papal Ministry in the Church*, ed. Hans Küng. New York, 1971. = *Concilium* 64:148–55.

3. The Presbyterate; the Priesthood

Brown, Raymond. *Priest and Bishop: Biblical Reflections*. New York, 1970.

Kilmartin, Edward J. *Church, Eucharist, and Priesthood*. New York, 1981.

Küng, Hans. *Why Priests?* London, 1972.

Moudry, J. "Bishop and Priest in the Sacrament of Holy Order." *Jurist* 31 (1971):163–86.

O'Meara, Thomas F. *Theology of Ministry*. New York, 1983.

Rahner, Karl. *The Priesthood*. New York, 1973.

Vatican II. "Decree on the Ministry and Life of Priests" *Presbyterorum Ordinis*.

4. The Diaconate

Martimort, Aimé Georges. *Deaconesses: An Historical Study*. San Francisco, 1983.

Nowell, Robert. *The Ministry of Service: Deacons*. London, 1968.

Paul VI. Motu Proprio. *Sacrum Diaconatus Ordinem*. 18 June 1967.

Rashke, Richard L. *The Deacon in Search of Identity*. New York, 1975.

United States Bishops' Conference on Permanent Diaconate. *Permanent Deacons in the United States*. Washington, 1971.

5. The Laity's Role in the World

Congar, Yves. *Lay People in the Church: A Study for a Theology of the Laity*. Westminister, MD, 1957; rev. ed. London and New York, 1985.

Congar, Yves. "My Pathfindings in the Theology of the Laity." *Jurist* 32 (1972):169–88.

Vatican II. "Decree on the Apostolate of the Laity" *Apostolicam actuositatem*.

XII. The Marks or Essential Attributes of the Apostolic Church

Sullivan, Francis. *The Church We Believe In: One, Holy, Catholic, and Apostolic*. New York, 1988.

Witte, Jan. "One, Holy, Catholic, and Apostolic." In *One, Holy, Catholic and Apostolic*, ed. Herbert Vorgrimler. London, 1968.

PART FOUR: THE CHURCH'S TASKS AND ITS WAYS TO SELF-REALIZATION IN THE WORLD

XIII. The Church's Unity and Unicity; Its Missionary Nature

1. *The Church's Unity and Unicity*

Craig, C. T. *The One Church in the Light of the New Testament*. New York, 1951.

Moltmann, J. *The Church in the Power of the Spirit: A Contribution to Messianic Ecclesiology*. London, 1977.

2. *The Church's Missionary Nature*

Anderson, Gerald H., ed. *The Theology of Christian Mission*. New York, 1961.

Anderson, Gerald H., and Thomas F. Stransky, eds. *Mission Trends*. Vols. 1ff. New York, 1974– .

Beyerhaus, Peter, and Henry Lefever. *The Responsible Church: The Foreign Mission*. Grand Rapids, 1964.

Bühlmann, Walbert. *All the Same God: An Encounter with the Peoples and Religions of Asia*. Slough, UK, 1979.

Bühlmann, Walbert. *The Coming of the Third Church*. Maryknoll, NY, 1977.

Bühlmann, Walbert. *The Church of the Future: A Model for the Year 2001*. Maryknoll, 1986.

Fahey, Michael A. "The Mission of the Church: To Divinize or to Humanize?" *Catholic Theological Society of America Proceedings* 31 (1967):56–69.

Harnack, Adolph von. *The Mission and Expansion of Christianity in the First Three Centuries*. 2d rev. ed. 2 vols. London, 1908.

Hillman, Eugene. *The Church as Mission*. New York, 1965.

The Jurist. "The Church as Mission." Vol. 39. Nos. 1–2.

Latourette, K. S. *A History of the Expansion of Christianity*. 7 vols. New York, 1937–1945.

Paul VI. Apostolic Exhortation. *On Evangelization in the Modern World*. Washington, 1976.

Provost, James H., ed. *The Church as Mission*. Washington, 1979.

Rahner, Karl, ed. *Rethinking the Church's Mission*. New York, 1966. = *Concilium* 13.

Schmemann, Alexander. *Church, World, Mission: Reflections on Orthodoxy in the West*. Crestwood, NY, 1979.

XIV. Ecumenism as an Essential Task of the Church in the World

Butler, B. C. *The Church and Unity*. London, 1979.

Desseaux, Jacques. *Twenty Centuries of Ecumenism*. New York, ca.1986.

Fries, Heinrich, and Karl Rahner. *Unity of the Churches: An Actual Possibility?* New York, 1985.

Lambert, Bernard. *Ecumenism: Theology and History*. New York, 1967.

Minus, Paul. *The Catholic Rediscovery of Protestantism: A History of Roman Catholic Ecumenical Pioneering*. New York, 1976.

Stormon, E. J., ed. *Towards the Healing of Schism (1958–1984)*. New York, 1987.

Wainwright, Geoffrey. *The Ecumenical Movement: Crisis and Opportunity for the Church*. Grand Rapids, 1983.

XV. The Church's Catholicity and Its Necessity for the Salvation of Humankind

Dulles, Avery. *The Catholicity of the Church*. Oxford, 1985.

Lubac, Henri de. *Catholicism*. London, 1950.

Meyendorff, John. *Catholicity and the Church*. Crestwood, NY, 1983.

Tavard, George. *The Quest for Catholicity: A Study in Anglicanism*. New York, 1964.

XVI. The Church's Tasks in the World: Church and State, Society, Economy, Science, and Culture

Bea, Augustin. *The Church and Mankind*. Chicago, 1967.

CELAM, ed. *Church in the Present-Day Transformation of Latin America*. 2 vols. Bogota, 1970.

Norman, Edward. *Christianity and the World Order*. Oxford, 1979.

Rahner, Karl. "Church and World." *Sacramentum Mundi* 1:346–57. New York, 1968.

Vatican II. "The Pastoral Constitution on the Church in the Modern World" *Gaudium et spes*.

1. *Work, Labor, Freedom*

Baum, Gregory, ed. *Work and Religion*. New York, 1980. = *Concilium* 131.

John Paul II. Encyclical. *Laborem exercens*. 1981.

Langan, Thomas. "The Changing Nature of Work in the World System." *Communio* 11 (1984):120–35.

Metz, Johann Baptist. *The Emergent Church: The Future of Christianity in a Post-Bourgeois World*. New York, 1981.

O'Brien, David J., and Thomas A. Shannon, eds. *Renewing the Earth: Documents on Peace, Justice, and Liberation*. New York, 1977.

Pohier, Jacques, and Dietmar Mieth, eds. *Unemployment and the Right to Work*. New York, 1982. = *Concilium* 160.

2. *The Rich and the Poor; the North/South Divide*

Boff, Leonardo, and Virgil Elizondo, eds. *Option for the Poor: Challenge to the Rich Countries*. New York, 1986. = *Concilium* 187.

Congar, Yves. *Power and Poverty in the Church*. Baltimore, 1964.

Elizondo, Virgil, and Leonardo Boff, eds. *Tensions between Churches of the First World and Third*. New York, 1981. = *Concilium* 144.

Fabella, Virginia, and Sergio Torres, eds. *Doing Theology in a Divided World*. Ecumenical Association of Third World Theologians [EATWOT]. New York, 1985.

Hengel, Martin. *Property and Riches in the Early Church: Aspects of a Social History of Early Christianity*. London, 1974.

3. *Guardianship of Nature and Ecology*

Carmody, John. *Ecology and Religion: Toward a New Christian Theology of Nature*. New York, 1983.

Murphy, Charles M. *At Home on Earth: Foundations for a Catholic Ethic of the Environment*. New York, 1989.

4. *Art and Learning in Relationship to Today's Church's Cultural Responsibility*

Balthasar, Hans Urs von. "Earthly Beauty and Divine Glory." *Communio* 10 (1983):202–6.

Collins, Mary, et al., eds. *Music and the Experience of God*. New York, 1989. = *Concilium* 202.

Cunningham, W. Patrick. "Toward an Aesthetic of Liturgical Music." *Communio* 5 (1978):363–81.

Rahner, Hugo. *Man At Play*. London, 1965.

XVII. The Church's Holiness and Its Definition as the Communion of Saints

Kuhn, Karl George, and Herbert Procksch, "*hagios* [holy]." In TDNT 1:88–115.

Otto, Rudolf. *The Idea of the Holy: An Inquiry into the Non-Rational Factor in the Idea of the Divine*. London, 1957.

Rahner, Karl. "The Church of the Saints." *Theological Investigations* 3:91–104. New York, 1974.

Rahner, Karl. "The Church of Sinners." *Theological Investigations* 6:253–60. Baltimore, 1969.

XVIII. The Church and the Kingdom of God; The Fundamental Marian Mystery of the Church

Congar, Yves. *Christ, Our Lady, and the Church: A Study in Eirenic Theology*. London, 1957.

Greeley, Andrew. *The Mary Myth: On the Femininity of God*. New York, 1977.

Heft, James. "Marian Themes in the Writings of Hans Urs von Balthasar." *Communio* 7 (1980):127–39.

Rahner, Hugo. *Our Lady and the Church*. New York, 1961.

Ratzinger, Joseph. *Daughter Zion: Meditations on the Church's Marian Belief*. San Francisco, 1983.

Suenens, Leon J. *Mary the Mother of God*. New York, 1959.

Suenens, Leon J. *Theology of the Apostolate of the Legion of Mary*. Westminister, MD, 1954.

Index of Names

Index of Subjects